D0094608

KEYGuide

The **AA** **KEY**Guide
Provence
and the Côte d'Azur

Contents

KEY TO SYMBOLS

- Map reference
- Address
- Telephone number
- Opening times
- Admission prices
- Métro station
- Bus number
- Train station
- Ferry/boat
- Driving directions
- Tourist office
- Tours
- Guidebook
- Restaurant
- Café
- Shop
- Toilets
- Number of rooms
- No smoking
- Air conditioning
- Swimming pool
- Gym
- Other useful information
- Shopping
- Entertainment
- Nightlife
- Sports
- Activities
- Health and beauty
- For children
- Cross reference
- Walk/drive start point

HOW TO USE THIS BOOK

Understanding Provence and the Côte d'Azur is an introduction to the region, its geography, economy and people. **Living Provence and the Côte d'Azur** gives an insight into the area today, while **Story of Provence and the Côte d'Azur** takes you through its past.

For detailed advice on getting to Provence and the Côte d'Azur—and getting around once you are there—turn to **On the Move**. For useful practical information, from weather forecasts to emergency services, turn to **Planning**.

Out and About gives you the chance to explore Provence and the Côte d'Azur through walks, drives and a bicycle ride.

The **Sights, What to Do** and **Eating and Staying** sections are divided geographically into six regions, which are shown on the map on the inside front cover. These regions always appear in the same order. Towns and places of interest are listed alphabetically within each region.

Map references for the **Sights** refer to the atlas section at the end of this book or to the individual town plans. For example, St-Tropez has the reference ✚ 295 M13, indicating the page on which the map is found (295) and the grid square in which St-Tropez sits (M13).

UNDERSTANDING PROVENCE AND THE CÔTE D'AZUR

In theory Provence is in France, but in truth it has always been a land apart. You'll know when you've crossed the border because in Provence everything is different: the pale rocky terrain, the herb-rich food, the outdoor life, the dry air and brilliant sunlight. There are markets bursting with life, shaded squares filled with café tables, astounding art galleries and world-class music festivals. The landscape ranges from mountains and lavender fields to coastline and wetlands. The Côte d'Azur is the glitzy side of Provence, with exclusive beaches and marinas packed with luxury yachts.

Fields of sunflowers are a familiar sight in Provence

Soaking up the atmosphere outside a bar in Eygalières

Preparing for an all-important game of boules in St-Tropez

GETTING YOUR BEARINGS

Provence has an enviable position in France's sunny southeastern corner, with the warm waters of the Mediterranean to the south and Italy to the east. The western reaches of the Alps stretch to the north of Provence—in early spring you can ski in the morning, then drive to the Côte d'Azur for a stroll by the sea in the afternoon. The Côte d'Azur, with its celebrity glitz, is the area of coastline running from the Italian border in the east to St-Raphaël in the west. It is also known as the French Riviera, although officially this stretches farther west along the coast. The tiny principality of Monaco sits on the eastern edge of the coast, between Nice and Menton.

TOURISM

Tourism encompasses the whole of Provence, and the Riviera coastal strip is one of the most popular holiday destinations in the world. The Côte d'Azur accounts for one per cent of the world market for overnight stays, with almost 70 million guest nights per year. Annual visitor spending reaches around €5 billion. There have been environmental costs, and quality of life in the busier areas has inevitably suffered. Nevertheless, both regional and national decision-makers are determined to ensure further tourism growth. Yet thanks to a diverse landscape, with rocky hill districts and dense wilderness areas that defy development, most of inland Provence (and even some coastal stretches) remains largely unspoiled and there are plenty of opportunities to escape the crowds.

THE ECONOMY

Provence by no means depends on tourism. Unlike some popular holiday destinations, Provence—even the Riviera tourist heartland—has a huge diversity of other industry. High-tech development, telecommunications and scientific research are major contributors to the region's economy. One of Europe's leading technology parks, Sophia-Antipolis, is a short distance from Cannes. Viniculture and horticulture remain an important part of the economy—grapes, melons, lemons, olives and cut flowers are among the local produce. Provence provides 70 per cent of the world's lavender oil and is home to around a tenth of France's vineyards.

CLIMATE AND LANDSCAPE

There's something absolutely joyous about the climate of Provence, with its balmy temperatures, the freshness of the shade on a summer afternoon and the comfortable warmth of long evenings outdoors. That, of course, is what has attracted visitors, from the aristocratic seekers of winter sun in the 19th century to today's holiday-makers here for two weeks in summer. Tour companies' brochures describe it as perfection, yet the climate of Provence has its harsher edge. The long rainless summer, zero humidity, high temperatures and sheer blue sky may sound like a dream come true, but for centuries such weather impoverished the population and made life hard. Only when the capricious rivers, especially the Durance, were tamed and the waters channelled for irrigation, did agriculture really begin to flourish. Storms can be spectacularly sudden and violent, menacing skies illuminated by endless lightning, with downpours that can flood towns and villages within hours and send dangerous torrents surging down river beds that are usually bone dry. Mont Ventoux, especially, towering above the Vaucluse in western Provence, draws stormy weather to itself.

Provence locals are aware of the shifting winds and the weather they bring. Wind from the east brings turbulence, from the south, rain. The prevailing wind is the *mistral*, dry air flowing from the Alps to the sea. In winter it can howl icily down the Rhône valley, fanning out along the coast as it approaches the sea. In summer, though, it's lighter, sometimes almost gentle, and keeps skies cloudless for weeks at a time.

Provence's landscape ranges from the watery plains of the Camargue to the Mediterranean

word for yes, *oc*, with the word northerners once used, *oïl*. While the word *oc* has vanished, the talk of rural southerners is still liberally peppered with local dialect words.

Though Provençal was officially suppressed from the 15th century onwards, it continued in everyday use until the Revolution. The poet Frédéric Mistral (1830–1914) then led a 19th-century revival with his Félibrige movement and won the Nobel Prize for Literature in 1904 for his novels and poetry written in Provençal. Mistral remains a local hero, but his movement failed, and French replaced the old tongue.

Yet Provençal will not go away. Under the name Occitan, it has resurfaced as a symbol of southern independence, part of a wave of pride in southern culture and traditions. While the authentic language survives only as a country patois, many towns and villages have put up

Explore inland to discover Provence's scenic hillside villages

Nîmes' amphitheatre is a reminder of Provence's Roman past

A basket of lavender

beaches, from the low inland hills to the snowy peaks of the Alps. To some extent, each of these areas has its own climate. The diversity is at its most striking in February, when spring flowers are opening on the Riviera, while an hour's drive north snow-covered mountain resorts in the Provençal Alps offer perfect skiing conditions.

LANGUAGE

It's easy enough to hear that the *accent du Midi*—the strong southern inflection, with its emphatic tones ringing like church bells—is different from French as spoken farther north. Here every word ending is vigorously sounded, often with a resounding nasal 'ang'. *Vin* (wine) becomes *vang*, *pain* (bread) becomes *pang*, *demain* (tomorrow) becomes *demang*, *beau temps* (good weather) is *beau tang*.

The Provençal accent is a last remnant of a completely separate language. The language of southern France—whether called Provençal, Langue d'Oc or Occitan—came directly from Latin (like Spanish or Italian). It was the everyday speech of both the educated and the ordinary people. Above all, it was the language of the troubadours, whose lyric poems and songs of gallantry were all told in the Provençal tongue. In those days, the language was called Romans or Lenga Romana. The later name, Langue d'Oc, contrasts the southern

streets signs and other public information in Provençal. Schools offer a chance to learn the local language, while in the universities of the south, it is possible to study Provençal more seriously. Many names, especially of southern dishes, are pure Provençal, like *anchoïade*, *aïoli*, *pistou* and *ratatouille*. At the same time, several towns still have their own historic patois, sometimes mixing Provençal with French and Italian, like the popular Nissart speech of Nice.

SOCIETY

Provence is distinctly more 'Latin' than the rest of France. Siestas shut some shops from noon until 3pm, bullfights remain a spectator sport (especially in Arles and Nîmes) and politics has sometimes followed the turbulent model more familiar from nearby Italy.

The lively village market remains an important occasion, giving the chance to buy seasonal produce and catch up on the local gossip. Festivals also play a key role in Provence life. Nice celebrates the early spring with its Carnival and Menton with the *Fête du Citron*. The partying continues in the summer, with around 300 towns and villages staging their own festival.

PROVENCE AND THE CÔTE D'AZUR AT A GLANCE

The Provence-Alpes-Côte d'Azur region is broken down into six *départements*. You can tell which *département* a town or attraction is in by looking at the first two digits of the postal code (these are given in brackets below). Also within Provence's boundaries, although not part of France, is the luxury-loving principality of Monaco.

Bouches-du-Rhône (13) is on the Mediterranean coast, on the western side of Provence. Its capital is the ancient port city of Marseille and its landscape includes the wetland reserves of the Camargue and the beautiful Chaîne des Alpilles hills. There are Roman reminders at Arles.

Var (83), farther east, has the Côte d'Azur beach resorts of Fréjus, Le Lavandou and Hyères, as well as the celebrity's choice, St-Tropez. The interior has tranquil sun-basking villages, wild hills like the Massif des Maures, thriving country towns such as Draguignan and Romanesque sites such as the Abbaye du Thoronet.

Alpes-Maritimes (06) includes the northeastern stretch of the Côte d'Azur. Its resorts extend along the scenic waterfront from Cannes and Antibes to Menton and the Italian border. The whole strip is dedicated to relaxation, style and the good life, plus generous helpings of superb history dating back to Roman times and beyond, and world-famous art museums like the Fondation Maeght. Nice is the *département's* ancient capital and Queen of the Riviera. Inland are perched villages like Èze and the mountainous Mercantour region.

Monaco, a short way up the coast from Nice, is the tiny principality that thinks big. Monaco-Ville, perched on its rock, is the stately little ceremonial capital, while Monte-Carlo is the principality's big-money quarter, dominated by its casino.

Alpes-de-Haute-Provence (04), north of Var, takes in the spectacular Grand Canyon du Verdon, as well as the appealing old hill towns of Castellane, Forcalquier and Sisteron, and the spa town of Digne-les-Bains.

Hautes-Alpes (05), in northern Provence, is popular for skiing in winter and hiking in summer.

Vaucluse (84), north of Bouches-du-Rhône, includes medieval Avignon, Roman Orange and the wine town of Châteauneuf-du-Pape. Southern Vaucluse has an array of impressive sights, man-made and natural, including the gushing Fontaine de Vaucluse spring, ochre-tinted Roussillon and Romanesque abbeys like Sénanque. Northern Vaucluse has mountain scenery but also remarkable Roman sights like Vaison-la-Romaine.

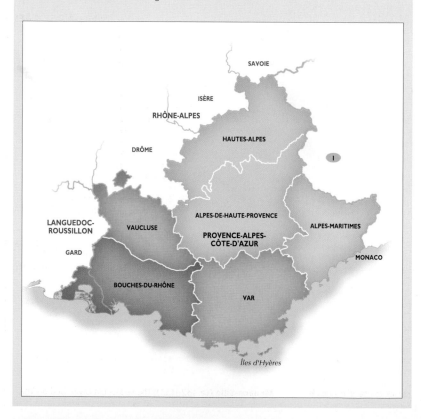

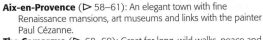

BOUCHES-DU-RHÔNE

Treat yourself to some Provençal chocolates

Aix-en-Provence (▷ 58–61): An elegant town with fine Renaissance mansions, art museums and links with the painter Paul Cézanne.

The Camargue (▷ 68–69): Great for long, wild walks, peace and quiet, horseback riding and birdwatching.

Chocolaterie de Puyricard (▷ 178): Sample some of the best chocolates in France, at this shop in Aix-en-Provence.

Fête des Gardians (▷ 185): Be entertained by the cowboys of the Camargue during this celebration in Arles.

Marseille (▷ 72–78): Soak up the history in the Vieux Port and Le Panier districts of this ancient city, then sample the lively nightlife…or the delicious local fish stew, bouillabaisse.

Oustau de Baumanière (▷ 235): Enjoy exquisite food in the restaurant of this 16th-century country-house hotel.

Sports range from horseback riding in the Camargue to windsurfing on the Med

VAR

Îles d'Hyères (▷ 94–95): Catch a ferry to these peaceful islands, which represent a different side of the Côte d'Azur.

Massif des Maures (▷ 97): Here's real wilderness, just minutes from the Riviera resorts.

St-Tropez (▷ 98–99): More film set than fishing village, it's still popular with celebs.

La Tarte Tropézienne (▷ 188): Visit this St-Tropez patisserie to try the famous Tarte Tropézienne cream cake.

Windsurf (▷ 176): L'Almanarre, near Hyères, is a popular spot with enthusiasts.

ALPES-MARITIMES

A statue in Cannes

Èze (▷ 110): Of all the perched villages of the Riviera, this is one of the most accessible and most impressive.

Cannes (▷ 106–108): Shop 'til you drop in Provence's most glamorous destination.

Fête du Citron (▷ 195): Visit Menton in late February to experience the lively Lemon Festival.

Fragonard (▷ 191): Treat yourself to a fragrance from this renowned perfumery, in Grasse.

Hôtel Negresco (▷ 253): If you're feeling wealthy, book yourself into this luxury hotel—if not, wander past to admire the landmark dome.

Nice (▷ 116–121): Stroll the Promenade des Anglais, see the great art galleries and experience the hectic nightlife.

Perfume from Fragonard

Nice Carnival (▷ 195): Join in the party at the Nice Carnival, in February. If you're visiting in summer, catch the Nice Jazz Festival (▷ 195) in July.

MONACO

Casino quarter (▷ 135): At its most impressive admired from outside, the ornate Casino symbolizes the lavish opulence of the principality.

Grand Prix (▷ 197): Monte-Carlo becomes a racetrack in May and welcomes the top names in Formula 1.

Le Louis XV (▷ 240): Spend your casino winnings (and you may need them) at this luxurious restaurant, part of the Hôtel de Paris.

Musée Océanographique (▷ 133): Dug into the cliff face of The Rock, this is one of the best sea-life museums in Europe.

Monaco-Ville (▷ 132–133): The sedate old city poised on The Rock has quiet pageantry and wonderful sea views.

A soldier of the Royal Guard stands to attention outside Monaco's Palais Princier

ALPES-DE-HAUTE-PROVENCE AND HAUTES-ALPES

The Rocher de la Baume looms over Sisteron

La Citadelle (▷ 242): This restaurant offers wonderful alpine views and tasty local dishes.

Digne-les-Bains (▷ 139): Relax in the thermal baths at this famous spa town.

Entrevaux (▷ 140): Vauban's fortifications add to the impressive natural defences of this mountain gateway to Provence.

Grand Canyon du Verdon (▷ 142–143): The deepest, longest river gorge in Europe makes a spectacular drive.

Sisteron (▷ 146): Napoleon Bonaparte paused at this dramatically sited fortified mountain town on his march back to Paris in 1815.

Ski (▷ 138): Hit the slopes surrounding the Val d'Allos or the Serre Chevalier resorts.

VAUCLUSE

Avignon (▷ 150–153): The main draws of this vivacious, riverside walled city are the magnificent Palais des Papes (Palace of the Popes) and the huge drama and dance festival held in July.

A woman in period costume, in Avignon

Châteauneuf-du-Pape (▷ 155): Discover a world-famous wine village nestled among immaculate vineyards.

Christian Étienne (▷ 243): Dine in a 14th-century palace in Avignon and enjoy creations by a former sous-chef at Paris' Ritz Hotel.

Théâtre Antique (▷ 160): Experience the wonderful acoustics of Orange's Roman amphitheatre during the *Chorégies* festival in July.

Vaison-la-Romaine (▷ 166–168): Step back 2,000 years by visiting the huge Roman sites of this pleasant market town.

The cloisters of the cathedral at Vaison-la-Romaine (above)

TOP 15 EXPERIENCES

Buy Provençal Check out vivid fabrics, local herbs, lavender toiletries and other evocative souvenirs of Provence.

Dance the night away—whether you're into clubbing or ballroom, Provence has it all.

Drink either a cooling Rosé de Provence wine or a rich Côte du Rhône red.

Eat bouillabaisse, ratatouille, *pan bagnat*, *salade niçoise* or one of the other delicious local dishes.

Escape the crowds and head for the mountains.

Get festive at one of the many *fêtes* on the Riviera or at an inland town.

Go to the market in almost any town for a glimpse of the vivacity and richness that is Provence.

Lie on a beach There are plenty to choose from. The sandiest are from Cannes westward.

Return to Rome by visiting Provence's remarkable amphitheatres in Arles, Nîmes and Orange.

Nice's flower market (above) and the Negresco Hotel (below)

See some art at the Chagall in Nice, the Fondation Maeght near St-Paul-de-Vence or the Villa Ephrussi de Rothschild on Cap Ferrat.

Ski Yes, if you're here in spring, combine skiing at Isola with relaxing on the beach at Nice.

Try luxury living with a meal in a top hotel, like the Martinez in Cannes or the Negresco in Nice.

Visit a monastery and relax in the serene setting of a Romanesque abbey like Sénanque.

Walk the ramparts at fortified medieval towns and cities like Avignon and Aigues-Mortes.

Watch the world go by from an outdoor café table.

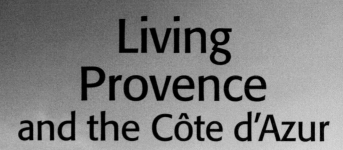

Living
Provence
and the Côte d'Azur

Café culture is an important part of French life, whether it's a trendy St-Tropez café (right) or a traditional *crêperie* (below)

Boats moored in an inlet sheltered by limestone cliffs

Provence Life

The day the sheep came to town

Spring sees the *trans-humance*, when shepherds take their flocks from winter to summer grazing grounds. As the sheep are driven through the narrow streets of historic towns, it is a time for thanksgiving, music and wine. From little known Vaucluse villages such as Jonquières to more established visitor destinations including St-Rémy-de-Provence and ski resorts in the Alps, thousands of sheep, dogs, donkeys and shepherds parade along the streets. Mass is said, tambourines are shaken and copious quantities of wine are quaffed until the animals are well on their way. Then, in autumn, the locals get ready for the return journey.

For a region with such rich and varied language, it is paradoxical that the greatest eloquence is in the shrug. The image of daily life in Provence is the most abiding of all pictures of regional France: pastel houses around dusty squares where old men while away the hours sipping pastis on a café *terrasse* and playing pétanque (bowls) under age-old plane trees. Taciturn they may be, but this very characteristic has inspired generations of writers and some of the most heartwarming tales of the land and the people who love it. Their stories help perpetuate the timeless charm of the place, but it is the landscape—background to isolated villages perched above rolling fields of lavender and craggy olive groves—that really preserves Provence's character, with locals living life the old way. The Mediterranean climate helps keep any aggressive movement for change safely at bay, and the patois and dialects (whose imminent demise has been predicted for the past 400 years) have been regularly rescued by successive generations, from the 19th-century poet Frédéric Mistral to the second-generation immigrants in modern Marseille, keen to embrace the original language of the area. These immigrants are part of the secret of Provence's success. The clichéd images of village life may be as true and vivid as ever. But new blood—whether trans-Mediterranean communities in the ports or artists settling in picturesque hamlets—and a vibrant cultural life prove Provence is as much an ideal of today as a mirror to the past.

Boules is a serious business in Provence (above).
Flowerpots hang from a sunny yellow shutter in Arles (left).
Larger-than-life characters parade through Nice for the famous Carnival (below)

Relaxing on the beach at Fréjus (above).
Precious truffles (right)

When one Mozart is not enough

Some people can never have too much sun, nor too much Mozart. Thus Provence in summer reverberates to the sound of popular arias in historic settings. To add to Provence's festivals of music, a new venue arrived in 2002, when fashion designer Pierre Cardin launched his own opera festival in the ruins of the Château Lacoste. The opening star-studded production was Mozart's condemnation of loose morals and licentiousness, *Don Giovanni*. This was apt because the chateau's most famous resident before Pierre Cardin was the Marquis de Sade.

Party time

Forget understated style—the Riviera has a gaudy party for a glorious two weeks, when the international visitors are looking the other way. Mardi Gras is the way to party out of winter and into spring. In Nice, massive papier-mâché heads join the marching bands and dancing crowds following floats parading daily through the streets and along the Promenade des Anglais to the sea. The giant papier-mâché King of the Carnival reigns supreme until he is set alight and put to sea, bringing the carnival to its dramatic close. Along the coast, the usually genteel folk of Menton provide a rival assault on the senses, when 130 tonnes of oranges and lemons are transformed into massive floats for the *Fête du Citron*.

The invisible market

On Parisian menus, the black diamonds of Provence are known as *truffes* (truffles). In Vaucluse, the delicacy is better known as *rabasse*. Legends of countrymen wandering off before dawn with hounds snuffling out truffles in secret locations help fuel the mystique and high prices. These days, they're virtually farmed around the roots of the downy oak. Rows of trees are planted in *truffière* fields. Saturday markets in Carpentras, Valréas and Grillon see farmers and dealers trading openly. But the big money, say locals, changes hands in the invisible truffle markets. Word of mouth, not maps, and deep pockets instead of picturesque stalls are the backdrop to hard-core trade. To the uninitiated, these markets don't exist. But anonymous deals in village bars and cafés are serious business.

Gypsies and cowboys by the sea

Gypsies dance with the Camargue's cowboys during one of the most lively events of the Provençal calendar, the *Pèlerinage des Gitans*. The village of Saintes-Maries-de-la-Mer is where, legend has it, saints Marie-Jacobé, Marie-Salomé and Mary Magdalene arrived with their maid Sarah, patron saint of gypsies. Every year in late May, gypsies from all over Europe make their pilgrimage to the coast. Dressed in vibrant, traditional costumes, gypsies and *gardians* (local cowboys who look after wild black bulls) carry jewel-encrusted statues of St. Sarah and the Maries into the sea to be blessed. During the evening and into the night, the beach echoes to the sound of celebrations.

Luxury living: Monte-Carlo's famous Casino (above and far right) and the Carlton Hotel, in Cannes (below)

Cannes, the Rich and

the Famous

The Cannes Film Festival is the ultimate A-List event. The Mediterranean boasts more movie stars per square yacht than ever and 4,000 journalists from 75 countries compete for interviews with directors and photographs of starlets on the Croisette. More than a mere photo opportunity, the festival has been the scene of fights, booing and mass walk-outs at screenings, with passion a lot closer to the surface than at other celebrity events. In the great spirit of 1968, when anarchy took to the streets of France, film makers François Truffaut and Jean-Luc Godard stormed the stage at the festival, reflecting the volatile political climate. Cannes has always been political. Its founding in 1939 was in itself a reaction to Mussolini's fascist takeover of the Venice Film Festival—although World War II meant Cannes didn't properly take off until 1947. Idealism is only part of the story. Money matters at Cannes too. Half the world's movie deals take place here, from blockbusters to small art-house flicks.

Not all today's celebrities on the Riviera come down to the Croisette to parade before the paparazzi. Dame Shirley Bassey and George Michael are among the legends of the music industry finding solace and inspiration in private villas behind the seafront.

Elton John

Since Elton John was granted honorary citizenship of Nice, he is often to be seen shopping for blooms at the world's oldest flower market. The cours Saleya, in the heart of the old town, is one of France's most picturesque markets, and fills the air with the scent of violets, mimosa and carnations for six days every week. Elton discovered the charms of the market back in the days when he was a regular guest at the Hôtel Negresco, and now hunts for exotic blooms for his luxury villa that perches high above the bay.

Rock superstar Elton John has a home on the Côte d'Azur

Dressing in style (left) and big names of fashion (below)

AVENUE DE MONTE-CARLO
GUCCI
VALENTINO
HERMÈS
LALIQUE
PRADA

Prince Albert, Prince Rainier and Princess Caroline of Monaco, at the opera

Director Michael Moore receives the Palme d'Or at the 2004 Cannes Film Festival for *Fahrenheit 9/11*

MADAME ZAZA OF MARSEILLE
PARIS MARSI

They can't stay away for long

British author Peter Mayle was not the first big name to discover the enchanting delights of the Lubéron village of Ménerbes. Former French president François Mitterrand and actress Jane Birkin had also been numbered among the VIP residents. But the publication of Mayle's 1980's best-seller *A Year In Provence* led to the Mayle Trail of tourists driving through the streets in search of locations from the book. The author finally left the village and moved to California. But such is the lure of the place, he returned to Provence within a decade—finding a house suitably off the beaten track, and less easily recognizable to keen-eyed readers.

Franco Zeffirelli's handprints, at Cannes

On the big screen

Provence is highly sought after for film locations, the landscape being wonderfully resistant to change. The link is not exclusively retro, though the perched village of Le Castellet had a starring role in *Jean de Florette* (1986), just as it had in the 1930s when Marcel Pagnol, on whose novel the movie is based, filmed *La Femme du Boulanger* here. Other films showing Provençal scenery include *Love Actually* (2003), *Herbie Goes to Monte-Carlo* (1977), *To Catch a Thief* (1955) and *French Kiss* (1995), with Meg Ryan.

There's something about Marianne

Marianne, symbol of the French Republic, adorns civic buildings, coins and stamps. While the latest image (launched in 2003) features a stylized multi-ethnic figure, her image has been inspired by stars and models such as Cathérine Deneuve, Inès de la Fressange and Laetitia Casta. However, the Marianne in Menton's *Salle des Marriages*, where townsfolk register their weddings, is a little unusual. The room was decorated by the artist and film director Jean Cocteau and includes a Marianne that bears a striking resemblance to the legendary actor Jean Marais, star of *Beauty and the Beast*, *Orpheus* and *Les Misérables*.

The Bébé grows up

Since Brigitte Bardot first stepped out in St-Tropez for Roger Vadim's classic film *Et Dieu Créa la Femme* in 1957, hers has been the face of the village resort, eclipsing previous high-profile residents such as the author Colette and artist Raoul Dufy. In her wake came the rock royalty of the 1960s, and the excesses of their front-page lifestyles, chic shopping and pricey wining-and-dining gave the resort the nickname *St-Trop* (too much!). The chances of seeing the famous Bardot pout in public these days are pretty slim, since the actress known to the French as *BB* (pronounced *Bébé*) famously gave up show-business on her 40th birthday, establishing an animal sanctuary and leaving town in 1989, returning only to keep an eye on the animals.

You might find yourself parking next to a Ferrari in Monaco

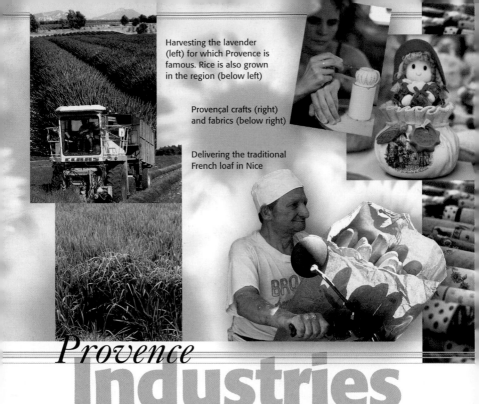

Harvesting the lavender (left) for which Provence is famous. Rice is also grown in the region (below left)

Provençal crafts (right) and fabrics (below right)

Delivering the traditional French loaf in Nice

Provence
Industries

The art of the blacksmith

When demand for traditional village crafts dries up, what should a fellow do but upgrade from artisan to artist and move the client base from a remote farmstead to a metropolitan salon? Raymond Moralès, born in 1926, spent the bulk of his working life as a blacksmith, before deciding to transfer his skills to the world of the arts. His passion for creating huge and dramatic sculptures led him to open his own museum in 1982. Now hundreds of looming metal figures fill the open-air park and gallery on his estate between Fos and Martigues. When not working on his latest artwork, Moralès greets visitors at the museum and escorts them around the exhibition.

With a natural backdrop most regions could only envy, a slow pace of life and a near-perfect climate, it would be easy simply to declare that Provence's single industry is tourism. But that would be to miss the point of those rolling fields of lavender and centuries-old village workshops. The dazzling blooms earn their keep as a viable crop. Provence is, after all, the heart of France's perfume industry. Across the Var and Alpes-Maritimes, growing flowers is such serious business that mere prettiness is but a luxury. So important is the cultivation of ornamental plants and cut flowers that growers raise them in vast plastic tunnels, producing mimosa and carnations for flower markets and ornamental palm trees for offices and restaurants. Alongside the traditional crops of vines and olives, horticulture turns the great outdoors into the thriving heart of the region's economy.

Provence's wealth comes not only from the land, but also the sea. Fishing fleets serve villages along the Med, but the days of the simple fishing boat putting out to sea are as numbered here as in the rest of the world. To meet demand, fish farming is developing, with sea bass (known as *loup*) and bream (*daurade*) being reared for the table as successfully as more traditional water crops such as mussels. Inland from the coast, France's first science park has created a silicon valley. The heart of trade has always been Marseille, whether the commodity was hemp, wine or grain. One Marseille product still manufactured in the region is the celebrated soap, *Savon de Marseille*.

Gîtes de France (above)—typically French places to stay. A fisherman mends his nets in Marseille (left)

Santons (above). High-tech industry at Sophia-Antipolis (below)

Bowls of scents, in Grasse

Little people, big business

For most of the country Christmas comes but once a year. In Provence, it's a 365-day industry. The production of nativity scene backdrops and figurines is a craft for which the region is justly famous. *Santons* (mini-saints) were wooden or wax dolls that were used in church displays. When the Revolution closed the churches, Marseille potter Jean-Louis Lagnel created the first mass production of the figures so each home could have its own crib, or *crèche*. Over the years the biblical cast was augmented with secular characters, such as doctors and farmers. In Aubagne, popular figures include actors Gérard Dépardieu and Yves Montand.

A new generation

Provence is famous for its crafts and rural professions. In many a rustic hamlet you'll find a *boulanger* up at the crack of dawn baking bread and a blacksmith hard at work beating horseshoes. Yet there is a place where the local skills are IT and cybernetics and you are more likely to encounter an astrophysicist than a basket weaver. On the Plateau de Valbonne, behind Antibes, is Sophia-Antipolis, dubbed France's silicon valley. New technology rules in the nation's first science park. Unlike nearby villages, where the past keeps the present alive, here 15,000 people with an eye firmly on the future work for over 800 companies at the cutting edge of technology. Pharmaceuticals, chemicals and life sciences are the new Provençal trades. Maybe the next generation of visitors to Provence will come here to photograph the village robotics expert.

How rice saved the region's greens

The fresh green vegetables on the plates at fashionable Provençal restaurants may well owe their existence to the humble paddy fields that have kept the wetlands of the Carmargue unspoiled by the march of progress. Surprising as it may seem, the very fact that the fields of the area can now yield a wide variety of tasty greens is due to the planting of rice paddies in the 1950s. Until then, the pastures of the Camargue were too rich in salt to be used for anything other than grazing cattle, horses and sheep. In its heyday, the Camargue produced a third of the rice served in France, but by the 1970s production had begun to drop. Now a fraction of the area covered 40 years ago, the rice fields have nonetheless revitalized arable production in the region by cleaning the soil of salt.

A nose by any other name

The hillside town of Grasse is famous for its gloriously intoxicating fragrance industry. Each talented expert who creates the cocktail of aromas is known as 'The Nose'. Less well publicized is that Noses may well earn as much for coming up with new smells for disinfectants as they do for designer scents in expensive bottles.

Marseille soaps are often scented with mountain herbs

Enjoying a drink and a chat at an outdoor café in place Rossetti, Nice

Antibes' market (right) bursts with local produce

Food and Drink

Olive oil, garlic, tomato, onions and herbs: The basic ingredients of Provençal cuisine came as something of a revelation to Northern Europe after the austerity of World War II. But before the recipe books from food writers such as Elizabeth David opened up the vista of French gastronomy to include something other than rich creamy sauces and complex combinations, the good folk of Provence had long cooked in the simple manner that has been credited with promoting longevity and good health.

The very simplicity of the diet owes much to the climate. *Primeur* vegetables are available weeks before their regular season in the rest of the country. The long coastline means fish is plentiful. The traditional soup dish is, of course, bouillabaisse, practically a stew, filled with sea bass, mullet and shellfish cooked in a rich stock seasoned with saffron, fennel and other herbs. Originating in Marseille, this dish is prepared differently in every restaurant on the coast, the only constants being the accompanying dishes of *rouille* (spicy mayonnaise), croutons and grated cheese.

No meal is complete unless served with a local wine. The heat of the summer sun encourages locals to sample a rosé at midday. The aperitif of choice is pastis. If you are looking for fast food, the not-quite-tart, not-quite-pizza of the area is a *pissaladière*, best munched cold on the beach. The seafront dish of the Riviera is the wonderful *salade niçoise*—tomatoes, peppers, onions, olives, olive oil, anchovy, hard-boiled eggs, green beans, basil and crisp lettuce.

One man and his melons

Cavaillon, in the Vaucluse region, is the heart of melon country. One man who has more than a passing respect for the rich succulent summer fruit is restaurateur Jean-Jacques Prévot. Not only does it feature on every menu from mid-May until the end of September (try the melon cocotte with lobster), but it is the heart of a local aperitif, *délice de melon*. Monsieur Prévot even makes paint from the pips and skins and these contribute to the restaurant's exhibition of 600 melon-related arts and crafts. The town itself hosts an annual melon parade in July, with music in the streets and melon tasting late into the night.

Eating out in Nice (left).
A plate of seafood (below)

The famous *Salade Niçoise* (below left).
Fresh produce at Avignon's market (below)

Wine from the Lubéron

A spicier cure

With their traditional distrust for authority figures, the French have long preferred to seek advice from people who stand behind a counter rather than sit behind a desk. Thus it is the village pharmacist who dispenses wisdom on what ails the pet cat, which mushrooms in the basket are safe to eat and how to treat a bad back. In the south, locals are as likely to ask the herb seller in the market for tips on swollen feet and cramps as for seasoning a bouillabaisse. In 1970, author Laurence Durrell was looking for a remedy for his eczema. He took the advice of Arles market trader Ludo Chardenon and brewed a pot of herbal tea. Chardenon then became a best-selling author in his own right. *In Praise of Wild Herbs* is still in print, with its suggested remedies for baldness, acne and cellulite.

Soup kitchens

Foodies from far afield pack their forks and prepare to tantalize the taste buds at the legendary Gastronomic Days festival in the Roman town of Vaison-la-Romaine in November. Master bakers, great chefs and award-winning wine-makers descend on the town for five days' lip-smacking competition. Locals, though, prefer the earthier contest between some 14 nearby villages that takes place a week or so earlier. Which village housewife makes the best bowl of soup? To decide all are invited to roll up their sleeves and dip their ladles in the pots, bowls and tureens of the makeshift soup bars in each village. Lots of music and dancing—and plenty of *potages, veloutés* and *consommés*—ward off the winter chill.

A Provençal Christmas

If you dine out in Provence at the end of December you'll find that Christmas dinner is both a sweet and savoury occasion. The table is decked with symbolism and tradition in mind. The *Gros Souper* (Big Supper) on Christmas Eve is one of the south's most cherished rituals. With 13 desserts, the meal is known for its abundance of sweets and, paradoxically, for its so-called austerity. Dishes include modest marinated vegetables, *anchoaïde* (anchovy paste), salt-cod and *escargots à l'aïoli* (snails in garlic), through to the finale of a spread of platters representing Christ and the apostles, with nougats, nuts and raisins, and plenty of fruit dishes, from delicious figs to sweet *confits* (candied fruits). The table is draped with three white cloths and set with bowls and candles symbolizing the Holy Trinity.

A twist in the tale

How does a winemaker while away the months and years before his replanted vines bear fruit? The answer, in Ménerbes at least, is to make sure he has enough corkscrews to open the bottles once they are ready for drinking. Yves Rousset-Rouard collected corkscrews, in ivory, gold, silver and wood, until he had enough to open a museum in his Côte du Lubéron cellars. At his Musée du Tire-Bouchon, in Cavaillon, you can see more than 1,000, dating from the very first models of the 17th century to the latest high-tech boys-toys gadgets. While his wines have garnered gold and silver medals for their quality, the vigneron has also won great reviews from the wine media for his collection of ornate tools.

HERBES DE PROVENCE

White-water rafting on the Verdon river

Horseback riding in the Camargue (above).
Fast action in the Monaco Grand Prix (right).
Boules in St-Tropez (below)

Sport and Leisure

Square balls

Pétanque, the great bowling sport of the south, is an essential part of Provence life. No village is without its *boulodrome*, the grand name for a dusty square where locals roll boules in the late afternoon. But what of those steep perched villages on the hillside behind the Riviera, where streets are on such a slope that front and back doors may be on different floors? The answer, in Haut-de-Cagnes, is simple: Use square balls. In creating their cubed bowling balls, the villagers invented a whole new sport. *Boules Carrées* now has its own world championship, with 300 players descending on Cagnes for the finals each summer.

France is a nation of sports lovers, even if, when it comes to participation, some may prefer to argue the latest scores and scandals over a drink at the local *bar des sports*. In Provence, those who like to take things easy choose the sedentary pleasures of pétanque, or bowls, in the town square. The game gets its name, depending on which story you prefer, from the patois version of the phrase *pieds tanques* (feet together) or the clanking sound of the balls clashing.

Traditional boules is played over a long course of some 20m (66ft), whereas pétanque uses a smaller area.

More energetic pursuits include white-water rafting, canoeing and other adventures on inland waterways. Water sports have grown up along the seaside resorts, with world-class windsurfing at Saintes-Maries-de-la-Mer. You can play golf at links along the coast or go horseback riding in the Camargue. Hikers can even travel with a donkey!

Spectator sports range from rugby to bullfighting in the Roman arenas. The local *Courses Camarguaises* are less bloody than the traditional bullfight, with the bull being allowed to survive the contest. Compassionate visitors beware: At *ferias*, or festival days, the arenas of Arles and Nîmes stage Spanish-style corridas in which the bull is killed.

Inline skating along the Promenade des Anglais, Nice

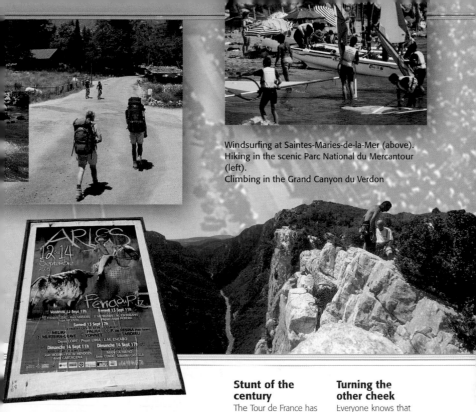

Windsurfing at Saintes-Maries-de-la-Mer (above).
Hiking in the scenic Parc National du Mercantour (left).
Climbing in the Grand Canyon du Verdon

A stroll with your snorkel

Ten per cent of France is protected parkland. However, should you fancy a ramble in the park of Port-Cros, don't forget your snorkel. This 687ha (1,700-acre) island, one of the Îles d'Hyères, is nestled in amazingly clear waters and was designated as a national park in 1963. The protected zone extends around the coast, some 600m (654 yards) out to sea. The nature trail here takes visitors under water more than a third of a mile along the seabed. Signposted visitor trails continue from the island's paths down into the unspoiled waters. To protect the wildlife, boats are not allowed to moor on the sandy beaches. Underwater guided tours from La Palud beach are free, but you should bring your own snorkel.

Bullfights are still staged at Arles

Rugby is a popular sport

Bicycling up one of Provence's many hills

Stunt of the century

The Tour de France has been going for more than a century, which is not bad for a marketing stunt. Originally staged in 1903 to publicize *l'Auto* magazine, the first *tour* saw 60 riders covering 2,500km (1,550 miles) over 19 days. There were only six stages, so riders had to pedal their boneshakers through the night. These days, not only are comfortable hotels provided, but vast tracts of the country are crossed by luxury train or plane between stages. The event has been dogged by tabloid headlines and intrigue almost since the first race. Dirty tricks of previous years included nails scattered on the road and allegations of poisoning.

Turning the other cheek

Everyone knows that Provence is the place to buy pétanque balls. However, less well known is Marseille's sideline industry selling reproduction buttocks to lovers of the sport. Traditionally players from the south of France have to pay a specific forfeit if they score no points at all in a match. The origins of the custom of kissing a sculpted or painted *derrière* after losing the game are lost in the mists of time. However, no self-respecting *boulodrome* is without a discreetly positioned pair of artificial buttocks. So do not be surprised when visiting the village potter to encounter a realistic looking backside among the olive bowls, fruit platters and garlic graters.

Contrasts in style: a rural gîte (above) and the eye-catching façade of the Fondation Vasarely (right), in Aix

Striking modern design at the Hi-hôtel, in Nice (right)

Urban vs. Rural

Cabins in the sun

While New Yorkers have their summer houses in the Hamptons, the good people of Marseille have their *cabanons*. Most casual visitors may well pass through the coastal area south of Marseille unaware of its unique *cabanon* lifestyle. This is focused on weekend and holiday houses where families decamp to party and play boules or cards with their friends in huts, cabins, shacks and boathouses. The *Route des Cabanons* takes you through the enchanting yet little-known villages of Montredon, Madrague and Morgiou, as well as better-known fishing ports such as Vallon des Auffes. The tourist office in Marseille can suggest an early evening driving itinerary through this hinterland of the south.

The arrival of the TGV (super-fast trains) cut journey times between Paris and Provence. But move from the city to the country and your journey will still be measured in decades not hours. Away from the urban buzz, Provence's villages eschew the cult of internationalism, choosing instead a celebration of all things rural. People nod and bid each other a friendly *bonjour* when passing in the street. Of course, time does leave its mark, and those same fast trains that are making France smaller are nudging away at those differences. The Mediterranean is now only three hours from Paris, and as local trains link up with TGVs, city families are leaving behind the cosmopolitan life to move to the country. These families are buying rural houses not just for weekends (a trend that threatens many village communities), but as their main homes. They believe their children will receive a better education in the country, so the breadwinner opts for a weekly commute to the city and staying in a studio pied-à-terre, while the rest of the family lives the country life.

Designer Hotel

The 21st century is the era of the designer hotel. Where once it was enough to have designer Philippe Starck come up with waiters' uniforms or a new chair, France's newest hotels vie for the most outrageous concepts. In Nice, the palatial elegance of the Negresco has a new rival in Matali Crasset's multi-concept Hi-hôtel, where you can choose the space that best suits your mood. Shower behind a plant screen in a room with an indoor terrace theme, relax on furniture created from computer monitors or sing along to the Sofablaster with its built-in music. Other options include a bathroom with a lava rockpool and, for total luxury, a champagne vending machine.

The Story of Provence and the Côte d'Azur

Prehistory, Greeks & Romans

Provence took its name because it was indeed a province of Rome, while all of France farther north was a mere colony. The region boasts more Roman buildings than anywhere outside Italy, with magnificent constructions ranging from arenas to the breathtaking Pont du Gard. However, beyond grand edifices remain legacies of local communities dating back many thousands of years. The first known settlement is Terra Amata, discovered behind the old port in Nice. Cro-Magnon hunters lived near freshwater springs by the beach. At Menton, Palaeolithic discoveries include a 30,000-year-old skull and burial sites with bodies draped in shell-jewellery. Neolithic and Bronze Age Ligurians, who farmed the region around 8,000 years ago, left their mark with impressive rock engravings in the Vallée des Merveilles.

At this time, the Ligurians began intermarrying with Celtic tribes and started the trading migrations that changed the face of the Mediterranean. First arrivals were the Greek Phocaeans, who established the bridgehead of Massalia (Marseille). It was a relatively peaceful settlement until conflict with local Celts led the Greeks to appeal to Rome for back-up in 124BC. Canny Romans, who marched in under the command of Sextius Calvinius, saw the area's potential and made their first settlement at Aquae Sextiae (Aix-en-Provence). Founding a capital at Narbonne (in modern Languedoc) in 118BC, the Romans soon held a territory stretching from the Pyrenees in the west to the Alps in the east, and as far north as Lyon. Roadbuilding included the Via Agrippa, north from Arles and Avignon, the Via Aurelia, towards Italy, and the Via Domitia, to Spain. Southern Gaul was now part of the empire.

Prehistory

To Greece with love

In surprising contrast to the warlike arrival of the Roman regime, the Greeks won Marseille in the most improbable manner: It was given as a wedding present. When a group of Greek traders dropped anchor at the Lacydon inlet on France's Mediterranean coast, they were fortunate enough to arrive just as the local king, Nann, was holding a banquet for his daughter to choose a husband. As luck would have it, the lass, Gyptis, was rather taken with Protis, the spokesman for the new arrivals. So she chose him as her fiancé. Better yet, King Nann gave Lacydon (the site of today's Vieux Port) to the couple. Thus, with no hint of aggression or unpleasantness, the Greeks were able to establish a colony at one of Europe's most strategic sites.

A Classical statue in Vaison-la-Romaine (below)

All Rhodes lead to Rhône

Provence's greatest river pays tribute to an island across the Mediterranean, thanks to the trading routes into Gaul established by the Greeks. The river Rhône provided an unrivalled trade corridor between the Mediterranean and key settlements in Provence, with local tin, copper, gold and silver exchanged for Greek ceramics. The Greeks planted exotic fruits and vines along the river bank, tended with Hellenic know-how, and established a wine and olive oil trade. The river itself was named after the Greek island of Rhodes, with the adjective *Rhôdéenne* still used today to describe the plains along the river valley.

A statue of Empress Sabine (left), found at Vaison-la-Romaine. Julius Caesar (below)

The unlikely capital

Proof, if any were needed, that political acumen is more than a match for natural resources is found in the speedy elevation of Arles to the capital of Roman Provence. The unlikely choice of Arles over the more obvious trading port of Marseille is due to the town's canny allegiances at the time of Julius Caesar's conflict with Pompey in the turmoil that followed Caesar's conquest of Gaul in 51BC. Marseille, or Massalia as it was then known, backed the wrong side, whereas Arles supported Caesar, even building a fleet of 12 boats for him. Thus Caesar sacked the port on the Med and elevated Arles to capital. Even when Marseille had re-established itself in later centuries, the legacy of Roman patronage guaranteed Arles success through the Renaissance and beyond.

A prehistoric rock carving of a chieftain, from the Vallée des Merveilles (right). An olive branch (far right)

Cavemen leave their mark

While cave paintings in the Dordogne are visible proof of prehistoric life in France, Provence had long lacked this type of artistic legacy from its earliest inhabitants. Then, in 1991, Henri Cosquer went diving along the coast near Cassis. The limestone cliffs are famous for their fjord-like *calanques* (inlets), and it was 37m (121ft) under the sea that Cosquer found an opening in one of them. Exploring further, he discovered a cave lined with hundreds of paintings of bison, deer, fish and horses—dating from around 25,000BC. The site became known as the underwater Lascaux and was listed as a historical monument in 1992. The caves are not on the visitor trail. They were walled up after other divers died trying to visit them.

The good life

Leisure is not a modern concept. Provence was something of an arts and entertainment hub for the Roman Empire. The area's incredible legacy of theatres, arenas and bathhouses owes much to the reign of Augustus, who established a large number of settlements to be governed by military veterans. Towns such as Arles, Avignon and Vaison soon developed into cities and cultural hubs with grandiose architecture reflecting the artistic and relaxed lifestyle of a prosperous peace. Temples, sporting arenas, theatres, aqueducts and bridges made the cities more desirable outposts of the empire. The luxuries of life were funded by Provence's natural resources and the development of a skilled workforce. The region produced oil, grain and ships for the empire.

AD300

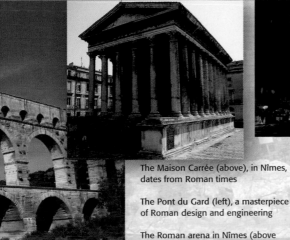

The Maison Carrée (above), in Nîmes, dates from Roman times

The Pont du Gard (left), a masterpiece of Roman design and engineering

The Roman arena in Nîmes (above right) is still used today

The Celts (right) arrived in Provence between the 8th and 4th centuries BC

23

Christianity and Feudalism

Feudalism

Christianity arrived in Provence towards the end of the Roman era. Preachers settled on the coast and St. Trophimus came to Arles quite early on, but it was after the open support of Emperor Constantine in the fourth century AD that Christianity established itself. The first Church Council took place in Arles in AD314 and the next century saw the construction of abbeys and monasteries around Marseille.

As Rome's influence declined, so peace evaporated. The Visigoths made incursions into Arles and other invaders encroached on Provence. By AD536 the Franks were the leading power. Saracens from across the Pyrenees in Spain, seeing the destruction of a formerly unified province, began taking key towns in the eighth century AD. This resulted in a period of conflict between the Saracens and the Franks, led by General Charles Martel. The Franks forced the Saracens out of Provence throughout the 730s, but this was no lasting peace. For more than a century, Saracens continued to raid towns from their bases such as La Garde-Freinet, besieging Marseille in AD838 and Arles in AD842.

Provence became a kingdom in its own right in AD855, but found itself subject to renewed attacks, from not only the Saracens but also the Normans. The Saracens were finally overwhelmed in 1032, when Guillaume le Libérateur banished them at the dawn of the era of the Counts of Provence. The feudal system saw local seigneurs governing their own fiefdoms. This coincided with a golden era of learning, thanks to the monasteries, and trade, developing after the Crusades.

An unsuccessful hermit

While other offshore attractions lure hordes of visitors, the island of St-Honorat, one of the îles de Lérins near Cannes, has managed to retain its monastic peace. A Christian community was accidentally established here in the fourth century AD by St. Honoratus, arch-bishop of Arles, a great teacher and one of history's least successful hermits. He chose the island as a place of solitary contemplation, yet, according to contemporary writers, he established an enormous monastery. The island soon earned an enviable reputation as a place of learning, despite not having any formal teaching structure. It produced many of the Church's best known saints, among them Ireland's St. Patrick and Marseille's St. Cassian. The tranquil setting of today's Abbaye de Lérins belies a tumultuous history. The monks were slaughtered by Saracens in the seventh century AD.

AD300

A statue of Charlemagne (above), who became king of the Franks in the eighth century

The monastic community at Lérins (above) dates back to the fourth century AD.
The Abbaye de Silvacane (right)

Revenge of the Hammer

Victor over the Saracens, Charles Martel (Charles the Hammer) famously began his own power-broking regimes towards the end of his life, arbitrarily announcing rulers and appointing leaders throughout the land. Charles did not put too much stock in the legal rules of succession, having suffered first hand from the vagaries of a step-grandmother who manipulated the fortunes of her own family, when Charles was in his 20s. To prevent Charles' objections to her policy, Plectrude, a lady with a will of iron, had arranged for the lad to be thrown into prison. He wrested power from Plectrude and, in a series of bloody battles, took on all Saracen uprisings, eventually defeating Saracen settlements in Avignon, Marseille and Aix-en-Provence, restoring Frankish Christian rule to the region.

Saracens' legacy

Pillaging, laying siege to entire communities and a general warlike stance have given the invading Saracens some bad press over the years. However, just as the Greeks left their vines, and the Romans their infrastructure, the Saracens also gave Provence a pretty decent legacy. Flat tiled roofs can be traced back directly to their arrival in Provence and (albeit less practical) the tambourine was their gift to music. The most profitable gift to the locals was the cork industry, which flourished for around 900 years after the Saracens left. In La Garde-Freinet, chestnut groves and eucalyptus trees surrounding the town are outnumbered by vast woods of cork oak trees. By the 19th century, La Garde-Freinet was France's principal producer of cork.

Les Baux-de-Provence (below) had its heyday in feudal times.

Miracle Madonna

The oldest Black Madonna statue in France is in the Église St-Sauveur, in Manosque (▷ 144). Said to have been found in a nearby forest in the sixth century AD, it mysteriously disappeared for generations before being rediscovered as the church was being built. The monks did not like the look of the statue (Black Madonnas were often the subject of fear and superstition) and decided to leave the Madonna outside the church door. Local legend has it that the Madonna walked into the church and made her way to the altar. Despite this, the monks removed the icon and placed her outside once again. Whereupon, so the story goes, she once again returned to the church altar, where she has stayed ever since.

From battle to ballads

Music hath charms to soothe the most savage beast. And so feuding feudal barons of Les Baux-de-Provence, whose regimes were marked with bloodshed, were responsible for a mini-musical renaissance as well as for military aggression. From the 10th century the lords, who claimed kinship with the magi kings attending Christ's nativity, fought to assert their authority with regard to land. However, in wooing for love, they preferred a more gentle approach and would hire troubadours to pen ballads and sing serenades at the windows of potential wives. This led to Les Baux becoming a musical hot spot, with strolling players from far and wide descending on the citadel to sing in the streets in European song contests.

Charlemagne

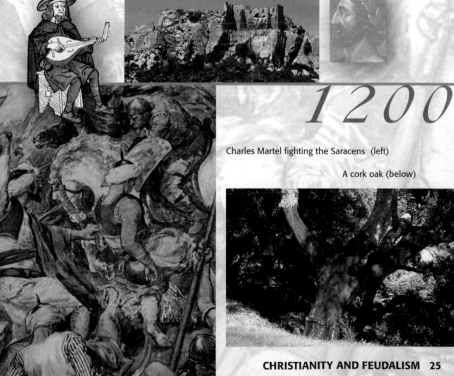

1200

Charles Martel fighting the Saracens (left)

A cork oak (below)

Conflict and Culture

The squabbles of the feudal lords were finally ended in the 13th century, when Count Raymond-Bérenger V of Barcelona took control of the region, establishing firm laws and an administrative structure based on his own Catalan regime. It was the marriage of his youngest daughter Beatrice that set Provence on the path to stability. In 1246 Beatrice married Charles of Anjou, brother to Louis IX, King of France, and part of a family with a strong track record of ruling. Britain's Plantagenet monarchs came from the same stock.

Earlier in the century, in Languedoc, France waged war against the Cathars (followers of a heretical Christian sect). Avignon made the mistake of allying itself with the losing side and was attacked by France and badly damaged in 1226. France seized control of the Comtat Venaissin, territories north of Avignon. This was in turn given to Rome in 1274, in a move that led to the Avignon papacy. This period brought an artistic and cultural boom to Provence. Under the patronage of the popes, a thriving university developed in Avignon and artists came from Sienna to decorate the new palaces and chapels.

Outside the charmed enclave, the rest of Provence found the 14th century less enjoyable. There was a great plague in 1348 and when Queen Jeanne died childless in 1382 it led to the inevitable warring over the succession. Louis II (d.1434) and the legendary Roi René (1409–1480) brought stability back to Provence. Meanwhile Nice, no longer part of Provence, spent the coming centuries until the French Revolution warring with France and the Duchy of Savoy.

Beginning of the end

When Louis XI inherited Provence after the death of King René in 1480, the French king set about bringing the region under closer royal control. As Louis began measures to dilute the powers of Provence's *États-Généraux* (States General), Aix's politicians voiced public opposition. Eventually, as Provence was a crucial buffer zone between the French and Italian provinces—after all, what is now the Riviera had long been ceded to Savoyard and Genovese control—the Crown relented. In 1486, a compromise treaty was signed granting Provence freedom to run its own legal institutions.

1200

A stone dragon on the Hôtel des Monnaies, Avignon

Tarascon's dramatic *tarasque* procession (left)

A medieval street in the *village perché* of Peille

The popes at Avignon

After years of violence at the hands of the citizens of Rome, the Pope fled to the safety of Avignon in 1309, after an invitation from King Philip, who lusted after papal money and influence on French soil. The popes lived in a fortress-like palace, which the poet Petrarch called 'a sewer where all the filth of the universe had gathered', and by 1377 the court was so threatened by thieves and swindlers that Gregory XI returned to Rome. The sovereigns of Europe then sponsored their own candidates, and by 1414 there was the spectacle of three popes, each vying for pre-eminence. The prelates of the Sorbonne, among others, put a stop to this, and in 1418 a sole pope again sat in Rome.

Renaissance René

Roi René was a popular figure and credited with the golden age of Aix-en-Provence. Indeed, some historians pun his name, claiming the Renaissance as 'René essence'. Good King René of the House of Anjou boasted several dukedoms and was also King of Aragon, Hungary, Mallorca, Naples, Sardinia, Sicily, Valencia and even Jerusalem. He enjoyed something of a front-row seat at history, escorting Joan of Arc to visit the Dauphin in Orléans and giving Christopher Columbus his first naval commission. He was a true Renaissance man, speaking six languages, writing a rule book for the sport of jousting, and excelling in the arts as painter, poet and musician. When jailed by the Duke of Burgundy, he passed time by perfecting his skills at engraving on glass.

When is a monk not a monk?

From the 12th century, Monaco belonged to Genoa, a city state split between two factions, the papist Guelfs and the Ghibellines. When the Guelf Grimaldi family was chased out of Genoa, they seized their rivals' land along the Riviera. The prize of Monaco was won when François Grimaldi and an accomplice, disguised as monks, gained access to the fortress, then drew swords from under their habits to take control of Monaco. This is remembered today on the family crest—two sword-wielding monks.

Hidden dragon

June visitors to Tarascon are often surprised to see a dragon dance in the streets—an event that might seem more at home in a New Year's celebration in Hong Kong than a midsummer carnival in Provence. However this is truly a Provençal tradition, even if the monster is not quite a dragon. The ritual was established in 1474 to commemorate the routing of the *Tarasque*, a legendary beast that supposedly emerged from the waters of the port and terrorized the town, eating children and cattle. The story goes that St. Martha tamed the beast by waving her crucifix at it. The monster then allowed itself to be put on a lead and trotted off, leaving the townsfolk in peace. The dragon dance, with its attendant bonfires and fireworks, represents the taming of the beast—a symbol of Christianity's supremacy over paganism.

The Grimaldi coat of arms (below), on Monaco's Palais Princier

Tarascon's 15th-century castle (below)

Pope Gregory XI (far left)

The procession of Roi René, at Aix-en-Provence (left)

1500

Avignon's Palais des Papes (above)

Finally French

Provence lost its language in 1539. With the Edict of Villers-Cotterêts, King François I delivered the death sentence on Provençal, one of several *langues d'Oc* (languages of the south). He made it illegal to use any language other than French in schools, churches and local administration.

The 16th century brought fresh religious conflict to Provence, with the rise of Protestantism, as much a challenge to the monarchy as to the Catholic Church. Various sects around the country were regarded as hotbeds of insurgency, and the State took revenge with bloody massacres in the Petit Lubéron: Around 3,000 people were slaughtered over five April days in 1545. Protestants attacked Orange Cathedral and churches across Haute-Provence, bringing an inevitable backlash of State-sanctioned massacre.

The return of plague and the coronation of the former Huguenot Henri IV at the end of the century calmed the situation, with the 1598 Edict of Nantes securing freedom of worship for Protestants. It was a short-lived peace, as after Henri's assassination in 1610, Louis XIII and Cardinal Richelieu flexed the monarchy's muscles against the regions. In 1685, Louis XIV revoked the Edict of Nantes, leading to a mass Protestant exodus.

Decadence in Louis' court and corruption in successive reigns, coupled with a decline in Provence's fortune after blighted harvests, meant the region was ready to follow Paris' lead when it came to Revolution in 1789. Chateaux and churches were looted and the guillotine was set up in Marseille.

Ultimate pest control

When a village calls itself Contes (stories), it is no surprise that its history is made up of myths and legends. Among many *contes* in the village, in the Alpes-Maritimes, was the tale of an invasion of voracious caterpillars in 1508. The grubs took to the streets, devouring everything in sight and secreting a poison causing rashes and illness among the residents. As the creatures munched their way through pine needles and foliage, the citizens appealed to the Bishop of Nice, who came to the village in order to perform the exorcism that finally rid Contes of its most unwelcome invaders.

Henri IV

Plague hits Marseille in 1792 (below)

Nostradamus (below) was born in St-Rémy-de-Provence. His writings (below left) are still popular today

1500

Man of the centuries

Michel de Nostre Dame was born in St-Rémy-de-Provence in 1503 into a family of recent converts from Judaism to Catholicism. A stargazer from his school days, Nostradamus studied medicine. He devoted his early years to finding a cure to the plague that ravaged 16th-century Provence, experimenting with herbalism and blending established medical practice with country lore. Gaining a reputation as a doctor, he moved to Salon-de-Provence in 1547, but within a decade he had become better known as the court astrologer, with his first book of predictions published in 1555. Nostradamus died in 1566, but his work lives on, his own immortality guaranteed by the *Siècles* (centuries), cryptic predictions re-appraised by each successive generation to reveal visions of tyrants and natural disasters.

The French flag (below), flying from a building in Arles

The price of freedom

Marseille rose up against Louis XIV in 1659 and the king retaliated by building a fortress to keep an eye on the city's citizens. However, in the early 18th century, the king granted Marseille the status of Free Port, increasing its fortunes. Unfortunately, as the port grew, so did the risk of infection from dubious cargoes. In 1720 a ship brought the third and worst outbreak of plague to Marseille, killing half the population of the city and claiming 100,000 lives across Provence.

The girl in the velvet mask, perhaps?

Not all prisoners in 17th-century France were granted the respect paid to the most famous resident of the Fort Royal, on the island of Sainte-Marguerite. Contemporary accounts state that the guards would take off their hats in his presence. For this was the Man in the Iron Mask. The writer Voltaire dropped hints as to his identity, suggesting he bore a stunning resemblance to a very famous Frenchman. A popular story is that the prisoner was the twin brother of Louis XIV. Another claims the man was in fact a woman, the female heir to the throne, and other conspiracy theorists say the prisoner had proof of the king's illegitimacy. It is not just the man who is the subject of conjecture. Experts dispute the nature of the mask. Some swear it was made of black velvet.

A menacing costume designed to protect doctors from the plague

How Marseille got its song

The French national anthem, *La Marseillaise*, is probably the best known link between the Republic and Marseille. So it is surprising to discover that it was written about an army that could not have been farther from Marseille, and by a loyal supporter of the monarchy. The Revolution was well under way when the aristocratic mayor of Strasbourg commissioned a marching song from Claude-Joseph Rouget de Lisle in 1792. The song of the Rhine army was then promoted as the song of the border armies. Then François Mireur came to Marseille to recruit volunteers to storm Louis XVI's Tuileries palace. The soldiers of the south sang the song so lustily when they marched into Paris that the Parisians renamed it *La Marseillaise*. It became a national anthem in 1795.

1800

The cover of a song sheet for *La Marseillaise* (left)

A ship leaves Marseille in the mid-18th century (below)

Religious conflict in the Petit Lubéron

The 19th Century

The 19th century was the hundred years that began to define modern France, politically and artistically. Napoleon Bonaparte seized power at the turn of the century, bringing an end to the Terror that had followed the French Revolution. Provence was less supportive of Napoleon's imperial wars and downright cross at losing a swathe of the Alpes-Maritimes to Sardinia on his defeat in the Russian campaign. After his abdication, the former emperor made one final march through the region after escaping from Elba before being defeated at Waterloo.

The subsequent return to power of the royal family led to a revival of the old political skirmishing in Provence. After a lull at the coronation in 1830 of 'Citizen King' Louis-Philippe, Provençal tempers flared up again in support of his overthrow in the 1848 revolution and passions still simmered during the reign of Napoleon III from 1850.

The second half of the century saw a flourishing of art and literary movements, with the poet Frédéric Mistral reclaiming local identity. Rail links brought tourism to the south of France and also moved artists from the dark skies of northern Europe to the vibrancy of the Riviera.

Commercially, Provence changed during this period, with modern shipbuilding and the opening of the Suez Canal reforming industries and establishing global markets. Marseille became a base for sugar refining and exporting soap.

The Côte d'Azur

British people of the upper class in the 19th century often went on the Grand Tour in Europe. In 1834, Lord Brougham, a member of the English aristocracy, was forced to spend the night in the village of Cannes and loved the place so much he built a villa there. His wealthy friends soon followed him and over the years British aristocrats opened up the rest of the coast, resulting in a rail line connecting London directly to Menton (via a ferry) by 1868. Royalty were not averse to the Riviera's charms—Queen Victoria spent winters at Nice in the 1890s, away from the chills and fogs of England. Even today there is a little bit of Nice that is forever England—the seafront is named Promenade des Anglais.

Napoleon III was among visitors to the Côte d'Azur in the 19th century

1800

A Côte d'Azur ticket

LE LAVANDOU

Côte d'Azur

STATION HIVERNALE ET BALNÉAIRE

12 Cartes Détachables

Nice in the 19th century (below) and one of its most famous visitors (below right), Queen Victoria

l'Hiver à Nice

Services Rapides
PARIS & NICE

A poster advertises winter in Nice

Looks familiar

The *tricolore* blue, white and red flag of the French Republic was a long time coming. At the start of the Revolution in 1789 a simple blue and red cockade was used as the national symbol. Blue, white and red were agreed as the republican colours in 1794. With the restoration of the monarchy, a combination of the *tricolore* with the national emblem of a cockerel proved an unsatisfactory compromise. By the revolution of 1848 the simple blue, white and red symbol came back into fashion, and the state adopted the *tricolore* we know today, taken from the original flag of the Provençal town of Martigues. The royalists never accepted the dismissal of their cockerel, but the blue, white and red was officially enshrined as a national symbol, with the blue stripe always flown closest to the flagpole.

A plaque of artist Paul Cézanne

Mistral blows away the cobwebs

The rediscovery of the once-banned Provençal language can be traced to the region's most famous poet, Frédéric Mistral (1830–1914), a Nobel-prize winner. After conventional schooling near his home in St-Rémy, Mistral studied in Avignon, where he found a fellow lover of the old tongue in Joseph Roumanille. On 21 May 1854, Roumanille, Mistral and five other writers founded the Félibrige movement for the revival of the traditional language of Provence. A year later, Mistral established the annual *Armanan Provençau*, the first publication to be written in Provençal since the 16th century. He opened a museum of traditional culture in Arles with his Nobel prize money. You'll find plaques featuring his poems across the area.

Recipe for fame

These days, television produces a never-ending stream of celebrity chefs, but in the 19th century, cooks remained anonymous. The first kitchen master to become a celebrity in his own right was Auguste Escoffier, who learned his trade in the family restaurant in Nice back in the 1880s. By the turn of the century he had launched the Ritz in Paris and Savoy in London. Escoffier was quick to see the advantages of fame, and he swiftly launched spin-off industries marketing his own brand of utensils and a stream of cook-books. His birthplace, in the village of Villeneuve Loubet, is home to the Fondation Escoffier museum, where foodies may salivate at exhibitions of simple country cooking and haute cuisine.

Celebrity chef Auguste Escoffier (left)

The Riviera coast, viewed from Èze (below)

Local boy paints good

Although the tortured artist most often associated with Provence is Vincent Van Gogh, his famous link with Arles and St-Rémy lasted just two years. The local boy with an intense passion for his art was in fact Paul Cézanne. Born in Aix-en-Provence on 10 January 1839, he moved to Paris in his twenties and joined the young Impressionists, but was disillusioned at the reception their work received and returned to his home town. Here he worked alone, developing his style in the Provence country-side and his attic studio in rue Boulegon. Like Van Gogh, Cézanne became extraordinarily prolific during his final years, creating more than 300 paintings after 1895. As he finally achieved recognition, he built a typical Provençal-style house, called Les Lauves, by Aix Cathedral. He died on 22 October 1906.

1900

The 20th Century

At the start of the 20th century, the artistic and literary boom of the Belle Époque continued, with a new generation of *arrivistes* including Pablo Picasso and Raoul Dufy. This, coupled with the high-profile celebrity status of selected resorts, highlighted the dramatic difference in the fortunes of the coast and the inland areas. As traditional rural occupations disappeared, people moved to the cities in search of work, often a fruitless journey.

World War II left key cities such as Avignon and Marseille battered and bruised, with their infrastructures and industries all but wiped out. The 1950s saw road building, including the *autoroute* Esterel–Côte d'Azur, and the 1960s brought major investment, with the first plans of a TGV rail network and huge concrete industrial plants bringing jobs to the region, if compromising the aesthetics. Petrochemical plants, oil refineries and tanker terminals gave fuel to the fortunes of Marseille and the outlying area. Hydroelectric power stations and the Canal de Provence boosted the agricultural and industrial economy inland.

The post-war period saw the area reinvented as a summer cultural capital. Cannes Film Festival and Avignon's theatre festival led the way to creating an international meeting place of the arts. The 1960s saw the first of the legendary jazz events in the Gould pine grove at Juan-les-Pins and brought Count Basie, Ella Fitzgerald and Charlie Parker to the coast. Aix's *Art Lyrique* opera festival sees an opera house built each summer in the courtyard of the Archbishop's palace and has been responsible for discovering some of the world's leading talents.

Arrivederci Mercantour

The 20th century saw the final Italian retreat from Provence. The Italianate architecture of the Riviera is the enduring testament to generations of cultural occupation. However the last corner of the region to remain part of the adjoining country has no architectural legacy. The Mercantour was Italy's 19th-century royal hunting ground, a sprawling natural landscape stretching from Piemonte to the Alpes-Maritimes and Alpes-de-Haute-Provence. The rocks, canyons, mountain peaks, alpine forests and meadows are home to eagles, kestrels, vultures, mouflons, chamois and wild boar and more than 2,000 varieties of plant life. In 1946 the area was finally split across national borders, and 68,000ha (168,000 acres) returned to France. Both nations granted the site national park status. The park has been designated a protected nature reserve since 1979.

1900

Charles Aznavour, Ella Fitzgerald and Eddie Barclay on the Côte d'Azur, in 1964

Shopping at the Marché des Ramparts, Avignon

Go build it on the mountains

The growth of air travel in the 1960s and the boom in affordable tourism led to an explosion in hotel and apartment building along the Côte d'Azur. Not all the construction projects reflected the traditional Provençal and Savoyard style of the region. Soon, concrete threatened to overshadow ochre cliffs and olive groves as the face of the coast, with controversial high-rises and schemes such as the Marina des Anges. Away from the Riviera, inland tourism promoted renovation and restoration of old village houses. Just 90 minutes from the Promenade des Anglais, the alpine ski villages also welcomed more visitors, and in the 1970s the first new winter sports resort, Isola 2000, at 2,000m (6,560ft) above sea level, was built above the traditional old village of Isola, 17km (10 miles) away.

Occupation and resistance

From 1940 to 1944, under the German occupation, the Vichy Government of Marshal Pétain ran the southern part of France. It's a painful episode that still divides French society. Klaus Barbie was convicted of war crimes in the 1980s. Vichy is remembered for deporting 70,000 Jews and 650,000 workers from France to Germany. But Vichy did not spring solely from Nazi occupation. Far-right politicians in 1930s France had spoken out against foreigners and pushed through the Family Code in 1939, setting down strict laws for women and sexual morality.

Philippe Pétain

Rise of the Right

After nearly 3,000 years of ethnic infusion, which started when Celts, Greeks and Romans settled along the coast, immigration is still a political hot potato. In 1962, as Algeria won independence from France, thousands of *Pieds Noirs*, former colonists, returned from Africa, bringing with them the first in a wave of racist outcries that was refuelled by the rise of Jean-Marie Le Pen's far-right Front National party in the 1980s. The Front achieved its biggest political successes in the ports and urban areas of the south. Orange and Toulon were among the other key strongholds of the far right towards the end of the century.

Prince Rainier and Grace Kelly, on their engagement in 1956 (right)

Jean-Marie Le Pen

America-sur-Med

If Paris was the home of 19th-century Americans in exile (Oscar Wilde said 'When good Americans die, they go to Paris'), the 20th century saw Provence stake a claim for the title. Luxury hotels and villas created a charmed combination of metropolitan society in an idyllic climate. Before World War II, author F. Scott Fitzgerald, composer Cole Porter and actor Rudolph Valentino were among the Juan-les-Pins crowd. In the 1940s, the Cannes Film Festival introduced Errol Flynn and Clark Gable to the Riviera. Most celebrated of all was film star Grace Kelly who, in the ultimate Hollywood love story, married Prince Rainier of Monaco and became Riviera royalty.

2000

Cap Ferrat, crowned by the Villa Ephrussi de Rothschild (above)

Crowds at the Cannes Film Festival (above)

Nice's Museum of Modern Art (left)

The 21st Century

The 20th century turned as the Riviera was discovering a new and unaccustomed humility. Just as the most chic resorts were launching and refurbishing ever more luxurious hotels, the area's traditional market shrank. The threat of global terrorism after 9/11 kept many wealthy overseas visitors at home, so the €3,000-a-week rents for holiday villas outside Avignon and Aix and the fortune-a-night room charges at pampering palaces on the Med were no longer bankable guarantees. Fortunately, low-cost air travel from the UK brought new visitors to the once exclusively millionaires' playgrounds, and people began exploring the backcountry in search of affordable second homes. A world away from the glitz of the 20th century, villages developed heritage tourism, focusing on country pursuits and traditional crafts.

It's a small world

Provence came closer to London in June 2001, when Eurostar launched a direct summer rail service non-stop from London to the heart of Avignon. The service, which travels through the Channel Tunnel, means you can go from the Thames to the Rhône in just over six hours.

Single currency, choice of emblems

On New Year's Day 2002, France said goodbye to its national currency, the franc, but Provence found itself with two local versions of the euro in its tills. Coins carry the euro symbol on one side and national emblems on the other. Those issued in France are stamped with various images of the Republic.

However, under a special treaty with the EU, Monaco, which is not a member of the union, was granted permission to issue its own euros, embossed with national symbols. Cherished by coin collectors, since fewer coins were minted than in most other euro states, these coins feature either the national crest or the head of Prince Rainier.

Traditional interiors

The architect Norman Foster is usually associated with modernist forward-looking designs, so at the start of a new century it was surprising to see him unveiling a new building boasting interior designs thousands of years old. In 2001, Europe's largest Museum of Prehistory opened in the village of Quinson, in the Parc Régional du Verdon. Provence welcomed the new millennium by turning the spotlight on its earliest inhabitants, the Verdon canyon having been the hub of the region's first communities. In 2001 Foster's almond-shaped museum opened, housing bones and other items from around 60 local caves and featuring a reconstruction of the Grotte de la Beaume Bonne.

The sleek interior of the Museum of Prehistory (abo...

2000–today

Painting faïences in Moustiers-Sainte-Marie

Old meets new in 21st-century Provence—medieval streets in Èze (above); a sign for a traditional workshop in Moustiers-Sainte Marie (left); Eurostar (far left)

On the Move

ARRIVING

Arriving by Air

Many visitors to Provence arrive by air, with Nice and Marseille being the main gateways to the region for visitors from Europe. Passengers from the US usually need to change in Paris or London, although there are currently a few direct services between New York and Nice-Côte d'Azur. The increasing number of flights from low-cost European airlines has encouraged visitors from the UK and the rest of Europe to take short breaks to Provence. The flight time from London to Provence is around two hours, from New York to Nice (direct) around eight hours and Paris to Nice around one hour 30 minutes.

● **Nice-Côte d'Azur** is the major airport for eastern Provence and is on the coast, 6km (4 miles) west of Nice. It is handy for reaching Monaco, Cannes and the other Riviera resorts. There are nearly 200 flights a week from Paris, as well as flights from around Europe, including low-cost airline services. Delta Air Lines currently has some services between New York and Nice. The airport's Terminal 1 serves the vast majority of international flights, with airlines including British Airways, Bmibaby and Aer Lingus. It has two restaurants, a post office, car rental offices and an information desk. Terminal 2 serves Air France, along with British Midland and Easyjet. Facilities include a restaurant, car rental offices and an information desk.

Marseille-Provence airport, 30km (19 miles) northwest of Marseille, caters mainly to business traffic and is the third-busiest airport in France, with both regional and international flights. The airport has two connected terminals, with shops, restaurants and a bureau de change in each. Terminal 1 has a pharmacy and first-aid station. **Toulon** airport is 22km (14 miles) east of Toulon and receives at least four Air France flights a day from Paris Orly. British Airways currently operates three flights per week from

GETTING TO THE CITY FROM THE AIRPORT		
AIRPORT	**TAXI**	**TRAINS**
Nice-Côte d'Azur (NCE)	Cost: €20–€25 (cash only). Journey time: 20 min.	None.
Marseille-Provence, also called Marseille-Marignane (MRS)	Cost: around €37 (day), €46 (night). Journey time: 45 min.	None.
Toulon (TLN)	Cost: around €40. Journey time: 40 min.	None.
Avignon (AVN)	Cost: around €22. Journey time: 15 min.	None.
Nîmes-Arles-Camargue (FNI)	Cost: around €20 to Nîmes. Journey time: 25 min to Nîmes.	None.
Montpellier (MPL)	Cost to Montpellier: around €20. Journey time: 20 min.	None.
Lyon St-Exupéry (LYS)	Cost to central Lyon: around €33 (day), €47 (night). Journey time: 45 min.	TGV trains travel from the airport to destinations in Provence, including Aix-en-Provence, Arles, Avignon and Marseille. Reserve ahead.

London Gatwick. There is one terminal, with a café/bar.

Avignon airport receives around four flights a day from Paris Orly. The single terminal, 10km (6 miles) southeast of Avignon, has a bar/restaurant and car rental offices.

Nîmes-Arles-Camargue is a small airport 12km (7.5 miles) southeast of Nîmes and has services from London Stansted by Ryanair. The small terminal has a car rental office.

Montpellier airport is 7km (4.5 miles) southeast of Montpellier and a 40-minute drive from Nîmes, on the western boundary of Provence. It has regular services from the UK with British Airways and Ryanair, as well as flights from Paris with Air France. *Autoroute* links with Provence are good. The airport's one terminal has a restaurant, café, car rental offices and information

kiosk. There is also a hotel on site.

Lyon St-Exupéry is 28km (17 miles) east of Lyon. Its TGV rail link makes the journey to Provence relatively quick, taking around one hour 30 minutes to Marseille and just over an hour to Aix-en-Provence. But there is currently only one train per day

to each destination, so check times carefully. The airport has two terminals, linked by a central area containing a currency exchange kiosk, ATM, business facilities, pharmacy, travel agency, car rental companies, restaurants, cafés and bars.

The international airport at Nice

BUS	CAR
Bus 23 runs to the heart of Nice every 20 min. Journey time: 20 min. Cost: €1.80. There are also regular services to Marseille, Aix-en-Provence and Monaco.	Take the N7 to Nice. Journey time: 15–30 min.
Buses to the Gare St-Charles train station run 6.10am–10.50pm and leave every 20 min. After 10.50pm they coincide with flight arrivals. Cost: €8.50. Journey time: 30 min.	Take the D20, D9, then A7 to Marseille. Journey time: 30 min.
A bus service runs several times a day, but does not necessarily tie in with flights. Cost: €8.80. Journey time: 45 min.	The A570 leads to the A57, which heads southwest to Toulon. Journey time: 45 min.
None.	Take the N7 to Avignon. Journey time: 15 min.
A bus service meets flights and takes passengers into Nîmes. Cost: €4.80. Journey time: 25 min.	Take the A54, northwest to Nîmes, southeast to Arles. Journey time: 25 min to Nîmes
Bus to Montpellier and the rail station departs 7 times a day (usually on the hour) from Pont A outside the terminal. Cost €4.80. (Local trains link Montpellier station with Marseille and Arles several times a day. The journey to Marseille takes around 1 hour 40 min and to Arles 50 min.)	Take the D21 northwest to Montpellier. Journey time: 20 min. (The A9, northeast, leads to Nîmes and Orange.)
Buses leave every 20 min. They run daily 6am–11.20pm from the airport to Lyon, and 5am–9pm from Lyon to the airport. Cost: €8.20. Journey time: 40–50 min.	Take the A432, A43 then N383 to Lyon. Journey time: 45 min. (To head to Provence from Lyon, pick up the A7 and drive 200km/125 miles south to Orange.)

AIRPORT CONTACTS

Nice-Côte d'Azur	0820 423 333
	www.nice.aeroport.fr
Marseille-Provence	04 42 14 14 14
	www.marseille.aeroport.fr
Toulon	04 94 00 83 83
	www.toulon-hyeres.aeroport.fr
Avignon	04 90 81 51 51
	www.avignon.aeroport.fr
Nîmes-Arles-Camargue	04 66 70 49 49
	www.nimes.cci.fr
Montpellier	04 67 20 85 00
	www.montpellier.aeroport.fr
Lyon St-Exupéry	04 26 00 70 07
	www.lyon.aeroport.fr

OTHER USEFUL CONTACTS

General airport information www.worldairportguide.com
Information on all French airports www.aeroport.fr
Air France 0820 820 820 www.airfrance.fr
American Airlines 1 800 433 7300 (US number) www.aa.com
British Airways 0870 850 9850 (UK number) www.ba.com
British Midland 0870 60 70 555 (UK number)
www.flybmi.com
Delta 1 800 241 4141 (US number) www.delta.com
Easyjet 0870 6000 000 (UK number) www.easyjet.com
Ryanair 0871 2460 000 (UK number) www.ryanair.com
United 1 800 538 2929 (US number) www.ual.com
Sunbus 04 93 13 53 13 www.sunbus.com (bus service from
Nice-Côte d'Azur airport to the city)
Régie des Transports de Marseille (RTM) 04 91 91 92 10
www.rtm.fr (public transportation in Marseille)

Nice airport welcomes flights from across Europe

AIRPORTS

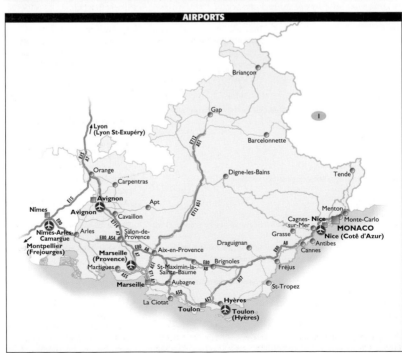

Arriving by Train

Provence has good rail links with the rest of France, into northern Europe through the hub of Paris and directly with Italy to the east. The French rail network is run by Société des Chemins de Fer (SNCF), which oversees the *Grands Lignes* (long-distance services) and *Lignes Régionals* (regional services). *Grand Lignes* have the regular Corail trains and the faster *Train à Grande Vitesse* (TGV), which can reach speeds of up to 300km/h (186mph). TGV services to Provence leave Paris from the Gare de Lyon.

TICKETS

● Most trains have first and second classes, both of which are perfectly acceptable.
● Fares are split into blue (normal) and red (peak). Reduced-rate fares are generally available for normal travel on mainline routes, excluding TGV and couchette services.
● Ticket prices vary according to the level of comfort (first or second class) and departure time. First-class fares are roughly 50 per cent more expensive than second class.
● Buy tickets in the stations, at SNCF offices and through some travel agents. Tickets for TGV trains must be reserved. You can do this up to a few minutes before departure, although in peak season it is best to book well in advance. Couchettes must be booked at least 75 minutes before the train leaves its first station.
● Stamp your ticket in the orange machines on the platforms before you start your journey. You'll risk a fine if you forget to do this.
● If you are under 26, you can get a 25 per cent discount (*Découverte 12–25*) on train travel. Seniors also receive discounts (*Découverte Senior*).
● When you travel second class, there are lower rates for booking more than eight days in advance (*Découverte J8*) and more than 30 days in advance (*Découverte J30*).
● A variety of rail passes allow travel either within France only, or within France and certain other countries, or within the whole of Europe. Buy these before you enter France, either through travel agents or Rail Europe (▷ 40).

Using a ticket machine can save time

● Ticket machines, with instructions in English, accept notes, coins and credit cards. They also dispense tickets you have ordered on the internet, by telephone or Minitel.

FASTEST JOURNEY TIMES TO MARSEILLE (APPROXIMATE)
Paris
3 hours
Lille
3 hours 30 min
Bordeaux
5 hours 30 min
Strasbourg
7 hours
Lyon
1 hour 30 min

CATERING SERVICES

● Catering facilities—ranging from sandwiches and salads to hot meals—are available on most TGV and Corail services, but can be quite expensive.
● Food can be served at your seat with first-class travel on most TGV trains. You'll need to reserve in advance, except on

TGV *Méditerranée* trains.
● You can reserve meals when you buy your train ticket. Ticket machines dispense meal vouchers.
● Hot and cold drinks, sandwiches and snacks are served on most trains.
● Overnight trains have vending machines dispensing hot and cold drinks and sweets (candy).

OVERNIGHT TRAINS

● Most overnight trains offer either reclining seats, couchette berths or a sleeper car.
● Reclining seats are available only in second class. They have adjustable head- and footrests.
● In first class, couchettes are in four-berth compartments; in second class they are in six-berth compartments.
● Sleeper car compartments are for two people in first class and three in second class.
● Overnight services include Reims to Nice; Bordeaux to Nice; Paris to Nice; Paris to Briançon.

STATION ASSISTANCE

● Larger stations have an information kiosk.
● If you need assistance, look for a member of the station staff, identifiable by their red waistcoats (vests).
● You'll need a €1 deposit to use the luggage trolleys (carts).
● Porters are on hand to help with your luggage in main stations. They wear red jackets and black or navy caps.

LEFT LUGGAGE

● Some stations have a baggage-storage office or coin-operated lockers. Electronic locks issue a printed ticket with a code number. You'll need to keep this ticket for when you

return to collect your items.
● Don't store valuables in
lockers.
● Security concerns mean that
baggage-storage facilities are not
always available. Ask at the
information kiosk.

UNDERSTANDING RAILWAY
TIMETABLES
● Pick up free timetables
(*horaires*) at stations.
● SNCF timetables are published
twice a year—the summer one
lasts from late May to late
September, and the winter one
from late September to late May.
● There are two styles of
timetable: one for the *Grandes
Lignes*, covering high-speed
TGV and other mainline services,
and another for the regional
TER trains.

● On *Grandes Lignes*
timetables, two rows of boxed
numbers at the top refer to the
numéro de train (train number)
and to the *notes à consulter*
(footnotes). On TER timetables,
the train number is not listed.
● Footnotes explain when a train
runs (*circule*). *Tous les jours*
means it runs every day; *sauf
dimanche et fêtes* means it
doesn't run on Sundays and
holidays. *Jusqu'au*, followed by a
date, indicates the service runs
only up until that date.

RAIL PASSES
● If you are staying in France for
a long time, consider buying a
rail pass that is valid for a year.
This entitles you to a 50 per cent
discount and is available to those
aged 12 to 25 (*Carte 12–25*),

those with a child under 12
(a *Carte Enfant+*) and the over
60s (*Carte Senior*).
● Foreign visitors can choose
from many attractively priced rail
passes. Buy these before you
enter France. To buy certain
passes you must have been
resident in Europe for at least six
months, and have a valid
passport with you.
● Rail Europe sells a variety of
rail passes (www.raileurope.com
for US visitors; www.raileurope.
co.uk for UK visitors).
● Once you are in France it
may be difficult to change
reservations made abroad.

CAR TRANSPORTER
SERVICES
● You can take your motorcycle
or car on board the *Auto-Train*.

MAINLINE RAIL NETWORK

The most useful service runs from Calais to Marseille.
- Pick up a *Guide Auto/Train* from SNCF stations and outlets.

TIMETABLE, FARE AND OTHER INFORMATION

- Timetable and fare information is available from SNCF stations, ticket outlets and travel agencies, by telephone (tel 08 91 67 68 69), the internet or Minitel.
- The websites www.sncf.com and www.tgv.com are a useful source of information and have pages in English.
- For timetable information for rail services in Provence, look for the brochures *Sud-Est* and *TGV-Méditerranée*.
- Ask for the *Guide Train+Velo* for information on taking your bicycle on the train.

TIPS

- If you plan to travel during peak times (mid-June to early September, holidays and rush hours), reserve your tickets well in advance.
- You must validate (*composter*) your ticket before boarding the train. Do this by inserting it into the orange machine on the platform.
- Bar and at-seat services on most long-distance trains are expensive. You may prefer to bring your own snacks.
- If all the seats on a TGV train have been reserved, you can be placed on standby. Your ticket entitles you to board the train but does not guarantee a seat.

EUROSTAR

- If you are starting from the UK, you can take the Eurostar from London to Paris (reserve ahead), then take a train to Provence.
- Up to 16 trains per day depart from Waterloo Station, London, to Gare du Nord, Paris. The journey time is 2 hours 40 minutes. Tel 08705 186 186 (UK); www.eurostar.com.
- To continue to Provence, you'll need to cross Paris to the Gare de Lyon. You can do this by taking the Métro or an RER train, but if you have a lot of luggage a taxi may be simpler.
- Eurostar also offers a weekly service direct to Avignon in summer, but tickets for this should be booked well in advance. The journey takes around six hours 15 minutes.

ON THE MOVE

RAIL JOURNEY TIMES

This chart shows the duration in hours and minutes of a train journey between various destinations in France.

TRAINS FROM PARIS

Trains usually depart hourly during the day from Paris' Gare de Lyon to Marseille. Most trains then go on to Nice. Some trains travel directly to Nice, cutting 40 minutes from the journey time.

	Amiens	Bayonne	Bordeaux (St-Jean)	Brest	Clermont-Ferrand	Dijon	Grenoble	Lille (Europe/Flandres)	Limoges (Bénédictins)	Lyon (Part Dieu)	Marseille (St-Charles)	Montpellier	Nantes	Nice (Ville)	Paris	Poitiers	Reims	Rennes	Rouen (Rive Droite)	Strasbourg
Bayonne	642																			
Bordeaux (St-Jean)	456	144																		
Brest	730	952	809																	
Clermont-Ferrand	556	1001	548	920																
Dijon	359	742	534	703	348															
Grenoble	509	1222	710	839	424	326														
Lille (Europe/Flandres)	120	648	501	642	513	245	448													
Limoges (Bénédictins)	504	441	203	822	341	521	656	431												
Lyon (Part Dieu)	325	908	545	648	238	136	120	251	509											
Marseille (St-Charles)	505	744	529	841	436	320	220	431	643	134										
Montpellier	538	605	400	909	455	327	229	447	514	143	126									
Nantes	420	559	358	401	548	452	623	355	508	424	602	622								
Nice (Ville)	727	1039	804	1217	718	602	507	724	918	414	218	401	925							
Paris	107	450	303	422	324	141	257	100	250	157	302	320	215	537						
Poitiers	330	322	138	623	527	357	540	308	208	410	615	627	242	831	126					
Reims	225	819	531	711	630	340	540	250	607	455	617	612	448	807	136	424				
Rennes	423	745	548	206	622	444	600	347	626	414	609	630	116	908	203	350	439			
Rouen (Rive Droite)	121	736	513	648	558	335	453	254	550	346	514	537	418	807	106	341	349	413		
Strasbourg	612	1049	839	641	840	356	652	541	754	437	705	723	711	950	356	651	328	736	643	
Toulouse (Matabiau)	711	315	158	1030	546	543	457	720	303	359	326	156	605	607	514	355	751	755	735	939

ARRIVING 41

Arriving by Road

Visitors from the UK and other European countries should find that driving to France is relatively easy. Plenty of car ferries, as well as Eurotunnel, link the UK with France. Once in France, a comprehensive system of *autoroutes* (motorways/expressways) fanning out from Paris enables you to cross the country with relative ease.

BRINGING YOUR OWN CAR
Legal Requirements
● You can take private vehicles registered in another country into France for up to six months (in any 12-month period) without customs formalities.
● You must always carry the following documentation: a current passport or national ID card, a full (not provisional) valid national driver's licence (UK drivers with a photocard licence will need the photocard and the counterpart), a certificate of insurance and the vehicle's registration document (as well as a letter of authorization from the owner if the vehicle is not registered in your name). If you are taking a UK-registered hired or leased car, ask the company to supply you with a Vehicle on Hire Certificate (VE103).
● You should always tell your insurer before you take your car abroad and buy extra cover where necessary. Third-party insurance (covering the other parties but not your own vehicle in the event of a collision) is the minimum requirement in France, but fully comprehensive insurance is strongly advised.
● Check that your insurance covers you against damage in transit, for example on the train or ferry when your car is not being driven.
● There are spot checks on cars and you may be asked to produce your documents at any time. To avoid a police fine and/or confiscation of your car, be sure that your papers are in order.
● Display an international distinguishing sign (for example GB for Britons) at the rear of your car and on any caravan or trailer. This is not necessary if your vehicle has Euro-Plates.

Most autoroutes in France are toll roads

● UK drivers should adjust the headlights of their vehicles for driving on the right. On older cars, use the simple black headlight beam converters that stick onto the glass. But don't use these on cars with halogen headlights—check in your owner's manual or with your dealer. If your vehicle has Xenon or High Intensity Discharge (HID) headlights, check with your dealer who may need to make the adjustment.

Breakdowns
● If you are taking your own car, make sure you have adequate breakdown cover. For information on AA breakdown cover, call 0800 444 500 (UK number) or visit www.theAA.com.

DRIVING FROM THE UK
Eurotunnel
● The Eurotunnel shuttle takes vehicles under the English Channel from Folkestone, in the UK, to Calais/Coquelles, in northern France. At 35 minutes, it is the shortest vehicular journey time from the UK to mainland Europe.
● For continuing travel from Calais, ▷ 43.

Ferries from the UK
● Numerous ferries link France with the UK. The cost varies widely according to the time, day and month of travel.
● Routes include Dover to Calais, Newhaven to Dieppe,

CONTACT DETAILS

Brittany Ferries
www.brittanyferries.com
Tel 08703 665 333 (UK)

Hoverspeed
www.hoverspeed.com
Tel 08702 408 070 (UK)

P&O Ferries
www.poferries.com
Tel 08705 202 020 (UK)

Seafrance
www.seafrance.com
Tel 08705 711 711 (UK)

Eurotunnel
www.eurotunnel.com
Tel 08705 353 535 (UK)

(To call these numbers from the US, dial 011 44, then omit the initial zero. To call from mainland Europe, dial 00 44 then omit the zero).

Portsmouth to Caen, Portsmouth to Le Havre, Poole to Cherbourg, Portsmouth to Cherbourg, Portsmouth to St-Malo and Plymouth to Roscoff.

Continuing Travel

● From Calais, the fastest and easiest route to Provence is to take the A26 towards Paris/Reims. At the intersection of the A1 take the A1 towards Paris. At Paris, the *Périphérique* road circling the city will take you to the *autoroute* A6 (Porte d'Italie junction). Take the A6 south to Lyon, then the A7, which enters Provence close to Orange.

● In good conditions, you can reach Provence from the northern coast of France in around 11 hours. It is less stressful to break up your journey. You'll find numerous chain hotels (▷ 258) near major *autoroute* exits. It's best to reserve rooms ahead, especially in summer.

● The journey to Provence from Normandy and Brittany is not as straightforward as from Calais since there are few fast roads running in a southeasterly direction across France. The simplest and quickest route from Normandy (Caen and Le Havre) is to head north on the A13, which leads to Paris to pick up the A6 south of the capital. From Brittany (Cherbourg and St-Malo) it is simpler to travel south on the N137, picking up the A10 (direction Bordeaux). From Bordeaux, the A62 swings west past Toulouse, then the A9 at Narbonne leads northeast to Nîmes and Orange in Provence.

● Bear in mind that *autoroutes* are toll roads and you should always have cash available to pay at the toll booths. The cost of a journey from Paris to Marseille is approximately €63 (www.autoroutes.fr).

● France's *autoroutes* have a good number of service stations and rest areas.

AUTOROUTES

The Autoroute du Soleil (A7/E15) is the main highway down to the south

DRIVING DISTANCES AND TIMES

Use the chart below to work out the distance in km (green) and estimated duration in hours and minutes (blue) of a car journey

```
        724 705 140 554 439 717 133 542 616 928 920 533 1059 158 507 150 448 139 511 846
            640 843 438 750 730 802 301 648 622 444 327 755 557 231 702 449 653 1023 223
 Amiens         745 851 856 1115 822 706 1014 1247 1109 323 1419 631 533 736 247 545 1057 848
   Bordeaux         713 535 826 115 701 725 1037 1028 633 1207 316 626 246 528 219 607 1005
     Brest              350 303 632 256 212 450 358 604 620 427 357 532 613 528 654 434
 723   Calais              302 454 520 201 513 504 640 643 329 533 253 618 443 332 720
 634 630  Clermont-Ferrand     745 546 114 311 303 845 442 549 637 543 837 702 544 519
 161 879 722   Dijon               620 644 956 947 620 1126 235 545 205 558 257 517 924
 567 359 804 723   Grenoble             456 717 539 353 850 415 150 520 515 516 824 318
 473 761 868 574 349   Lille               317 308 754 447 448 547 442 736 601 505 524
 746 776 1127 876 295 303   Limoges             154 933 207 800 824 754 1041 913 811 410
 119 809 767 111 653 504 806   Lyon               756 327 751 700 746 918 905 802 233
 539 228 609 695 177 436 545 625   Marseille         1106 414 220 519 126 426 840 535
 639 542 1020 769 179 196 109 699 429   Montpellier          930 955 925 1211 1044 816 543
 972 652 1278 1102 479 529 310 1032 714 318   Nantes           340 143 353 148 504 719
 954 488 1114 1085 344 511 293 1015 550 300 169   Nice             445 342 436 806 439
 518 330 300 599 483 656 764 611 309 648 978 814   Paris            458 304 324 824
 1127 810 1436 1258 635 684 466 1188 872 473 205 327 1136   Poitiers          328 819 657
 143 582 596 294 426 312 571 224 398 464 797 779 384 952   Reims              625 820
 478 249 524 634 318 516 599 564 121 482 783 733 224 938 337   Rennes                1018
 177 718 732 278 562 298 601 208 534 494 827 809 520 982 144 473   Rouen
 443 445 245 532 556 620 879 575 424 772 1021 929 106 1176 348 339 484   Strasbourg
 123 620 504 211 513 461 720 256 485 613 946 929 384 1102 141 375 284 313   Toulouse
 520 1061 1076 621 661 341 541 523 748 508 824 807 863 792 488 816 346 827 628
 840 245 871 996 384 753 535 926 307 542 411 247 571 569 699 490 835 686 785 1049
```

GENERAL DRIVING
The Law
- In France you drive on the right (*serrez à droite*).
- The minimum age to drive is 18, although to rent a car you must be at least 21.
- You must wear a seatbelt.
- Children under 10 must travel in the back, with a booster seat/child safety seat, except for babies under nine months with a specially adapted rear-facing front seat (but not in cars with airbags).
- Do not overtake where there is a solid single central line on the road.
- Never drive under the influence of alcohol.
- Always stop completely at stop signs, or you may be fined.
- Remove any device to detect radar speed traps from your car.

Road Signs
- Road signs are split into three categories. Triangular signs with a red border are warnings, circular signs are mandatory (such as speed limits or No Entry) and square signs display text information.
- Before you take to the road, familiarize yourself with the French highway code on www.legifrance.gouv.fr.
- For more road sign information see www.permiscnligne.com.

SELECTED ROAD SIGNS

No entry except for buses and taxis

Toll booth

A yellow diamond (top) indicates a priority road

Speed limits for various road types, in km/h

Give way to traffic

Parking 150m to the left

Parking only for those with disabilities

No left turn

A town sign, with the road number displayed above

FRENCH	ENGLISH
Allumez vos phares	Switch on your lights
Attention travaux	Roadworks/construction
Cédez le passage	Give way
Chantier	Roadworks
Chaussée déformée	Uneven road/temporary surface
Déviation	Diversion/detour
Gravillons	Loose surface
Nids de poules	Potholes
Passage protégé	Priority
Péage	Toll
Priorité à droite/gauche	Priority to the right/left
Rappel	Reminder (continue with the previous instruction)
Route barré	Road closed
Sens interdit	No entry
Sens unique	One way
Serrez à droite/gauche	Keep to the right/left
Sortie	Exit
Stationnement interdit	No parking
Vous n'avez pas la priorité	You don't have right of way

SPEED LIMITS	
Urban roads	50km/h (31mph)
Outside built-up areas	90km/h (56mph); 80km/h (49mph) in wet weather
Dual carriageways (divided highways), and non-toll motorways	110km/h (68mph); 100km/h (62mph) in wet weather
Toll motorways (*autoroutes*)	130km/h (80mph); 110km/h (68mph) in wet weather

Visiting drivers who have held a licence for less than two years are not allowed to exceed the wet-weather limits, even in good weather.

ON THE MOVE

Roads
- The *autoroute* is the French counterpart of the British motorway or US expressway and is marked by an 'A' on maps and road signs. A few sections around key cities are free, but tolls are charged on the rest (*autoroutes à péage*). Have cash available as foreign credit cards may not be accepted.
- There is a comprehensive network of other roads, with surfaces that are generally good. A trunk road/federal highway is called a *Route Nationale* (N). The next level down is the *Route Départementale* (D), which can still be wide and fast. There are also quieter country roads.

Equipment
- Carry a red warning triangle in case you break down. Even if your car has hazard lights, a triangle is still strongly advised as

a breakdown may affect the electrical system in your car.
- Keep a spare-bulb kit (buy before you go) on hand as it is illegal to drive with faulty lights.
- Snow chains must be fitted to vehicles using snow-covered roads, in compliance with road signs. You could be fined for non-compliance. Snow chains can be rented from most tyre stores in France or you can buy them from hypermarkets, especially in mountain areas.

Fuel
- Fuel (*essence*) comes as unleaded (95 and 98 octane), lead replacement petrol (LRP or *supercarburant*) and diesel (*gasoil* or *gazole*).
- Many filling stations close on Sundays and at 6pm other days. It may be difficult to find a 24-hour station and some may not accept foreign credit cards.
- Prices are high at filling stations on *autoroutes*.
- Filling stations can be far apart in rural areas, so never let your tank get too low.

Car Breakdown
- If your car breaks down on an *autoroute*, look for an emergency telephone on the roadside, which will connect you with roadside assistance.
- If you break down on an *autoroute*, you must call the police or the official breakdown service operating in that area, rather than your own roadside assistance company.

Road Conditions
- To find out about traffic conditions visit www.bison-fute.equipement.gouv.fr (in French only).
- For the National Road Information Centre call 0836 682 000 (French only).
- For road conditions on *autoroutes* call 0892 681 077.
- For regional road conditions call 0826 022 022.

BY LONG-DISTANCE BUSES
- Taking a long-distance bus can be an option if you are on a tight budget, although the journey from Paris to Provence takes more than 10 hours, much longer than the train.
- Eurolines runs services from countries across Europe, with UK starting points at Victoria Coach Station (London), Canterbury and Dover (Kent).
- Destinations that Eurolines serves in Provence include Avignon, Marseille, Nîmes, Aix-en-Provence, Arles and Cannes.

Eurolines buses travel from Paris to Provence

BUS CONTACTS

Eurolines
www.eurolines.co.uk
Tel 08705 143 219 (UK)

Eurolines offices in Provence
Avignon Gare Routière, Boulevard St-Roch
Tel 04 90 85 27 60

Marseille Gare Routière, Place Victor Hugo
Tel 04 91 50 57 55

Nîmes Gare Routière Rue Sainte-Félicité
Tel 04 66 29 49 02

GETTING AROUND

Driving in Provence

Driving is a good way to get around Provence's more rural areas. Roads in the region are generally in excellent condition and signposting is good.

RENTING A CAR
- Most major car rental agencies have offices at airports, main rail stations and in the large towns and cities.
- Renting a car in France can be expensive because of high taxes. Arranging a fly-drive package through a tour operator or airline from home could be a less expensive option. SNCF, the national rail company, has inclusive train and car-rental deals from mainline stations.
- To be able to rent a car in France you must be at least 21 years old and have held a full driver's licence for at least a year. However, some companies either do not rent to, or else add a surcharge for, drivers under the age of 25. The maximum age limit varies, but the average is 70.
- You will have to show your licence and passport or national ID card.
- As a guide, companies should include the following in their rental agreement: unlimited mileage, comprehensive insurance cover, theft protection and 24-hour emergency roadside assistance.
- Some agencies include mileage in the cost but others may charge you extra above a certain distance, so check before you rent.

- Make sure you have adequate insurance and that you are aware of what you are covered for in the event of an accident.
- Bear in mind that low-cost operators may have an extremely high excess charge for damage to the vehicle.
- Most rental companies supply vehicles with roadside assistance, so refer to your documentation or to the information regarding breakdowns in the car, which is often kept in the glove compartment or under the sun visor.
- If your car breaks down on an *autoroute*, look for emergency telephones on the roadside. You can contact roadside assistance from here.

PROVENCE WAYS
- Despite the many benefits of exploring Provence by car, you'll also meet several challenges. Cities such as Avignon, Nice and particularly Marseille are a confusing pattern of one-way streets linked by a grid of major boulevards. Parking is difficult and car crime is rife, so do not leave valuables in view. In cities, park only in designated spaces.
- Once in the countryside, the roads become less crowded but they can be narrow and steep, especially in the mountains. Pay special attention on blind corners. If you want to admire the stunning views, pull off into a designated rest stop.
- Summer brings lots of drivers. They too may be unfamiliar with the roads so extra patience is needed. Summer also means traffic jams are a problem, particularly on the coast—it is worst on weekends, when locals also head to the beach. Traffic heading to Nice and St-Tropez is particularly heavy.

Parking
- Authorized parking spaces are indicated by road markings (white dotted lines). In those marked *payant*, you have to pay a fee.
- Charges usually apply from 9am to 7pm, Monday to Saturday. Sundays and holidays are generally free, but always check before parking your car.
- To pay for parking, buy a ticket from a machine at the side of the road and display it in your car.
- Some towns also have multi-level or underground parking areas.
- Many of Provence's medieval villages offer ample parking (paid) just outside the walls.

RENTING AUTOMATIC CARS
If you are keen to rent an automatic, rather than manual, car it is best to reserve in advance, as there are fewer available in France than in countries such as the US. You may also have to pay a premium for the vehicle.

CAR RENTAL COMPANIES

Company	Telephone number	Website
Avis	0820 050 505	www.avis.com
Budget	0825 003 564	www.budget.com
Europcar	0825 352 352	www.europcar.com
Hertz	0825 861 861	www.hertz.com
Sixt	0820 007 498	www.sixt.com

Trains, Buses and Taxis

TRAINS

● The mountainous terrain in Provence means that not all areas are served by trains. But there are places where the regional TER trains will enhance your sightseeing, freeing you from having to find parking and avoiding traffic jams.

● Reliable services link Nice, Cannes and Fréjus with Marseille. The Rhône valley towns of Avignon, Orange, Arles and Nîmes are also connected by train. Lines from Nice run through the Roya valley and northwest into the pre-Alps.

● For journey planning try www.ter-sncf.com.

● You can take bicycles onto all suitable trains outside the peak hours (Mon–Fri 7am–9am and 4.30pm–6.30pm).

● Buy tickets at stations. You must validate your ticket in the orange machine on the platform before you board the train. If there is no ticket office or it is closed you can pay the

conductor on board the train. Some TER platforms do not have validation machines. In this case, the conductor will validate your ticket on the train.

BUSES

● Bus services between towns and villages in Provence range from very useful to impractical. You'll find services linking the key towns, but the scattered villages are another matter.

● Services are severely limited on Sundays and official holidays.

● Buses usually leave from either the bus station or the central town square. You should be able to find timetable details here or at the bus company offices.

● Buses will display the route number and final destination on the front.

● You can normally buy tickets on the bus or at kiosks/*tabacs* around the town. You must validate tickets in the machine on the bus.

TAXIS

● Taking a taxi is not the most cost-effective way of getting around, but you may consider it worthwhile for convenience, especially in the major towns and cities.

● Some taxi firms provide chauffeur-driven cars by the day if you wish to visit several locations around Provence without driving or using buses or trains.

● Taxis charge for a pick up and a separate charge per kilometre (0.6 mile) driven. There will be an extra charge for luggage and for journeys during the evening and on Sundays. All taxis use a meter (*compteur*). Make sure that this is reset for your journey.

● The best way to find a taxi is to head to a taxi stand (indicated by a blue *Taxi* sign). Phoning for a taxi means the meter starts from the moment it sets off to pick you up.

● Some taxis accept credit cards but most will accept only cash.

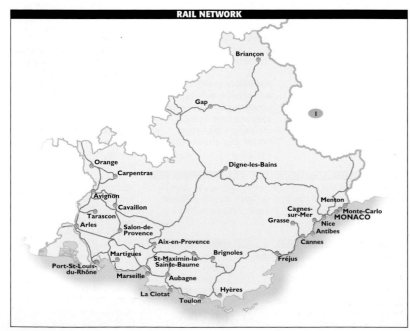

RAIL NETWORK

Briançon

Gap

Orange
Carpentras

Digne-les-Bains

Avignon
Cavaillon

Tarascon
Arles

Salon-de-Provence

Menton
Cagnes-sur-Mer
Monte-Carlo
MONACO
Grasse
Nice
Antibes

Aix-en-Provence

Martigues

Brignoles

Fréjus

Cannes

Port-St-Louis-du-Rhône

St-Maximin-la-Sainte-Baume

Marseille
Aubagne

La Ciotat
Toulon

Hyères

Getting Around in Major Towns and Cities

All the major towns and cities have buses linking outlying districts to the central areas and it is sometimes easier to use these rather than taking your car and having to hunt for a parking space. Marseille also has an efficient Métro system, with two lines. Remember that on most buses in Provence you must validate your ticket by inserting it into the machine near the driver.

AIX-EN-PROVENCE
Buses
A shuttle bus links the heart of town with the TGV station, 15km (9 miles) away. This operates from 4.25am to 8.45pm, every 15 minutes at peak times and every 30 minutes at other times. Autobus Aixous (tel 04 42 26 37 28) runs 20 lines around town and the suburbs. Buses depart from the bus station at avenue de l'Europe.

Tickets
Buy tickets from the bus station office or on the buses (exact change only). One ticket costs €1.10, 10 tickets €7.70.

ARLES
Arles and the Camargue are served by three bus companies—call 0810 000 816 for information on all three. Buses depart from the bus station at 24 boulevard Clemenceau. Societé des Transports d'Arles runs four lines. Ceyte Tourisme Méditerranée links the town with Tarascon, Salon, Marseille and Avignon. Cars de Carmargue runs services to Saintes-Maries-de-la-Mer.

Tickets
Prices for town buses are €0.80 per ticket or €7 for 10 tickets. Example prices for longer routes are €11.40 to Aix-en-Provence and €14.60 to Marseille.

AVIGNON
Transports en Commun de la Region d'Avignon (TCRA), based at avenue de Lattre de Tassigny (tel 04 32 74 18 32; www.tcra.fr), runs 28 bus lines around Avignon and to surrounding towns such as St-Rémy-de-Provence. But there are no bus services within the walls of Avignon. Buses run from 7am to 8pm. STDGard (▷ 50, Nîmes) runs services linking Nîmes, Avignon and Tarascon.

Tickets
Tickets cost €1.05 and last for one hour after validation. They can be purchased on the bus or from the bus-company office. A two-trip ticket, valid for two people making the same trip at the same time or two trips by one person, is €1.80. You can also buy 10 tickets for €8.

Traffic approaching toll booths on the autoroute near Marseille

CANNES
Bus Azur runs 20 services in Cannes and to surrounding towns. You'll find information at the bus station at place Cournou Gentille, next to the town hall (tel 0825 825 599). Buses run from 6am to 8.30pm. Sillages runs services from Cannes north into the hills around Grasse (tel 0800 095 000/04 93 64 88 84; www.sillages-stga.tm.fr).

Tickets
Single trips cost €1.30, ten tickets are €8.50 and a one-week pass is €9.45. You can buy single tickets on the bus but all others must be purchased from the bus station.

The pace of life is slower in Provence's villages

MARSEILLE

Métro

The city has two fast, well-maintained Métro lines. Métro 1 runs from La Timone in the eastern suburbs through the northeast suburbs to La Rose and is due to be extended by 2006. Métro 2 runs roughly north to south, from Bougainville to Sainte-Marguerite Dromel and is also due to be extended. The Métro runs Monday to Thursday from 5am to 9pm, and Friday to Sunday until 12.30am.

Régie des Transports de Marseille (www.rtm.fr) runs the Métro. The main office is at Espace Infos, 6–8 rue des Fabres (Mon–Fri 8.30–6, Sat 9–5.30).

Buses

Régie des Transports de Marseille also runs the city's bus services, with 140 lines during the day and 10 at night.

Tickets

A single trip on the bus or Métro is €1.50. You can make a change within an hour of validation. A one-day pass is €4, a three-day card €9.50 and a seven-day card €10.

MONACO

Compagnie des Autobus de Monaco (www.cam.mc) runs bus services in Monaco, with six routes spanning the principality. Services run between 7am and 9pm and are less frequent on weekends. Lines 1 and 2 are most useful for visitors, linking Monaco Rock with Monte-Carlo. Single tickets cost €1.40, although they are slightly cheaper if you buy a pack of four

or eight. A day ticket for visitors costs €3.40. Buy tickets on the bus. You can change buses on the same ticket if the second leg starts no more than 30 minutes after the start of the first, but you must still validate the ticket a second time.

NICE

Service Urban de Nice (SUN) (tel 04 93 13 53 13; www.sunbus.com) runs 44 routes in the city and outlying districts. The bus station is at boulevard Jean Jaurès and the Gare Routière (long-distance bus station) is next door, although buses also depart from surrounding streets. Daytime buses run from 7am to 9pm. There are also four evening routes departing from place Masséna from 9.10pm Monday to Saturday and 8.10pm on Sundays.

Tickets

Buy tickets on the bus and also at Bel Canto, 29 avenue Malausséna (Mon–Fri 8–5.45, Sat 8–12.15) and Grand Hotel, 10 avenue Félix Faure (Mon–Fri 7.15–7, Sat 7.15–6), plus various *tabacs* and kiosks around the city. A single ticket costs €1.30; a Sunmaxi ticket of 14 trips costs €16. You can also buy a day pass for €4 or a pass covering five or seven days, including transfers from Nice airport.

NÎMES

Transports en Commun Nîmois (TCN) runs the city buses (tel 04 66 38 15 40), while Navette serves the airport (tel 04 66 29 27 29). Société des Transports Departmental du Gard

(STDGard; tel 04 66 29 11 11; www.stdgard.com) runs services in the Gard department but includes routes between Nîmes, Avignon and St-Rémy-de-Provence and outlying towns. Services run between 6am and 7pm.

Tickets

Tickets cost €1 per journey within the city and can be purchased on the bus.

ORANGE

Transports en Commun de la Ville d'Orange (TCVO; tel 04 90 34 15 59) runs four lines within the town from 7am to 7.30pm.

Tickets

Tickets cost €1 per journey and can be bought on the bus.

ST-RÉMY-DE-PROVENCE

TCRA from Avignon (▷ 49) runs bus services for St-Rémy-de-Provence. STDGard (▷ Nîmes, this page) runs services between St-Rémy-de-Provence and Tarascon.

Tickets

▷ 49, Avignon.

ST-TROPEZ

There are no bus services within the town itself. SODETRAV runs bus services around the Golfe de St-Tropez from the Gare Routière at St-Tropez, just outside the parking du Port. It also provides services to markets in the area and to the SNCF rail stations at Toulon and St-Raphaël.

Tickets

Buy tickets on the bus.

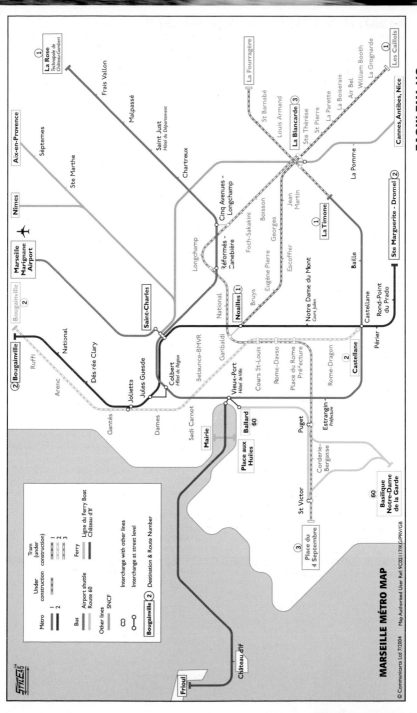

MARSEILLE MÉTRO MAP

© Communicarta Ltd 7/2004   Map Authorised User Ref 9C02117/K/PRV/GB

VISITORS WITH A DISABILITY

Getting around Provence is becoming easier for people with disabilities thanks to improvements to buses, trains and platforms. Most airports have special facilities and Eurostar and TGV trains are accessible to wheelchair-users. But you'll still find challenges when getting around the region. Before you travel it's worth checking that facilities are available at your arrival airport and your hotel, as older buildings may not have an elevator.

ARRIVING BY AIR

- Nice airport has dedicated parking and toilets for wheelchair-users.
- Marseille airport has a help service for passengers with disabilities (tel 04 42 14 27 42). The airport has dedicated parking spaces and wheelchair-accessible toilets.
- Lyon airport has covered car parking close to the terminals and offers a 50 per cent discount on parking charges. The set-down point is outside Terminal 1 and there is reserved parking at the airport TGV station. All toilets and phones are accessible to wheelchair-users.
- Aeroguide publishes a guide to French airports for people with disabilities. For further details look up www.aeroguide.fr or call 01 46 55 93 43.
- If you are a wheelchair-user, inform your airline when you reserve your ticket.

GETTING AROUND
By Train

- France's long-distance trains are equipped for people with reduced mobility. On TGV and Corail trains, spaces for wheelchair-users are reserved in first class, although only a second-class fare is payable. Reserve at least 24 hours in

Road markings indicate parking spaces reserved for drivers with disabilities

advance. There are also adapted toilets.
- Most large stations have elevators or ramps to the platform. If you need assistance, it is best to request it at the time of reserving your ticket. For more information, look up SNCF's

website (www.sncf.com).
- Facilities on regional trains tend to be more varied. It is always best to check before you travel. For more information, call SNCF (tel 0800 154 753).

By Bus
Bus services vary in usefulness. Bus Azur in Cannes and Sunbus in Nice have vehicles with access ramps but services in rural areas may prove more problematic. Local tourist offices should be able to give you information.

General Information
- All new buildings must have suitable access for people with disabilities and many of the modern museums, such as the Musée d'Art Moderne et Contemporain in Nice, have good facilities. With older buildings, you may find that access for wheelchair-users involves a member of staff unlocking a side door.
- In some towns, curbs have been lowered at street crossings. Many large towns have traffic-free zones with reasonably flat pavements, but medieval villages often have steep cobbled lanes.
- Most parking areas have places for cars displaying the official registered disabled sticker.

USEFUL WEBSITES AND ORGANIZATIONS

Holiday Care Service
Tel 0845 124 9971 (from UK); +44 208 760 0076 (from outside UK)
www.holidaycare.org.uk
Travel and holiday information for people with disabilities.

Maison de la France
www.franceguide.com
The website of the French tourist office has useful information for people with disabilities.

Mobile en Ville
www.mobile-en-ville.asso.fr
A website packed with information on disability access and related issues.

Mobility International USA
www.miusa.org
Promotes international travel and exchange schemes for people with disabilities.

Society for Accessible Travel and Hospitality (SATH)
Tel 212 447 7284 (from US)
www.sath.org
A US-based organization offering advice for visitors with disabilities and promoting awareness of their travel requirements.

This chapter is divided into six regions, which are identified on the map on the inside front cover. Places of interest are listed alphabetically within each region. Major sights are listed at the start of each region. To locate all the sights, turn to the atlas on pages 280–295.

The Sights

BOUCHES-DU-RHÔNE

Ancient Provence starts here. Greek traders settled at
Marseille and the Romans built the handsome cities of
Arles, Aix-en-Provence and Nîmes. The violent Middle
Ages saw the rise of feudal towns, including Saintes-
Maries-de-la-Mer and Les Baux-de-Provence.
Bouches-du-Rhône also includes the vast salty wetland
of the Camargue.

THE SIGHTS

The Abbaye de Silvacane, one of the 'Three Cistercian Sisters'

ABBAYE DE SILVACANE

🔲 292 F10 ✉ Abbaye de Silvacane, 13640 La Roque d'Anthéron ☎ 04 42 50 41 69 🕒 Apr–end Sep daily 9–7; Oct–end Mar Wed–Mon 10–5 💶 Adult €5.50, under 17 free

This long-suffering, much-damaged masterpiece, standing close to the south bank of the Durance, could so easily be overlooked as it nestles in its deliciously peaceful waterside setting. The Abbey of Silvacane, completed in 1144, was the last of three Cistercian abbeys in Provence—known as the Three Cistercian Sisters. The others are Sénanque (▷ 148) and Le Thoronet (▷ 89). Silvacane is considered the loveliest of them, and a perfect example of the simple austere elegance promoted by the Cistercians.

The isolated setting was more wild than rural at first—the name, from *Silva Cana*, is Latin for Forest of Reeds. The monks gradually drained the soil and made it cultivable. The remoteness from the world was a deliberate attempt to encourage prayer and spirituality.

The surrounding greenery enhances this assembly of very sober buildings under Provençal red roof tiles. The abbey barely looks like an ecclesiastical building, an impression strengthened by its modest tile roof and low, damaged square tower. The church is interesting for being built on a steep slope, and having several different styles of ceiling vaults encompassing different periods. Below the church, the 13th-century cloisters with a fountain are very attractive. **Don't miss** Most striking is the refectory, rebuilt in 1423 in Gothic style. It has a rose window and is not as austere as other parts of the abbey, with more natural light.

Sunlight spills through the arches of the Abbaye de Montmajour

ABBAYE DE MONTMAJOUR

These awesome, beautiful ruins of a large Romanesque fortified abbey just outside Arles include a tranquil church, beautiful cloisters and a superb view.

🔲 291 C11 ✉ Abbaye de Montmajour, route de Fontvieille, 13200 Arles ☎ 04 90 54 64 17 🕒 Apr–end Sep daily 9–7; Oct–end Mar daily 10–1, 2–5 🚌 Mon–Sat 8 buses daily from Arles; Sun 2 buses only 🚆 Arles, then bus 💶 Adult €5.50, under 18 free

RATINGS			
Historic interest	●	●	●
Photo stops	●	●	●	●
Walkability	●	●	●

TIP
● See photo exhibitions at the church from June to September.

Montmajour was among the most powerful religious communities in medieval Provence, its wealth boosted by its landholdings and its status as an important pilgrimage site. The fortified Romanesque Benedictine monastery is on a small hill 3km (2 miles) north of Arles. Today, you can wander around the extensive ruins. The sheer scale of the buildings is striking and local people have carried out much restoration in recent years. The incomplete 12th-century Upper Church is austere but impressive. To the right of the nave is the crypt, partly built into the hillside, with fine stone carvings on the bases and capitals of the columns depicting demons and wild beasts. Note several mason's marks in the church vaulting and graffiti dating back to medieval times in the cloister.

RISE AND FALL OF A MONASTERY
Montmajour's story began with the early Christian St. Trophimus, who fled here from Arles to hide in a cave, which became known as a holy place. Later a group of Christian ascetics came to reside at the site where he had lived. Their community grew and eventually the monastery was founded in the 10th century. The community was never large in numbers of monks but, thanks to its importance as a pilgrimage site, Benedictine Montmajour become one of the biggest monastic structures in Provence. Their growing wealth appears to have so corrupted the community that when, in 1639, the Benedictines sent a group to inspect and reform Montmajour, the monks in residence attempted to destroy the abbey. The community was disbanded in 1786. Restoration of the buildings began in 1907.

Don't miss If you can face a steep climb of 124 steps, there are exceptional views of the Alpilles and Crau landscapes from the top of the 14th-century keep, 26m high (85ft).

Aigues-Mortes

●

This awesome medieval town, within powerful ramparts, stands in the flat Camargue landscape like a bizarre piece of art.

Wandering past the 13th-century ramparts　　*Wednesday and Sunday are market days*　　*A statue of Louis IX dominates place St-Louis*

RATINGS	
Historic interest	● ● ● ●
Photo stops	● ● ● ●
Walkability	● ● ●

BASICS

✚ 290 A11

🚌 Infrequent buses from Nîmes and Montpellier

🚆 Aigues-Mortes (for trains to and from Nîmes)

ℹ️ Place St-Louis, 30220 Aigues-Mortes, tel 04 66 53 73 00; May–end Sep daily 9–12, 2–6; Oct–end Apr Mon–Sat 9–12, 2–5

🅿️ Outside the walls, beside Porte de la Gardette

🍴 Many bars and cafés in and around place St-Louis

www.ot-aiguesmortes.fr
Informative, multilingual and up-to-date.

TIPS

● The Chapelle des Capucins, in the main square, is now a gallery displaying high-quality works by local artists.
● Try the Camargue delicacy *taureau gardian* (beef and olive stew) in the town's restaurants.

SEEING

The perfectly preserved, sturdily fortified walled town of Aigues-Mortes, in the sparsely populated western Camargue, is a phenomenal sight. It is just outside Bouches-du-Rhône, across the Provence border in the Gard *département,* but is an important part of the Provence experience. Though often crowded with visitors, with many restaurant tables and souvenir shops, it remains strongly evocative of the Middle Ages. Now, though, Aigues-Mortes has less of its traditional appearance of defensive isolation, with areas of industry, vineyards and modern housing lying outside the walls.

Within its ramparts, Aigues-Mortes is a simple grid of old streets—five running east to west and five running north to south. In the heart of town is the busy main square, place St-Louis, with a statue of St. Louis in the middle. It takes about half an hour to walk on the path around the ramparts. In July and August, trips by boat, horse-and-carriage or *petit train* leave from outside the town's main gate and take you into the Camargue's salt marshes.

HIGHLIGHTS

THE RAMPARTS

Aigues-Mortes' ramparts stretch for more than 1.5km (1 mile) around the town and are in remarkably good condition. Work started on them in the 13th century, at the command of Philip III, and took nearly 30 years. The fortifications, including 15 towers and 10 gates, remain almost entirely intact today, partly because almost as soon as they were built Aigues-Mortes went into decline, as the seashore retreated in the mid-14th century.

TOUR DE CONSTANCE

• Logis du Gouverneur, place Anatole France, 30220 Aigues-Mortes
☎ 04 66 53 61 55 🕐 May–end Aug daily 10–6; Sep–end Apr daily 10–4.30
🎟️ Adult €6.10, under 18 free

The impregnable Tour de Constance is by far the most impressive of the towers. It can be reached only via the Logis du Gouverneur, starting point for the official tour of the ramparts. The tower was built as

part of the town's defences but became a prison early on in its life, after the town ceased to be a royal port. Philippe le Bel imprisoned 45 Templars here in 1307, but its most notorious period was in the 17th century, when hundreds of Protestant women from the Cévennes were locked up in terrible conditions. One of these women, Marie Durand, was kept here for 38 years because she refused to renounce her faith. You can still see where she carved the one word *register*—'resist' in her local dialect—into the stone wall.

BACKGROUND

King Louis IX (St. Louis) began building a port here in 1241. He was desperately anxious to have a French royal port on the Mediterranean so he could launch his long-dreamed-of crusades to conquer the Holy Land. His options were limited as much of the coast was controlled by the Counts of Provence and the Kings of Aragon. The land around Aigues-Mortes belonged to the monks of the powerful Abbaye de Psalmody, but they agreed to exchange their Camargue territories for the Château de Villevieille, near Sommières. By 1248, the port was ready. With 30,000 knights, Louis set off in an armada of 1,500 ships to Jerusalem. This Seventh Crusade, like the others, was a disaster, but the king survived. Unperturbed, he set off for the Eighth Crusade, this time to North Africa. He died of typhoid at Tunis in 1270—Aigues-Mortes had been his final sight of France.

Aigues-Mortes means 'dead waters', an uninviting title intended to distinguish it from the more endearingly named town of Aigues-Vives ('living waters') 20km (12.5 miles) farther north. Today, salt-production is an important industry for the town.

A view of the Tour de Constance from across the water

NOTRE-DAME-DES-SABLONS
• Place St-Louis, Aigues-Mortes
🕐 Summer daily 9–5; winter daily 9–12, 2–5 🏛 Free
The town's main church, Our Lady of the Sands, was originally built of wood in the 12th century, then rebuilt in stone in the 13th. It has been much changed since and has modern stained glass.

Découvrez la Camargue au rythme de ses canaux

Aix-en-Provence
●

**This elegant, historic university town has an impressive array of Renaissance buildings and an arty, youthful feel.
It hosts a distinguished annual arts festival and was home to artist Paul Cézanne.**

Brightly painted shutters at the former home of Paul Cézanne | *An outdoor restaurant in the lively cours Mirabeau* | *The Tour de l'Horloge* | *Aix has more than 100 fountains*

RATINGS
Cultural interest	● ● ● ● ●
Historic interest	● ● ● ● ●
Photo stops	● ● ● ● ●
Walkability	● ● ●

BASICS
✚ 292 G12

ℹ 2 place Général-de-Gaulle, tel 04 42 16 11 61; Apr–end Sep Mon–Sat 8.30–8, Sun 10–1, 2–6; Oct–end Mar Mon–Sat 8.30–7, Sun 10–1, 2–6

🚆 TGV Aix-en-Provence station is west of the city, in the l'Arbois district. The station in the heart of town is off rue G. Desplaces, 400m (440 yards) south of place Général-de-Gaulle.

www.aixenprovencetourism.com
A full and detailed site about the city.

TIPS
● Reserve lodgings as far ahead as possible at festival time (June and July).
● Aix has seven annual festivals, including the important Festival d'Aix (*Festival International d'Art Lyrique et de la Musique*), an opera festival lasting for around three weeks in July.

A door carving at the Cathédrale St-Sauveur (right)

SEEING AIX-EN-PROVENCE
Aix, historic capital of Provence, has a quintessentially southern feel—joyful, busy and relaxed. For centuries a town of art and culture, it is famous as the home of Paul Cézanne (1839–1906), who was born here and did most of his work here. The tourist office produces a map showing locations in and around Aix where Cézanne lived or worked. Many visitors are content to get no farther than the town's tree-shaded main street, cours Mirabeau, where it is perfect just to stroll on the wide pavement or sit at an outdoor table under the trees and watch the saunter-ing crowds. This leisurely avenue is the epitome of all that's agreeable about a Provençal city. Yet there is a good deal to enjoy within a short walk of Mirabeau, not least the enticing, tangled lanes of Vieil Aix, the more sober Renaissance streets of the Quartier Mazarin and several good art museums.

The 'Visa for Aix and its Region' card (€2) gives reductions on the entry price to various museums, as well as discounts on bus tickets. Buy it from the tourist office and museums.

HIGHLIGHTS

COURS MIRABEAU
This broad central boulevard is the town's main attraction, appealing for its quiet bustle and broad, leaf-shaded walkway. Its double row of leafy plane trees shades hundreds of café tables on the north side, where the classic brasserie Les Deux Garçons (▷ 179) dates from the 1790s. Across the road there's a duller workaday air with banks and offices—yet these are housed in 17th- and 18th-century mansions with elaborate ironwork balconies supported by huge caryatids. Down the middle of the boulevard are four natural fountains, including the hot-water Fontaine d'Eau Thermale (▷ 60).

QUARTIER MAZARIN
The Quartier Mazarin, off cours Mirabeau on the south side, is the neatly laid out district constructed in grid style by Archbishop Mazarin in 1646 as a grand residential area for the lawyers and noblemen attending the Parlement de Provence. The streets are curiously quiet,

FONDATION VASARELY

• 1 avenue Marcel Pagnol, Jas de Bouffan, 13090 Aix-en-Provence ☎ 04 42 20 01 09 🕙 Mon–Sat 11–1, 2–7 💶 €7

This gallery is devoted to modern abstract artist Victor Vasarely, a great admirer of Cézanne.

FOUNTAINS

Aix has more than 100 fountains. The moss-covered Fontaine d'Eau Thermale, on the cours Mirabeau, is a natural hot spring, with water pouring out at 34°C (93°F).

MUSÉE DU VIEIL AIX

• 17 rue Gaston de Saporta, 13100 Aix-en-Provence ☎ 04 42 21 43 55 🕙 Apr–end Sep Tue–Sun 10–12, 2.30–6; Nov–end Mar Tue–Sun 10–12, 2–5 💶 €4

Curiosities here include marionettes of characters from the medieval *Fête-Dieu* festival.

MUSÉE DES TAPISSERIES

• 28 place des martyrs de la Résistance, 13100 Aix-en-Provence ☎ 04 42 23 09 91 🕙 Wed–Mon 10–12, 2–6 💶 €2

The former Archbishops' Palace now shelters a tapestry museum.

The cours Mirabeau

with little commerce and few visitors. Among the many Renaissance houses is the remarkable former home of art collector and bibliophile Paul Arbaus, with hand-crafted ceilings and fireplaces, silk wallpaper and carved wooden doorways. The house, at 2A rue 4 Septembre, has been turned into a museum, the Musée Paul Arbaud (Mon–Sat 2–5), displaying his collection of faïence from Moustiers-Sainte-Marie and Marseille, works by Puget and Fragonard, sculptures and an enormous collection of manuscripts, rare editions and books on Provence.

VIEIL AIX

At the heart of Aix is its attractive medieval and Renaissance old quarter, enclosed by a ring of avenues and squares that have replaced the town's ramparts—cours Mirabeau marks the district's southern boundary. Vieil Aix is a place to explore at a leisurely pace—there are markets, pretty little squares with splashing fountains and lively narrow lanes, many for pedestrians only. Strolling in these lanes, you'll discover many Renaissance and medieval buildings, and a few small museums. This is also a district for fine restaurants and elegant shopping. The town's main square, place de l'Hôtel de Ville, with its Italianate town hall, is here. Rising from one corner of the building is a 16th-century belfry, the Tour de l'Horloge, its tower adorned with an astronomical clock. Three days a week (Tuesday, Thursday and Saturday) the vivid hues and scents of a flower market fill the square. Place Richelme, close by, has a daily produce market and is a main hang-out for street musicians and students. Just north of the Tour de l'Horloge, in rue Gaston de Saporta, is the Musée du Vieil Aix (▷ this page, More to See).

MUSÉE GRANET

• Place St-Jean-de-Malte, 13100 Aix-en-Provence ☎ 04 42 38 14 70 🕙 Wed–Sun 10–12, 2–6 (closed for refurbishment until 2006) 💶 €2

Until the 1980s, Aix did not possess a single work by its most famous son, artist Paul Cézanne. This was remedied when the town's main art museum, Musée Granet, was given a small collection of minor early Cézanne paintings. Untypical of the artist's work, and not doing justice to his later greatness, these are displayed in their own

Cézanne Gallery. The bulk of the museum's art collections are European paintings, collected by François Granet (1775–1849), but there are also extensive archaeological finds dating to Roman Aix. Perhaps the most interesting exhibits in the museum are the Ligurian masks, statuary and other items discovered at nearby Entremont. These are among the oldest pre-Roman artworks in France. The museum is currently closed for refurbishment and will open in time for the centenary of the anniversary of Cézanne's death, in 2006.

ATELIER CÉZANNE

• 9 avenue Paul Cézanne, 13090 Aix-en-Provence ☎ 04 42 21 06 53 🕓 Jul, Aug daily 10–6; Apr–end Jun, Sep daily 10–12, 2–6; Oct–end Mar daily 10–12, 2–5
💶 Adult €5.50, under 16 free
www.atelier-cezanne.com

Cézanne's studio is of interest simply as a perfectly preserved house and studio of the 1900s, although it contains none of the artist's work. The story is that Cézanne was mocked by locals, and with difficulty endured their daily ridicule as he made his way out to paint, carrying his easel and palette and ignoring his tormentors. In addition, he felt that his work was unappreciated in artistic circles. Near the end of his life, after the death of his mother, Cézanne became highly productive and began to earn an income from sales of his work in Paris, Berlin and Vienna (but not in Aix). He had a handsome studio-house built on a hill above the cathedral. From 1897 to his death in 1906, Cézanne spent most of his time here, leaving each afternoon for his landscape painting out of town.

The Fontaine de la Rotonde (left); parasols offer diners shade from the Provence sun on the cours Mirabeau (middle); the simple façade of the house where artist Paul Cézanne lived (right)

CATHÉDRALE ST-SAUVEUR

The cathedral is an interesting mix of styles from Romanesque to baroque, spanning the 5th to the 17th centuries. Look for the 16th-century Flemish tapestries in the chancel, which were stolen from Canterbury Cathedral during the English Civil War. The ancient baptistery, off the right-hand nave, contains traces of the main street of the Roman town. There are superb pieces of medieval art, notably Nicolas Froment's triptych of the *Burning Bush* in the central nave, painted for King René in 1476; the king and his queen are depicted kneeling in prayer.

The Cathédrale St-Sauveur

BACKGROUND

Aix started life as a Roman spa, Aquae Sextiae. It remained an important place, especially under Good King Réné of Provence (▷ 27), a great patron of the arts, who retired here to write poetry, novels and moral treatises. It is to this day a hub for art and culture. The university opened in 1409 and is an important presence today, with more than 40,000 students. When Provence came under the French crown, the establishment in 1501 of the Parlement de Provence—which was based here and which represented royal authority—brought a wealthy class of nobility and clerics to the town. That's when the many Renaissance mansions were built. In recent years, Aix has become one of the south's main cultural, commercial and high-tech industrial hubs.

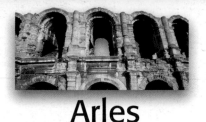

Arles

Arles is a lively, arty, market town with exceptionally well-preserved Roman buildings.

Carved archways at the Cathédrale St-Trophime

Two lions stand guard over Arles

An outdoor café in place du Forum

SEEING ARLES

On the Rhône's left bank, at the northern edge of the Camargue, Arles is a thriving commercial town. Locations in and near the town are reproduced in several paintings by Vincent Van Gogh. Extraordinarily ancient, Arles has an impressive array of historical places. Most are in the largely traffic-free old quarter, so it is convenient to stay in or near here. Especially notable are the Roman arena and, next to it, the Roman theatre, but there are considerable medieval sights too. Most of the main sights can be reached on foot. The busy main street, boulevard des Lices, runs alongside the old quarter and has many shops, bars, hotels and restaurants, as well as the tourist office. It is well served by buses.

HIGHLIGHTS

LES ARÈNES

• Place des Arènes, 13200 Arles ☎ 04 90 49 35 36 ◉ May–end Sep daily 9–6; Mar, Apr, Oct daily 9–5.30; Nov–end Feb daily 10–4.30 💶 Adult €4, child €3
The Roman arena stands at the quiet heart of historic Arles. Much damage has been done over the years to its sturdy structure—it was even largely dismantled in the 1820s to be used as building stone and in the 12th century was turned into a walled village. The medieval towers at each end are a relic of that time, when there were 200 houses, and even a church, within the arena. Yet enough remains of this circle of ancient walls, corridors and steps to be an awesome sight. It is still used for bullfights and performances.

THÉÂTRE ANTIQUE

• Rue de la Calade, 13200 Arles ☎ 04 90 49 38 34 ◉ May–end Sep daily 9–6; Mar, Apr, Oct daily 9–11.30, 2–5.30; Nov–end Feb daily 10–11.30, 2–4.30 💶 Adult €3, child €2.20
Near the arena is the large Théâtre Antique, or Roman theatre. Only the bare bones have survived thanks to years of destruction as the stonework was gradually removed to build houses and churches. All that remains are two columns of the stage wall and twenty rows of seats. Even this remnant creates a powerful impression. The theatre ruins are used for concerts, drama and the July folklore festival.

RATINGS	
Cultural interest	●●●●
Historic interest	●●●●
Photo stops	●●●●
Walkability	●●●●

BASICS

✚ 291 C11
ℹ **Main office:** Esplanade Charles de Gaulle, boulevard des Lices, tel 04 90 18 41 20; Apr–end Sep daily 9–6.45; Oct, Nov Mon–Sat 9–5.45, Sun 10.30–2.15; Dec–end Mar Mon–Sat 9–4.45, Sun 10.30–2.15 **Gare SNCF office:** mid-Jun to mid-Sep daily 9–1, 2–6
🚆 Gare SNCF, avenue Paulin Talabot

www.tourisme.ville-arles.fr
A full, detailed and lively site.

Bright yellow shutters on a house in Arles (left).
Roman columns in the Théâtre Antique (below)

MORE TO SEE

CRYPTOPORTICUS

• Rue Balze, 13200 Arles ☎ 04 90 49 32 82 ◉ May–end Sep daily 9–6.30; Mar, Apr, Oct 9–11.30, 2–5.30; Nov–end Feb daily 10–11.30, 2–4.30 👟 Adult €3.50, child €2.60

Beneath the street in the heart of the old quarter is the grim Cryptoporticus, two parallel galleries built by the Romans to give underground support to the Forum. The galleries were then used by the Romans as a storage area for grain, wine, produce, unused statuary and even slaves. During World War II it proved a useful public bomb shelter.

FONDATION VAN GOGH

• 26 rond-point des Arènes, 13200 Arles ☎ 04 90 49 94 04 ◉ Apr–end Oct daily 10.30–8; Nov–end Mar Tue–Sun 11–5 👟 Adult €7, child (8–18) €5, under 8 free

www.fondationvangogh-arles.org/ Facing the Roman arena, the small Fondation Van Gogh is an art museum but has no works by Van Gogh; it is simply named in his memory. The works too, by leading modern artists including Francis Bacon, Jasper Johns and Olivier Dubré, are supposed to have been inspired by him.

THERMES DE CONSTANTIN

• Rue D. Maisto, 13200 Arles ☎ 04 90 49 36 36 ◉ May–end Sep daily 9–12, 2–6; Mar, Apr, Oct daily 9–11.30, 2–5.30; Nov–end Feb daily 10–11.30, 2–4.30 👟 Adult €3, child €2.20

The Roman town reaches down to the banks of the Rhône, where the last remnants of the vast spa baths of Roman Arles are spread out close to the river. What can still be seen are vestiges of the tepidarium (warm baths), caldarium (hot baths), two pools and a steam room. It seems that the baths were part of the palace of Emperor Constantine, or at least were attached to it, but nothing remains except the baths, thought to have been the largest in Provence.

CATHÉDRALE ST-TROPHIME

• Place de la République, 13200 Arles ☎ 04 90 49 33 53 ◉ May–end Sep daily 9–6.30; Mar, Apr, Oct daily 9–5.30; Nov–end Feb daily 10–4.30 👟 Adult €3.50, child €2.60

St-Trophime Cathedral, dating from the sixth century AD, was one of the first Romanesque churches in France. However, there's little left of that original structure and the present building is mainly 12th century. Its ornate west front doorway is among the finest pieces of Provençal Romanesque stone carving. Go through the church and adjacent Bishops' Palace to reach the delightful cloisters, combining Gothic and Romanesque. The upper gallery is an exhibition space.

Outdoor café tables in a prime position next to Les Arènes

MUSÉE RÉATTU

• 10 rue du Grand Prieuré, 13200 Arles ☎ 04 90 49 37 58 ◉ May–end Sep daily 10–12.30, 2–7; Mar, Apr, Oct daily 10–12.30, 2–5.30; Nov–end Feb daily 1–5.30 👟 Adult €5.50, child €4

This museum, in a 15th-century Templar priory within the old quarter but close to the river, takes its name from its founder, local painter Jacques Réattu (1760–1833). It houses his own works, but more importantly, his remarkable collection of works by other artists. Donated to the town, it became Arles' main fine art museum, and in recent years has acquired some exceptional paintings representing all periods from the 16th century to today, especially by 19th- and 20th-century artists including Dufy, Gauguin, Léger, de Vlaminck and Rousseau. The greatest surprise is a set of 57 small line sketches by Picasso, a regular at the Arles bullfights. These are curiosities rather than important examples of his work; all date from early 1971.

MUSÉON ARLATEN

• 29 rue de la République, 13200 Arles ☎ 04 90 93 58 11 ◉ Jun–end Aug daily 9.30–1, 2–6.30; Apr, May, Sep daily 9.30–12.30, 2–6; Oct–end Mar daily 9.30–12.30, 2–5 👟 Adult €4, child €3

Provençal poet Frédéric Mistral used his 1904 Nobel Prize for Literature to set up this important ethnographic museum of Provençal folk culture, and many of the displays are still exactly as he arranged them. Appropriately, the name is in Provençal dialect, meaning 'Museum of Arles', and the staff wear traditional local costume. The compendious collection includes items from all aspects of life in the region during the 17th to the19th centuries. Household items sit alongside *santons* (figurines) and a delightful collection of pre-Revolution women's clothes. Archaeological finds are on the upper floor and there are ruins of a Roman temple in the courtyard.

MUSÉE DE L'ARLES ANTIQUE

• Presqu'île du Cirque Romain, avenue de la 1ere DFL, 13635 Arles ☎ 04 90 18 88 88/04 90 18 88 89 ◉ Mar–end Oct daily 9–7; Nov–end Feb daily 10–5.30 👟 Adult €5.50, child (12–18) €4, under 12 free 🚼

www.arles-antique.org/ Beside the Rhône, about 2km (1.2 miles) from central Arles, the Musée de l'Arles Antique is a startling modern construction, a pointed triangular building with blue enamel walls. It stands at the site where a huge cache of Roman gold coins was found, next to the Roman circus, or racetrack. The N113 overpass crosses the Roman circus. On display in the museum are numerous Classical items found at Arles, including rich Roman mosaics, sculptures of Augustus and Venus of Arles, and the finest collection of carved marble sarcophagi outside Rome. In what appears to be a deliberate contrast, these ancient items are displayed in an bright, ultra-modern setting.

LES ALYSCAMPS
• 13200 Arles ☎ 04 90 49 36 87 ⏱ May–end Sep daily 9–5.30; Mar, Apr, Oct daily 9–11.30, 2–5.30; Nov–end Feb daily 10–11.30, 2–4.30 💰 Adult €3.50, child €2.60

A short walk from boulevard des Lices (follow avenue des Alyscamps), the remarkable Alyscamps cemetery was once one of the most renowned burial grounds in the world. The name comes from the Latin *Elysii Campi* (the Elysian Fields). Already famous in Roman times, the cemetery continued to be used right into the Middle Ages, with tombs stacked on top of one another. It was claimed that miracles and magic occurred here. Then, in the 15th century, the grandest sarcophagi began to be stolen by clergy and officials, who coveted the fine stonework, and the cemetery was rapidly destroyed. The 20th-century construction of a railway through the grounds brought further decline, and today factory chimneys add to the ugliness. What survives is the last of the pathways between the tombs, a peaceful, melancholy and evocative tree-lined walkway leading to a church. The graves are empty. The site was given added poignancy in the paintings of *Les Alyscamps* by Vincent Van Gogh.

BACKGROUND

GREAT CITY
Arles was founded by the Greeks in 600BC as a trading outpost of Massalia (Marseille). It was later taken over by the Romans, who for political reasons preferred Arles to Marseille, and built Arles up as a large port, linked to the Mediterranean by canal. It became one of the Roman Empire's most important cities (they called it Arelate). Emperor Constantine was born here. The town's fourth-century Roman baths are believed to have been the largest in Provence. In the medieval period, too, Arles remained the greatest city of Provence, until overtaken by Aix. Arles is proud of its strongly Provençal cultural identity, and it was here that 19th-century poet Frédéric Mistral based himself in his struggles to revive the Provençal language.

VINCENT VAN GOGH
Vincent Van Gogh came to live in Arles during his most productive period. In search of a change of scene, he took the train from Paris in 1888 and was immediately satisfied with what he found. However, his depression did not lift. He set up home in place Lamartine, for part of the time living with fellow artist Paul Gauguin. Vincent fell out with Gauguin, and also with a prostitute that he visited, and ended up mutilating himself by partly severing his ear. Yet this was to prove a prolific, highly creative period. It is surprising that there are no Van Gogh paintings in Arles, nor any other traces left of his two-year stay. Even his house—the little yellow house featured in his paintings—no longer exists, destroyed by wartime bombing. After cutting his ear, Van Gogh was admitted to a hospital, which has now become the Espace Van Gogh, a *Mediathèque* devoted to the study of the artist. It stands opposite the Muséon Arlaten, and still has the garden seen in his painting *Jardin de l'Hôpital à Arles*. In 1889, Van Gogh was moved at his own request to the mental hospital out of town at St-Paul-de-Mausole (▷ 85). A year later, his mental condition not having improved, he returned north, and in 1890 he committed suicide at Auvers-sur-Oise, near Paris.

The Thermes de Constantin, where Romans once bathed

THE SIGHTS

Van Gogh's Jardin de l'Hôpital à Arles *(above) and the garden as it is today (top)*

Les Baux-de-Provence

This ruined citadel is poised on a high stony plateau among jagged Alpilles hills on the northern limits of the Camargue.

The setting sun throws a golden glow over Les Baux-de-Provence

A flower-filled window (above). Traditional santon figures (top)

There are wonderful views from the village

The entrance to the bizarre Cathédrale des Images

SEEING LES BAUX

The medieval fortress-village of Les Baux-de-Provence, with its atmospheric alleys, has an awesome location. It receives up to one million visitors a year and has almost no permanent residents. Cars must be parked in designated areas. When the upper parking areas are full, no cars are allowed on the access road, and you must park at the foot of the village. Occasionally the lower parking area is full too, and no further access to the village is possible except for pedestrians. A second entrance, the original Porte Eyguières, has no vehicle access. In reality, Les Baux has little to offer except atmosphere and views—but these are exceptional. The citadel and place St-Vincent give sweeping vistas across Vallon de la Fontaine to the hills all around.

HIGHLIGHTS

CITADELLE

● Rue du Château, 13520 Les Baux-de-Provence ☎ 04 90 54 55 56 🕐 Mar–end Nov daily 9–7.30 (until 9 Jul, Aug); Dec–end Feb daily 9–6 💶 Adult €7, child (7–18) €3.50, under 7 free 🎧 Audioguide is included in entry price 🌐 www.chateau-baux-provence.com/les_baux/index.htm

The dominant feature of Les Baux, especially from below, is the gaunt and impressive walled enclosure of the medieval citadel, whose ruins occupy most of the site. This large and bleak area is also evocatively known as the Ville Morte, or Dead City. Inside the enclosed area are about a dozen buildings still standing, including a 13th-century keep and other medieval towers, an olive musuem, a chapel and a pigeon house cut out of the rock, interspersed by reconstructions of medieval siege machines. A map directs you around the site. The views from this high cliff-edge location are the main attraction, taking in a landscape of wild rocky terrain broken up with vineyards and woods.

MODERN VILLAGE

Alongside the ruins of the Citadelle's Dead City is the handsome, busy modern Les Baux, with shops, houses and a town hall. Though referred to as the 'modern' village, it dates mainly from the 16th to 17th centuries. This area occupies a narrow strip outside the original fortress. Rue du Trencat, the main street, has been carved directly from the rocky terrain. Holiday crowds saunter the streets between the ice-cream stores, souvenir shops, *crêperies*, large areas of café tables and art galleries. Sights to pause at include the 16th-century town hall, with its façade of mullioned windows, lovely Renaissance courtyard and, inside, a folksy *santons* (figurines) museum.

ART IN LES BAUX

The picturesque site has long attracted artists of renown, including Vincent Van Gogh. The medieval village has now been taken over almost entirely by seasonal artists and craftspeople, and there are many galleries and craft stalls. Several places in town are used for temporary exhibitions, including the town hall. There are festivals of art and music throughout the summer.

ÉGLISE ST-VINCENT

• Citadelle, rue du Château, 13520 Les Baux-de-Provence ☎ 04 90 54 55 56 ⊙ Mar–end Nov daily 9–7.30 (until 9 Jul, Aug); Dec–end Feb daily 9–6 🎟 Adult €6.50, child (7–18) €3.50, under 7 free 🎧 Audioguide included in entry price 📧 This 12th-century church, partly hewn out of the rock, has a tower (Lanterne des Morts) and windows designed by the 20th-century stained-glass master Max Ingrand. On Christmas Eve, the popular *Fête du Pastrage* festival takes place here. In a chapel on the right-hand side of the church is the *Charette de l'Agneau* (The Lamb's Cart), which plays a key role in the festival. In a tradition dating back to the 16th century, during midnight mass, an angel hidden behind the altar announces the Nativity to shepherds at the back of the church. The shepherds come forward, dancing and singing Christmas songs, accompanied by shepherdesses with flowers and fruits strung about them. They are followed by the chariot bearing a new-born lamb.

CATHÉDRALE DES IMAGES AND VAL D'ENFER

• 13520 Les Baux de Provence ☎ 04 90 54 38 65 ⊙ Mid-Mar to mid-Nov daily 10–7; mid-Nov to end Jan, early to mid-Mar daily 10–5.30. Closed Feb 🎟 Adult €7, child (8–18) €4.10, under 8 free 🎧 30-min guided tour included in entry price www.cathédrale-images.com
There are also impressive sights at the foot of the village: Les Baux gave its name to bauxite, which was first quarried in what is now called the Val d'Enfer (the Valley of Hell), when geologists in the 1820s discovered that the red rock from the hills surrounding Les Baux could be smelted to produce aluminium. The Val d'Enfer is a spectacular gorge of wild rocks and caves to the north of the village. Its tortured-looking rock formations were supposedly the inspiration for Dante's *Inferno*. Jean Cocteau shot scenes from *Orphée* in the deserted quarries here in 1950 and one of the huge underground caverns has now been converted into the extraordinary Cathédrale d'Images, which offers an incredible sound and light experience.

BACKGROUND

Les Baux came into being as a refuge for locals in the 8th century, when Saracen raiders were attacking Provence. It later became a fortress of the powerful local lords. Up to the 12th century, the Lords of Les Baux controlled a wide area of western Provence. During the 14th century, the citadel became the base of the brigand-nobleman Raymond de Turenne, who lived by kidnapping noblemen and demanding a ransom. Those whose families did not pay were thrown off the edge of the cliff. To ensure his own control over western Provence, in 1483 Louis XI ordered the destruction of the Les Baux Citadelle, but during the religious wars of the 16th century, the village was reborn as a Protestant fortress. It was defeated and largely dismantled under Richelieu in 1632. The Prince of Monaco inherited the village, as Marquis des Baux, but it remained in ruins until the 19th century, when it was taken up by well-to-do artists and romantics. It was given a boost by the opening in the 1940s of l'Oustau de Baumanière, an exclusive luxury hotel-restaurant at the foot of the hill (▷ 235).

MUSÉE D'HISTOIRE DES BAUX

• Citadelle, rue du Château, 13520, Les Baux-de-Provence ☎ 04 90 54 55 56 ⊙ Mar–end Nov daily 9–7.30 (until 8.30 Jul, Aug); Dec–end Feb daily 9–6 🎟 Included in Citadelle entry ticket 🎧 Audioguide in English available free 📧
The Musée d'Histoire des Baux is at the entrance to the old citadel. Its contents trace the eventful history of the fortress village. A tour of the museum is essential for a better understanding of what can be seen on a visit to the citadel.

MUSÉE YVES BRAYER

• Hôtel des Porcelet, place de Hérain, rue de l'Eglise, 13520 Les Baux-de-Provence ☎ 04 90 54 36 99 ⊙ Apr–end Sep daily 10–12.30, 2–6.30; Oct to mid-Jan, mid-Feb to end Mar Wed–Mon 10–12.30, 2–5.30 🎟 Adult €4, child €2.50 www.yvesbrayer.com/pages/fr/baux/baux.htm
The Yves Brayer Museum houses vivid works by this figurative painter (1907–1990), as well as pieces by other modern artists, in the 16th-century Hôtel des Porcelet. The former 17th-century Chapelle des Penitents Blancs was also decorated by Yves Brayer.

A reminder of the time when the area was ruled by the Lords of Les Baux

THE SIGHTS

Camargue

The Rhône river opens out into Europe's largest wetland, where fresh water, sea water and land meet together in a unique and haunting world of wildlife, tranquillity and wide open spaces.

RATINGS	
Outdoor activities	● ● ● ● ●
Photo stops	● ● ● ● ●
Walkability	● ● ● ● ●

A statue of a Camargue bull (above)

SEEING THE CAMARGUE

The Camargue is a vast delta formed where the Grand Rhône and the Petit Rhône meet the sea. Much of this curious terrain is submerged in wide, shallow *étangs*—saltwater lagoons. The most sensitive areas have been classified as nature reserves and are closed to the public, including the Réserve Nationale Zoologique et Botanique de Camargue, covering 13,500ha (33,360 acres) around the Étang de Vaccarès. There are also towns here—notably Saintes-Maries-de-la-Mer (▷ 83), Aigues-Mortes (▷ 56–57) and, north of the Camargue margins, Arles (▷ 62–65). The best way to explore the Camargue is to get out of your car: Walk, ride a horse, rent a bicycle or go on safari. Jeep safaris and boat tours of the canals operate from Saintes-Maries-de-la-Mer.

HIGHLIGHTS

WILDLIFE

The Camargue is famous for its elegant half-wild white horses and black cattle, but many other creatures shelter in its ecosystems. The saltwater marshes attract colonies of terns and black-headed gulls, as well as species such as the oystercatcher, shelduck and redshank. In the *étangs*, pink flamingos pick their way through the shallows in search of food, while birds of prey stand sentinel on the fence posts by the road. The silence is almost total, apart from the honking of geese as they move in fluttering ribbons across the sky. Farther inland, and closer to the Rhône, there are freshwater areas where herons, moorhens, coot, mallards and egrets thrive.

Elegant flamingos in the shallows

THE COAST

The western Camargue coast has wide sandy beaches and dunes next to Saintes-Maries-de-la-Mer. These are among the most threatened areas in the Camargue, as the natural flows of silt have been destroyed by industry. Dikes, groynes and fences have been put in place to prevent the sands disappearing. In winter, rainwater collects in the dunes and nourishes plants such as sea wormwood, sand lilies, sea rocket and sea stock. In summer, sea holly and sea spurge appear.

ETANG DE VACCARÈS

🏠 Centre d'Information de la Réserve Nationale de Camargue, La Capelière, tel 04 90 97 00 97; Apr–end Sep daily 9–1, 2–6; Oct–end Mar Wed–Mon 9–1, 2–5
From Saintes-Maries you can hike along the *digue-à-la-mer*, a sea wall that divides the unspoiled beaches and lagoons around the southern side of the Étang de Vaccarès. The reserve of the Étang de Vaccarès itself is open only to permit-holders, but there are many points just off the surrounding roads (especially the D37) from where you can watch bird life. The reserve's headquarters is on the eastern side of the *étang*, where the Centre d'Information de la Réserve Nationale de Camargue has one of the best displays on the Camargue. There are three observatories within a few minutes of here and a walking trail, 1.5km (1mile) long. On the west side of the *étang* there are two more observation points.

PONT DE GAU

🏠 Parc Naturel Régional de Camargue, Pont de Gau, tel 04 90 97 86 32; Apr–end Sep daily 10–6; Oct–end Mar Sat–Thu 9.30–5
The Maison du Parc Naturel Régional de Camargue, 4km (2.5 miles) north of Saintes-Maries-de-la-Mer, has environmental displays and huge viewing windows. To get closer to the bird life, go to the adjacent Parc Ornithologique du Pont de Gau (Apr–end Sep daily 9–dusk; Oct–end Mar daily 10–dusk), which has trails around the Étang de Pont de Gau (a half-hour walk), or the more extensive Étang de Ginès sanctuary, where bulls graze in the summer. Large aviaries house predators such as buzzards, Egyptian vultures and eagle owls. The park looks after injured predators sent here from all over Europe.

BACKGROUND

Monks came to the Camargue in the Middle Ages to collect salt and reclaim the swampland. They were followed in the 17th century by ranchers, who bred black, longhorn bulls and the Camargue's famous white horses. In the 1970s, much of the area was designated as the Parc Naturel Régional de Camargue. In 1993 horses, sheep and bulls had to be evacuated by helicopter and lorry after the Rhône burst its banks.

Enjoying the salty view at the Salin-de-Giraud

BASICS

🗺 290 C11
🏠 Centre d'Information de la Réserve Nationale de Camargue, La Capelière, 13200 Arles, tel 04 90 97 00 97; Apr–end Sep daily 9–1, 2–6; Oct–end Mar Wed–Mon 9–1, 2–5

www.reserve-camargue.org
Packed with wildlife information, photos and maps; French only

TIPS

● Take precautions against mosquitoes, which breed prolifically in the marshes.
● Always take plenty of drinking water with you when you set out to explore the area.
● You can see flamingos throughout the year, but there are larger numbers in spring and summer.
● For guided tours in the Camargue ▷ 180, 184 and 230.
● For a drive in the Camargue ▷ 210–211.
● For a bicycle ride ▷ 212– 213.

It took over a century to build the Château de Barbentane

Boats and their reflections in the calm waters of the port at Cassis

BARBENTANE

🞖 284 D9 🇮 Le Cours, 13570 Barbentane, tel 04 90 90 85 86; Jul, Aug Mon–Sat 9–12.30, 2–6.30, Sun 10–12; Sep–end Jun Tue–Fri 10–12, 2–5.30, Sat 10–12 **Château de Barbentane** • 1 rue du Château, 13570 Barbentane ☎ 04 90 95 51 07 🕓 Jul–end Sep daily 10–12, 2–6; Apr–end Jun, Oct Thu–Tue 10–12, 2–6; Nov, mid-Feb to end Mar Sun 10–12, 2–6. Closed Dec to mid-Feb 💷 Adult €6, child (7–17) €4.50

The pretty village of Barbentane sits near the confluence of the Durance and the Rhône, south of Avignon. It is dominated by its chateau. Founded by the Marquis of Barbentane in 1674 and finished more than a hundred years later, the classic grace of the great Château de Barbentane owes much to the great chateaux of the Île de France, around Paris. Still occupied by the Barbentane family, it has rich furnishings that reflect 400 years of acquiring the finest items—the opulent interior is often used for magazine shoots. It is adorned with 18th-century tapestries, Aubusson carpets, porcelain, statues and chandeliers.

On the outskirts of Barbentane is the Parc Floral Provence Orchidées, which has an exotic garden with tropical plants, orchids and butterflies.

LES BAUX-DE-PROVENCE

See pages 66–67.

CAMARGUE

See pages 68–69.

CASSIS

🞖 293 G13 🇮 Oustau Calendal, quai des Moulins, 13260 Cassis, tel 04 42 01 71 17; Jul, Aug Mon–Fri 9–7, Sat, Sun 9.30–12.30, 3–6; Mar–end Jun, Sep, Oct Mon–Fri 9.30–12.30, 2–6, Sat 10–12, 2–5, Sun 10–12; Nov–end Feb Mon–Fri 9.30–12.30, 2–5, Sat 10–12, 2–5, Sun 10–12
www.cassis.fr

Handsome cliffs rise behind this busy little modern resort and older port. The town is close to the city of Marseille and popular with residents of that city. It is backed by wild wooded country, as well as vineyards. This is a very old vineyard area, producing a range of local wines, especially white. Cassis has a leisurely, civilized feel to it, with memories of artists who used to meet and paint here—about a century ago it was a popular spot with painters Matisse, Dufy, Derain and de Vlaminck. There's a small beach of sand and pebbles, and among other modest attractions is an old castle. The town is popular with walkers taking the easy clifftop paths that lead from here towards Marseille. **Don't miss** Take a boat trip from Cassis to see the coastline's scenic *calanques* (inlets).

CHAÎNE DES ALPILLES

🞖 291 D10

This narrow range of small, pretty, rocky hills, along the northeastern edge of the Camargue plain, is an isolated extension of the Lubéron range. Among the hills are villages, vineyards, densely wooded areas of cork oak and wild Mediterranean flora. Les Baux-de-Provence (▷ 66–67), in the heart of the Alpilles, attracts many visitors, but much of the rest of the area is almost unknown to tourists. A few narrow roads penetrate the heart of the range and reach interesting places around the base of the Alpilles.

The small town of Eygalières, on the northern edge of the Alpilles, is worth a visit. You can see the ruins of the 12th-century castle keep, as well as the 17th-century Chapelle des Penitents Blancs.

For a scenic drive through the Alpilles, head south from Eygalières on the D24. The narrow, winding road is bordered by vineyards and pine forests.

Each Easter there is a pilgrimage from Eygalières to the nearby 12th-century Chapelle de St-Sixte, on a small hill. (The chapel is closed the rest of the year.)

At the foot of Les Alpilles, near Les Baux-de-Provence, is the wealthy village of Maussane. Its fortunes came from the surrounding olive groves. A century ago it had more than a dozen olive mills, producing high-quality olive oil. Today one survives, which is still at work pressing olives in the traditional way.

Outside the nearby village of Le Paradou, in avenue de la Vallée des Baux-de-Provence, there's a huge indoor miniature village called La Petite Provence du Paradou (daily 10–6.30). This features over 300 figures of local characters—shepherds, gypsies, farmers, fishermen and so on—integrated into a vast, wonderfully detailed tableau, called a *village des santons*, with working windmills and other features. The attractive lane D78 snakes from Maussane around the south face of the Alpilles along an ancient route once used for the annual transhumance (▷ 10).

The imposing towers of the Château de la Barben

The elegant 17th-century town hall in Gémenos

The tower of La Ciotat's church watches over the port

CHÂTEAU DE LA BARBEN

✚ 292 F11 • 13330 La Barben
☎ 04 90 55 25 41 🕐 Jul, Aug daily
10–12, 2–6; Sep–end Dec, Feb–end Jun
Wed–Mon 10–12, 2–5 💰 Adult €6 plus
€10 for zoo and vivarium, child €3 plus
€5 for zoo and vivarium ❓ People with
disabilities may find it difficult to get
around the site ✦ 40-min guided tours
of the chateau are available in French
🍴 🏛 🎎 🛍

An awesome, magnificently
fortified castle on the top of a
rocky hill, daunting La Barben
looks almost like a film set.
Originally a medieval fortress,
today's castle is in reality more
like a stately home, and dates
largely to a 17th-century
reconstruction. Probably first built
before the year 1000, the castle
belonged to Marseille's St-Victor
Abbey. In the 15th century it was
acquired by King René (▷ 27),
who kept it as a private residence
before selling it to the de
Fortins—a powerful Provençal
noble family close to the French
monarchy. They owned it right up
until the 19th century and turned
it into a luxurious home.

The highlight is a spectacular
terraced garden in formal French
style. This was created by André
Le Nôtre, the landscape designer
of Versailles, at the meeting of
the Touloubre et Quatruie
streams. The formality of the
flower borders, statuary and
basins is emphasized by the
surrounding untamed woodland.

There are lavish period furnishings and fine craftsmanship
inside the chateau, including
striking 16th- and 17th-century
Flemish and Aubusson tapestries
and elegant 18th-century painted
ceilings. The entrance hall is
covered with 17th-century
Cordoban leather. Napoleon's
sister, Pauline Borghese, once
lived here, and you can visit her
bedroom, which is in the Empire
style. The kitchens have a bread

oven made of volcanic stone
brought from the Massif Central.

Other attractions include a
Vivarium (reptile collection), in
the castle's vaulted sheep pen,
and a zoo (daily 10–6), with
bears, lions, hippos and more.
Don't miss The chateau's lofty
main terrace has a grand double
staircase, which gives a dramatic
view of the Étang de Berre and
the town of Salon-de-Provence
(▷ 87) below.

LA CIOTAT

✚ 293 H14 ℹ Boulevard A. France,
13600 La Ciotat, tel 04 42 08 61 32;
May–end Sep Mon–Sat 9–8, Sun 10–1;
Oct–end Apr Mon–Sat 9–12, 2–6
www.laciotatourisme.com

La Ciotat's history as a port town
stretches back to the fourth
century AD. The town, southeast
of Marseille, is still dominated by
industrial architecture, including
vast gantries and cranes that
have stood idle since the dock-
yard closed in 1990. The port is
now home to fishing boats and
pleasure craft.

The town hosts a film festival
in June, in memory of the
Lumière brothers' first showing of
a motion picture, which took
place here in 1895.

West of town, behind the
dockyards, is the Parc Naturel
du Mugel, a wilderness area
dominated by the Bec de l'Aigle
(eagle's beak) promontory, 70m
(230ft) high.

GÉMENOS

✚ 293 H13 ℹ Cours Pasteur, 13420
Gémenos, tel 04 42 32 18 44; May–end
Sep daily 10–12, 3–6; Oct–end Apr
Mon–Sat 10–12, 2–5
www.gemenos.fr

Despite being close to the
autoroute and the spreading
edges of Marseille, Gémenos is a
typical Provençal village, with
narrow streets and steps and old

houses. It is set back from the
sea at the foot of the Massif de la
Sainte-Baume in 'Pagnol country',
the Provence of films *Jean de
Florette* and *Manon des Sources*.
Director Marcel Pagnol
(1895–1974) was born in
nearby Aubagne.

At the main square you can
look inside the courtyard of the
Granges du Marquis d'Albertas, a
huge 17th- to 18th-century
building that once housed agricultural workers. The beautiful
17th-century chateau of the
marquis is now the town hall.
Outside the village on the D2 is
the Parc de St-Pons, a protected
parkland of fine deciduous
trees—unusual in this region—
around the ruins of the early
13th-century Cistercian ladies'
abbey of St-Pons (free access).
Just behind the abbey, the
source of the river Fauge gushes
out of a small fissure in the rockface. The abbey ruins host
religious music concerts
in summer.

GLANUM

See page 86.

GROTTES DE CALÈS

✚ 292 E11 ✉ 13113 Lamanon
🕐 Free access, but site and path may
be closed in dry periods if there is a risk
of fire 🚌 Salon–Avignon buses stop
here 🚉 Lamanon 💰 Free

This bizarre troglodyte village has
dwellings carved into caves in
the steep rocky woods outside
Lamanon, 10km (6 miles) north
of Salon-de-Provence (▷ 87).
The caves were inhabited from
Neolithic times to the 16th
century and were still in use as
late as the 19th century. There
are more than 100 different
dwellings and steps lead down
into them. To reach them takes
about 15 to 20 minutes: Walk
out of Lamanon following signs
to the Grottes de Calès.

THE SIGHTS

Marseille

This ancient yet irresistibly dynamic city is a Mediterranean melting pot, with an intriguing atmosphere and exhilarating joie de vivre. There's a wealth of sightseeing, art and culture, and at its heart is the Old Port district, home of the classic Provençal fish stew, bouillabaisse.

The Cathédrale de la Major soars above the traffic

The arcaded galleries of La Vieille Charité, in Le Panier district

Taking a boat trip to the Château d'If

A gilded Madonna and Child crown the belfry of Notre-Dame de la Garde (top).
The Marché aux Poissons is a great place to buy fresh fish (right)

SEEING MARSEILLE

On the west coast of Provence, close to the Camargue, Marseille is an energetic city with a long history. It is France's premier Mediterranean sea gateway and has a distinctive mix of ethnic and cultural influences. The city has plenty to offer, including museums and art galleries, and boat trips to offshore islands. There are two Métro lines (▷ 50, 51). The grandly beautiful Vieux Port (Old Port) and its surrounding streets form Marseille's focal point. Here are bars, art galleries, music venues and scores of little restaurants. You can walk or drive the shore road a few minutes south from Le Vieux Port to the old-fashioned little port at Anse des Auffes, where bright fishing boats are pulled up in front of a choice of fish restaurants. And the city makes a good base for some out-of-town sightseeing on the western Provence coast. While there are areas where you should be careful, on the whole the 'crime and drugs' image of the city is exaggerated.

HIGHLIGHTS

LE VIEUX PORT

✚ 76 B3 🚇 Vieux Port

The focal point of the city heart, for both visitors and residents, is the large, westward-facing rectangular Old Port. Fortified, enclosed by spacious 17th-century quays, surrounded by the pale stone façades and red roofs of high, handsome old buildings, and with scores of boats jostling against one another, the port is an inspiring sight. Steep hillsides slope down to the port, overlooked on the south side by the sturdy defences of Fort St-Nicolas (no entry to visitors) and the powerfully fortified Romanesque basilica of St-Victor, which has a fifth-century crypt. Farther back is the hilltop Notre-Dame de la Garde, a 19th-century basilica topped with a huge gilded Virgin, strikingly lit at night, that locals traditionally believed gave divine protection to the city. At the foot of the hill, close to the port behind quai de Rive Neuve, is the grid of streets called the Quartier de l'Arsenal; now full of restaurants, it was once a notorious shipyard area where galley slaves were housed among the workshops. Stretching up the coast away from the Vieux Port are the city's extensive modern dockyards.

MUSÉE D'HISTOIRE DE MARSEILLE

✚ 76 C2 • Square Belsunce, Centre Bourse, 13001 Marseille ☎ 04 91 90 42 22
🕐 Mon–Sat 12–7 💶 Adult €2, child (6–16) €1, under 6 free 🚇 Vieux Port

The fascinating Musée d'Histoire de Marseille stands alongside the Jardin des Vestiges. It sets out the complete history of the city, with a third-century Roman ship as its focal point. The Jardin des Vestiges is an archaeological site transformed into a pretty garden. A walkway enables an overview of the ruins of the original Greek ramparts, traces of a roadway and parts of the dock as it was in the first century AD. Many of the items found in the excavations are now in the museum.

LE PANIER

✚ 76 B2 🚇 Vieux Port

Stepped alleys and rundown tenements with laundry lines strung between windows climb the Panier hill from the docks. In 1943 the occupying Nazi regime destroyed 2,000 buildings here and expelled or murdered around 25,000 residents. Among the buildings that survived is the 16th-century Maison Diamanté, so-called for a façade of stones carved into diamond-like points. It houses the Musée du Vieux Marseille (closed until 2006), with sections dedicated to Provençal furnishings, *santons* (figurines) and the esoteric playing cards called the Tarot Marseillaise. Another survivor, in Grand Rue, is the 16th-century Hôtel de Cabre. After World War II, it was taken apart and rebuilt on a different street, which is why it says Rue de la Bonneterie on the wall. At the top of Le Panier district is the former 17th-century hospice called La Vieille Charité, a rectangle of lovely, three-floor arcaded galleries, set around a large courtyard with a small baroque chapel. Originally a place of detention and shelter for vagrants, La Vieille Charité now hosts art exhibitions and the Musée de l'Archéologie Mediéranéenne (Jun–end Sep Tue–Sun 11–6; Oct–end May Tue–Sun 10–5). Beyond is the 19th-century neo-Byzantine Cathédrale de la Major, with its domes and striped façade. The sad, damaged little building beside it is the 12th-century Romanesque Ancienne Cathédrale de la Major (closed to the public).

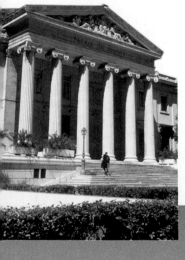

The neoclassical columns of the Palais de Justice

PALAIS LONGCHAMP

✚ 77 F1 • 142 boulevard Longchamp, 13004 ☎ Palais: 04 91 14 59 50. Musée des Beaux-Arts: 04 91 14 59 30 🕐 Musée des Beaux-Arts: Jun–end Sep Tue–Sun 11–6; Oct–end May Tue–Sun 10–5 🚇 Cinq-Avenues-Longchamp

This palace is home to the Musée d'Histoire Naturelle (Jun–end Sep Tue–Sun 11–6; Oct–end May Tue–Sun 10–5), which has a zoo behind it, and the Musée des Beaux-Arts. The latter has 16th- and

17th-century French and Italian paintings, a room devoted to local architect, sculptor and painter Pierre Puget, and another room dedicated to local cartoonist Honoré Daumier.

CHÂTEAU D'IF

✚ Off map at 76 A3 ☎ 04 91 59 02 30 🕐 May–end Sep daily 9.30–6.30; Oct–end Apr Tue–Sun 9.30–5.30 👆 Adult €4, under 18 free 🚢 From quai des Belges
It's a 15-minute ferry ride to the island of If, with its nightmarish prison fortress, built in the 16th century and made famous by Alexandre Dumas in *The Count of Monte Cristo* (1844). The journey gives great views of the city and guided tours take you to the cells once occupied by various aristocratic prisoners.

MORE TO SEE

LA CANEBIÈRE

✚ 76 C3 🚇 Vieux Port
Leading through the heart of the city in a majestic straight line from the Vieux Port's quai des Belges is the broad avenue La Canebière. Built in the 17th century, the street was for a long time rather seedy, but today is an inspiring sight. Most of the main shopping streets branch off it.

BACKGROUND

Founded as the trading port of Massalia by the Greeks 2,600 years ago, Marseille has been the western Mediterranean's main port ever since. After the Roman conquest of Provence, the port was sacked and stripped of its fleet, although Marseille remained a busy town. A period of decline followed the Saracen raids of the seventh century, which curtailed Mediterranean trade. By the 11th century, the city had revived and continued to develop until the plague arrived in 1720, killing 50,000. By the 1760s, the city was the major port trading with the Caribbean and Latin America. The republican zeal of Marseille's oppressed workers proved a backbone of the Revolution, the city giving its name to the new national anthem, *La Marseillaise*, even though it was composed in Alsace. The city sustained extensive damage during World War II. In the second half of the 20th century, large numbers of people from Africa, particularly North Africa, moved to the city. Today, Marseille has a total population of around one million.

Greek ruins in the Jardin des Vestiges, framed by trees and a newer building (left); the yellow façade of the Bazar du Panier (middle); crowds fill La Canebière (right)

MUSÉE CANTINI

✚ 76 C3 • 19 rue Grignan, 13006 Marseille ☎ 04 91 54 77 75 🕐 Jun–end Sep Tue–Sun 11–6; Oct–end May Tue–Sun 10–5 👆 Adult €3, under 5 free 🚇 Estangin-Préfecture
This modern art gallery, with a good Surrealist collection and works by Matisse, Dufy, Miró, Kandinsky and Picasso, was a private home in the 17th century.

MUSÉE DES DOCKS ROMAINS

✚ 76 B3 • 28 place Vivaux, 13002 Marseille ☎ 04 91 91 24 62 🕐 Jun–end Sep Tue–Sun 11–6; Oct–end May Tue–Sun 10–5 👆 Adult €2, under 5 free 🚇 Vieux Port
At the foot of Le Panier district are several important relics and museums of the Classical period. The Museum of the Roman Docks displays a collection of first- to third-century AD Roman objects discovered during post-war rebuilding work. It has a good collection of Roman *dolia* (large ceramic storage jars).

A view over the Vieux Port from the Esplanade de la Tourette

MARSEILLE

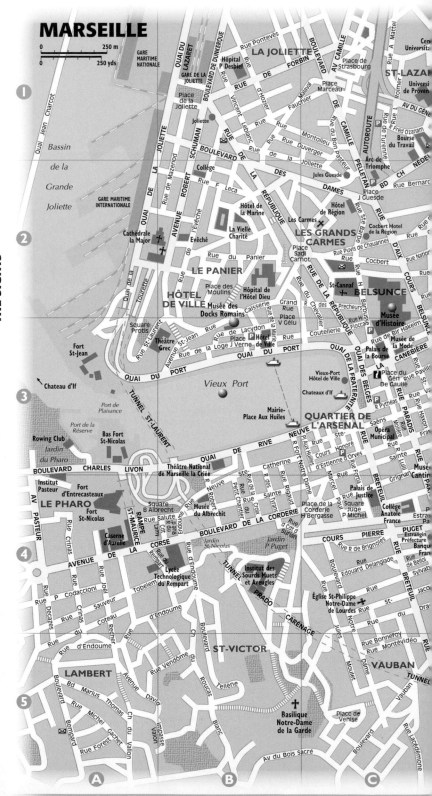

THE SIGHTS

0 ———— 250 m
0 ———— 250 yds

GARE MARITIME NATIONALE

QUAI DU LAZARET

BOULEVARD DE DUNKERQUE

Rue Ponteves

LA JOLIETTE

Rue Forbin

BOULEVARD

AV CAMILLE

Rue A Mattei

Place de Strasbourg

Cen. Universita

ST-LAZAR

Hôpital P Desbief

Place Marceau

Universi de Proven

AV DU GÉN

GARE DE LA JOLIETTE

QUAI DE LA JOLIETTE

Place de la Joliette

RUE d'Hozier

Rue Vincent Leblanc

Rue

DE

Manatl

Faucher

DE

CAMILLE

Rolmer

Rue Fréd Ozanam

AUTOROUTE

Joliette

Rue

BOULEVARD DE SCHUMAN

Montolieu

Rue du Bon pasteur

DES

PELLETAN

Rue de Turenne

Bourse du Travail

Bassin

de la

Grande

Joliette

GARE MARITIME INTERNATIONALE

QUAI DE LA JOLIETTE

AVENUE ROBERT

Collège

Rue de Mazenod

Rue de l'Evêché

Rue Leca

DE

LA

Rue Duverger

de la

Joliette

Jules Guesde

DAMES

Arc de Triomphe

Place J Guesde

BD

CH NÉDE

Rue Bernarc

Cathédrale la Major

Evêché

de l'Evêché

Hôtel de la Marine

La Vielle Charité

RÉPUBLIQUE

Les Carmes

Hôtel de Région

LES GRANDS CARMES

Cocbert Hotel de la Région

D'AIX

Rue Ste Barbe

Place Sadi Carnot

Rue Puvis de Chauannes

Rue

Cocbert

COURS

Rue

LE PANIER

Rue du Panier

St-Cannaf

BELSUNCE

HÔTEL DE VILLE

Place des Moulins

Hôpital de l'Hôtel Dieu

RUE DE LA RÉPUBLIQUE

Precheurs

Musée d'Histoire

Musée de la Mode

CANEBIÈRE

Musée des Docks Romains

Caisserie

Grand Rue

Rue du Chevalier

R des

Rue H Flocoaq

Rue de Bir Hakeim

Square Protis

Théâtre Grec

Rue St-Laurent

Avenue St-Jean

Rue de la Loge

Rue de Lacydon

Place J Verne

Hôtel de Ville

Rue

Coutellerie

QUAI DE LA BOURSE

Palais de la Bourse

Place du Gén De Gaulle

Fort St-Jean

QUAI DU PORT

Vieux Port

QUAI DU PORT

Vieux-Port Hôtel de Ville

QUAI DES BELGES

R Pythéas

RUE PARADIS

Chateau d'If

TUNNEL ST-LAURENT

Port de Plaisance

Mairie-Place Aux Huiles

Chateaux d'If

QUAI DE LA FRATERNITÉ

Port de la Réserve

Bas Fort St-Nicolas

QUARTIER DE L'ARSENAL

Saëns

Opéra Municipal

Mont...

Sainte

Rowing Club Jardin du Pharo

BOULEVARD CHARLES LIVON

NEUVE

Pl Aux Huiles

Cours

Honoré

d'Estienne d'Orves

Muse Cantin

Institut Pasteur

Théâtre National de Marseille la Criée

Ste-

Catherine

Rue Rigaud

Marcel

Grignan

Muse Cantin

AV PASTEUR

LE PHARO

Fort d'Entrecasteaux

Fort St-Nicolas

Square B Albrecht

Musée du Albrechit

R du Petit Chantier

Ste-

Rue Sainte

Palais de Justice

Square Juge P Michel

Collège Anatole France

Estra Pa

Caserne d'Aurelle

RAMPE ST-MAURICE

AVENUE DE LA CORSE

Rue Salute

Cdt Lamy

BOULEVARD DE LA CORDERIE

Place de la Corderie

H Bergasse

PUGET

Estrangin

Préfecture

Banqu

Fran

de Belol

AVENUE DE

Lycée Technologique du Rempart

Jardin St-Nicolas

Jardin P Puget

COURS PIERRE

Rue R de Brignoles

Rue Edouard Delanglade

BRETEUIL

Sylvab

Rue P Codaccioni

Rue Decazes

Rue Crinas

Rue Coteau

Rue d'Endoume

Institut des Sourds Muets et Aveugles

TUNNEL PRADO

Église St-Philippe Notre-Dame de Lourdes

Rue St-

CARENAGE

Rue Bonnefoy

Rue Montevidéo

Jaco

Dra

LAMBERT

Bd Marius Thomas

Rue Michel

Rue Forest

Boulevard

Bompard

Avenue David

ST-VICTOR

Rue Vendôme

Ch du Vallon

Impasse

Blanc

Basilique Notre-Dame de la Garde

Place de Venise

VAUBAN

TUNNEL

Rue Jardedmon

Av du Bois sacré

A ———— B ———— C

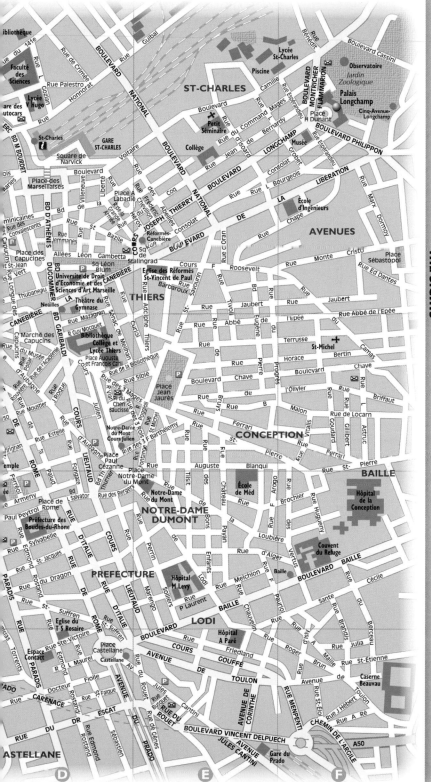

THE SIGHTS

Pretty houses on the quai Brescon, in Martigues

Artist Paul Cézanne painted the Montagne Sainte-Victoire on many occasions

MARTIGUES

✚ 292 E12 ⓘ Maison du Tourisme, Rond Point de l'Hôtel de Ville, 13500 Martigues, tel 04 42 42 31 10; Mon–Sat 9–6.30, Sun 10–12.30
🚉 Gare Martigues-Caronte
www.martigues-tourisme.com

Once a popular spot among the Impressionists, and still beloved by artists for its picturesque quaysides, Martigues is curiously located on a narrow strip of land with the Mediterranean on one side and the large Étang de Berre on the other. Linking the two is the Canal de Caronte, the town's main canal, while other picturesque waterways link the three separate 'villages' that make up Martigues.

Jonquières, on the southern side of the main canal, is the best village to try if you are looking for a meal or a drink. Among its tangled lanes and narrow traffic-free streets are markets, shops and bars.

As its name suggests, the second village, L'Île (The Island), sits in the middle of the canal. Here you'll find the lovely Église Sainte-Madeleine-de-l'Île, as well as several 17th- and 18th-century houses.

For art, head to the Musée Ziem, in Martigues' third village, Ferrières. The museum, on boulevard du 14 Juillet, has works by the artist Félix Ziem (1821–1911) and others (Jul, Aug Wed–Mon 10–12, 2.30–6.30; Sep–end Jun, Wed–Sun 2.30–6.30).

A picturesque range of low hills, called the Chaîne de l'Estaque, runs along the coast between Martigues and Marseille. Here you can follow woodland walking trails and enjoy some good sea views.
Don't miss Stand on the bridge at quai Brescon, next to the Église Sainte-Madeleine-de-l'Île, to admire the famous view of fishing boats moored on a curve of the canal. The scene, known as the *Miroir des Oiseaux* (the bird's mirror), was painted by Ziem.

MIRAMAS-LE-VIEUX

✚ 291 E11 ⓘ 24 place Jean Jaurès, 13140 Miramas, tel 04 90 58 08 24; Mon–Fri 9–12, 1.30–5 🚉 Miramas
www.miramas.org/tourisme

Overlooking the thriving modern town of Miramas is its fortified hilltop quarter, Miramas-le-Vieux. Here the streets have been recobbled to create the kind of medieval *village perché* you are more likely to come across in the Vaucluse. On summer evenings you can enjoy music concerts in the evocative ruins of the old chateau.

MONTAGNE SAINTE-VICTOIRE

✚ 293 G–H11

Nineteenth-century artist Paul Cézanne loved this huge sunlit wedge of limestone rising in the Provençal countryside east of Aix. Each afternoon he would walk from the city to capture views of the mountain, repeating this same subject endlessly, exploring the ideas of structure, form and light that it inspires, often conveying it as a blue-grey pyramid rising strangely above ochre soil and dark green trees.

To the ordinary eye it might appear less awesome— its highest peak, Pic des Mouches, rises to only 1,010m (3,300ft)—but more satisfying as part of a rugged, dry, unchanging landscape that epitomizes Provence. The mountain is encircled by minor roads (the D10 on the north, D17 on the south) giving easy access to its viewpoints and trails. Just off the D10, the Barrage de Bimont (7km/4 miles from Aix) is an impressive structure that forms a small lake by damming the river Infernet. The area has been turned into a pleasant park (for a walk there ▷ 207).

Farther along the D10, a marked trail near Les Cabassols farm leads up the steep 3km (2-mile) path to La Croix de Provence, the peak at the western end of the mountain. Allow several hours to do this walk, as the path is difficult in places, but the reward is an awesome vista extending across waves of blue and purple hills.

Vauvenargues (▷ 208), on the D10, is a small, pretty village. The 17th-century chateau standing on a rock nearby was the home of artist Pablo Picasso.

At the southeastern end of the mountain is the village of Pourrières, supposedly named (from *pourri*, rotten) for the thousands of corpses of Teutons piled here after their defeat by Romans in 102BC. From here to Puyloubier, south of the mountain on the D17, is vine country producing rosé wines. For a drive ▷ 208–209.

The Montagne Sainte-Victoire has inspired many artists

Nîmes

A town of wonderful Roman buildings, including one of the best-preserved amphitheatres of the ancient world.

One of the city's many fountains

Corinthian capitals on the Maison Carrée

A café in place aux Herbes (above). A Classical figure on a fountain (right)

RATINGS

Historic interest	●●●●○
Photo stops	●●●●○
Walkability	●●●●○

BASICS

✚ 290 B10
ℹ️ 6 rue Auguste, 30000 Nîmes, tel 04 66 58 38 00; Jul, Aug daily 8–8; Easter–end Jun, Sep Mon–Fri 8–7, Sat 9–7, Sun 10–6; Oct–Easter Mon–Fri 8.30–7, Sat 9–7, Sun 10–5
🚉 Nîmes

www.ot-nimes.fr
A guide to the sights and history of Nîmes, and hotels.

TIPS

● The brass studs in the pavements feature the city symbol, a crocodile and a palm tree.
● Also worth visiting are the Musée de Vieux Nîmes, in place aux Herbes, and the Musée des Beaux-Arts, in rue de la Cité-Foulc.
● Once you've taken in the history, enjoy some retail therapy at La Coupole, a small shopping mall of 50 high-class stores.

SEEING NÎMES

Though Nîmes is outside the Bouches-du-Rhône *département*—it is in the Gard about 16km (10 miles) from the western edges of the Camargue—it was a vital part of Roman Provence and rewards today's visitors with exceptional buildings from that period. The size of Nîmes is one of its key attributes. It is large enough to offer the facilities necessary for its visitors, yet small enough—especially in its old city—to generate a feeling of intimacy. Most of the sights are within walking distance of each other. The old heart of the city has been tastefully preserved and the narrow alleys are full of expensive boutiques.

HIGHLIGHTS

LES ARÈNES

✚ 81 B2 • Place des Arènes, 30000 Nîmes ✉ 04 66 76 72 77 🕐 Mid-Mar to mid-Oct daily 9–7; mid-Oct to mid-Mar daily 10–5; closed during some events 🎫 Adult €4.45, child (10–18) €3.20, under 10 free
Nîmes' amphitheatre is one of the best preserved from the Roman world and is the city's top attraction. Once inside, visitors can explore the tiers of seating surrounding the amphitheatre. Those at the top (21m/69ft above the ground—and with no guard rail) enjoy panoramic views of Nîmes. Behind the scenes, there is a complicated arrangement of arches and passages (those beneath the arena are closed to the public), inspiring wonder at the sheer scale of the 2,000-year-old building, still much used today, not only for bullfights but for a succession of events and trade fairs. Between October and Easter, a dome-shaped inflatable cover is in place to keep out the rain.

MAISON CARRÉE

✚ 81 B2 • Place de la Maison Carrée, 30031 Nîmes ✉ 04 66 36 26 76 🕐 Jun–end Sep daily 9.30–6.30; Oct–end May daily 9–5 🎫 Free
The Maison Carrée, in the heart of town, is a fully preserved Roman temple. The interior contains a display of panels describing the history of the temple and some beautiful small examples of Roman mosaic work. Built in the first century AD and based on the Temple of Apollo

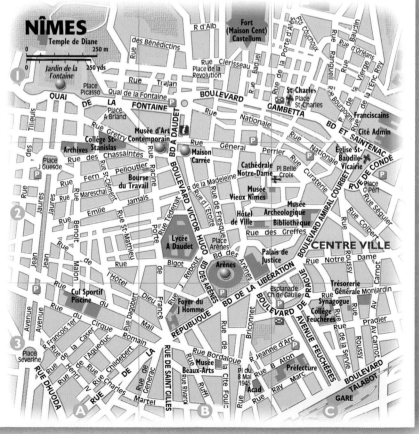

NÎMES

Temple de Diane

0		250 m
0		250 yds

Jardin de la Fontaine

R d'Alb

Fort
(Maison Cent)
Castellum

des Bénédictins

Rue Clérisseau
Place de la
Révolution

Rue Trajan

Place
Picasso

Quai de la Fontaine

QUAI DE LA FONTAINE

BOULEVARD GAMBETTA

St-Charles
Place
St-Charles

Nationale

Franciscains
BD ET SAINTENAC
Cité Admin

Place
A Briand

Rue Grétry

Musée d'Art
Contemporain

Collège St-
Stanislas

Archives

Rue des Chassaintes

Rue
Général Perrier

Rue Nationale

Maison
Carrée

Cathédrale
Notre-Dame

Pl Belle
Croix

Église St-
Baudile
Vicairie

RUE DE CONDÉ

Place
G Péri

des Tilleuls

Place
J Guesde

Rue

Pelloutier

Bourse
du Travail

Fern St-Clément

Mareschal

Rue de la Madeleine

Rue de l'Étoile

Musée
Vieux Nîmes

Musée
Archéologique

Bibliothèque

Rue Séguier

Rue Colbert

Jaures

Jaures

Rue

Emile

Benoit

Jamais

Rue St-Mathieu

Rue Tédenat

Porte

Rue

BOULEVARD VICTOR HUGO

Hôtel
de Ville

Rue des Greffes

BOULEVARD AMIRAL COURBET

CENTRE VILLE

Jean

Jean

Rue

Malon

Racine

Lycée
A Daudet

Bigot

Rebout

Place
Arènes

Bd des Arènes

Arènes

Palais de
Justice

Rue Notre Dame

Rue Roussy

Av Carnot

Cul Sportif
Piscine

Rue

de

l'Hôtel

du

Dieu

Rue Dagobert

Rue Daudet

Foyer du
J Homme

BD DE LA LIBÉRATION

Esplanade
Ch de Gaulle

Trésorerie
Générale Monjardin

Synagogue

Collège
Feuchères

Pradier

Avenue

Avenue

Rue

R Francois 1er

Place
Séverine

Rue de la Caser

Rue Henri

Cirque
Romain

Mail

RÉPUBLIQUE

BOULEVARD DE PRAGUE

France

Rue Jeanne d'Arc

AVENUE FEUCHÈRES

Bricconet

Préfecture

Rue de la Servie

Av Carnot

BOULEVARD TALABOT

RUE DHUODA

RUE

Rue Charles

IV

Rue Childebert

Rue de Générac

RUE DE SAINT GILLES

de l'Aqueduc

LA DE

Rue Rivaro

Rufti

Rue Bordaloue

Musée
Beaux-Arts

Rue de la Cité Foulc

Pl du
8 Mai
1945

Acad

Rue B Aton

Rue Ray

Marc

GARE

Martel

A

B

C

PONT DU GARD

✚ Off map at 290 C10

🅸 Exhibition Centre, Pont du Gard, 30210, tel 04 66 37 51 10 ◉ Exhibition hall: Easter–end Sep daily 9.30–7; Oct–Easter daily 10–6. Site: daily 7am–1am 🅿 Parking ticket (€5) gives entrance to the site. Exhibition hall: €5. 25-min film: €3. Ludo, children's discovery zone: €4

🍴 📷 ♿

A UNESCO World Heritage Site, this aqueduct was built in the first century BC to channel huge amounts of water to the Roman settlement at Nîmes. City engineers carved out the aqueduct from a source near Uzès, 50km (30 miles) away, which necessitated spanning the Gardon river gorge at a height of 48m (156ft). Details such as the fact that no mortar was used, or that the average drop over the entire length of the aqueduct was only 24cm (10in) per km, add to the fascination of the site.

On the left bank, there is a huge parking area, information panels and a pathway leading directly to the exhibition hall, which has been carefully designed and positioned so as not to detract from the site. The exhibition shows how water was used to enrich the civilized lifestyle of the Romans—wealthy households had their own piped supply, public baths were constructed, fountains graced public areas and water powered industry. It also deals with the geological challenges that were overcome during construction. Various multimedia and participatory displays make this an excellent facility.

Although people are no longer allowed onto the Pont itself, you can walk over the bridge that runs alongside it at the same level as the first tier of arches. By so doing you fully realize the size and weight of the building blocks used in the aqueduct's construction, but to appreciate it fully, you'll need to go up- or downstream for an unimpeded view from a distance.

A figure from one of the fountains in the delightful Jardin de la Fontaine (above)

in Rome, it was dedicated to Augustus' grandsons, Caius and Lucius. Surrounded by elegant Corinthian columns, it remains almost perfectly intact, despite having been used as a stable, among other things, in the Middle Ages.

MUSÉE D'ART CONTEMPORAIN

✚ 81 B2 ✉ Carrée d'Art-Musèe d'Art Contemporain, place de la Maison Carrée, 30031 Nîmes ☎ 04 66 76 35 70 ◉ Tue, Thu 10.30–7, Wed, Fri, Sat 10.30–6 🅿 Adult €4.45, child (10–18) €3.20, under 10 free

Rising impressively beside the Maison Carrée, and making a striking contrast, is a gallery of contemporary art and a library designed by Sir Norman Foster. Completed in 1993, the museum has a pleasingly spacious feel and lots of natural light. The artworks date from the 1960s to today, with occasional visiting exhibitions. The gallery has an excellent third-floor bar/restaurant, with an outside terrace overlooking the Maison Carrée.

JARDIN DE LA FONTAINE

✚ 81 A1 ◉ Mar–end Oct daily 9–7; Nov–end Feb daily 9–5 🅿 Adult €2.40, child (10–18) €1.90, under 10 free

A short walk from the old quarter, the Jardin de la Fontaine is a beautiful park with flowing water, fountains and statues, developed in the 18th century on an ancient site that features an enigmatic

temple to Diana. The area above and behind the park, on rising ground, is planted with Mediterranean evergreens, intertwined with paths up to the Tour Magne. The tower has an internal spiral staircase leading to a small viewing platform and excellent views.

BACKGROUND

Nîmes was an important settlement even before Roman times—a Celtic tribe known as the Volcae-Arecomici chose it as their capital and named it Nemansus. The Romans arrived in the first century BC and Nemansus became Nemausensis. Augustus heaped privileges on the town, encircling it with a monumental wall, 8km (5 miles) long. Soon after, the large amphitheatre was added, as well as the Maison Carrée and the Pont du Gard aqueduct (23km/14 miles away), which brought fresh water to the baths and fountains. In the Middle Ages, Nîmes went into decline, and suffered much bloodshed during the Religious Wars, when it sided with the Protestants. When peace returned, the city built up a thriving textile industry, employing thousands of workers in the 18th century. One of its best-selling lines was a hard-wearing blue serge called De Nîmes. This became known as denim after Levi Strauss began, in 1848, to manufacture his famous blue jeans in California. Today, Nîmes has invested heavily in culture, commissioning world-class architects to embellish the city with impressive buildings and monuments.

THE SIGHTS

SAINTES-MARIES-DE-LA-MER

A picturesque medieval coastal town with sandy beaches, Saintes-Maries makes a perfect base for visits into the heart of the Camargue.

Saintes-Maries-de-la-Mer is the main town in the scenic Camargue (▷ 68–69). As a medieval fortified port on the Mediterranean, with its own sandy beaches to the east, it has become the visitor capital of the Camargue region. Sports facilities include bicycle rental, horseback riding and plenty of water sports. A profusion of bird life lives in the adjacent lagoons and herds of half-wild white horses roam free in the watery terrain just outside town. The unusual name ('Holy Maries of the Sea') comes from a medieval legend that Mary Magdalene, together with St. Marie-Jacobé, sister of the Virgin Mary, and St. Marie-Salomé, mother of the Apostles James and John, sailed across the Mediterranean from the Holy Land and landed here on the Camargue coast. Accompanying them were other Biblical characters and their Ethiopian servant Sarah.

MAIN SIGHTS
The town is dominated by the sturdy fortified Romanesque church (May–end Sep daily 8–12, 2–7; Mar, Apr, Oct daily 8–7; Nov–end Feb daily 8–6) with its curious open bell tower. Its heavy defences date from the 12th century, and were put in place as a protection against Saracen raiders then harassing the Provençal coast. Inside the church are ancient wooden statues of Sarah. A tower standing on a corner next to the church, in rue Victor Hugo, houses the Musée Baroncelli (Jun–end Sep Wed–Mon 10–12, 2–6), which displays some interesting local historical finds. The museum tower and the church tower both give wonderful views of the town, the sea and the Camargue flatlands.

A GYPSY CAPITAL
On landing, Mary Magdalene went farther into Provence, while the other two Maries and Sarah remained at Saintes-Maries, where Sarah became patron saint of gypsies. Huge, vibrant, traditional gypsy gatherings and processions in her memory are held here annually on 24 and 25 May. Although they come from all over Europe, most of the gypsies are Spanish. Gypsy caravans are a permanent feature of the area around the town, as is Spanish entertainment such as flamenco, put on for visitors.

Browsing for souvenirs (above).
Enjoying lunch (top)

RATINGS				
Good for kids	●	●	●	●
Historic interest	●	●	●	
Photo stops	●	●	●	●
Walkability	●	●	●	●

BASICS

✚ 290 B12

🚹 5 avenue Van Gogh, 13460 Saintes-Maries-de-la-Mer, tel 04 90 97 82 55; Jul, Aug daily 9–8; Apr–end Jun, Sep daily 9–7; Mar, Oct daily 9–6; Nov–end Feb daily 9–5

www.saintesmaries.com
This useful, informative site has most pages available in English, and includes a weather forecast for the town.

TIP
● The area beside the beach is the best place to find somewhere to park.

St-Rémy-de-Provence

This busy, charming old winemaking town has a strong cultural and artistic heritage, while nearby are the ruins of Graeco-Roman Glanum.

Delicious olives, sold in the market　*Exploring the ruins at Glanum*　*A hunting scene from a bas-relief at Les Antiques*

BASICS

✚ 291 D10

🛈 Place Jean Jaurès, 13210 St-Rémy-de-Provence, tel 04 90 92 05 22; Jun–end Sep Mon–Sat 9–12.30, 2–7, Sun 10–12, 3–6; Oct–end May Mon–Sat 9–12, 2–6

www.saintremy-de-provence.com
An attractive site in French and English, with comprehensive information.

TIPS

● There are interesting wineries all around the town, such as Château Romanin, off the D99.
● It's worth joining one of the themed guided tours run by the tourist office.
● St-Rémy makes an attractive base for visits to Les Baux-de-Provence (▷ 66–67) and Les Alpilles (▷ 70).
● To find out more about local folklore, geology and ethnology, head to the Musée des Alpilles, in place Favier.

The 16th-century Hôtel Mistral de Mondragon (top) houses the Musée des Alpilles

SEEING ST-RÉMY-DE-PROVENCE

In countryside 5km (3 miles) north of the Alpilles hills, St-Rémy is a bustling little town noted for its fruit, vegetables and wine. It has many good small shops specializing in local gastronomy, antiques, pottery and traditional Provençal arts and crafts. There are few sights of importance within the town itself, but the small old quarter is pleasant, with narrow streets, plant-filled alleyways, quiet tree-shaded squares and cooling fountains. Many fine 16th- to 18th-century mansions can be seen in this quarter, and there are some small art galleries and museums. From April to October the tourist office runs a 90-minute guided tour, called 'In the steps of Van Gogh', visiting sights that he painted (Tue, Thu, Sat at 10am). The tour gives reduced entry fees for St-Paul-de-Mausole and the Centre d'Art Présence Van Gogh. Alternatively, there is a self-guided tour using a map from the tourist office.

St-Rémy's main sights are about 1km (0.6 miles) south of town, where the archaeological site of the important Graeco-Roman town of Glanum is located. You can take a taxi to Glanum, or reach it on foot in 10 to 15 minutes.

HIGHLIGHTS

OLD QUARTER

Encircled by a boulevard of plane trees, the heart of town is a warren of narrow streets and small squares with many grand houses. On the edge of the boulevard is place de la République, with an outdoor café. The Hôtel de la Ville Verte has been here for some 150 years—Charles Gounod composed the Provençal opera *Mireio* while staying here in 1864, and American author Gertrude Stein had a room here for a year in the 1920s. Facing the square is Collegiale St-Martin, with its famous modern organ, installed in 1983 and said to be one of the best contemporary organs in Europe. Recitals take place on Saturday evenings throughout the summer. Behind St-Martin, in place Favier, are several fine Renaissance mansions—some house museums devoted to local folk culture, Nostradamus and archaeology. Part of the house where Nostradamus was born in 1503 can be seen in rue Hoche, though it is not open to the public.

LES ANTIQUES
• Avenue Vincent Van Gogh/Routes des Baux (D5), 1km (0.6 miles) south of St-Rémy-de-Provence 🚇 Free (unsupervised) access

Standing beside the road (D5) across from the entrance of Glanum (▷ 86), two remarkable Roman structures survive, known as Les Antiques. For many centuries, these two structures were the only visible remnants of Glanum, and it was not known that they were Roman. One of these is a two-level memorial, 18m (59ft) high and very well-preserved, decorated with carvings and reliefs, dating to about 30BC and traditionally known locally as the Mausolée des Jules. It is not, however, a mausoleum and appears to have been erected by members of a Roman family in memory of their parents. Alongside is an arch, probably by Greek craftsmen (though the tiled roof was added in the 18th century), which is now thought to have marked the entrance to the town of Glanum.

ST-PAUL-DE-MAUSOLE
• St-Paul-de-Mausole, avenue Vincent Van Gogh/Routes des Baux (D5), 13210 St-Rémy-de-Provence 📞 04 90 92 77 00 🚇 Apr–end Oct daily 9.15–7; Nov–end Mar daily 10.15–4.45 🎫 Adult €3.20, child €2.40

Just outside the Glanum site is the beautiful old monastery of St-Paul-de-Mausole, where Van Gogh committed himself voluntarily for a year's rest and treatment in 1889 after mutilating his ear. It was one of the most productive periods of his life—he turned out 150 paintings and 100 drawings in 12 months, mainly set in and around the town and the sanatorium. It is still a private sanatorium for those with mental health problems. The monastery's Romanesque church and cloisters are open to the public. There is a permanent exhibition of pictures painted by the patients. These paintings are available for sale together with Van Gogh prints—all proceeds go towards the upkeep of the hospital.

The organ at the Collegiale St-Martin was installed in 1983

Glanum's Mausoleum

GLANUM

- Glanum, avenue Vincent Van Gogh/Routes des Baux (D5), 1km (0.6 miles) south of St-Rémy-de-Provence ☎ 04 90 92 23 79 🕐 Apr–end Sep daily 9–7; Oct–end Mar daily 9–12, 2–5 💰 Adult €5.50, under 18 free

Roman ruins at Glanum

The archaeological site of Glanum, extending over a large enclosed area of ruins next to Les Antiques and St-Paul-de-Mausole and running beside the road (D5), has been under excavation for more than 20 years. It covers three cultural periods, all of which have left extensive relics—Greek, early Roman and late Roman. Glanum is important in the study of the spread of Greek culture. It is a site rich in significance for the expert, and for the casual visitor, too, the layered excavations are fascinating. Especially interesting are the Forum (or main square) of the Roman town, the Baths and a sacred well of the Greek period. The sites of several large private houses can be made out, as well as Greek temples—one of which has been partly reconstructed using ancient tools and techniques.

1. Basin of fountain

GREEK PERISTYLE HOUSES
2. Maison des Antes
3. Maison de Cybèle
4. Maison d'Atys

ROMAN BATHS
5. Heating Chamber
6. Caldarium (hot water)
7. Tepidarium (tepid water)
8. Frigidarium (cold water)
9. Palaestra (courtyard)
10. Natatio (swimming pool)

OTHER EXCAVATIONS
11. Maison de Capricorne
12. Building with apse
13. Basilica
14. House of Sulla
15. Covered water channel
16. Forum
17. Hall with apse
18. Monument or altar
19. Roman theatre
20/21. Roman temple
22. Well
23. Buleuterion (council chamber)
24. Hall with Doric columns
25. Fortified Gate
26. Nympheum (presumably above the sacred well of Glanum)
27. Altars (dedicated to Hercules)
28. Celtic shrine

BACKGROUND

Long before St-Rémy existed, Glanum had been built by Greek merchants from Massalia (Marseille) and had become a large, prosperous town. Taken over by the Romans, it continued to thrive until it was destroyed by Visigoths in the third/fourth century AD, after which the medieval town of St-Rémy grew up about 1km (0.6 miles) away. St-Rémy became an important hub for the Alpilles and surrounding region. One of its most illustrious sons was the astrologer Nostradamus (1503–1566), whose predictions in his book *Centuries* extend even to today. St-Rémy also has connections to the 19th-century writer Frédéric Mistral, who grew up in a nearby village.

VAN GOGH

St-Rémy has strong associations with Vincent Van Gogh, who came for a year (1889–1890) to the nursing home at St-Paul-de-Mausole monastery to seek help for his depression. Cared for there by doctors and nuns, he tried to find peace of mind and to a large extent succeeded, albeit temporarily. He spent much time walking in and around the town, painting and drawing constantly. He left St-Rémy on 16 May 1890 to go to a clinic at Auvers-sur-Oise. He committed suicide a few weeks later on 29 July 1890. The Van Gogh connection has helped to make St-Rémy popular with artists and writers, such as the American novelist Gertrude Stein, who lived here in the 1920s.

THE SIGHTS

The belfry of the Porte de l'Horloge, Salon-de-Provence

ST-CHAMAS

➕ 291 E11 ℹ️ Montée des Pénitents, tel 04 90 50 90 54; Mon–Sat 9–12, 3–7

St Chamas, near the Étang de Berre, was once a fishing village but has now turned its attention to yachting and tourism. Its church has a striking 17th-century baroque façade.
Don't miss The Pont Flavien, just outside the village, is a first-century AD Roman bridge framed by two triumphal arches.

SALON-DE-PROVENCE

➕ 292 E11 ℹ️ 56 cours Gimon, 13300 Salon-de-Provence, tel 04 90 56 27 60; Jun–end Sep Mon–Sat 9–12.30, 2.30–7, Sun 12–2; Oct–end May Mon–Sat 9–12, 2–6 🚂 Salon

The large industrial town of Salon sits between the Crau plain and the hills of western Provence and at the crossroads of roads linking Arles, Avignon, Aix and Marseille. Its fortunes were founded on soap-making and olive oil.

Sights include the Maison de Nostradamus, at 11 rue Nostradamus, in the old quarter, (Mon–Fri 9–12, 2–6, Sat, Sun 2–6). This was home to the astrologer Michel de Nostradame and is now a museum of his life. Nostradamus moved here from St-Rémy in 1547 and remained until his death in 1566. It was here he wrote the prophetic tome *Centuries*. Nearby is a 17th-century gateway, Porte de l'Horloge, with a beautiful encrusted 18th-century fountain, called the Grand Fontaine, opposite. Nostradamus' tomb is in the Église St-Laurent, in the north of the town.

The imposing Château de l'Empéri, in place des Centuries, dates back to the 10th century and houses the Musée de l'Art et d'Histoire Militaire (Wed–Mon 10–12, 2–6).

TARASCON

The magnificent white castle at Tarascon is a fairytale spectacle on the bank of the River Rhône.

➕ 291 C10 🚂 Tarascon ℹ️ 59 rue des Halles, 13150 Tarascon, tel 04 90 91 03 52; Jul, Aug Mon–Sat 9–7, Sun 9.30–12.30; Sep–end Jun Mon–Sat 9–12, 2–6, Sun 9.30–12.30
www.tarascon.org

RATINGS	
Good for kids	● ● ●
Historic interest	● ● ●
Photo stops	● ● ● ●

A former river port rising from the banks of the Rhône midway between Avignon and Arles, Tarascon is at the heart of a busy enterprise zone and calls itself La Plus Douce des Villes Industrielles—the gentlest of industrial towns. The main commercial activities revolve around food, especially preserves and canned fruit. There is also a tradition of cloth-making using vivid hues in the Provençal style, which can be explored at the beautiful Musée Souleïado, in a handsome private mansion at 39 rue Proudhon, in the old quarter (May–end Sep daily 10–6; Oct–end Apr Tue–Sat 10–5). The town is frequently in a festive mood, with several markets and fairs during the year including an Orchid Festival in February, a medieval fête in September and a market in November dedicated to *santons* (traditional figurines).

Above all, Tarascon is dominated by its immaculate castle, on boulevard du Roi René (Apr–end Sep daily 9–7; Oct–end Mar Tue–Sun 10.30–5), by the river. In the Middle Ages, the equally mighty fortresses of Tarascon and Beaucaire faced each other across the Rhône. While Beaucaire has fallen into ruin, Tarascon has been restored to near-perfect condition, complete with massive walls, turrets and towers and a bridge across the moat.

Once the luxurious palace of Good King René, Tarascon is now one of the finest medieval chateaux in France. Built from 1400 to 1449, the daunting, defensive exterior is in sharp contrast to an elegantly styled interior, with grand rooms, spiral stairways and galleries. Particularly notable are the great fireplaces, mullioned windows, banquet hall and flamboyant *cour d'honneur*, where a spiral staircase makes its way to royal apartments decorated with sumptuous tapestries. There are also interesting working areas, including kitchens. From the Revolution to the 1920s, the castle was used as a prison—there is some graffiti by 18th-century English prisoners. Tarascon is known too for its legendary or fictitious personalities—the *Tarasque*, a monster banished by St. Martha (▷ 27), and the over-sized *Tartarin*, a 19th-century comic character created by Alphonse Daudet.

The tightly packed, red-tiled rooftops of Tarascon

VAR

The Var is a fortunate land, a *département* of wild inland beauty and breathtakingly lovely Mediterranean seashore, long hours of sunshine and productive small farms and vineyards. On the coast there are working ports and thriving Riviera resorts. Tourism, which started here more than a century ago at Hyères, continues in style at St-Tropez and popular family resorts.

The abbey's simple, tranquil Romanesque church (above).
The square bell tower, rising above the pale red roofs (right)

ABBAYE DU THORONET

Hidden deep in woodland, Le Thoronet Abbey is in one of the most evocatively picturesque areas of the Provençal interior.

In the rustic interior of the Var, lying just off the D79 country road from Brignoles to Draguignan, the abbey of Le Thoronet was the first to be built of the three 12th-century Cistercian abbeys known as the 'Three Sisters of Provence'. The buildings themselves, of great stone blocks without mortar, have survived the centuries in excellent condition, and there are beautiful, unusual cloisters. The woodland setting still conveys a sense of serenity to the site despite the easy accessibility today.

CISTERCIANS AT LE THORONET

The Cistercians, based at Cîteaux in Burgundy, promoted the ideal of a rigorous, harshly simple, chaste life of religious devotion and hard work. They were rebelling against the corrupt riches of the Church. As their movement grew, it founded three great abbeys in Provence—Le Thoronet, Silvacane (▷ 55) and Sénanque (▷ 148). Building started at Le Thoronet in the 1130s. The isolated forest setting fitted the Cistercian ideas of shunning the world. The present building, in Provençal Romanesque style, was completed in 1190, and despite its austerity, soon became extremely wealthy through substantial donations. In the 14th century, Le Thoronet, like other abbeys, was the target of many raids, suffered poor harvests and was attacked during the Wars of Religion. It was gradually abandoned, seized by the State in the Revolution and sold, though in 1854 it was repurchased by the State and restored.

INSIDE THE ABBEY

Going through the gatehouse, you see ahead the beautifully proportioned but rather low church, built in lovely pinkish stone, with a square bell tower and red tile roof. The interior is very plain and undecorated. Beside the church are attractive cloisters, built on three levels because of the uneven ground. In the middle of the cloisters is a hexagonal structure containing a fountain used by the monks for hand-washing before meals. Other buildings around the cloister include the chapter house, in the early Gothic style. It has a dormitory upstairs. There's also a tithe barn, which originally stored goods given as tithes but later became an oil mill.

RATINGS			
Historic interest	●	●	●
Photo stops	●	●	●
Walkability	●	●	●

BASICS

✚ 294 K12 • Abbaye du Thoronet, 83340 Le Luc

☎ 04 90 55 25 41

◉ Apr–end Sep daily 9–6; Oct–end Mar Mon–Sat 10–1, 2–5, Sun 10–12, 2–5

Adult €5.50, under 18 free; free to all first Sun of month

Guided visits are available, depending on demand

🖩

👫

The abbey is 11km (7 miles) from Carcès. It lies off the D79 between the D13 and D84

TIP

● Mass is sung by the Sisters of Bethlehem in the church every Sunday at noon.

Red rooftops of Aups, nestling amid woodland

The beach resort of Bandol was popular with D. H. Lawrence

Beautiful blooms in Bormes-les-Mimosas

THE SIGHTS

LES ARCS-SUR-ARGENS

✚ 295 L12 ❖ Place Général-de-Gaulle, 83460 Les Arcs-sur-Argens, tel 04 94 73 37 30; Jul, Aug Mon–Fri 9–12, 2–5.30, Sat 9–12, Sun 10–12; Sep–end Jun Mon–Fri 9–12, 2–5.30, Sat 9–12
🚉 Draguignan-Les-Arcs

Lying in the Argens valley south of Draguignan, this attractive medieval village has an old quarter called Le Parage, which rises to the ruins of a 13th-century castle. From here, there is a wonderful vista encompassing the Massif des Maures and the surrounding vineyard country. A large Provençal-style *crèche* tableau inside St-Jean-Baptiste church (daily 10–2, 2–5) shows Le Parage as it once was. There is also a 15th-century polyptych by Jean de Troyes.

AUPS

✚ 294 K11 ❖ Place F. Mistral, 83630 Aups, tel 04 94 84 00 69; Jul, Aug daily 9–1, 3.30–7.30; Sep–end Jun Mon–Sat 9–12, 2–5.30

Dominated by the Montagne des Espiguières, the small town of Aups lies in the Haut Var woodlands. Although still mainly a farming town, Aups is also a popular base for exploring the Haut Var and visiting the Grand Canyon du Verdon, 23km (14 miles) to the north (▷ 142–143). As well as the remains of its medieval ramparts, several fountains and a 16th-century tower with a fine wrought-iron belfry, the town also has an attractive Gothic church, Église St-Pancrace, entered through a restored Renaissance doorway.

BANDOL

✚ 293 H14 ❖ Service du Tourisme, allée Vivien, 83150 Bandol, tel 04 94 29 41 35; Apr–end Oct daily 9–7; Nov–end Mar Mon–Fri 9–12, 2–6, Sat 9–12
🚉 Bandol
www.bandol.fr

The beach resort of Bandol, between Marseille and Toulon, is popular with local families. In the past, it was a haunt of intellectuals and literati: D.H. Lawrence, Aldous Huxley and Katherine Mansfield all spent time here in the 1920s. It has a pleasant tree-lined promenade running the length of the port, and all the trappings of the Riviera—discos, nightclubs, water sports, casino—without the sky-high prices.

The hills behind the town are rather unsightly with apartments, but in town the port is picturesque and there are sandy beaches. The best of them is Anse de Renecros beach, in a sheltered position on the west of town. A frequent ferry service connects the waterfront to the Île de Bendor, where there are two hotels, diving and windsurfing facilities and a museum of wines and spirits.
Don't miss Bandol produces a good wine of its own.

LE BEAUSSET

✚ 293 H13 ❖ Place Général-de-Gaulle, 83330 Le Beausset, tel 04 94 90 55 10; Jul, Aug Mon–Sat 9–12.30, 3–7.30, Sun 9–12.30; Apr–end Jun, Sep Mon–Sat 9–12, 2.30–6; Oct–end Mar Mon–Fri 9–12, 2.30–6, Sat 9–12
www.ot-lebeausset.fr

Inland, on the main road between Toulon and Aubagne, the town of Le Beausset keeps its pleasant typically Provençal old heart. Napoleon Bonaparte stayed for a month at a house in rue Pasteur in 1793. The town square has a lovely fountain dating from 1832. On a hillside above the town is Le Beausset Vieux, site of the original Ligurian settlement, abandoned when the inhabitants moved downhill to the present location in 1506.
Don't miss You'll get wonderful views of Ciotat Bay from the tower on top of the Romanesque chapel, Notre-Dame du Beausset Vieux (Apr–end Sep Wed–Sun 9–12, 3–6; Oct–end Mar Wed–Sat 10–12, 2.30–5, Sun 10–12, 3–5).

BORMES-LES-MIMOSAS

✚ 295 L14 ❖ 1 place Gambetta, 83230 Bormes-les-Mimosas, tel 04 94 01 38 38; summer daily 9–12.30, 2.30–6.30; winter Mon–Sat 9–12.30, 2.30–6.30
www.bormeslesmimosas.com

At the heart of Bormes is the steep medieval village with its pretty houses, evocative lanes, passageways and steps, and a restored fortress at the top of the hill. Perched on a Massif des Maures hilltop just inland from the beaches, Bormes is special because of its abundant bright yellow vanilla-scented mimosa, which flower throughout the village in springtime. Winding up the hillside from its modern coastal annex, the whole hillside is a puff of yellow blossoms. In summer, mimosa is replaced by bougainvillea and geraniums. There's a mimosa festival in February and another flower festival in June. A *Parcours Fleuri* (flower walk), starting from near the church, leads up around the castle.

Much attention and improvement has been lavished on Bormes-les-Mimosas by the artists and second-homers who have bought property here in recent years, and there is a plethora of potteries, art galleries and craft shops. The Musée d'Art et d'Histoire, in 61 rue Carnot (Tue–Sat 10–12, 2.30–5.00, Sun 10–12), traces the history of the village and holds frequent temporary art exhibitions throughout the year.

There are good views from the ruins of a chateau, at the top of the village.

A narrow street in Cogolin

Strolling along a cobbled street in the perched village of Le Castellet, with the château in the background

BRIGNOLES

🕂 294 J–K12 🛈 Hôtel de Claviers, 10 rue du Palais, 83170 Brignoles, tel 04 94 69 27 51; Mon–Fri 9.30–12.30, 2–5.30 www.tourisme.fr/office-de-tourisme/brignoles.htm

In the rustic heart of Provence, Brignoles is a large, lively town with an extensive medieval quarter. The rather odd star attraction is the Musée du Pays Brignolais, in the 13th-century summer palace of the Counts of Provence (Apr–end Sep Wed–Sun 9–12, 3–6; Oct–end Mar Wed–Sat 10–12, 2.30–5, Sun 10–12, 3–5). Exhibits include a 13th-century wine-press, first-century sarcophagus, local art and an automated Provençal Nativity tableau.

LA CADIÈRE D'AZUR

🕂 293 I113 14 🛈 Maison des Gardes, place Général-de-Gaulle, 83740 La Cadière, tel 04 94 90 12 56; Jul, Aug Tue–Sat 9–12, 3–7; Sep–end Jun Tue–Sat 9–12, 2 6 www.la-cadiere.com

This *village perché* may not be as scenic as nearby Le Castellet (▷ this page) but it has fewer visitors and so is quieter. Jazz fans should visit in the summer, when concerts are held in the Chapelle Notre-Dame-de-la-Miséricorde. The chapel was built by the Pénitents Noirs monks in 1634. The Pénitents Gris monks built the Chapelle Sainte-Madeleine, at the top of the village, which is now a private house. There is an impressive marble altarpiece in the 12th-century Église St-André.
Don't miss Buy olive oil and other local produce at the Moulin de St-Côme, on the D266 just outside the village.

LE CASTELLET

🕂 293 H13 🛈 Hôtel de Ville, 83330 Le Castellet, tel 04 94 98 57 90

Surrounded by vineyards, the delightful, flower-filled Le Castellet was one of the first perched villages to be taken up by artists and craft workers, who began to move in during the 1950s. The photogenic medieval streets have several times served as film sets, most notably for Marcel Pagnol movies like *Manon des Sources*. The cinematic associations go back further to the very origins of film-making, for it was here that the Lumière brothers bought a house (now the Castle Lumière hotel) to use as a production studio in 1895 for the making of the first-ever moving pictures.

COGOLIN

🕂 295 M13 🛈 Place de la République, 83310 Cogolin, tel 04 94 55 01 10; mid-Jun to mid-Sep Mon–Sat 9–1, 2–7, Sun 10 1; mid-Sep to mid-Jun Mon–Fri 9–12.30, 2–6.30, Sat 9–12.30 www.cogolin-provence.com

Cogolin, a short distance inland from St-Tropez and on the edge of the Massif des Maures, is known for its crafts, pipes and rugs. Craftsmen in the village specialize in ironwork, pottery, corks for wine bottles, top-quality reeds for wind instruments, and cane furniture. But what many shoppers come for are the famous pipes, made at La Fabrique de Pipes Courrieu, in avenue G. Clemenceau (daily 9–12, 2–6). They are worth a look even if you don't smoke, with quirky varieties including pipes with faces and pipes with frills.
Another good buy in the village is rugs, produced in the work-shops of La Manufacture de Tapis, on boulevard Louis Blanc (daily 8–12, 2–6; closed Aug, Dec). Armenian immigrants brought the tradition of rug-making to the village when they arrived in the 1920s.

COLLOBRIÈRES

🕂 294 L13 🛈 Boulevard Charles Caminat, 83610 Collobrières, tel 04 94 48 08 00; Tue–Sat 10–12.30, 2–6.30

In the heart of the Massif des Maures coastal hills, Collobrières keeps its traditional feel, the only modern touch being a factory processing the chestnuts produced by the surrounding forests. The village has modest sights, including a 12th-century bridge and the curiously arcaded place Rouget de l'Isle, but is mainly a rest stop on the road up to the Chartreuse de la Verne (mid-May to mid-Oct Wed–Mon 11–6, mid-Oct to mid-May Wed–Mon 11–5; closed all reli-gious holidays). This Carthusian nunnery stands isolated among the dense Maures forest, 12km (7 miles) from Collobrières. Founded in 1170, it has been damaged and rebuilt many times, and has recently been restored. It is a rambling complex of cloisters, chapels and cells—each with its own garden—in the rich shades of the local stone, red schist and green serpentine.
Don't miss If you have a sweet tooth, try some *marrons glacés* (candied chestnuts).

COTIGNAC

🕂 294 K11 🛈 2 rue Bonaventure, 83570 Cotignac, tel 04 94 04 61 87; Apr–end Sep Tue–Sat 9.45–12.45, 3.30–6.30; Oct–end Mar Tue–Fri 9–1, 3–6, Sat 9–12 www.tourisme.fr/office-de-tourisme/cotignac.htm

Wine, olive oil and honey form the main produce of this scenic village in the Haut Var. Two ruined towers sit on top of a cliff, 80m (260ft) high, riddled with caves. The Romanesque parish church has a façade rebuilt in the 19th century. Summer concerts are held in the nearby Théâtre de Verdure.

Hillside houses in the pretty village of Entrecasteaux

Pleasure boats moored in front of the pastel villas of Port Grimaud

THE SIGHTS

DRAGUIGNAN

✚ 295 L11 ℹ Maison de Pôle Touristique de la Dracénie, 2 avenue Carnot, 83300 Draguignan, tel 04 98 10 51 05; Jul, Aug Mon–Sat 9–7, Sun 9–1; Sep–end Jun Mon–Sat 9–6
🚉 Draguignan-Les-Arcs
www.ot-draguignan.fr

Draguignan is a busy working town in the Riviera backcountry, and former capital of the Var *département*. It has also been a military town since Roman times. The approach to the town is not particularly attractive—you pass a conglomeration of *hypermarchés* and second-hand car lots. But persevere to the well-preserved central medieval quarter, the *vieille ville*. Of the medieval fortifications, the two gateways Porte de Portaiguières and Porte de Romaine survive. The façade of the synagogue in rue de la Juiverie dates from the same time. The Musée Municipal (Mon–Sat 9–12, 2–6), in a former Ursuline convent on rue de la République, has European fine art from the 17th to 19th centuries, as well as faïence and other porcelain. In nearby rue Joseph Roumanille, the Musée des Traditions Provençales (Tue–Sat 9–12, 2–6, Sun 2–6) is an excellent ethnography museum, focusing on Provençal culture, as well as changes in local landscapes.
Don't miss The market (Wed, Sat) in place du Marché is one of the region's best.

A metal dragon in Draguignan

ENTRECASTEAUX

✚ 294 K12 ℹ 21 cours Gabriel Péri, 83570 Entrecasteaux, tel 04 94 04 40 50; summer daily 10–12, 3.30–5.30; winter open if staff available

This pleasant inland village on the banks of the Bresque is dominated by its large chateau (open daily from Easter to Nov), a rare example of the Provençal style of the 17th century, including a fine wrought-iron gateway. The building replaced an earlier fortress—you can still see the 11th-century entrance.

The chateau was restored in the 1970s by Scottish artist Ian McGarvie-Munn. Inside, the decor mixes period furnishings with modern art. Temporary art exhibitions are often held here. At the foot of the chateau is a formal garden designed in the 17th century by André Le Notre.

EVENOS

✚ 293 J14 ℹ Hôtel de Ville, 83330 Evenos, tel 04 94 90 37 02; Mon–Fri 8.30–12, 2–5.30
www.evenos.com

The walls of Evenos' daunting 12th-century castle rise high above the Ollioules gorge. A twisting road reaches the castle itself (the interior is closed to the public but you can walk around the outside). Surrounding the castle and a 13th-century church is the tiny village.

LA GARDE-FREINET

✚ 295 L13 ℹ 1 place Neuve, 83680 La Garde-Freinet, tel 04 94 43 67 41; Mon–Fri 9–12, 3–5.30, Sat 9–12
www.ville-lagarde.fr

Groves of cork oaks, eucalyptus and sweet chestnut encircle this peaceful village, known as the 'capital' of the Massif des Maures

(▷ 97). Alleys, fountains and courtyards make it pleasant to wander through the village, perched 360m (1,180ft) above sea level. La Garde-Freinet was France's main producer of cork in the 19th century and was one of the last Saracen strongholds in Provence in the 10th century.
Don't miss Take a 20-minute walk up to the Fort Freinet, to the west, for lovely views of the Le Luc plain and beyond to the foothills of the Alps.

GRIMAUD

✚ 295 L13 ℹ 1 boulevard des Aliziers, 83310, Grimaud, tel 04 94 43 26 98; Jul, Aug Mon–Sat 9–12.30, 3–7; Apr–end Jun, Sep Mon–Sat 9–12.30, 2.30–6.15; Oct–end Mar Mon–Sat 9–12.30, 2.15–5.30. Annexe Port Grimaud, Chemin Communal, tel 04 94 56 02 01; Jul, Aug Mon–Sat 9–12.30, 3–7; Jun, Sep Mon–Sat 9–12.30, 2.30–6.15
www.grimaud-provence.com

The atmospheric medieval hillside village of Grimaud stands on the eastern flanks of the Massif des Maures (▷ 97) just inland from St-Tropez. The main street, rue des Templiers, with Gothic doorways and arcades, climbs to the Romanesque church of St-Michel and the Hospice of the Knights Templar. The village was a possession of the noble Grimaldi family, whose chateau ruins give broad vistas down to the Gulf of St-Tropez.

Down on the coast is Port Grimaud, an elegant marina designed in the 1960s. Its canals have earned it the name 'Provençal Venice'. The resort is appealing, with its quays, lively waterside cafés and pastel-hued apartments. But it is enclosed by fences, has overpriced facilities, and drivers must use an expensive parking area outside the resort.
Don't miss Boats leave from the main square for canal tours.

Relaxing on the beach at Fréjus

FRÉJUS

This animated, long-established little beach resort, close to the Esterel hills, makes a good base for drives along the coast and inland.

On the east bank of the river Argens estuary between the wild coastal hills of the Massif des Maures and Massif d'Esterel, Fréjus was a busy little Roman town and seaport. Over the centuries it moved 3km (2 miles) inland, where the medieval and Renaissance town was based. Today, it has extended back to the seashore, with the development of an appealing marina at Fréjus-Port and a narrow beachside strip called Fréjus-Plage. The town and its surroundings offer plenty of interest, including several medieval buildings, Roman ruins and modern family attractions.

ROMAN AND MEDIEVAL REMINDERS
Although it merges into nearby St-Raphaël (▷ 100), Fréjus remains more of an inland town, St-Raphaël more of a beach resort. In the heart of Fréjus town, 17th- to 20th-century districts enclose a medieval quarter of narrow streets. At the hub of the old town is a curious *Cité Épiscopale* (Cathedral Close) with a medieval cathedral, cloisters and a fifth-century AD baptistery, possibly the oldest in France (Jun–end Sep daily 9–6.30; Oct–end May Tue–Sun 9–12, 2–5). Near the cathedral close are considerable Roman ruins, including remnants of an aqueduct, a theatre, an army barracks and a fortified quay. There is also an amphitheatre called Les Arènes (Apr–end Oct Wed–Mon 9–12, 2–6.30), where concerts are still held, although it is not the most impressive amphitheatre in Provence.

OUT OF TOWN
Out of town attractions include an extraordinary mosque in red stone, standing off the D4, built by sailors from Mali based at Fréjus in the 1920s. There's a zoo almost opposite, the Parc Zoologique de Fréjus (▷ 187). Aquatica (▷ 187) is a huge water park west of town on the N98.

CELEBRATIONS
Fréjus enjoys an extraordinary array of events, festivals and fairs, including water jousting, a *bravade* (religious festival and procession) at Easter and a grape festival in August.

The medieval cloisters of the Cité Épiscopale

RATINGS	
Cultural interest	●●●
Good for kids	●●●●
Historic interest	●●●
Photo stops	●●●

BASICS

✚ 295 M12

🛈 325 rue Jean Jaurès, 83600 Fréjus, tel 04 94 51 83 83; May–end Sep Mon–Sat 10–12, 2.30–6.30, Sun 10–12, 3–6; Oct–end Apr Mon–Sat 10–12, 2–6, Sun 10–12, 3–6

🚉 Fréjus

www.ville-frejus.fr
An attractive site with up-to-date information; French only.

TIPS
● There are markets on Wednesday and Saturday, as well as additional summer markets.
● The Roman ruins are an often-overlooked treasure of Fréjus.

Hyères and the Îles d'Hyères

A sense of remoteness and a sultry warmth greet visitors to the Côte d'Azur's most southerly resort and its unspoiled offshore islands. Exotic plants and palm trees flourish: The town is also known as Hyères-les-Palmiers.

Looking towards the church of St-Paul, in the old quarter

Enjoying a drink under blue skies, in place Massillon

SEEING HYÈRES AND THE ISLANDS

The most southerly part of the Provence coast, once an aristocratic resort, is now a budget destination near the airport of the industrial and military town of Toulon (▷ 100). For all that, Hyères has much to recommend it, with a hotter climate and a flatter, richly cultivated fertile landscape. If you're arriving by car, it is best to park in the new town, in avenue A. Denis or avenue J. Jaurès, as parking in the old town is difficult.

You reach the Îles d'Hyères (known locally as the Îles d'Or) by public-transport ferry from two harbours: Port St-Pierre near the heart of Hyères town or the harbour on the Giens peninsula to the south. The Île de Porquerolles is the easiest island to visit as the direct ferry from Giens takes only 20 minutes. The island has enough of interest to fill a full day. Ferries from Port St-Pierre go to Port-Cros (taking one hour) and Le Levant (taking 90 minutes). You can take more expensive private excursions from Giens to the Île de Porquerolles and Port-Cros in high season. Ferries to Port-Cros also leave from Le Lavandou (▷ 96), farther east along the coast.

HIGHLIGHTS

HYÈRES OLD QUARTER

The old quarter uses the backs of houses to create a defensive wall, penetrated by a Gothic gateway that leads into this atmospheric residential district of narrow streets lined with tall buildings, many with Renaissance doorways. The area climbs a slope to the ruins of a chateau in a park with wide views. The main square is the triangular place Massillon marketplace, overlooked by the Tour des Templiers, once under the command of the medieval Knights Templar. Other remnants of the Middle Ages include two Romanesque–early Gothic churches, St-Paul and St-Louis. Villa de Noailles, beside the park, was a famous address in the 1920s, when the Noailles family gave parties whose guests included Pablo Picasso and Salvador Dalí.

HYÈRES NEW TOWN

The area on the flat land below the old town is laid out with wide, busy boulevards edged with palm trees. In this district the Anglican church, in avenue Godillot, is evidence of the many English visitors who came in the resort's heyday. The Jardins Olbius-Riquier, covering 6.5ha (16 acres) to the southeast of the old town, are glorious tropical gardens with palm, cactus and flowering trees, a small animal enclosure and an interesting indoor area with other exotic plants and some rarer animals (May–end Sep daily 7.30am–8pm; Oct–end Apr daily 7.30–5.30). The gardens surround a villa in Moorish style. On the seashore, there are sandy beaches and a marina.

GIENS

The Giens Peninsula used to be one of the Îles d'Hyères, but is now connected to Hyères by a curious double sandbar, 4km (2.5 miles) long. In between the two arms of the sandbar, salt pans attract numerous wading birds. The small resort village of Giens has castle ruins with an extensive view. At the eastern tip of the peninsula, La Tour Fondue is the departure point for ferries to Porquerolles.

The tower of St-Paul's church rises above flower beds

ÎLE DE PORQUEROLLES

🚢 Daily throughout the year from Giens, with more frequent departures in Jul, Aug; adult €15, child (4–10) €13.50

At around 18sq km (7sq miles), Porquerolles is the largest of the Îles d'Hyères. Covered with Mediterranean woodland and heath, and preserved as a nature reserve, its forest paths are a haven for walkers and bicyclists. The south coast of the island has rocky cliffs, while the north coast, some 40 minutes' walk away, has a couple of sandy beaches. Ferries arrive at the enticing little quayside of Porquerolles village on the north coast, overlooked by the 19th-century Fort Sainte-Agathe (with an older corner tower), now an exhibition venue.

ÎLE DE PORT-CROS

🚢 Apr–end Sep daily; Nov–end Feb Mon, Wed, Fri, Sat; Mar, Oct Mon, Wed, Fri–Sun; €22; Île du Levant and Île de Port-Cros €25

Ferries pull in at the harbour of a small village with unpaved quays on the most southerly of the Îles d'Or. The whole island of Port-Cros, around 10sq km (4sq miles), is covered with dense unspoiled Mediterranean woodland protected as a national park. There's no bicycling here, but walkers may use a network of pretty paths. The Route des Forts is a marked trail leading up to the Fort de l'Estissac and Fort du Moulin, beside the village. You can take guided snorkelling tours (▷ 19) from La Palud beach.

Beautiful coastline on the Île de Porquerolles

ÎLE DU LEVANT

🚢 Apr–end Sep daily; Nov–end Feb Mon, Wed, Fri, Sat; Mar, Oct Mon, Wed, Fri–Sun; €22; Île du Levant and Île de Port-Cros €25

Tiny, rocky Île du Levant, just 8sq km (3sq miles), is the most easterly of the Îles d'Or. Eighty per cent of the island is in the hands of the army and cannot be entered. The other 20 per cent is a nudist resort, with hundreds of permanent residents and visitors. Their small chalets rise up the wooded slopes behind the port.

BACKGROUND

Greek traders built a port here called Olbia and the Romans renamed it Pomponiana. After the Roman withdrawal, the residents moved onto the nearby hill within fortifications built by local feudal lords. The medieval town survives today as the old quarter. In the 17th century, Hyères began to decline as Toulon grew in importance. However, by the 18th century the town had become the first holiday resort on the French Mediterranean, attracting large numbers of winter visitors. In the 19th century, many British aristocrats came for holidays— even Queen Victoria. Other 19th-century sunseekers included the writers Robert Louis Stevenson and Victor Hugo. The expression 'Côte d'Azur' was first coined (by journalist Stephen Liegeard in 1887) as a description of Hyères.

Le Lavandou has 10km (6 miles) of sandy beaches

LE LAVANDOU

🔲 295 L14 🔳 Quai Gabriel-Péri, 83980 Le Lavandou, tel 04 94 00 40 50; Mon–Sat 9–12.30, 3–7
www.lelavandou.com

The resort of Le Lavandou stands at one end of the beautiful Corniche des Maures coast. Together with its seafront extensions La Fossette, Aiguebelle, the nudist beach of Le Layet, and Cavalière, it has 10km (6 miles) of sandy beaches. A popular package holiday destination, it also attracts many locals. The town's lovely setting, yachting port and good amenities make this one of the more popular spots west of the Riviera. You can take ferries to the Île du Levant and Île de Port-Cros (▷ 95) from the port.

The resort also makes a good base for exploring the Massif des Maures (▷ 97).

LES LECQUES

🔲 293 H14 🔳 Place de l'Appel du 18 Juin, Les Lecques, tel 04 94 26 73 73; Jul, Aug Mon–Sat 9–7, Sun 10–1, 4–7; Jun, Sep Mon–Sat 9–6; Oct–end May Mon–Fri 9–6, Sat 9–12, 2–6

The small seafront resort of Les Lecques, west of Toulon, has a safe, sheltered sandy beach that attracts many local families in this built-up section of the coast. The family appeal is enhanced by a massive water park, Aqualand, at the nearby town of St-Cyr. Les Lecques Cyr is thought to be the site of the ancient Greek settlement of Taurois, later Latinized to Tauroentum. However, no Greek relics have been found here. St-Cyr's Musée Tauroentum, on route de la Madrague (Jun–end Sep Wed–Mon 3–7; Oct–end May Sat, Sun 2–5) displays the Roman finds made locally.

The red-tinged peaks of the Massif de l'Esterel

MASSIF DE L'ESTEREL

This ancient massif of volcanic rock is impenetrably wild, serene and astonishingly beautiful.

🔲 295 N12

RATINGS	
Outdoor activities	●●●●
Photo stops	●●●●
Walkability	●●●

TIPS
● Some paths in the massif may be closed in summer because of fire risk.
● Pick up a walking map of the massif, published by the Office National des Forêts, from tourist offices at Fréjus or St-Raphaël.

The small range of the Esterel hills rises behind the coast between Fréjus and Cannes, bounded by the N7 main road and the sea. The jagged red-tinted terrain plunges into the azure sea creating exquisite bays and inlets. Until the 19th century, the Esterel was thickly covered with pine trees and Mediterranean undergrowth. However, a number of disastrous forest fires, together with an outbreak of a parasitical disease afflicting pine trees, have savagely cut back the vegetation. The animals and birds too, including wild boar, deer, hares and partridges, have suffered from the damage to the plant cover, but are recovering. Since 1984, the massif has been a protected conservation area. Two valley zones have been designated biological reserves—the Ravin du Mal Infernet and the Ravin du Perthus—which both have cool humid conditions that have produced exceptional flora unique on the Mediterranean coast. They are both easily reached by road.

Don't miss The wonderfully scenic Esterel coast road, from St-Raphaël to La Napoule, was carved into the impressive seafront cliffs a century ago. Known as the Corniche de l'Esterel or the Corniche d'Or, it is one of the most spectacular (and tortuous) drives on the Côte d'Azur.

A sign warns of the risk of starting forest fires

THE SIGHTS

MASSIF DES MAURES

The sun-dried, half-wild Maures hills, threaded by lanes winding through the vegetation, encapsulate much that is magical about Provence.

The ancient Maures hills, reaching heights of less than 800m (2,500ft), spread behind the coast from Hyères to Fréjus. In places they fall short of the seashore, while at other points—notably between Le Lavandou (▷ 96) and Cavalaire—they plunge directly into the sea to create a stunning coastline of dramatic views, small beaches, impressive bays and high cliffs. Detached a little from the rest of the massif stands the St-Tropez peninsula. All along the Maures shoreline, beaches are sandy and resort prices tend to be lower than farther east along the Riviera. The popular resort of Sainte-Maxime makes a good base for exploring the eastern Maures country. The massif is bordered by the D12 on the west, D7 on the east and N7 on the north.

DIFFICULT ACCESS

Most of the hill country can be reached only on foot. Napoleon Bonaparte laid out a network of paths to enable law enforcement officers to reach areas where bandits and smugglers had their hide-outs. Just one road traverses the whole length of the Massif des Maures, the N98 from St-Raphaël to Hyères, which runs along the coast as far as Port Grimaud. Three roads cut across the hills from north to south. The other zig-zagging little roads that reach into the interior reveal a hidden world of scenic landscapes thickly covered by *garrigue* (Mediterranean heath) and woods of holm oak, cork and low, aromatic pinewoods. There are also simple wine villages.

THE INTERIOR

The village of La Garde-Freinet (▷ 92), once a remote haven of bandits and pirates in the heart of the Massif, is the little 'capital' of the Maures. North of here, on the D75, the low-key Village des Tortues (▷ 187) is both a delightful and entertaining outing and at the same time a serious conservation facility for tortoises, including the rare Hermann's Tortoise, a native of the Massif des Maures. Nearby is another attraction, the Hameau des Ânes (Donkey Village; Mar–end Nov daily 9–7). Another attractive but difficult road from Grimaud winds through *garrigue*, small vineyards and cork oak forests to rustic Collobrières (▷ 91), a little village noted for its *marrons glacés* (candied chestnuts).

The Maures scenery (above). Chestnuts growing in the woods surrounding Collobrières (top)

RATINGS

Outdoor activities	●●●○
Photo stops	●●●○
Walkability	●●●○

BASICS

✚ 294 K–L13 ℹ Maison du Golfe de St-Tropez et du Pays de Maures, Carrefour de la Foux, 83580 Gassin, tel 04 94 55 22 00; summer Mon–Fri 9.30–7.30, Sat 9.30–6, Sun 10–6; winter times vary

Admiring a large piece of cork: Forests of cork oaks grow on the Maures hills

St-Tropez

Once a Provençal seaside village, St-Tropez has become a playground of the
rich and famous. Ordinary mortals come to stargaze—or to enjoy St-Tropez for
what it originally was and still is, an exceptionally pretty coastal village.

Boats fill the port • An exhibit in the Musée de l'Annonciade • Watching the world go by in the Café de Paris

BASICS

➕ 295 M13

ℹ Quai Jean-Jaurès, 83990 St-Tropez,
tel 04 94 97 45 21; Jul, Aug daily
9.30–8; Apr–end Jun, Sep, Oct daily
9.30–12.30, 2–7; Nov–end Mar
daily 9.30–12.30, 2–6

www.saint-tropez.st
Includes 360° photographs of the
town's sights and views.

TIPS

• Visit in mid-May or mid-June
to catch one of the town's two
spectacular *bravades* festivals.
• Minutes away from the
crowds of St-Tropez are
the beautiful unspoiled villages
of the St-Tropez peninsula,
such as Gassin and Ramatuelle
(▷ 99).
• For a walk in St-Tropez,
▷ 214–215.

SEEING ST-TROPEZ

The small town of St-Tropez faces out across the large St-Tropez
gulf from the north coast of the St-Tropez peninsula. The resort
really does attract celebrities from the world of pop music,
movies and TV, who stay in five-star luxury. If you want to spot a
celeb try Les Bronzes or Tropezina beaches. Don't attempt to
drive to St-Tropez—traffic is terrible, with waits of an hour or more
to get into town and nowhere to park. Instead, use the large
public parking areas at Port Grimaud and take the passenger
ferry across the bay. If you want to relax on one of the beaches to
the south of the port, the best way to get there from the town
(unless you have your own speedboat) is by the bus that leaves
from place des Lices in July and August. Some beaches are free
but most are owned privately and you'll have to pay.

HIGHLIGHTS

PORT

St-Tropez is based around its picturesque old quayside, which, despite
large numbers of visitors and huge luxury yachts moored alongside,
still somehow has a villagey charm. The quay curves along the edge
of a beautiful blue bay. At one end of the quay are the Tour Vieille,
Tour Suffren and Tour de Portalet, all remnants of the old fortifications,
and the jetty called Môle Jean Réveille. Beyond it, the tiny, endearing
quarter called La Ponche was once a waterside fishermen's district.
Another surviving fragment of the fortifications, Tour Jarlier, stands
close by. At the other end of the quay is the Annonciade museum
(▷ 99).

CITADELLE–MUSÉE NAVAL

• Montée de la Citadelle, 83990 St-Tropez ☎ 04 94 97 59 43 🕐 Apr–end Sep daily
10–12.30, 1.30–6.30; Oct–end Mar daily 10–12.30, 1.30–5.30 🎫 Adult €4, child
(8–18) €2.50, under 8 free
East of town, on a hilltop clothed with pine and oleander, the
Citadelle is an area of ruined 16th- and 17th-century defences.
The fortress houses the Musée Naval, dedicated to the history of
St-Tropez, with an interesting room on the 1944 Allied invasion.

VIEILLE VILLE

Turning away from the quay, the old quarter or *Vieille Ville* (closed to traffic in summer) consists mainly of narrow streets of small old houses, with several chic little boutiques. Despite the large numbers of people sauntering on the nearby quayside, the streets of the old quarter are relatively uncrowded. On the edge of the quarter is the town's large main square, place des Lices (also known as place Carnot), where local men play boules under the trees. From here the town extends into more modern areas.

MUSÉE DE L'ANNONCIADE

• Place Georges-Grammont, 83993 St-Tropez ☎ 04 94 97 04 01 ③ Apr–end Oct daily 10–1, 3–10; Dec–end Mar Wed–Mon 10–12, 2–6; closed Nov 🏷 Adult €5.50, child (12–25) €3.50, under 12 free

At the other end of the quay is the rather enticing Annonciade Museum, a cool and stylish art museum in a former 16th-century religious building. Good paintings of the pointillist, fauvist and nabis schools by Seurat, Signac, Cross, Matisse, Vlaminck, Van Dongen, Derain, Vuillard and Bonnard, including paintings of the Riviera a century ago, are displayed. You can also see personal memorabilia of Misia Godebska, friend of Bonnard, Renoir and others. Unusual drawings by Picasso show the circle of artistic friends.

BEACHES

There are no proper beaches in town, so for sandy beaches travel out onto the Cap de St-Tropez, on the peninsula. Along a sandy strip bordering the legendary Pampelonne Bay, pricey beach bars offer music, drinks and beach chairs to a cool clientele. Beaches include Tahiti-Plage, which once attracted stars such as Errol Flynn and Clark Gable, Les Bronzes, popular with celebrities, and the trendy Club 55. For water sports head for Pago Pago and for seafood try Bora Bora.

BACKGROUND

St-Tropez is named after Tropez, or Torpes, a Roman centurion martyred for his Christian faith. However, he had no connection with the site, other than in a legend that he was beheaded and cast adrift in a boat with a cock and a dog, the boat striking the shore again at this point. In the 15th century it became a fortified independent town belonging to a group of Genoese familles. They started the *bravade* festival in memory of the saint. This festival was the first of two spectacular *bravades* now held in the town each year. The other commemorates the involvement of the men of St-Tropez in the defeat of Spanish raiders farther along the coast in 1637. The town's obscurity continued to the 19th century, when the writer Guy de Maupassant (1850–93) happened to pause here and recommended it to his friend, artist Paul Signac (1863–1935), who set up house here. In the 1920s it became a haunt of writers and artists, including Colette. In the 1950s film star Brigitte Bardot made it her home, putting St-Tropez firmly on the media map. It remains the epitome of unconventional, carefree wealth and glitz.

The Musée de l'Annonciade is a museum of modern art

MORE TO SEE

ÉGLISE DE ST-TROPEZ

• Rue de l'Église, St-Tropez ③ Closed Mon and 12–2

You'll notice this 19th-century church for its unusual yellow and pink bell tower. Inside is a golden bust of the town's patron saint.

RAMATUELLE

✚ 295 M13

On a high point at the heart of the St-Tropez peninsula, Ramatuelle is a pretty village, lovingly restored by well-to-do second-homers. Vineyards all round the village produce the local Côtes-de-Provence wines. Above Ramatuelle on the D89, three ancient windmills give magnificent views over the peninsula and out to sea. You can climb the Moulin de Paillas (Mar–end Oct Tue 10–12). Farther up the same road, the village of Gassin, originally a lookout guarding against Saracen invaders, has similarly fine views—and restaurant tables where you can sit and enjoy them.

There are good views from the Citadelle

THE SIGHTS

The high, curved prows of pointus boats, in Sanary-sur-Mer

ST-RAPHAËL

⊞ 295 N12 **i** Rue Waldeck-Rousseau, 83702 St-Raphaël, tel 04 94 19 52 52; Jul, Aug daily 9–7; Sep–end Jun Mon–Sat 9–12.30, 2–6.30, Sun 10–12, 2–5 ⊠ St Raphaël www.saint-raphael.com

Merging with Fréjus (▷ 93), the popular resort of St-Raphaël has a big sandy beach curving around the bay between its marinas. Once a much grander resort than today, its fine hotels and Belle-Époque villas were destroyed by bombs in World War II. However, remnants survive of the medieval village surrounding the Romanesque church, Église St-Pierre. Beside the church, the Musée Archaeologique displays many finds discovered not just on shore but also underwater, including an enormous number of Roman jars and jugs, evidence of the town's busy trade during Roman times. The town hosts a New Orleans Jazz Competition every July, with outdoor performances along the promenade.

SANARY-SUR-MER

⊞ 293 H14 **i** Les Jardins de la Ville, 83110 Sanary-sur-Mer, tel 04 94 74 01 04; Jul, Aug Mon–Sat 9–12.30, 2–7, Sun 9.30–12.30; May, Jun, Sep, Oct Mon–Fri 9–12, 2–6, Sat 9–12, 2–5; Nov–end Apr Mon–Fri 9–12, 2–5.30, Sat 9–12, 2–5

Palm trees and pastel-hued buildings border the picturesque port at Sanary-sur-Mer. There is also a 13th-century watchtower. Look out for *pointus*—traditional boats with high, curved prows. The port dates back to Roman times, and ovens and jugs for exporting wine, dating from the second century AD, have been found nearby. Every second year (odd years), on the last weekend in June, the resort holds a St. Peter's Day procession and bouillabaisse feast.

TOULON

This naval port has successfully re-invented itself as a pleasant resort city at the western end of the Côte d'Azur.

⊞ 294 J14 **i** Place Raimu, 83000 Toulon, tel 04 94 18 53 00; Jun–end Sep Mon, Wed–Sat 9–6, Tue 10–6, Sun 10–12; Oct–end May Mon, Wed–Sat 9.30–5.30, Tue 10.30–5.30, Sun 10–12 ⊠ Toulon www.toulontourisme.com

RATINGS	
Cultural interest	● ● ●
Historic interest	● ● ●
Walkability	● ● ●

TIP
● Ollioules, on the outskirts of Toulon, has pretty streets and a ruined 11th-century chateau.

Toulon, France's second-largest naval port, became a naval base soon after Provence joined France in 1481. Under Louis XIV it became the strategic base for the Mediterranean fleet, a role it maintains today. While it lacks the glitz of other Riviera towns, Toulon has a lively atmosphere and its vast natural port is an impressive sight, backed by a ring of hills.

FOUNTAINS

In the heart of the city, look out for the Fontaine des Trois Dauphins, in place Puget. Made in 1782, this is one of the best of the town's 17 fountains; the three dolphins in the middle are now completely obscured by fig trees, oleander, ferns and ivy.

A NAVAL CITY

The powerful Atlantes figures by the baroque sculptor Pierre Puget, on either side of the old town hall doorway, are based on stevedores Puget had seen unloading ships in Marseille. Boats leave regularly for trips around the port from quai Stalingrad and, for those interested in maritime history, there's the Musée National de la Marine on quai de Norfolk (Apr to mid-Sep daily 10–6.30; mid-Sep to end Mar Wed–Mon 10–12, 2–6).

A CULTURAL CITY

Toulon has other good museums, with themes including natural history, Asian art and photography. The excellent Musée d'Art de Toulon, in boulevard Maréchal Leclerc (Tue–Sat 2–5.45) has more than 500 Provençal paintings from the 17th century onwards. The richly decorated opera house, the grandest in Provence, stages opera, drama and ballet.

Don't miss You'll find wonderful Provençal produce at the Marché de Provence, in the cours Lafayette every morning.

The neoclassical opera house

ALPES-MARITIMES

Here is the golden Riviera of legend—and it's stunningly beautiful. Corniche roads cling to rocky sunlit hills that press close to the azure sea. On craggy ledges, medieval 'perched villages' defy modern development. Farther inland are tranquil hill towns and the mountain wilderness of the Mercantour range. On the coast, Cannes, Nice, Antibes and Menton offer style, art and pleasure.

THE SIGHTS

Antibes and Cap d'Antibes

This likeable, fortified Riviera town has a world-class art museum and lovely beaches on the nearby cape.

The port at Antibes has been busy since Roman times

Buy local produce at the market

Cap d'Antibes has plenty of beaches

RATINGS

Cultural interest	●●●○
Good for kids	●●●○
Historic interest	●●●○

BASICS

✚ 288 P11

🛈 11 place Général-de-Gaulle, tel 04 92 90 53 00; Jul, Aug daily 9–7; Sep–end Jun Mon–Fri 9–12.30, 1.30–6, Sat 9–12, 2–6

🚊 Antibes

www.antibes-juanlespins.com

SEEING ANTIBES AND CAP D'ANTIBES

Antibes is one of the most rewarding and important resorts on the Riviera. A thriving, densely packed small town, heavily fortified by Louis XIV's military engineer Vauban in the 17th century, it stands on a very attractive stretch of coast just east of Cannes and the Cap d'Antibes peninsula. The old town meets the sea in a ring of fortifications, including the Grimaldi castle, now housing the Picasso Museum. Just outside the walls, Antibes' large yacht port, Port Vauban, is noted for the fine array of millionaire yachts usually moored alongside. Within the ramparts, the old town consists of busy, crowded squares and narrow streets lined with a lively mix of shops and restaurants. If you are driving, it is easier to find a parking space near the port rather than in the heart of town. If you are relying on buses, town bus number 2 is handy for reaching the *cap*.

HIGHLIGHTS

VIEIL ANTIBES

The attractive central historic quarter, Vieil Antibes, is bordered by Vauban's ramparts. The area is full of life, with tall 17th- and 18th-century houses lining squares and streets busy with shoppers. An open-air market in cours Masséna every morning except Monday, crowded with locals rather than visitors, gives the feel of a typical country town. Antibes is the largest horticultural hub in the Alpes-Maritimes *département* and is well known for its flowers, with top-quality roses, tulips and carna-tions—all on show in the market, along with barrels of the local olives and an abundance of freshly gathered melons, figs, asparagus and other seasonal produce.

The Église de l'Immaculée Conception (left) has a 16th-century altarpiece

The cours Masséna market (right)

MARINELAND

• On the N7, east of town ☎ 04 93 33 49 49 ⏰ Jul, Aug daily 10am–midnight; Sep–end Jun daily 10–6 🎫 Adult €24, child (4–12) €16, under 4 free 🅿 Parking available www.marineland.fr

This big marine-life park (▷ 189) just outside Antibes has dolphins, sea lions, sharks and more.

MUSÉE PEYNET

• Place Nationale, 06600 Antibes ☎ 04 92 90 54 30 ⏰ Jun–end Sep Tue–Sun 10–6; Oct–end May Tue–Sun 10–12, 2–6

This museum houses the work of comic and romantic cartoonist Raymond Peynet. His creations featured in books and French magazines from the 1960s onwards.

MUSÉE D'HISTOIRE ET D'ARCHÉOLOGIE

• Bastion St-André, 06600 Antibes ☎ 04 92 90 54 37 ⏰ Dec–end Oct Tue–Sun 10–12, 2–6 🎫 Adult €3, under 18 free

The town's archaeology and history museum, inside a bastion south of the Château Grimaldi, contains many important archaeological finds made here. The museum draws together Etruscan, Greek, Roman and medieval items, as well as objets trouvés from shipwrecks. Next door, the old cathedral contains a 16th-century altarpiece attributed to the Niçois religious artist Louis Bréa.

MUSÉE PICASSO–CHÂTEAU GRIMALDI

• Château Grimaldi, place Mariéjol, 06600 Antibes ☎ 04 92 90 54 20 ⏰ May–end Oct Tue–Sun 10–6; Dec–end Apr Tue–Sun 10–12, 2–6. Closed Nov 🎫 Adult €4.60, under 18 free 🎧 Audioguides in English, €3

The town's major sight is the acclaimed Picasso Museum, housed in the Grimaldi's striking fortress on the cliff edge. The museum displays many ceramics, paintings and other works by Pablo Picasso (1881–1973), encompassing a range of themes and periods but with the emphasis on work done while he had a studio here in 1946. Much of the work reflects the artist's joyous post-war mood, and much explores the mythological themes that had begun to fascinate him. Photographic portraits of Picasso, by Bill Brandt and Man Ray, give further insight into the artist. Also on display are works by Nicholas de Staël, as well as Fernand Léger, Amedeo Modigliani and Joan Miró.

CAP D'ANTIBES

Out of town, the Cap d'Antibes, a promontory of land extending south into the sea, is a luxury haven of palatial villas, expensive hotels and sandy beaches. One of the beaches on the east side, La Salis, is a large public beach. Farther south are smaller free beaches Plage de la Garoupe and Plage Joseph, as well as private beaches open to the public. A footpath follows the tip of the cape for 3km (2 miles). Beneath the Garoupe plateau, Jardin Thuret covers 4ha (10 acres) with rare and exotic plants, while on boulevard Cap d'Antibes are the world-famous rose gardens of Roseraies Meilland.

BACKGROUND

Antibes is a town of great age. It was founded by the Greeks in 400BC and named Antipolis, meaning Opposite the City, because it faced Nice across the Baie des Anges. Subsequently, Antibes grew and became a busy Roman port. In the Middle Ages, it was harassed and almost destroyed by Saracens. It became a possession of the powerful Grimaldi dynasty, who controlled much of the Riviera coast, and it was they who first fortified the town and began to rebuild it. In the 17th century, the military engineer Vauban constructed further defences. Antibes became part of France in 1860.

The Musée Picasso, in the Château Grimaldi (above), and one of the art works inside (below), Antipolis (1946)

A craftsman at work in the Verrerie de Biot

The Romanesque bell tower of the Église Collégiale St-Martin, in the mountain village of La Brigue

LE BAR-SUR-LOUP

✚ 288 N10 ℹ️ Place Francis Paulet, 06620 Le Bar-sur-Loup, tel 04 93 42 72 21; Jul, Aug daily 9–6; Mar–end Jun, Sep, Oct Mon–Sat 9–12.30, 2–6; Nov–end Feb Mon–Fri 9–12.15, 2–5, Sat 9–12.15
www.bar-sur-loup.com

Pretty Le Bar-sur-Loup sits high above the Gorges du Loup (▷ 111). The tourist office is housed in the dungeon of the medieval chateau, which once dominated the village. The only other remains of this building are the two cylindrical towers. The Celts, Gauls, Ligurians and Romans had military encampments here. A Roman tombstone is set into the base of the clock tower of the Église St-Jacques. **Don't miss** Inside the church is a curious 15th-century painting known as the *Danse Macabre*, thought to depict the legend of the Count of Bar, who dared to throw a party during Lent.

BEAULIEU-SUR-MER

✚ 289 Q10 ℹ️ Place Georges-Clemenceau, 06310 Beaulieu-sur-Mer; tel 04 93 01 02 21; Jul, Aug Mon–Sat 9–12.30, 2–7, Sun 9–12.30; Sep–end Jun Mon–Fri 9–12.15, 2–6, Sat 9–12.15, 2–5 🚂 Beaulieu-sur-Mer
www.ot-beaulieu-sur-mer.fr

Beaulieu is a prosperous little waterfront hideaway between Nice and Monaco. In the lee of the Maritime Alps, which press close to the shore here, and in a sheltered bay protected by Cap Ferrat and Cap d'Ail, the town has a famously mild winter climate and early spring. It was popular with well-to-do English visitors in the late-19th century, and still has its Anglican church, Belle-Époque villas and lush gardens, as well as a delightful palm fringed waterfront. The town's outstanding curiosity is the Villa Kérylos, in Impasse Gustave

Eiffel, (Feb–end Oct daily 10–6; Nov to end Jan Mon–Fri 2–6, Sat, Sun 10–6), on the tip of the northern headland. This extraordinary house, with the sea on three sides, constructed in the 1900s by archaeologist Theodore Reinach and architect Emmanuel Pontremoli, is a perfect reproduction of a Greek villa of the second century BC.

BIOT

✚ 288 P11 ℹ️ Maison du Tourisme, 46 rue St-Sébastien, 06410 Biot, tel 04 93 65 78 00; Apr–end Sep Mon–Fri 10–7, Sat, Sun 2.30–7; Oct–end Mar Mon–Fri 9–12, 2–6, Sat, Sun 2–6 🚂 Biot, 3km (2 miles) from the village

This little town, set back from the sea between Antibes and Nice, is famous for handmade glassware. Largest of the glassworks in the lower village is the Verrerie de Biot, in Chemin des Combes (Mon–Sat 9–6, Sun 10.30–1, 2.30–6.30). The earthenware tradition established here by the Romans continued until the 19th century, but then began to die out. It was the arrival in the 1950s of the innovative painter and sculptor Fernand Léger (1881–1955) that turned the town's attention to glass and ceramics. The Musée National Fernand Léger, in Chemin du Val de Pome (Jul–end Sep Wed–Mon 11–6; Oct–end Jun Wed–Mon 10–12.30, 2–5) has a Léger mosaic on the exterior and, inside, some 400 of his works. Biot has a picturesque medieval hilltop village with 16th-century fortifications and an arcaded main square. The town was founded by the Greeks, before becoming a Roman settlement devoted to pottery. To find out more, visit the Musée d'Histoire et de la Céramique Biotoises, in rue St-Sébastien (Jul–end Sep Wed–Sun 10–6; Oct–end Jun Wed–Sun 2–6).

BREIL-SUR-ROYA

✚ 289 R9 ℹ️ 17 place Blancheri, 06540, Breil-sur-Roya, tel 04 93 04 99 76; Jul, Aug Mon–Sat 8.30–12.30, 1.30–6, Sun 9–12; Sep–end Jun Mon–Fri 9–12, 2–5, Sat 9–12 🚂 Breil-sur-Roya
www.breil-sur-roya.fr

Breil, close to the Italian border, straddles the river Roya, with the old quarter on the eastern bank. The bell towers of the Église Sancta-Maria-in-Albis are topped with cheerful Niçois tiles. Inside the 18th-century baroque church is an altarpiece by religious artist Louis Bréa. The Ecomusée du Haut Pays (Jul–end Sep Thu, Sun 10.30–5.30), in railway carriages at the station, will fill you in on the local flora and fauna.

LA BRIGUE

✚ 289 R8 ℹ️ Place St-Martin, 06430 La Brigue, tel 04 93 04 60 04; daily 9–12, 2–5 🚂 La Brigue (Brigue-Gare)
www.labrigue-tourisme.org

Attractive La Brigue sits in the Provençal Alps close to the Italian border. Mont Bégo, in the Mercantour mountains, can be seen to the west. Built largely of the local grey-green rock, the village is in the lovely green valley of the river Levenza. Soaring over the village is the Lombardic Romanesque tower of the 13th- to 14th-century Église Collégiale St-Martin, which has paintings by the Niçois religious artist Louis Bréa.
Don't miss There's more remarkable medieval art 4km (2.5 miles) up the valley to the east, in the remote Chapelle Notre-Dame des Fontaines (May–end Sep Fri–Mon 10–12, 2–5; Oct–end Apr ask at tourist office). Here, 15th-century frescoes show the life of Christ in 38 sometimes gruesome scenes.

CAGNES-SUR-MER

See page 109.

Cannes

One of the world's most glamorous resorts is loaded with style and luxury—as well as having a good sandy beach, an excellent market and fine dining.

Luxury cruisers in the port

Taking a break on the beach

The Musée de la Castre, on the hill at Le Suquet

SEEING CANNES

The name Cannes conjures up high life and big money, an image stemming partly from the International Film Festival held here every May, with many of the world's top film stars in attendance. However, Cannes is not all about luxury. The resort, at the western end of the 'Old Riviera', has almost no 'must-see' sights, but there are many things to enjoy, including good entertainment, top-quality shopping and beach restaurants. The town's long beach is one of the few on the Riviera that is sandy, although payment is required for access to most of it. There are free sections at both ends. The hilltop old quarter, Le Suquet (▷ 108), is worth the walk for the wonderful sea view. The number 8 minibus connects Le Suquet with La Croisette.

HIGHLIGHTS

BOULEVARD DE LA CROISETTE

A stroll on La Croisette is the quintessential Riviera experience. The beautiful beachside promenade, with its tamarisk and palm trees, has a glorious blue bay on one side and luxury hotels on the other. This busy seafront road, divided by a green central strip, runs from the Palais des Festivals and old port (Vieux Port) in the west of town to the new private Port Canto in the east. (After this, Boulevard de la Croisette continues along the emptier coastal stretch to bleak Pointe de la Croisette.) The beach is divided into private sections, each with its own distinctively themed parasols. Opulent hotels across the street rank as sights in their own right: The 'top four' are the domed Carlton, the Majestic, the more recent Noga-Hilton and the white art deco masterpiece the Martinez (▷ 252). Along here, the 19th-century mansion La Malmaison houses the city's most important temporary art exhibitions. In the walkway in front of the Palais des Festivals, film stars have made handprints in the concrete. The whole of La Croisette is especially attractive at night thanks to floodlighting.

OLD CANNES

Boulevard de la Croisette ends at the Palais des Festivals. On the other side of the Palais is the Cannes that existed before La Croisette

BASICS

✚ 288 P11

🛈 **La Croisette office:** Palais des Festivals, La Croisette, tel 04 92 99 84 22; Jul, Aug daily 9–8; Sep–end Jun daily 9–7. **Station office:** Gare SNCF, rue Jean-Jaurès, tel 04 93 99 19 77; Jul, Aug daily 9–8, Sep–end Jun daily 9–7. **Le Cannet office:** avenue du Campon, 06110 Le Cannet, tel 04 93 45 34 27; Jul, Aug daily 9–8; Sep–end Jun daily 9–7

🚏 Cannes (in rue Jean-Jaurès)

www.cannes.com
Suitably sophisticated, high-tech and slick, including videos of the town and online booking for shows

TIPS

● Book a long way ahead for any kind of accommodation in Cannes at any time of year.
● Unless you want to star-gaze, the film festival in May is not the best time to come. Hotel prices skyrocket and the town is packed.

Celebrity handprints in the 'allée des Stars', on the boulevard de la Croisette (left)

PALAIS DES FESTIVALS ET DES CONGRÈS

• 1 La Croisette ☎ 04 93 39 24 53
🕐 Daily 9–7

This unsightly building is where the real work takes place during the film festival. Options change hands at astronomical prices at its basement screenings. Outside the building, see the handprints of film stars in the concrete of the allée des Stars.

ÎLES DE LÉRINS

✚ 288 P12 🚢 Journey times from Cannes Vieux Port: 15 min to St-Honorat, 30 min to Sainte-Marguerite; tel 04 93 39 11 82

The Lérins islands, a short ferry ride offshore from Cannes, make an enjoyable excursion. The peaceful, traffic-free islands enjoy an unspoiled simplicity in contrast with the glitz of nearby Riviera resorts. Frequent ferries run to the larger Île Sainte-Marguerite, where there are paths and picnic areas under the pine trees and the shore is broken by coves and bays. By the quayside are simple fish restaurants. Close by, a Vauban fortress called Fort Royal (or Fort Vauban) houses a marine museum, the Musée de la Mer, a Huguenot Memorial Chapel and former prison cells (Apr–end Sep Wed–Mon 10.30–12.15, 2.15–5.45; Oct–end Mar Wed–Mon 10.30–12.15, 2.15–4.45).

There are a few ferries to the Île St-Honorat, dominated by an abbey, the Ancienne Monastère Fortifiée, which you can visit (Jul, Aug Mon–Sat 10–12, 2.30–4.30, Sun 2.30–4.30; Sep–end Jun Mon–Sat 9–4, Sun 2.30–4).

THE SIGHTS

was built. Here is the extensive old port area and its spacious waterside esplanade called La Pantiero, with large popular brasseries along one side. Behind this tree-shaded square—adorned with a statue of Lord Brougham (▷ Background, below)—run narrow shopping streets that reach the town's large covered market (Tue–Sun). Steep lanes climb to the small, medieval district called Le Suquet, fortified in the 14th century by the monks of the Îles de Lérins. At the top of the hill is a 16th-century church, a terrace with lovely sea views, and the monks' watchtower, the Tour du Suquet. The exceptional Musée de la Castre (Jul–end Sep Tue–Sun 10–12, 2–7; Oct–end Jun Tue–Sun 10–12, 2–5), in the chateau at Le Suquet, is a large ethnographic museum with collections on all sorts of themes, including musical instruments and tribal masks.

MODERN TOWN

Modern Cannes has spread far inland, embracing the formerly separate village of Le Cannet, which made an arty, less expensive alternative to Cannes for pre-World War II visitors but is now a crowded, picturesque visitor haunt with good views. To the east, Cannes encompasses the prosperous heights of Super-Cannes, where several extravagant pre-World War II villas survive. Parallel to the seashore, a couple of blocks inland, is Cannes' main shopping street, rue d'Antibes. Along here are many fashion boutiques, designer stores, perfumeries, jewellers and art specialists, as well as chocolatiers and *salons de thé*.

BACKGROUND

An ancient Ligurian settlement here was taken over by the Romans, but was not a key site for them. In the 10th century, Cannes was a Genoese port called Canois, and in the 12th century it was given to the monks on the Îles de Lérins. It remained a fishing community until 1834, when Englishman Lord Brougham stayed here. He enjoyed his visit so much that he had a villa built—the Château Eleonore, behind avenue du Docteur Picaud—and returned each winter for the rest of his life. Lord Brougham was no ordinary English aristocrat. He was a former Lord Chancellor and inventor of the Brougham carriage and was a fantastically popular man. Numerous wealthy English visitors followed his example and built winter villas here. In the 1920s, a more artistic element began to arrive, many staying in summer. In the 1940s the film festival took off (▷ 12), attracting top Hollywood actors, directors and producers as well as hundreds of self-promoting starlets who gave the festival, and the town, a particular air of glitz and frivolity. More than half the hotel rooms in Cannes are rated four-star or four-star Luxe.

Wandering along La Croisette (right), with its grand hotels

The Carlton Hotel, with its striking dome

A narrow tree-shaded lane in Coaraze

The mountain village of Roquestéron

CAGNES-SUR-MER

🕀 288 P10 ℹ 6 boulevard Maréchal Juin, 06800 Cagnes-sur-Mer, tel 04 93 20 61 64; Jul, Aug Mon–Sat 9–7, Sun 9–12, 3–7; Jun, Sep Mon–Sat 9–12, 2–7; Oct–end May Mon–Sat 9–12, 2 6 www.cagnes-tourisme.com

Impressionist artist Renoir moved to this seaside town in 1907, hoping the warmer weather would ease his arthritis. He lived and painted here until his death in 1919. You can visit his house and gardens, the Domaine des Collettes, now known as the Musée Renoir (Wed–Mon 10–12, 2–6. Closed Nov).

The seaside section of Cagnes, known as Cros-de-Cagnes, is not as attractive as other places along the coast. More picturesque is Haut-de-Cagnes, with its medieval streets, steep steps and chateau built by Rainier Grimaldi in 1309. Here you'll find the Musée d'Art Méditerranéen Moderne (Wed–Mon 10–12, 2–6) and an olive museum. The chateau hosts the *Festival Internationale de la Peinture* from July to September.

COARAZE

🕀 289 Q9 ℹ 7 place Sainte-Cathérine, 06390 Coaraze, tel 04 93 79 37 47; Apr–end Sep daily 10–12, 2–5; Oct–end Mar Mon, Tue, Thu, Fri 10–12, 2–5

This picturesque village, perched on a cliff, calls itself *Village du Soleil* (Sun Village). Sundials have been a feature here since Jean Cocteau decorated the town hall with them. The chic village has attractive cottages, cobbled lanes, fountains and stone steps. A short walk away, the Chapelle Bleue (formerly Chapelle Notre-Dame des Sept Douleurs) is named after the blue murals—pierced by green stained-glass windows—created in 1965 by Ponce de Léon.

CLUES DE HAUTE-PROVENCE

Narrow river gorges, *clues*, make spectacular routes through the dramatic mountain scenery.

🕀 288 N9 ℹ Office de Tourisme Intercommunal Provence Val d'Azur, Maison de Pays, 06260 Puget-Théniers, tel 04 93 05 05 05; Apr–end Sep daily 9–12.30, 2–7; Oct–end Mar daily 9–12.30, 2–6 www.provence-val-dazur.com

RATINGS			
Outdoor activities	●	●	●
Photo stops	●	●	● ●
Walkability	●	●	● ●

The *clues*—a southern word meaning openings or keys—are narrow gorges and passes in the spectacular, stark wild mountains in the Provençal backcountry, on the border between the Alpes Maritimes, Haute-Provence and Var *départements*. Several of them provide abrupt openings in the harsh landscape between the broad valleys and plains of the Var and Alpes-Maritimes and the higher Alpine mountain country to the north. The area is popular with cross-country skiers in winter and walkers in summer.

HOSTILE BUT BEAUTIFUL

In the sparsely populated mountains north of Grasse (▷ 112), bounded approximately by the N202 and N85 roads, the limestone hills close up and create a difficult, inhospitable and often beautiful landscape of pale rock and dense wild *garrigue* or forest. The *clues* are narrow gorges with high steep sides, providing openings in the rocky terrain through which man and animals—and rivers—may pass. The focus of the region is the 1,777m (5,828ft) Montagne du Cheiron.

RIVER ESTERON

Many of the most dramatic sites are on the River Esteron, on the north flank of the mountain. Here is the strange fortified village of Roquestéron, with a river—formerly the border between Savoy and France—running through its heart. Before 1860, each half of the village was in a different country.

MORE *CLUES*

West from Roquestéron is the Clue du Riolan. Beyond is the spectacularly narrow Clue d'Aiglun, with a river gushing straight down through it as if under pressure from the mountains above. Farther west, the steep sides of the Clue de St-Auban are riddled with caves. The village of St-Auban stands at its opening.

A cobbled street in medieval Èze

ÈZE

Cacti thrive on the terraces of the Jardin Exotique

Beautiful Èze is one of the most perfect examples of a *village perché* and is also one of the most easily accessible.

RATINGS

Historic interest	●●●○
Photo stops	●●●●○
Walkability	●●○

BASICS

✚ 289 Q10

🛈 Place Général-de-Gaulle, 06360 Èze; tel 04 93 41 26 00; May–end Sep Mon–Sat 9–7, Sun 2–7; Oct–end Apr Mon–Sat 9–6.30, Sun 9.30–1, 2–6.30

www.eze-riviera.com
The town's lively site for visitors covers everything from local history to regional attractions to hotel packages; in French and English.

www.ville-eze.com
The website for local people.

TIPS

● The café terrace of the Château Eza has one of the best views in the village.
● Vehicles cannot enter the old village. There is a large parking area at the foot of the village.

The small old village of Èze, midway between Nice and Monaco, stands on top of a 430m (1,375ft) spike of rock rising beside the Corniche Moyenne road and just a short (if steep) distance from the Riviera resorts. A more modern Èze lies along the Corniche road at the foot of the medieval village. The fortified perched village is exceptionally pretty, with narrow medieval lanes and steps, and several viewpoints looking straight down onto the sea. Èze has survived with few changes since the 14th century, when the Saracens were forced out and the village reconstructed on more defensive lines to prevent further attacks.

POPULAR
Its closeness to the coastal resorts and to the Corniche Moyenne has made Èze a chic, arty, sometimes overcrowded attraction, with a stream of visitors and tour buses arriving during the day. Yet the village has an indomitable charm and in the evenings, when visitor numbers drop, feels surprisingly unspoiled. For a better understanding of how remote and inaccessible Èze was before the invention of the car, come here on foot: A precipitous path up from the shore is known as Sentier Friedrich-Nietzsche because Nietzsche, living by the sea, often took this strenuous walk up to the medieval village.

ATTRACTIONS
If you are arriving by car, park in the parking area at the foot of the village, then walk up the steep road to the large 14th-century fortified gateway into old Èze. Inside is a magical, maze-like world of pretty lanes and stairways. Head upwards to reach the ruins of a fortress, giving dazzling views out to sea. The ruins are surrounded by a brilliant, unusual cactus garden called the Jardin Exotique (Jul, Aug daily 9–8; Easter–end Jun daily 9–7; Sep–Easter daily 9–5), which gives unforgettable views along the Riviera coast. Below the fortress, the Chapelle des Pénitents Blancs is noted for its enamelled panelling. Within the medieval village, there are deluxe chateau-hotels, fine restaurants and little shops selling (sometimes pricey) souvenirs. On the main road below the old village there are several good shops, including branches of the Fragonard and Galimard perfumeries, a few paces up the road towards the old village.

The eye-catching architecture of the Fondation Maeght

Spectacular scenery in the Gorges du Loup area

FONDATION MAEGHT

288 P10 • Fondation Maeght, route de Pass-Prest, 06750 St-Paul-de-Vence 04 93 32 81 63 Jul–end Sep daily 10–7; Oct–end Jun daily 10–12.30, 2.30–6 Adult €11, child (10–18) €9, under 10 free www.fondation-maeght.com/

This art museum, in an intriguing modern building hidden in woodland outside St-Paul-de-Vence (▷ 125), has one of Europe's leading collections of 20th-century and contemporary art. The Fondation Marguerite et Aimé Maeght was opened by the Maeghts, successful art dealers, in 1964 to house their private art collection and as a memorial to their son, who died in childhood. It is still financed by their foundation. The building, designed by Catalan architect Josep-Lluis Sert, is a low simple structure with a pair of strange curved shapes resting on the roof. The interior is gloriously lit with natural light from above. The museum has several sculptures standing in the grounds, by Joan Miró, Marc Chagall, Georges Braque and others. These artists feature prominently inside the museum, together with Pierre Bonnard, Kandinsky, Alexander Calder and Fernand Léger, among others.
Don't miss A tiny chapel inside the building has Braque's *White Bird on a Mauve Background* (1958–62), a striking stained-glass window created in memory of the Maeghts' son.

GORBIO

289 Q10
www.menton.com/gorbio

The best time to visit this attractive *village perché* is during the *Fête Dieu* (Corpus Christi) in May–June, when you can see the entrancing night-time parade known as the *Procession dai limaca*. The

spectacle takes its name from the flickering lamps made from snail shells (*limaca* in Provençal) and olive oil that illuminate the village during the parade. The tradition dates back to a pagan ritual giving thanks for the winter's olive harvest.

At other times of the year, Gorbio's attractions are less arresting, but include at least half a dozen chapels and churches in or around the village. Gorbio's residents are sometimes known as '*Les nebuleux*' ('the cloudy ones') as the village is often enveloped in clouds.

GORGES DU LOUP

288 N10

The Loup river threads down through remarkable rocky ravines in the hilly country between Grasse and Vence. Many strange hollows have been carved into the rock by the rushing stream. Narrow roads alongside the ravines provide a spectacular country drive with some interesting little towns along the way. As the river approaches the small town of Pont-du-Loup, the start of the impressive gorge is marked by the curious Saut-du-Loup, a large hollow in the river bedrock, and the Demoiselles

waterfall, where minerals in the water spray have 'petrified' the surrounding greenery. Farther down is the mossy Courmès waterfall, just before the river enters Pont-du-Loup. After another 3km (2 miles) is the attractive small town of Le Bar-sur-Loup (▷ 105), among fruit groves and flowers. Its 15th-century church is noted for a vivid *Danse Macabre* mural. Also close to the right bank, the perched village of Gourdon (▷ below) soars above the river. On the left bank, the pretty D2210 continues to the lovely medieval village of Tourrettes-sur-Loup, standing on a rocky ridge, and known for its violets.

GOURDON

288 N10 Place Victoria, 06620 Gourdon, tel 04 93 09 68 25; May–end Sep daily 10.30–7; Oct–end May daily 2–6
www.Gourdon-France.com

A fascinating perched village poised on a high platform of rock in the hills behind Cannes and Nice, Gourdon justly calls itself a *nid d'aigle* (eagle's nest). With its fountains, steps, lanes and stunning views across the gorge of the river Loup, it attracts many visitors. The best view is from outside the church. The 17th-century chateau is still a private home. It also has two museums (Jun–end Sep Wed–Mon 11–1, 2–7; Oct–end May Wed–Mon 2–6). The Musée Historique has intriguing items including suits of armour, 16th-century furniture and a painting by Rubens. The Musée de Peinture Naïve, upstairs, has naïve art, including a self-portrait by Primitive painter Douanier Rousseau (1844–1910). The chateau gardens were designed by landscape architect André Le Nôtre.

THE SIGHTS

Hundreds of scents are created in the fragrance factories of Grasse

GRASSE

There's more to the 'world capital of perfume' than visiting a fragrance factory—Grasse also has an attractive medieval quarter and wonderful views.

Grasse is a large town 15km (9 miles) inland from Cannes, on the Route Napoléon. At its heart is an attractive medieval quarter, while away from here are the perfume factories that have made it famous as the 'world capital of perfume'.

THE OLD TOWN
The narrow pedestrian-only streets of the old quarter have been attractively restored. There are many fine old mansions, and a wide terrace, place du Cours, giving thrilling views towards the sea. Place aux Aires, in the heart of the old town, has a three-tiered fountain at its core. A busy flower and vegetable market takes place here every morning except Mondays. Other focal points in the old town are the 12th-century watchtower, the Tour de Guet, and the cathedral, which was originally 11th century but reconstructed in the 17th century, with an impressive stone double staircase added in the 18th century.

Sheltering in the shade in place aux Aires

PERFUMERIES
The town's major perfume makers are Molinard, Galimard and Fragonard. All three offer free guided tours in English. Fragonard offers a highly enjoyable tour of its museum and shop, a short walk from the old town in boulevard Fragonard (Feb–end Oct daily 9–6.30; Nov–end Jan daily 9–12, 2–6). Fragonard has a larger, modern site, called the Fabrique des Fleurs, 3km (2 miles) out of town on the Route de Cannes (Feb–end Oct 9–6.30; Nov–end Jan daily 9–12, 2–6), which is its modern perfume factory. A less poetic, more industrial approach is taken to the subject at the tours here. In the same area are Galimard, at 73 route de Cannes (Apr–end Oct daily 9–6.30; Nov–end Jan daily 9–12.30, 2–6.30), and Molinard, in boulevard Victor Hugo (May–end Sep daily 9–6; Oct–end Apr daily 9–12, 2–6). If you want to learn more about the perfume business, try the Musée International de la Parfumerie, in place du Cours (Jun–end Sep Wed–Mon 10–7; Oct, Dec–end May Wed–Mon 10–12, 2–5). Grasse owes its perfume industry to the manufacture of scented gloves, which began in the mid-17th century. After the Revolution, gloves fell out of fashion and the town switched its attention to perfume.

RATINGS
Historic interest	● ● ●
Photo stops	● ● ●
Specialist shopping	● ● ● ●
Walkability	● ● ●

BASICS
✚ 288 N11

🛈 Palais de Congrès, 22 cours Honoré Cresp, tel 04 93 36 66 66; Jul–end Sep Mon–Sat 9–7, Sun 9–1, 2–6; Oct–end Jun Mon–Sat 9–12.30, 2–6

www.grasse-riviera.com
A very attractive site with plenty of information on the town's perfume heritage

Isola 2000 is the highest ski resort in the Sud-Alpes

Sunbathers on the sandy, tree-fringed beach at Juan-les-Pins

Levens was encircled by double ramparts in medieval times

GUILLAUMES

✚ 288 N8 ℹ Mairie, 06470 Guillaumes, tel 04 93 05 50 13

Guillaumes is a large village perched 800m (2,625ft) above the confluence of the Var and the Tuébi rivers and dominated by the ruins of a chateau. Visit the chapel of Notre-Dame-du-Buyei to see a painting of a fire that ravaged the village in 1682. **Don't miss** From Guillaumes the D2202 takes you south through the dramatic Gorges de Daluis, towards Entrevaux (▷ 140).

ISOLA 2000

✚ 283 P7 ℹ Immeuble Le Pélevos, Isola 2000, tel 04 93 23 15 15; Jul, Dec–end Apr daily 8.30–12, 2–7; Sep–end Nov, May, Jun Mon–Fri 8.30–12, 2–7
www.isola2000.com

This fashionable high-quality modern ski resort is in the upper Tinée valley on the west flank of the Parc National du Mercantour, in the Provençal Alps. It offers excellent skiing, within a couple of hours' drive of the Riviera. The main part of the resort is at 2,000m (6,560ft), hence the name, while the older Isola village stands at 860m (2,800ft).

Isola 2000 was conceived as a place where holidaymakers could combine winter sports with Riviera beaches. It also makes a good summer base for exploring the peaks of the Parc National du Mercantour (▷ 122–123).

JUAN-LES-PINS

✚ 288 P11 ℹ 51 boulevard Guillaumont, 06600 Juan-les-Pins, tel 04 92 90 53 05; Jul, Aug Mon–Fri 9–12, 2–6, Sat 9–12; Sep–end Jun Mon–Fri 9–12.30, 1.30–6
www.antibes-juanlespins.com

Merging with Antibes at the head of the Cap d'Antibes peninsula (▷ 102–104), Juan-les-Pins is a popular little resort with a sandy beach, appealing to the young because of its lively nightlife. There are few traces of the large pine forest behind the coast that gave the town its name. A resort was laid out here in the 1880s by the Duke of Albany, Queen Victoria's son. It remained obscure until the 1920s, when Nice restaurateur Monsieur Baudoin went into partnership with American railway tycoon Frank Jay Gould to launch the Riviera's first summer resort, at a time when holidaying in summer was something of a novelty. Success followed, helped by the scandal of being the first beach where women wore modern-style swimsuits, and Juan developed a racy, hedonistic air.

Since 1960, the resort has hosted a popular Jazz Festival every July (▷ 195).

LANTOSQUE

✚ 289 Q9 ℹ Mairie, 06450 Lantosque, tel 04 93 03 00 02

Perched on a rocky spur over-looking the Vésubie valley, Lantosque looks as if it is about to slide down the hill. Indeed, it has done so many times. Few other villages in Provence have suffered so many landslides and earth movements, almost the whole village falling into the ravine on several occasions during the 15th to 17th centuries. The village had historic importance as a trading post on the Route du Sel (the salt route), along which pack animals carried salt from coastal salt pans to the mountain towns. In winter, the village is a popular little ski resort.

LEVENS

✚ 289 P9 ℹ 3 placette Paul Olivier, 06670 Levens, tel 04 93 79 71 00; Jul–end Sep Mon–Sat 9.30–12, 3–6, Sun 10–1; Oct–end Jun Mon–Sat 9.30–12, 3–6

Levens dominates the plains at the mouth of the Gorges de la Vésubie. The late 18th-century friary Chapelle des Pénitents Blancs stands on the north side of the village and the Chapelle des Pénitents Noirs, with a fine baroque façade, on the east side. The Maison du Portal gateway is all that is left of the castle.

There are some scenic drives from the village: The D19 and D2565 snake round the gorges before meeting up at St-Jean-la-Rivière. A hair-raising, 6km (4-mile) detour from here leads up to the isolated sanctuary of Madone d'Utelle. **Don't miss** There are wonderful views from the peak just past the Madone d'Utelle chapel.

MENTON

See pages 114–115.

MOUGINS

✚ 288 N11 ℹ 15 avenue Jean Charles Mallet, 06250 Mougin, tel 04 93 75 87 67; Mon–Sat 10–5.30
www.mougins-coteazur.org

Mougins, a beautiful medieval *village perché* in the hills behind Cannes, has become a fine dining resort for wealthy Riviera residents and visitors, with several acclaimed restaurants (▷ 239). Even if you're not here to eat, it's rewarding to explore Mougins' streets of carefully restored houses. There's also a Musée de la Photographie (Jul, Aug Wed–Sun 2–8; Sep–end Jun Wed–Sat 10–12, 2–6, Sun 2–6) next to the Porte Sarrazine. Art exhibitions are held in the old washhouse, La Lavoir, on the place de la Mairie. Southeast, on the D3, the Chapelle de Notre-Dame de Vie stands on a hilltop flanked by cypress trees. Originally 12th-century, it was rebuilt in 1646. Picasso (1881–1973) owned a villa hidden among trees opposite.

THE SIGHTS

Menton

This quiet resort with an Italian feel is famous for its gardens, lemon festival and exceptionally mild winter climate.

Italianate Menton is only 1.5km (1 mile) from the Italian border

RATINGS

Cultural interest	●●●●
Historic interest	●●●
Photo stops	●●●●

BASICS

✚ 289 Q10

ℹ️ 8 avenue Boyer, 06506 Menton, tel 04 92 41 76 76; Apr–end Sep Mon–Sat 9–7, Sun 9.30–12.30; Oct–end Mar Mon–Fri 8.30–12.30, 1.30–6, Sat 9–12, 2–6

🚃 Menton

www.villedementon.com
The site has an orange-and-lemon theme, with information on local sights

TIPS

● The *Fête du Citron* (Lemon Festival; ▷ 195) starts on Shrove Tuesday and lasts for 10 days.
● A chamber music festival is held in August in the Parvis St-Michel.

SEEING MENTON

This sedate, long-established Riviera resort is close enough to the border that Italians sometimes walk here. Menton is enclosed by high mountain slopes that offer a protective barrier against wind and weather from the north. Its balmy climate—there are around 300 days of sun each year—encourages the cultivation of local gourmet varieties of lemons and oranges.

There is a choice of parking areas in the town, including two underground areas at the Hôtel de Ville and St-Roch. From June to the end of September there is free parking at parking Rondelli. The Service du Patrimoine, based at 5 rue Ciappetta (tel 04 92 10 33 66), runs guided tours of Menton and its gardens.

HIGHLIGHTS

LA VIEILLE VILLE

The older part of town, with its alleys and covered stairways, rises steeply from the sea on the eastern side of Menton. Dating mainly from the 17th century, this Vieille Ville has an Italianate feel and gives a glimpse into the period before Menton became French. Climb along narrow rue Longue, the medieval main street, to little place de la Concepcion. With its pair of ornate ochre-painted churches, each with an Italian campanile, this square is the heart of the historic quarter.

SALLES DES MARRIAGES

• Hôtel de Ville, place Ardoïno, Menton ☎ 04 92 10 50 00 🕐 Mon–Fri 8.30–12.30, 2–5 💶 €1.65

Overlooking the Biovès gardens in the lower town, Menton's attractive 17th-century Italianate town hall contains a *Salle des Marriages*

(Wedding Room) decorated with wall and ceiling murals by artist and writer Jean Cocteau (1889–1963). Marriage is the fitting theme for the paintings.

MUSÉE JEAN COCTEAU
• Quai Napoléon III, Menton ☎ 04 93 57 72 30 🕐 Wed–Mon 10–12, 2–6 ✋ €3.05

The little Bastion du Port, projecting from the shore, is the 17th-century Grimaldi fortress that Cocteau restored to house his work. It is now the remarkable Musée Jean Cocteau, displaying his mosaics and ceramics, tapestries, poems and photographs.

HISTORIC GARDENS
A century ago several wealthy Edwardian horticulturalists came to Menton and the adjacent Garavan district to create remarkable parks and gardens on the steep sea-facing slopes just outside town–Serre de la Madone, Val Rahmeh, Jardin des Colombieres, Clos du Peyronnet and others. Catching the sun during the warmest part of the winter day, these gardens enabled aristocratic experimental gardeners to cultivate an astounding variety of exotic plants from around the world. They are well worth visiting in late winter, for example in February, when spring flowers are in bloom attended by butterflies and bees.

BACKGROUND
Menton was considered Italian until annexed by Napoleon III in 1860, although it had long belonged not to Italy but to the Grimaldis of Monaco. Even in those days it was already a winter resort popular with Russian and English aristocrats. Queen Victoria visited in 1882. A number of exotic Edwardian gardens planted behind the town are still beautifully maintained.

Menton's lively lemon festival takes place in February

MORE TO SEE
THE LOWER TOWN
The Promenade du Soleil skirts Menton's beach, close to which is the long-established—but no longer very glamorous—casino and the public gardens called the Jardin Biovès. During the town's visually stunning Lemon Festival, in February, the Biovès gardens are filled with 'sculptures' and set pieces made of oranges and lemons.

MUSÉE MUNICIPAL DE PRÉHISTOIRE RÉGIONALE
• Rue Lorédan Larchey, Menton ☎ 04 93 35 84 64 🕐 Wed–Mon 10–12, 2–6 ✋ Free

See rock carvings from the Vallée des Merveilles, the 30,000-year-old skull of 'Menton Man' and other items from prehistoric times.

PALAIS CARNOLÈS
• 3 avenue de la Madone, Menton ☎ 04 93 35 49 71 🕐 Wed–Mon 10–12, 2–6 ✋ Free

Enjoy various works of art at this Musée des Beaux-Arts. The luxurious 18th-century palace was once a summer home for the Princes of Monaco.

Menton has been a chic seaside resort since the 1860s

Nice

Nice is the Riviera's vivacious capital, backed by the foothills of the Provençal Alps.
It is an art lover's dream, with several major art galleries.

The Negresco is one of Nice's most famous hotels *Shopping for blooms in the Marché aux Fleurs* *The wonderful view from the Colline du Château*

SEEING NICE

With excellent road, rail and air connections, Nice is the busiest point of entry into Provence. The heart of town is bypassed by major roads, keeping it relatively free of through traffic. Parking is easy in the many covered parking areas, notably the useful parking area underneath place Masséna. Sights are not especially close together, but a good inexpensive bus system makes them all easily accessible. The 'visitor area' is mainly concentrated along the Promenade des Anglais and Le Vieux Nice.
The park-like Promenade du Paillon, constructed over the concealed Paillon river, divides the old town from the new and is home to several museums. The Chagall and Matisse art museums and Cimiez hill farther back in the town deserve a special trip.

HIGHLIGHTS

LE VIEUX NICE
➕ 119 C3 🅿 Underground parking area at cours Saleya
Set back from the sea at the eastern end of the beach is the historic and atmospheric old quarter called Le Vieux Nice. This is a delightful tangle of picturesque narrow lanes, many lined with bars, popular restaurants and little shops selling souvenirs or traditional Provençal fabrics. Side streets lead into quiet, undiscovered corners. There are several interesting small baroque churches too; if their doors are open, it's worth looking inside to see the elaborate workmanship of the interiors. The focal point of the old quarter is cours Saleya, a long esplanade edged with restaurant tables and filled for much of the day with a big, vibrant flower market.

PROMENADE DES ANGLAIS
➕ 119 B3 🅿 Street parking and underground parking areas
A wide seafront road edged by mimosa and palms follows the coastal strip where Nice meets the dazzling blue curve of the Baie des Anges. Running for several kilometres beside the town's stony beach, this is the famous Promenade des Anglais. Although it's now beside a busy highway, it remains an attractive sight, and on fine days is full of people sauntering, sitting in the sun or skating. Grand façades look

RATINGS	
Cultural interest	●●●●●
Photo stops	●●●●
Shopping	●●●●

BASICS

➕ 289 Q10
ℹ️ **Main office:** Gare SNCF, avenue Thiers, tel 0892 707 407; Jun–end Sep Mon–Sat 8–8, Sun 9–12; Oct–end May Mon–Sat 8–7, Sun 9–6 **Beach office:** 5 Promenade des Anglais, tel 0892 707 407; Jun–end Sep Mon–Sat 8–8, Sun 9–7; Oct–end May Mon–Sat 9–6 **Ferber office:** Promenade des Anglais, tel 0892 707 407; Jun–end Sep Mon–Sat 8–8, Sun 9–7 **Nice-Côte d'Azur Airport:** Terminal 1, tel 0892 707 407; Jun–end Sep daily 8am–10pm; Oct–end May daily 8am–9pm
🚇 Nice (in avenue Thiers)

www.nicetourism.com
Lots of information on what to see, what's on, hotels, restaurants and getting around; in French, English, Italian and German

A stepped alley in atmospheric Vieux Nice (left)

across from the other side of the road, including the sumptuous, traditional Hôtel Negresco and the Palais de la Méditerrannée, a state-of-the-art luxury hotel behind an art deco exterior. The Promenade des Anglais ends at the Jardin Albert I, but the promenade continues east as quai des États-Unis.

LE CHÂTEAU

✚ 119 C3 🅿 Street parking

The seafront promenade ends at the Château, which is not a castle but a high headland rising up between the beach area and the port. Le Vieux Nice is just below. The medieval fortress and other buildings that stood here were demolished in 1706, leaving almost no trace. Today the hilltop is a pleasant shaded park with fantastic views of the sea and town. At the foot of the hill, the coast road turns to reach the old port, a busy area with some popular restaurants.

Evening on the cours Saleya *This store sells olive oil made in Nice*

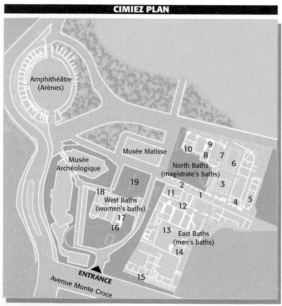

CIMIEZ PLAN

Amphithéâtre (Arènes)

Musée Matisse

Musée Archéologique

North Baths (magistrate's baths)

West Baths (women's baths)

East Baths (men's baths)

ENTRANCE
Avenue Monte Croce

1. Decumanus I
2. Early boundary wall (1st century AD)
3. Natatio (swimming pool)
4. Latrine
5. Reservoir
6. Courtyard
7. Frigidarium (cold water)
8. Tepidarium (tepid water)
9. Laconicum (sweat bath)
10. Caldarium (hot water)
11. Fourth-century AD building
12. Praefurnium (stove)
13. Great Courtyard (Palaestra)
14. School
15. Decumanus II
16. Foundations of baths (3rd century AD)
17. Choir of 5th-century AD Christian basilica
18. Baptisterium
19. Cardo

The Musée Henri Matisse (left)

NICE

BD BURKILL
Rue Michelet
Bellevue
BVD DE CESSOLE
BD AUG RAYNAUD
Rue Mollé
R Mich
A BINET
Cros de Capeu
Av de Pessicart
Av Gutenberg
Pl du de Cal
BD J GARNIER
R Clément Roas
Rue St-Etiénne
Vern
BOULEVARD
RUE TRACH
Av Paul Arène
Lycée
ST-ETIENNE
Cathédrale Orthodoxe Russe
GARE NICE VILLE
Bd du Tzarewitch
CAMBETTA
VOIE RAPIDE SUD
Bd Fr Crosso
Place Franklin
Rue Fr Passy
AVENUE
Rue Berlioz
Pl Mo
Ver
Place St-Philippe
Rue Caffarelli
AV D FLEURS
Rue Bottero
Rue François Grosso
CAMBETTA
BOULEVA
R de Rivoli
R de Cronstadt
France
Musée des Beaux-Arts
Rue Dante
Sq Cal Bouvier
Musé
Palai
DES
Massé
PROMENADE
98
Blue Beac
Forum Plage
Voilier Plage
Florida Plage
A

LES ARÈNES

⊞ Off map at 119 C1 • Musée Archéologique and Parc des Antiquités, 160 avenue des Arènes, Cimiez, 06000 Nice ☎ 04 93 81 59 57 ⏰ Wed–Sun 10–6. Closed mid-Nov to early Dec 🚌 15, 17, 20, 22, 25 💶 Adult €4, child €2.50; free on 1st and 3rd Sun of month 🅿 Street parking nearby ⛳ Guided tours (€3) in French on Wed and 1st Sun in month, at 3 🏛

On higher ground in the north, the Cimiez district is the site of Roman Nice. There are Roman ruins and a museum at the Parc des Antiquités, an archaeological site now laid out as a pleasant little park, known locally as Les Arènes. The oval-shaped arena itself, still within the ruins of its original Roman walls, now hosts open-air concerts, including jazz. Other first- to third-century AD ruins at the site include a good example of Roman baths. Beside the park, the Musée Archéologique displays objects found here and elsewhere in Nice.

MUSÉE HENRI MATISSE

⊞ Off map at 119 C1 • 164 avenue des Arènes, Cimiez, 06000 Nice ☎ 04 93 81 08 08 ⏰ Apr–end Sep Wed–Mon 10–6; Oct–end Mar Wed–Mon 10–5 🚌 15, 17, 20, 22, 25 💶 Adult €4, under 18 free; free on 1st Sun of month 🅿 Street parking nearby ⛳ Guided tours (€3) Wed at 3 in French; other languages by appointment 🏛

www.musee-matisse-nice.org/

Entered directly from the archaeological park, the Musée Henri Matisse houses the most important collection of his work. The museum is largely hidden from view, being mainly in a modern underground building, but above ground it also includes a 17th-century mansion. It deals comprehensively with the development of Matisse's work, from exquisite line drawings to vivid gouaches

Decorative archways

Going for a ride along the Promenade des Anglais (left)

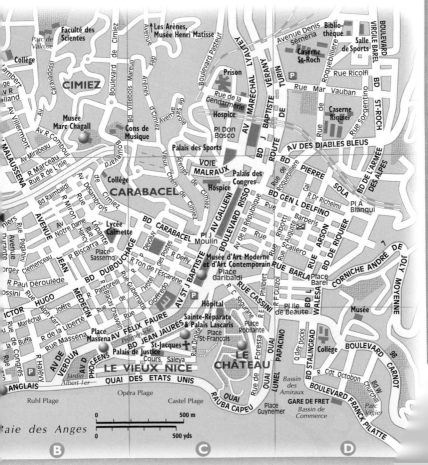

to a model of his chapel at nearby Vence. There are also personal possessions and photos. Henri Matisse (1869–1954) and Raoul Dufy (1877–1953) are both buried in nearby Cimiez cemetery.

MUSÉE MARC CHAGALL
119 B1 ✉ Avenue du Docteur Ménard, 06000 Nice ☎ 04 93 53 87 20
🕐 Jul–end Sep Wed–Mon 10–6; Oct–end Jun Wed–Mon 10–5 🚌 15 💶 Adult
€5.50, under 18 free; free on 1st Sun of month
🎧 Guided tours (€3) Wed at 3.30 in French, Thu at
3.30 in English; also 1st Sun in month at 3 in French
and at 4 in English 🏧 👥
www.musee-chagall.fr

Down a side road at the bottom of the Cimiez hill is the Musée Marc Chagall, with the alternative name Musée du Message Biblique. This is a phenomenal collection of Chagall's enigmatic work, including his stained glass, mosaics and art books, as well as the vast, vivid, dreamlike canvases devoted to Biblical stories *(message biblique)* and Jewish subjects, including scenes from his childhood shtetl home. The museum shop has excellent books on Chagall, as well as other art books, posters, prints and souvenirs.

PLACE MASSÉNA AND CENTRAL NICE
119 B3 🅿 Street parking and underground parking area
Masséna

The Paillon promenade runs into place Masséna and the busy heart of town. This central district is largely 18th- to 20th-century, with the distinctive attractive Niçois style of shallow roofs and ornate frontages with balconies and sectioned slatted

Narrow rue Droite (above)

The Promenade des Anglais (top) was funded by Nice's English visitors in the 1820s

A winged statue in the Jardin Albert I

shutters. Here are many stores, including Galeries Lafayette, as well as a pedestrian-only zone of narrow streets filled with specialist shops and inexpensive restaurants. The district is bisected by the city's main thoroughfare, avenue Jean Médecin.

MUSÉE DES BEAUX-ARTS
🕇 Off map at 118 A3 • 33 avenue des Baumettes, Nice ☎ 04 92 15 28 28
🕐 Tue–Sun 10–6 💰 Adult €4, under 18 free
At the western end of the beach, on avenue des Baumettes, a handsome 19th-century mansion houses the prestigious Musée des Beaux-Arts. Here you can see European fine arts of the 17th to 19th centuries, including paintings of the Riviera by Edgar Degas, Alfred Sisley and Raoul Dufy. Other exhibits include sculptures by Jean-Baptiste Carpeaux and Auguste Rodin and paintings by 17th-century Italian Old Masters.

╺╸ MORE TO SEE ╺╸

CATHÉDRALE DE SAINTE-RÉPARATE
🕇 119 C3 • Place Rossetti, Nice
☎ 04 93 62 34 40 🕐 Mon–Fri
8.30–11.30, 2–6 💰 Free
This 17th-century baroque extravaganza, with a roof of bright Niçois tiles, is named after Nice's patron saint.

MUSÉE D'ART MODERNE ET D'ART CONTEMPORAIN
🕇 119 C2 • Promenade des Arts, Nice ☎ 04 93 62 61 62 🕐 Tue–Sun 10–6
💰 Adult €4, under 18 free; free to all on 1st and 3rd Sun of month
www.mamac-nice.org
The avant-garde Museum of Modern and Contemporary Art has the definitive collection of the 'Nice school' of 1960s artists who lived and worked in the town. See Pop Art from names such as Andy Warhol and Roy Lichtenstein. Many of the pieces were created as a send-up of consumer society and even of the art world itself. The building is unusual—four octagonal marble towers are linked by walkways.

CATHÉDRALE ORTHODOXE RUSSE
🕇 118 A2 • Avenue Nicolas II, Nice ☎ 04 93 96 88 02 🕐 Mon–Sat 9.30–12, 2.30–6, Sun 2.30–6 💰 €3
Tsar Nicolas I commissioned this striking cathedral in 1903, in memory of his son, Nicolas, who died of consumption in Nice. The glistening green cupolas are a reminder of the building's Russian origins. Inside, the cathedral follows the shape of a Greek cross.

There's plenty to choose from at the market in cours Saleya (left); the Musée Archéologique, in the Cimiez district (middle); an outdoor café in Vieux Nice (right)

PALAIS LASCARIS
🕇 119 C3 • 15 rue Droite, Nice
☎ 04 93 62 05 54 🕐 Wed–Mon 10–6
💰 Free
See paintings, tapestries and furniture from the 17th and 18th centuries, in this baroque palace.

The eye-catching domes of the Cathédrale Orthodoxe Russe

BACKGROUND
Nice has changed location several times. The original Ligurian settlement, from 1000BC, was near the seafront at the mouth of the River Paillon. The Greek town of Nikaea, from 600BC, was built on the waterfront hill now called the Château. The Roman town of Cemenelum, from 200BC, was a short distance inland on today's Cimiez hill. After the fall of Rome in the fifth century AD, the town was again based on the Château hill and the port.

Medieval Nice, what is now Le Vieux Nice, belonged to the Counts of Provence and then to the Counts of Savoy. French troops occupied the area from 1792, but it was handed back in 1814. In 1860, it again became French when Napoleon III annexed the whole County of Nice, moving the Franco-Italian border to its present position. By then, Nice was already a winter resort, wealthy visitors building grand villas and extending the town westward along the seashore. By the end of the 19th century, 20,000 visitors came to Nice each winter. The 1920s brought a big growth in summer tourism, and many artists and writers stayed in or around Nice. Tourism continues to flourish: Nice airport is now the second-busiest air gateway into France.

Parc National
du Mercantour

An awesomely beautiful mountain region with superb wildlife, the Mercantour combines the warmth of the Mediterranean with the harsher world of the Alps.

A river flows past the mountains *Tackling the mountain terrain on two wheels* *Mountain flora*

RATINGS	
Outdoor activities	● ● ● ● ●
Photo stops	● ● ● ● ●
Walkability	● ● ●

BASICS

✚ 288 P8

ℹ Mercantour information office: Parc National du Mercantour, Centre Accueil Valberg, 1 rue St-Jean, 06470 Valberg, tel 04 93 02 58 23; summer daily 10–1, 3–7; winter hours vary

www.parc-mercantour.com
Beautiful site with facts, figures and photos of the Mercantour protected region.

TIPS

● The following are not allowed in the park: pets, fires, camping, waste disposal or removing any plant or natural object.
● The park's main office is in Nice, at 23 rue d'Italie, 06006 Nice, tel 04 93 16 78 88.
● Col de la Cayolle refuge (tel 04 92 81 24 25) is open from mid-June to mid-September.

SEEING MERCANTOUR

Mercantour National Park lies along the Franco-Italian border in the Provençal Alps, and can be reached relatively easily from the Riviera coast on roads climbing the Tinée, Vésubie and Roya valleys. The main entry point is the small town of Tende (▷ 126), on the Roya river. The landscapes are extremely varied, ranging from gentle green pasture and alpine forests to glacial lakes, canyons and soaring peaks in the inaccessible protected zone. Popular with walkers and climbers, this is a genuine adventure land, but carefully managed, with guides, park rangers and facilities. Refuges or chalets on well-marked mountain trails offer shelter or overnight lodgings, but these must be reserved well in advance. There are 600km (370 miles) of paths in the park and several nature trails, such as those at Lac d'Allos (▷ 138) and Col de la Bonette. Two long-distance hiking trails, GR5 and GR52, also cross the area. Most of the park's higher reaches are covered in snow from mid-October to mid-June, limiting accessibility for all but the most experienced climbers.

HIGHLIGHTS

VALLÉE DES MERVEILLES

🚌 Guided tours leave Refuge des Merveilles at 7.30, 11 and 3 daily in Jul, Aug (email: mercantour@wanadoo.fr) 🅿 On the D91 at Lac des Mesches there is a parking area at the start of the path to the Refuge des Merveilles (a 3-hour walk away)

The most popular and remarkable excursion into the Parc is the trek to the Vallée des Merveilles (▷ 216–217). This is a valley on a high tributary of the Roya, just below Mont Bégo (2,872m/9,420ft), where thousands of odd, repetitive drawings are inscribed on the rocks. Many more can be seen in the nearby Vallée de Fontanalbe. In a simple style resembling stick men, and actually rather hard to discern, these images are thought to have been made in the Bronze Age

(1800–1500BC) and depict hands, weapons, tools and horns. No one knows what purpose the pictures served, if any, but an explanation popular with the guides and others is that the Bronze Age inhabitants of the site here worshipped Mont Bégo as a sacred place of the Bull God and Earth-Goddess religion. There is, however, no convincing evidence for this. The most striking of the drawings have been given names, such as *The Sorcerer*. The walk to the Vallée takes you through a dramatically wild scene of forests, flower meadows, lakes and mountains.

Don't be surprised if you hear cow bells while out walking

FLORA AND FAUNA

For walkers and climbers venturing deep into the national park, there is a great wealth of animal and plant life to be seen. Pines and larches on the lower slopes give way to Alpine meadows at higher altitudes. There is permanent snow above 3,000m (9,840ft). Hovering overhead are birds such as eagles, kestrels and falcons, and the rare lammergeyer vulture. Smaller birds include the ptarmigan, great spotted woodpecker, hoopoe, citril finches, ortolan and rock buntings. Mouflons (wild sheep) were reintroduced in the 1950s, while red deer, chamois, blue hare, ibex and boar are increasing. There are numerous other animals, and 200 rare plant species, including 35 endemic to this region. In spring, mountain meadows are dotted with bellflowers and blue gentians. You may sometimes see saxifrage, the symbol of the park.

VALLÉE DE
LA ROYA

84

Vallon de la Minière
Baisse de Vallaurette

Vallée des Merveilles
Refuge des Merveilles
Baisse de Valmasque

BACKGROUND

In contrast to its current status as a protected area, the Mercantour was a hunting reserve for the Italian royal family in the second half of the 19th century. It remained in Italian hands until after World War II, when it was split between Italy and France. The two halves were symbolically joined in 1980 to form the Argentera National Park.

Houses cling to the rock in the perched village of Peille

Boats moored at St-Jean-Cap-Ferrat

PEILLE

🕂 289 Q10 🛈 Mairie, 06440 Peille
☎ 04 93 91 71 71

Reached by steep narrow roads that switchback up to a 630m (2,066ft) altitude from the Paillon valley, the peaceful perched village of Peille stands on a ridge some 20km (13 miles) inland from Monaco. Its remote, inaccessible, staunchly defended location gave the village an independent air—it even has its own dialect, called *Peilhasc*. There are several lovely old buildings in the cobbled alleys and passageways, and many fine doorways, fountains and other stonework of the Renaissance and Gothic periods. The appearance of the village in the Middle Ages can be seen from a painting that hangs inside the Église Sainte-Marie (ask at the Mairie for the key). The picture shows the feudal castle of the Counts of Provence, whose ruins still stand at the top of the village. Also inside the church is a fine 16th-century polyptych of the Rosary by Honoré Bertone of the Niçois school.

PEILLON

🕂 289 Q10 🛈 Mairie, 672 avenue de l'Hôtel de Ville, 06440 Peillon, tel 04 93 79 91 04

The dramatically perched village of Peillon, soaring above the river Paillon, enjoys an 'eagle's nest' setting among rocky peaks just inland from Monaco. Thanks to its position, it was accustomed to protecting itself from invaders, and today guards itself against unsightly tourism development. As a result, although much restored, the village remains remarkably unspoiled and uncommercialized. Its 16th-century mansions line vaulted alleys and steep stairways that climb up through the village.

Don't miss Dramatic frescoes of *The Passion of Christ*, painted in 1485 by Giovanni Canavesio, decorate the interior of the Chapelle des Pénitents Blancs, at the entrance to the village. Telephone the Mairie in advance to arrange a visit.

PUGET-THÉNIERS

🕂 288 N9 🛈 Mairie, 06260 Puget-Théniers, tel 04 93 05 05 05; May–end Sep daily 9–12, 3–7; Oct–end Apr Mon–Fri 9–12, 2–5

Puget-Théniers is a handsome town on the border of the Alpes-Maritimes and Alpes-de-Haute-Provence, strategically located where the Var valley broadens as it leaves the higher Alps. The Redoule river, which meets the Var at this point, also flows through the town. Once a possession of the Grimaldis (the Monaco ruling family), the town is dominated by their ruined Château des Trainières, dismantled in 1691.

The old town, whose heart is the place A. Conil, was in earlier centuries a Templar stronghold. It features many fine old doorways with carved shields on the lintels. Inside the church of Notre-Dame-de-l'Assumption are two remarkable 16th-century altar-pieces, the *Polyptyque de Notre-Dame-de-Secours* by Antoine Ronzen, and the carvings of the *Passion* by Mathieu d'Anvers. The town was the birthplace of Auguste Blanqui, a leader of the Paris Commune in 1870: A bronze by Aristide Maillol commemorates him.

At nearby Puget-Rostang is the excellent Ecomusée du Pays de la Roudoule (Apr–end Oct daily 9–12, 2–6; Nov–end Mar Mon–Fri 9–12, 2–6), whose displays capture the identity of this region. The museum also runs interesting guided tours focusing on local heritage.

ST-JEAN-CAP-FERRAT

🕂 289 Q10 🛈 59 avenue Denis-Semaria, 06230 St-Jean-Cap-Ferrat, tel 04 93 76 08 90; summer Mon–Fri 9–6, Sat, Sun 9–5; winter Mon–Sat 9–5
www.ville-saint-jean-cap-ferrat.fr

St-Jean is the small main town of the exclusive Cap Ferrat peninsula. Part ordinary village, part luxurious marina, St-Jean has an appealing quayside with a few bars and restaurants. Away from the port, the streets and houses have an Italianate appearance. St-Jean is the only part of Cap Ferrat that feels approachable to visitors who don't have a millionaire's bank balance. The rest of this rich person's hideaway consists mainly of palatial homes in vast, lush gardens half-hidden by walls, gates and hedges. The main site on the Cap is Villa Ephrussi de Rothschild (▷ 127), but also of interest for those with young children is the Zoo du Cap-Ferrat (▷ 195), west of St-Jean.

Don't miss Paths around the Cap's 14km (9 miles) of coastline give wonderful sea views.

ST-MARTIN-VÉSUBIE

🕂 289 P8 🛈 Place Félix-Faure, 06450 St-Martin-Vésubie, tel 04 93 03 21 28; summer daily 9–12.30, 3–7; winter Mon–Sat 9–12, 2.30–5.30, Sun 9–12
www.vesubian.com

The upper Vésubie valley and surrounding peaks form a spectacularly scenic landscape on the edge of the high-altitude Parc National du Mercantour (▷ 122–123). The main town of the region, St-Martin-Vésubie, is a popular little resort among the green hills on the twin streams of Le Boréon and La Madone de Fenestre, which pour down from the Mercantour heights and meet in the town to form the river Vésubie. Water even flows down the heart of the cobbled

An outdoor café in St-Paul-de-Vence

Vivid frescoes in the Église St-Sauveur, in Saorge

Brightly painted houses and an 11th-century toll gate, in Sospel

main street, rue Dr. Cagnoli, over-hung with chalet-style houses. The effect is delightful—but was not always so, since this stream once served as the town's main sewer. Rue Dr. Cagnoli runs from the main square, place Félix-Faure, down to a Gothic mansion, the Maison des Contes de Gubernatis, on the way passing the bulbous tower of the Chapelle des Pénitents-Blancs and the parish church.

Inside the church is an altarpiece from the Bréa school and, for part of the year, the polychrome wooden statue of the Madone de Fenestre, brought to the town by 12th-century Templars. In July the statue is carried in procession to its summer quarters, the Sanctuaire de la Madone de Fenestre, 12km (7.5 miles) northeast. It returns in September. The chapel gets its curious name ('Madonna of the Window') from a natural opening in the rocks above it, through which you can see the sky.

ST-PAUL-DE-VENCE

➕ 288 P10 ℹ️ 2 rue Grande, 06570 St-Paul-de-Vence, tel 04 93 32 86 95; Apr–end Sep daily 10–7; Oct–end Mar daily 10–8
www.saint-pauldevence.com

Visually stunning, the hilltop village of St-Paul is well-defended within its ring of ramparts. The busy, commercialized streets lead to picturesque sights like the old washhouse, while steps lead up to the church, with its fine medieval art. The village is in a constant battle to preserve something of its authentic atmosphere. Thousands of visitors come each day from Riviera resorts just 30 minutes' drive away. Packed with workshops, art galleries, antiques stores and gift shops, it is a wonder that St-Paul does not come to a standstill with shoppers clogging the

narrow streets in summer.

The village appealed to the Riviera's artists of a century ago, such as Pablo Picasso and Marc Chagall. They used to meet at a tavern called the Auberge de la Colombe d'Or and pay for meals by donating art every now and then. Some of these still hang on the walls of the auberge, now one of the region's most prestigious restaurants. The Musée d'Histoire (daily 10–5), in a 12th-century keep next to the town hall, has photos of some of the celebrities who have visited or lived in the village.

SAORGE

➕ 289 R8 ℹ️ Mairie: tel 04 93 04 51 23 🚉 Saorge-Fortan station 1km (0.6 miles) from the village

Seen from below, this perched village in the Roya valley in the Provençal Alps is a jumble of dark fortifications, towers and tall houses, with glazed rooftiles catching the light. The precipitous drive up to the village is well worth it to see how this peculiar place has been built, with houses piled one on top of the other and connected by stairways and alleyways where daylight hardly penetrates. The village stands

guard over the entrance to the awesome Roya Gorge and the approaches to the Col de Tende. It was a key defensive post in the Middle Ages, but the fort was destroyed by Napoleon Bonaparte in 1794. The church at the heart of the village has some intriguing trompe l'oeil frescoes. The fine carved organ was built in Genoa and brought up here by pack mules. At the end of the main street, a path leads across terraces to a 17th-century Franciscan monastery with an 11th-century chapel, La Madone del Poggio.

SOSPEL

➕ 289 O9 ℹ️ Place St-Nicolas, 06380 Sospel, tel 04 93 04 15 80; Jul, Aug daily 9–12.30, 2–6; Sep–end Jun daily 9.30–12, 2.30–6.30 🚉 Sospel

The charmingly Italianate town of Sospel sits among terraces and groves on the banks of the river Bévéra, in the hills that separate Provence from Italy. It is the starting point for some lovely walks. Located on an important medieval trade route, the town grew up around its distinctive fortified toll bridge over the river. The 11th-century bridge—still with its toll gate halfway across—remains an evocative sight. It was damaged during World War II and restored in 1947.

In the western half of the town, narrow streets open up into place St-Michel, lined with baroque façades. The 17th-century Église St-Michel has a Romanesque bell tower from the 12th-century church it replaced.

Out of town on the D2204 is Fort St-Roch, a Maginot Line fortress built in 1932. It now houses a museum of the Alpine resistance (Jul–end Sep Tue–Sun 2–6; Oct–end Jun Sat, Sun 2–6). **Don't miss** Inside the Église St-Michel are magnificent altarpieces by Louis Bréa.

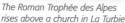

The Roman Trophée des Alpes rises above a church in La Turbie

Vence's Chapelle du Rosaire was created by artist Henri Matisse

THE SIGHTS

TENDE

✚ 289 R8 ℹ Avenue du 16 Septembre 1947, 06430 Tende-Val-des-Merveilles, tel 04 93 04 73 71; May to mid-Oct Mon–Sat 9–12.30, 2–6; mid-Oct to May daily 9–12.30, 2–5.30 🚉 Tende www.tendemerveilles.com

Tende is the last town in France on the mountain road from Provence into Italy's Piedmont—and until 1947, Tende itself was in Italy. It remained in Italy when the rest of the County of Nice became French in 1860 because Victor Emmanuel II begged Napoleon III to let him keep these high hills, where he loved to hunt chamois. As a gesture of goodwill, Napoleon III agreed to the request. Tende joined France after World War II.

The town is a curious steep collection of high balconied houses under dark stone roofs rising one above the other, a warren of little streets running between, all dominated by a rather bizarre bulbous church spire. Many of the houses, stone built and roofed with stone slabs, date from the 15th century. Ruins of a castle stand above the town. The unusual church, St-Marie des Bois, has a handsome Renaissance doorway and 17th-century organ.

The town has become the principal base for excursions into the Mercantour (▷ 122–123), especially walkers headed to the Vallée des Merveilles (▷ 216–217). The Musée des Merveilles, in avenue du 16 Sept 1947 (May to mid-Oct Wed–Mon 10–6.30; mid-Oct to end Apr Wed–Mon 10–5; closed for two weeks in Mar and Nov) has displays explaining the history, archaeology and mythology of the valley and the rock drawings, as well as giving insight into the local culture. The museum is also an information venue for walks to the Vallée des Merveilles.

LA TURBIE

✚ 289 Q10 www.ville-la-turbie.fr/

La Turbie sits on a lofty ridge in beautiful sunlit hills above Monaco. The small town dates back to early Roman times, when it was the highest point on the Via Julia highway (480m/1,575ft above sea level). Here in the first century BC, the massive Trophée des Alpes was erected as a triumphal monument to commemorate Augustus' conquest of the Alpine tribes. A small part is still standing, on cours Albert 1er, and its chunky silhouette is a memorable landmark overlooking the town. The Trophée (mid-Jun to mid-Sep daily 9.30–7; Apr to mid-Jun daily 9.30–6; mid-Sep to end Mar Tue–Sun 10–5) was originally 50m (165ft) high and 38m (125ft) wide, with a statue of Augustus on top. In the Middle Ages it was used as a fortress, and later much vandalized, eventually being largely dismantled on the orders of Louis XIV in 1705. It was further destroyed in the 19th century when the stonework was quarried to build the nearby church. Despite all this damage, enough of the vast monument survived to make partial restoration feasible (financed by an American, Edward Tuck). The present structure has a height of 35m (115ft). A long inscription on its base lists all 44 local tribes conquered by Augustus.
Don't miss The gardens surrounding the trophy offer wonderful panoramic views of the Riviera.

VENCE

✚ 288 P10 ℹ 8 place du Grand Jardin, 06140 Vence, tel 04 93 58 06 38; Jul, Aug Mon–Sat 9–6, Sun 9–2; Apr–end Jun, Sep, Oct Mon–Sat 9–6; Nov–end Mar Mon–Sat 9–5 www.ville-vence.fr

Vence is best known for its artistic connections, especially Henri Matisse's chapel. The town is an easy drive inland from Cannes or Antibes and is in an attractive part of the Riviera backcountry. It has an enjoyable old town, with surviving sections of the ramparts including five gateways. At the heart of town are place du Frêne, dominated by an ancient ash tree, and place du Peyra, with a fountain of drinkable mineral-rich water. Next to the square, Château de Villeneuve has a 13th-century watchtower; today the chateau is used for exhibitions of 20th-century art. Head down rue du Marché, which is crammed with excellent little patisseries, charcuteries, cheese specialists and fishmongers with sacks of mussels and mounds of freshly cooked prawns.

Rue du Marché leads to place Clemenceau, at the heart of the old quarter, where Roman tombstones are incorporated into the walls of the 10th-century cathedral—the site was formerly a Roman temple. In the baptistery at the back there's a mosaic by Marc Chagall (1887–1985).

Vence is noted for artistic and literary connections. André Gide, Paul Valéry and D.H. Lawrence are among the writers who have lived in the town. Vence's main attraction is in the modern suburbs in the north: the exquisite little Chapelle du Rosaire, created entirely by Henri Matisse (1869–1954). Stained glass throws patterns of yellow, green and blue onto walls of white tiles on which line drawings depict Biblical scenes. A rule of silence inside the chapel greatly enhances the effect. Matisse built the chapel as a thank you to Dominican nuns who cared for him when he was gravely ill. After five years of work, he declared that this was his masterpiece.

Fountains play in front of the Villa Ephrussi de Rothschild

VILLA EPHRUSSI DE ROTHSCHILD

This luxurious Italianate villa contains around 5,000 works of art.

Béatrice de Rothschild, wife of wealthy banker Baron Ephrussi, created the spacious villa and gardens here in 1912, wanting a place for banquets and entertaining. She also needed somewhere to house her huge collection of important items gathered from around France and the rest of the world. She chose a delightful setting, on the quiet and exclusive Cap Ferrat peninsula (▷ 124) close to Beaulieu, with sea views on both sides. Construction took seven years, with a succession of around 40 architects—some didn't last more than a few hours, thanks to the baroness' capriciousness. The baroness died in 1934, leaving the villa to France's Académie des Beaux-Arts. Now, visitors can wander around the beautiful gardens and the ground floor of the villa, although to see the collections on the first floor you have to take a guided tour.

THE ART
The art collection is diverse, with some 5,000 works, ranging from French period furniture and tapestries to Renaissance religious art, fine 18th-century porcelain and bas-reliefs. The Far Eastern art is also remarkable, with a wonderful display of pink jade and some rare Chinese chests.

OUTSIDE
The grounds are divided into a series of separate areas encapsulating different garden styles from around the world. Along the length of the central garden are musical fountains (you can have *Happy Birthday* played for you as the waters dance for your delight), surrounded by the seven other gardens in such styles as Spanish, Florentine and Japanese.

TEA AND SHOPPING
The villa has an elegant tea room with wonderful views of the Bay of Villefranche from its large windows. The site's shop has an interesting range of jewellery, porcelain and good-quality rugs and wallhangings.

Don't miss The Salon des Singes (Monkey Room) on the first floor reflects the Baroness' love of monkeys and other animals.

A painting of a dancer, by Frédéric Schall

RATINGS	
Cultural interest	● ● ● ○
Historic interest	● ● ● ○
Photo stops	● ● ● ○

BASICS
✚ 289 Q10 • Fondation Béatrice Ephrussi de Rothschild, Chemin du Musée, 06230 St-Jean-Cap-Ferrat
☎ 04 93 01 33 09
🕐 Jul, Aug daily 10–7; Feb–end Jun, Sep, Oct daily 10–6; Nov–end Jan Mon–Fri 2–6, Sat, Sun, school hols 10–6
🎫 To visit the collections on the first floor, you must take a guided tour; guided tours of the whole site are also available by arrangement
🍴 Elegant tea room
🚌 Buses from Nice every half hour to Beaulieu, which is around 2km (1.2 miles) from the Villa
🚆 Beaulieu, around 2km (1.2 miles) from the Villa
💶 Adult €8.50, child (7–17) €6.50
🅿 ⊞ 👫

www.villa-ephrussi.com

Picturesque Villefranche-sur-Mer

VILLEFRANCHE-SUR-MER

With fishing boats in the port and pastel-painted houses climbing steep narrow lanes, Villefranche-sur-Mer is thought by many to be one of the loveliest places on the Riviera.

Pretty, unpretentious Villefranche-sur-Mer is a small port town so close to Nice that visitors and locals often drive out here for a waterfront fish dinner and an evening stroll on the long quayside. Historically a military base as well as a fishing village, Villefranche still sometimes sees warships in its deep, sheltered port. The rue Obscure, a dark vaulted 13th-century street running beneath the houses close to the port, has often been used as a community bomb shelter, including during World War II.

FAMOUS RESIDENT
Writer and film director Jean Cocteau lived here from 1924 to 1926 and in 1957 he decorated the Chapelle St-Pierre (Jun–end Sep Tue–Sun 10–12, 4–8.30; Oct–end Mar Tue–Sun 9.30–12, 2–6; Mar–end Jun Tue–Sun 9.30–12, 3–7; closed mid-Nov to mid-Dec) near the waterfront. His dazzling, richly symbolic frescoes show the life of St. Peter as if among the people of the town, including fisherwomen and gypsies.

SIGHTS
Above the port, the massive walls of the 16th-century Citadelle enclose the Mairie (town hall), an open-air theatre and two museums. Fondation-Musée Volti (Dec–end Oct Wed–Sat 10–12, 3–6, Sun 3–7) is dedicated to sculptures of voluptuous female figures by local artist Volti. The Musée Goetz-Boumeester (Mon, Wed–Sat 10–12, 3–6, Sun 2–5) contains the works of modern artists Christine Boumeester and Henri Goetz, together with two works by Pablo Picasso and one by Joan Miró, as well as various displays of ceramics. At the citadel entrance you can see archaeological finds from the wreck of a Genoese trading ship that sank in Villefranche port in 1516.

Don't miss Wander past the brightly painted buildings and look out for sculptures.

As this sign (above) explains, the Chapelle St-Pierre was decorated by Jean Cocteau. The town remembers him with a sculpture (right)

RATINGS			
Good for food	● ● ● ○
Historic interest	● ● ● ○
Photo stops	● ● ● ○

BASICS

✚ 289 Q10
ℹ Jardin François-Binon, 06230 Villefranche-sur-Mer, tel 04 93 01 73 68; Jul, Aug daily 9–7; Jun, Sep Mon–Sat 9–12, 2–6.30; Oct–end May Mon–Sat 9–12, 2–6
🚆 Villefranche-sur-Mer

www.villefranche-sur-mer.com

MONACO

There's something faintly unreal about this awesome patch of rock, hanging off the Provençal coast, an independent nation-state though it covers just 2sq km (less than 1sq mile). More than a millionaires' playground, it also has several worthwhile sights, including the Musée Océanographique, Monte-Carlo and the world-famous casino.

MAJOR SIGHTS

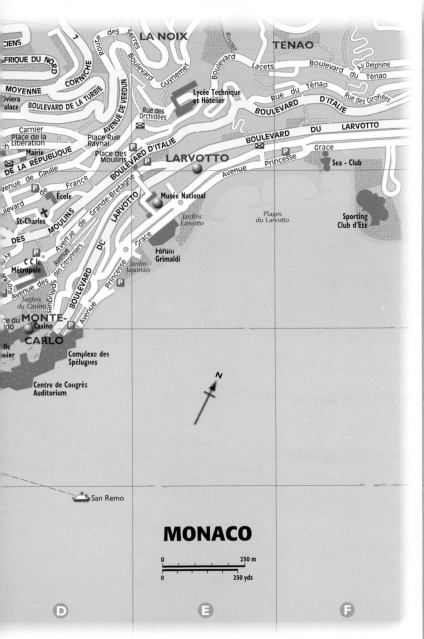

MONACO

0 — 250 m

0 — 250 yds

Monaco-Ville

The exquisite Prince's Palace makes The Rock the most extraordinary of all the Riviera's 'perched villages'.

| *The rooftops of Monaco-Ville* | *The imposing entrance to the Musée Océanographique* | *Looking down to the sea from the Jardin Exotique* |

BASICS

✚ 289 Q10

🛈 2A boulevard des Moulins, Monte-Carlo, Monaco, tel 377 92 16 61 16; Mon–Sat 9–7, Sun 10–12. In summer, additional tourist information kiosks are set up at the railway station and main sites

🚉 Monaco (avenue Prince-Pierre)

🚌 Frequent bus services run the length of Monaco from 7am to 8pm (€1.40 for a single trip)

www.visitmonaco.com
Monaco's site for visitors is slick, up-to-date and user-friendly.

www.monaco.gouv.mc/PortGb
The Government of Monaco's official website, in English.

www.monaco-tourisme.com
Photos and information

TIP

● The currency in Monaco is the euro.

Two members of the Royal Guard (top)

SEEING MONACO-VILLE

Although so small, Monaco today is made up of several districts. However, the original town was Monaco-Ville, poised in isolation on top of its legendary rock, Le Rocher, which projects into the Mediterranean with a port on either side. It remains a tranquil, historic, relatively uncommercialized area. Unlike most other Provençal villages perched on high crests and ridges, the terrain on top of The Rock is quite flat. The prince's palace stands at one end and a village-like old quarter covers the rest of the area.

Monaco-Ville is closed to visitors' vehicles and can be reached either on a long steep walkway from place d'Armes, or by elevator from parking des Pecheurs on the seafront.

HIGHLIGHTS

PALAIS PRINCIER

✚ 130 A3 • Place du Palais, 98000 Monaco ☎ 377 93 25 18 31 🕐 Jun–end Sep 9.30–6; Oct 10–5 (entry is by guided tour only) 🎫 Adult €6, child €3 www.palais.mc

The sturdily fortified Prince's Palace occupies the western end of The Rock. The first Grimaldi palace here was a defensive castle built in 1215. In the 17th century it was restructured to create the present elegant building. In front is a large esplanade, place du Palais, where members of the crisply immaculate Prince's Guard are on duty. The Changing of the Guard ceremony takes place daily at 11.55am. Guided tours inside the palace reveal sumptuous rooms richly decorated and furnished, adorned with frescoes, tapestries and art. Also in the palace is a museum devoted to Napoleon Bonaparte, with an assortment of personal items, including one of his hats. The palace is open to visitors only when Prince Rainier is away, in summer.

OLD QUARTER

✚ 130 B4

The Palais Princier and surrounding gardens and plaza take up a large proportion of Monaco-Ville. The rest of The Rock is covered by Monaco's small historic town. Several narrow streets run parallel from

LA CONDAMINE

✚ 130 B3

La Condamine, the old port district at the foot of The Rock and extending between Monaco-Ville and Monte-Carlo, is a busy shopping area with plenty of everyday stores. Here too is the principality's main covered market, opened in 1880. The main shopping street is rue Grimaldi. Monaco's rail station, and some of the most reasonably priced hotels, are in this part of town. The port area is packed with unpretentious restaurants—several of the best are Italian. La Condamine is the starting point for the Formula 1 Grand Prix.

FONTVIEILLE

✚ 130 A4

Fontvieille is the area west of Monaco-Ville that has been artificially extended into the sea. This 22ha (54-acre) residential and business district stands on specially constructed platforms of rock, with a yachting port alongside. Its Roseraie Princesse Grace, in avenue des Papalins, is an exquisite rose garden dedicated to Princess Grace of Monaco. Formerly the actress Grace Kelly, the Princess died in a car accident in 1982. Other attractions include the Musée des Timbres et des Monnaies (focusing on stamps and money), the Musée Naval (model ships), the Collection des Voitures Anciennes (gleaming historic motor vehicles) and the Parc Animalier (a zoo).

MONEGHETTI

✚ 130 A1

Climbing the steep slope between Monaco-Ville and the French border are the residential districts of Les Moneghetti and Les Révoires. At the top, just below the Moyenne Corniche road (N7), which is just outside Monaco, is the Jardin Exotique (mid-May to mid-Sep daily 9–7; mid-Sep to mid-May daily 9–5). This dazzling display is made up of succulents and cacti. The ticket includes a tour of the Grotte de l'Observatoire caves.

Statues in front of the Palais Princier (top)

A statue of Princess Grace, who died in 1982 (left)

place du Palais at one end of The Rock, to place de la Visitation at the other. They are spotlessly clean and pretty, with well-kept, pastel-shaded houses. Several of the buildings have good Renaissance doorways, especially along rue Comte Félix Gastaldi. However, there are few shops. Monaco-Ville's cathedral, in rue Colonel Bellando de Castro, has a Louis Bréa altarpiece, some fine paintings and the tombs of all Monaco's past princes.

MUSÉE OCÉANOGRAPHIQUE

✚ 130 B4 • avenue St-Martin, 98000 Monaco ☎ 377 93 15 36 00 🕐 Jul, Aug daily 9.30–7.30; Apr–end Jun, Sep daily 9.30–7; Oct–end Mar daily 10–6 💰 Adult €11, child (6–18) €6, under 6 free
www.oceano.mc

Carved into the flank of The Rock beside the sea is the Oceanography Museum, a world-class marine biology museum and study facility. Several floors high, it is educational and entertaining, with superb aquariums holding hundreds of thousands of creatures representing 350 species. There is a giant aquarium for sharks, a rare example of a living coral reef and sections on the human culture that has developed by the sea. The terrace offers fantastic coastal views.

BACKGROUND

Monaco was originally a medieval perched fortress, its castle a possession of Barbarossa. In the 13th century, the powerful aristocratic Grimaldi family of Genoa acquired The Rock and made it their headquarters, refashioning themselves as the Princes of Monaco in the 17th century. Under Napoleon Bonaparte, most of the many such independent fiefdoms of Provence were incorporated by force into France. But the Grimaldi influence in Provence and Italy remained very powerful, and for strategic reasons Napoleon decided to make an ally of Monaco's royal family instead of seizing their land. Monaco's income had come from high taxes on its domains, but it now found a role for itself as a refuge for the aristocracy.

Monte-Carlo

The millionaire resort of Monte-Carlo is devoted to gambling, luxury shopping and glitzy nightlife.

Cooling off in the pool

Shimmering lights of Monte-Carlo (above). The famous casino (top)

The man-made Larvotto beach

SEEING MONTE-CARLO

Monte-Carlo is the large modern district along the narrow slope, close to the seafront, in the north of the principality. This is Monaco's 'Casino quarter', with restaurants, luxurious hotels, opera and theatre, beautifully kept gardens, exclusive nightclubs and chic pricey shops, all within a short walk of the ostentatious Casino. Monte-Carlo's main street, boulevard des Moulins, is lined with jewellers and boutiques selling luxurious designer clothes and expensive accessories. Avenue Princesse-Grace has exclusive sports clubs, beach clubs and nightclubs. Near the Larvotto beach area is the Jardin Japonais, a Shinto garden and a quiet, meditative refuge from the glitz that is Monte-Carlo.

Unless you are into motor racing, don't come during the Grand Prix in May, when many thousands of visitors cram into the principality and many roads are closed.

HIGHLIGHTS

CASINO

✚ 131 D3 • Place du Casino, Monte-Carlo, 98000 Monaco ☎ 377 92 16 29 00
🕐 Daily from 12 noon, except Salons Privés, from 4pm 💶 €10, over 18s only
❓ Passport or similar required for entry. No casual dress in Salons Privés (a jacket and tie is obligatory for men after 9pm) 🅿 Underground parking area
www.casino-monte-carlo.com

The wedding-cake extravagance of the Casino, along with its spacious sunlit square front-edged with café tables and the beautiful gardens, make a set-piece of gloriously ostentatious turn-of-the-19th-century style. The smart, white-gloved police officers briskly waving on the traffic complement the scene. Inside the Casino, the first halls reached are the Salons Européens and Salons Américains, which have a less-than-glamorous feel with their slot machines. You must pay to go into the more lavish Salons Privés, which is the real casino. Here is an air of riches, with high stakes and a strict dress code—and few ordinary tourists. A grand staircase leads down to an expensive nightclub featuring slick and exotic cabaret. Attached to the Casino is the equally richly decorated Monte-Carlo Opera, created by the same architect, Charles Garnier (1825–1898).

RATINGS	
Photo stops	●●●○
Special interest (Grand Prix)	●●●●
Shopping	●●●○

BASICS

✚ 289 Q10
ℹ 2A boulevard des Moulins, Monte-Carlo, Monaco, tel 377 92 16 61 16; Mon–Sat 9–7, Sun 10–12. In summer, additional tourist information kiosks are set up at the railway station and main sites
🚉 Monaco (avenue Prince-Pierre)
🚌 Frequent bus services run the length of Monaco from 7am to 8pm (€1.40 for a single trip)

www.montecarloresort.com
A high-tech site in English capturing something of the Monte-Carlo lifestyle

- Monte-Carlo's open-air pool is the venue for many international swimming contests—and the view from the top diving board is excellent!
- Law enforcement is rigorous in Monaco, with 24-hour surveillance of the entire principality, including inside public buildings.
- All driving laws (and most other laws), road signs and drink-driving limits are the same in Monaco as in France.

THE SIGHTS

A café outside the Casino (bottom)

A doorman stands at the entrance of the Casino (below)

MUSÉE NATIONAL

⊞ 131 E2 • 17 avenue Princesse-Grace, 98000 Monaco ☎ 377 93 30 91 26
🕒 Easter–end Sep daily 10–6.30; Oct–Easter 10–12.15, 2.30–6.30. Closed the four days of the Grand Prix 💷 Adult €6, child (6–14) €3.50

A grand villa designed by Charles Garnier north of the Casino houses this curious, eclectic collection of hundreds of dolls. Most are 19th-century, with some dating back to the 18th century, but also some modern dolls. Dressed in impeccable period costume, they are amid miniature furnishings of their time. The most interesting and weird are automata—dolls that move. The mechanisms that work the dolls are fantastically delicate, and are open to view. The automata are set in motion several times a day. The museum also has a rose garden.

LARVOTTO

⊞ 131 E1

Take a break from sightseeing and lie on the beach. What Monaco does not have naturally, it creates artificially. The Larvotto area of Monte-Carlo, close to Beausoleil on the French side of the border, offers man-made beaches and swimming facilities. Next door is Le Sporting Club (including Jimmy'z nightclub), a legendary, exclusive 6ha (15-acre) seafront area. Making a sharp contrast, near the Larvotto beach is a space for quiet reflection at the extensive authentic Shinto garden called the Jardin Japonais (daily 9–sunset).

BACKGROUND

Until the 19th century, Monaco consisted of Monaco-Ville (on The Rock, ▷ 132–133) and La Condamine (at the foot of The Rock, ▷ 133). In 1866 Prince Carlo III set out to develop the territory along the remainder of the Monaco shore. The result was the glamorous new district called Monte-Carlo. The architect Charles Garnier was commissioned to create a casino in similar style to his acclaimed Paris Opera House. The casino opened in 1878 and succeeded so well in raising more funds for the royal family that all taxes were eventually abolished for Monaco citizens, and kept very low for other residents of the principality. Today, Monte-Carlo also hosts a large number of international fairs and festivals, as well as its Grand Prix motor races, which attract visitors from all over the world.

ALPES-DE-HAUTE-PROVENCE AND HAUTES-ALPES

Here the landscape becomes soaring mountains and lofty plateaux, with impressive natural sights including the Grand Canyon du Verdon. Trails lead through forests and open pastures. At even greater heights are the peaks of the High Alps. All is snow-covered in winter, though skiers can drive to the Riviera in under two hours.

MAJOR SIGHTS

THE SIGHTS

Mountain peaks in the Val d'Allos

A glimpse of the mountains at the end of a Barcelonnette road

THE SIGHTS

ALLOS AND VAL D'ALLOS

➕ 283 M7 ℹ️ Place du Presbytère, 04260 Val d'Allos, tel 04 92 83 02 81 or 04 92 83 80 70; winter and summer daily 8.30–12, 2–6.30; autumn and spring Mon–Sat 9–12, 2–5, Sun 9–12 www.valdallos.com

The Allos valley is a large modern mountain resort area just south of the Col d'Allos pass, on the edge of the beautiful Parc National du Mercantour. In winter it's the largest skiable area in the southern Alps; in summer it's a good starting point for walks and drives.

On the northern side is the Alpine-style resort called Val d'Allos 1800 (or La Foux). To the south is the sports-based Val d'Allos 1500 (or Le Seignus). It is next to Val d'Allos 1400 (or Allos), the valley's original village. The greener lower slopes, formerly sheep pastures, are now dotted with ski chalets and summer holiday homes.

The most important outing is to the spectacularly beautiful Lac d'Allos, in the peaks to the east of Allos village. Located at 2,220m (7,300ft), and covering some 60ha (150 acres), it's the largest lake in the High Alps. To reach the lake involves a 15km (9-mile) drive zig-zagging upwards on the D266 (open mid-Jun to mid-Oct only), then a walk of some 40 minutes to the amphitheatre of slopes looking across the lake itself. Its still water, reflecting the surrounding peaks like a giant mirror, is so cold that, reputedly, nothing can grow in it.

BARCELONNETTE

➕ 283 M6 ℹ️ Place Frédéric Mistral, 04400 Barcelonnette, tel 04 92 81 04 71; Jul, Aug daily 9–8; May, Jun, Sep-end Nov Mon–Sat 9–12, 2–6; Dec–end Apr daily 9–12, 2–7 www.barcelonnette.com

Far up in the Alpine northern limits of Provence, close to ski resorts, this tranquil and rather remote old town is surrounded by high peaks, tiny farms and mountain meadows. The town, in the valley of Ubaye, is well worth seeing for its curious Mexican cultural connection.

The Mexican link arose by chance in the 19th century, when many local young men went to Mexico to seek their fortunes. The first were the two Arnaud brothers, Jacques and Marc-Antoine, whose huge financial success tempted others to follow in their footsteps. In Mexico itself, the men of Barcelonnette and its nearby villages assisted each other and many had a degree of success—a few even became millionaires. After some years, a number of them returned to the Provençal Alps, building houses in a strange mix of styles reflecting their New World culture and prosperity.

Barcelonnette is especially popular in summer as a starting point for walks and drives into the Mercantour National Park (▷ 122–123). The Maison du Parc, near the heart of town, is an information point for the park. Downstream from the town, organizations offer kayaking, canoeing and rafting.

Barcelonnette was built by the Counts of Barcelona (hence its name) and vestiges survive of their 13th-century fortifications. It is a picturesque and atmospheric town, with cobbled lanes and small squares. Place Manuel, the main square, is especially attractive, surrounded by old buildings. There are fine old houses in several streets, as well as villas in a bizarre mix of styles influenced by the town's Latin American links. The Musée de la Vallée de l'Ubaye, in avenue de la Libération, (Jul, Aug Tue–Sat 10–12, 2.30–7; Sep–end Jun

Tue–Sat 2.30–6), itself in one of the Mexican villas, tells the town's story.
Don't miss Wander along avenue de la Libération to see some of the grander Mexican houses.

BRIANÇON

➕ 280 M3 ℹ️ 1 place du Temple, 05100 Briançon, tel 04 92 21 08 50; Mon–Sat 9–12, 2–6, Sun 10–12.30, 3–5 🚇 Briançon www.ot-briancon.fr

Briançon is the highest town in Europe, at 1,320m (4,330ft), and is surrounded by mountain peaks. Two national parks, the Parc National des Écrins and Parc National Régional du Queyras, are in the surrounding area.

The town is on the Col de Montgenèvre, one of the major Alpine passes linking France and Italy, and has been settled since pre-Roman times. It now promotes itself as a ski station of the Serre Chevalier ski area, with more than 250km (155 miles) of ski runs between four villages.

At the end of the 17th century Louis XIV's military planner, Vauban, turned Briançon's old medieval town into an impenetrable walled city. Now known as Cité Vauban, this area is traffic free and the focus of visitor interest. Go through Porte de Pignerol into Grande Rue, with its impressive houses.

Other highlights include the Maison des Templier (which houses the tourist information office), the 14th-century Église des Cordeliers and the Fort du Château, where 19th-century defences replaced the last vestiges of the original chateau, built in the 11th century. The 18th-century Collégiale (Notre-Dame de St-Nicolas) was built to Vauban's design, with its strong walls as much for protection as for worship.

Castellane's Notre-Dame du Roc, dwarfed by the rock on which it sits

CASTELLANE

🔲 287 L10 ℹ️ 34 rue Nationale, 04120 Castellane, tel 04 92 83 61 14; Jul, Aug Mon–Sat 9–12.30, 2–7, Sun 9–12.30; Sep–end Jun Mon–Sat 9.15–12, 2–6
www.castellane.org

In some ways a typical attractive old Provençal hill town arranged around a main square, Castellane becomes exceptional because of its dramatic location. It stands on the Route Napoléon (the Emperor rested here on 3 March 1815) and is the key starting and finishing point for a trip along the Grand Canyon du Verdon (▷ 142–145).

Alongside the town, and rising above it, soars a remarkable narrow ridge of rock, 184m (603ft) high, with the chapel of Notre-Dame du Roc perched on the top. Though a steep climb, it's accessible on a trail that winds up to the summit. The walk takes about 30 minutes. The old town of Castellane was once fortified, and has remnants of its 14th-century walls. The town is a little bit spoiled by tourism: It is incongruously surrounded by campsites and is terribly crowded in summer.

COLMARS

🔲 287 M8 ℹ️ Place Joseph Girieud, 04370 Colmars, tel 04 92 83 41 92; Jul, Aug daily 8–12.30, 2–6.30; Sep–end Jun Tue–Sat 9–12, 2–5.45
www.verdon-provence.com/hautverdon.htm

Colmars is a lovely old fortified town nestled amid woodland and mountain peaks just down the Haut Verdon Valley from Allos (▷ 138). It is dominated by two forts, the Fort de France to the south and the Fort de Savoie to the north, built at the end of the 17th century, when the border town faced constant attacks by the Savoyards.

The striking west front of Notre-Dame du Bourg

DIGNE-LES-BAINS

This bright, airy, prosperous spa resort is the largest town in the mountainous backcountry of Provence.

🔲 287 K8 ℹ️ Place du Tampinet, 04000 Digne-les-Bains, tel 04 92 36 62 62; Jul, Aug Mon–Sat 8.45–12.30, 1.30–6.30; Sun 9–12.30, 4–6.30; Sep–end Jun Mon–Sat 8.45–12, 2–6
🚉 Digne
www.ot-dignelesbains.fr

RATINGS	
Health and Beauty	●●●●
Photo stops	●●●
Specialist shopping	●●●●

TIP

● The town hosts a lavender festival, the *Corso de Lavande*, for five days in early August.

Digne is an excellent base for touring the hills by foot, by car or on the old narrow-gauge Chemin de Fer de Provence railway that connects the town to Nice. A spa during Roman times, Digne flourished into the Middle Ages, as can be seen from the large, beautiful 12th-century Romanesque church, Notre-Dame du Bourg, in the main boulevard. The old town, which also has some modern buildings, encloses a crumbling 15th-century hilltop Gothic cathedral, St-Jerome.

SPA
At Digne's renowned ultra-modern spa (▷ 199), 3km (2 miles) south of town, you can enjoy anti-stress remedies and other treatments. The natural mineral waters emerge from eight hot springs and one cold spring. In town, a 150-year-old 'Great Fountain' in boulevard Gassendi is heavily cloaked with deposits from the calcium-rich water.

MUSEUMS
The Musée de la Seconde Guerre Mondiale (Museum of World War II), in place Paradis, is in a former bomb shelter carved into the mountain (Jul, Aug Mon–Fri 2–6; mid-Apr to end Jun, Sep to mid-Nov Wed 2–5). Here you can learn about Digne's curious fate during the war, when it was occupied by the Italians. Out of town, at 27 avenue Maréchal Juin, is a Tibetan museum, the Fondation Alexandra David-Neel (Jul–end Sep tours daily at 10, 2, 3.30, 4.30; Oct–end Jun tours daily at 10, 2, 4). It is named after the explorer who established it in the 1980s.

Don't miss Digne is the lavender capital of Provence and you can buy wonderful lavender products at the market on Wednesdays and Saturdays, in place du Général-de-Gaulle.

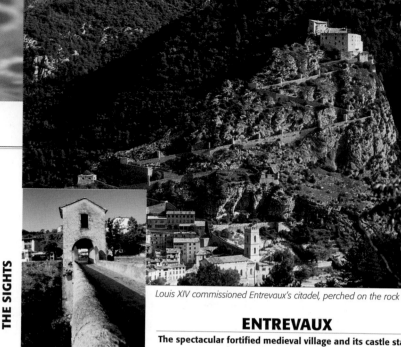

Louis XIV commissioned Entrevaux's citadel, perched on the rock

A fortified bridge

RATINGS	
Historic interest	●●●○
Photo stops	●●●○
Walkability	●●●○

BASICS

✚ 288 N9

🛈 La Mairie, 04320 Entrevaux, tel 04 93 05 46 73; Jul, Aug daily 9–6.30; mid-Jan to end Jun, Sep, Oct Mon–Fri 9–12, 2–5.30. Closed Nov to mid-Jan

🚆 Entrevaux (on the Chemins de Fer de Provence line from Digne to Nice)

TIP

• The village hosts concerts and festivals in summer.

A carving from the cathedral

ENTREVAUX

The spectacular fortified medieval village and its castle stand guard over a dramatic mountain scene.

Entrevaux, above a narrow gorge in the mountains between Nice and Digne, is an impressive sight. The compact medieval village—originally a Ligurian settlement, then a Roman garrison—has a fortified draw-bridge and an awesome 17th-century citadel. Approaching Entrevaux from either direction along the Var valley, it is easy to see why it was such an important town in the 17th century, when this was the French border with Savoy. The gorges here narrow to just a few hundred metres across—plug this and you block a major route between France and Savoy. On the west bank of the Var, a jagged curtain of rock makes the hillside impassable. On the east bank, this natural barrier is reflected in the grand fortifications, built by Vauban, Louis XIV's military architect, which zigzag up to La Citadelle, perched 135m (440ft) above the town.

CITÉ VAUBAN

The main access to the town is via a fortified single-arch river bridge, built by Vauban, which enters through the Porte Nationale or Porte Royale. A remarkable ramp, strikingly punctuated by a score of bastions, goes from the town up a sheer rock face to reach Vauban's ruined Citadelle, crowning a steep crest of rock. There is little to see at the fortress, but the view is exceptional. Vauban's work started in 1692 and was completed in 1706. When Napoleon Bonaparte annexed the County of Nice to France, Vauban's defences became redundant and the village returned to its previous obscurity, but with its remarkable legacy of military architecture. During most of the 19th and 20th centuries, Entrevaux was unknown, and few visitors found their way here. In recent years, the dramatic setting and Vauban's work have been rediscovered, and Entrevaux has been revitalized.

THE OLD TOWN

Within the town walls, the narrow streets keep their historic appearance, especially around the fortified cathedral, the walls of which form part of the city's defences. The town's other gateway, Porte d'Italie, opens onto a pleasant riverside walk. There's plenty to see around the village, including a restored oil mill and flour mill, a communal bread oven and a collection of historic motorcycles. Much restoration is under way throughout the village.

Red-roofed buildings climb the hillside (above).
An angel seranades the town from the roof of the Chapelle Notre-Dame-de-Provence (right)

FORCALQUIER

A historic town in beautiful hill country, Forcalquier makes a popular base for bicyclists and walkers.

This quiet, attractive market town in the Provençal hills has a peaceful hardworking atmosphere. Originally a small Roman town, it became the seat of a powerful independent county controlling a wide area in the 12th century and was capital of Haute-Provence from the end of the 11th century to the beginning of the 13th century. Its old buildings are reminders of these times. Today, the surrounding countryside attracts bicyclists and walkers, who set off on the many marked trails.

EXPLORING THE TOWN

The former citadel is raised up on a hill, but everything has now vanished except the ruins of just one tower. In town, in place du Bourguet, the large Romanesque and Gothic Cathédrale Notre-Dame du Marché, dating partly from the 12th century, survives. South of the cathedral is the old quarter, including what was once an enclosed Jewish ghetto. The convent in place du Bourguet now houses a cinema and the Musée Municipal (Apr–end Sep Thu–Mon 3–6), with displays of local costumes, furnishings and other examples of folk culture. Outside the town gate (the Porte des Cordeliers) is the Couvent des Cordeliers, in boulevard des Martyres (one-hour guided tours Jul to mid-Sep Wed–Mon 10, 2.30, 4.30; May, Jun, mid-Sep to Oct Sun 2.30, 4), a 12th-century monastery much changed in modern times, though with fine cloisters. It is one of the oldest Franciscan monasteries in France.

STAR-GAZING

The Observatoire de Haute-Provence sits on a plateau southwest of Forcalquier, near the village of St-Michel-l'Observatoire. Its 14 domes house various telescopes pointed at the stars. You can take tours on Wednesday afternoons (tel 04 92 70 64 00), although as it's daylight you're unlikely to discover any new constellations. The observatory was built here in 1936, after experts spent much effort hunting for the place in Provence with the clearest atmosphere.

Don't miss Forcalquier's citadel gives sweeping views across the surrounding countryside.

RATINGS

Historic interest	●●●
Photo stops	●●●●
Walkability	●●●

BASICS

⊞ 286 H9

🗓 L'Office de Tourisme Intercommunal du Pays de Forcalquier et Montagne de Lure, 13 place du Bourguet, 04310 Forcalquier, tel 04 92 75 10 02; mid-Jun to mid-Sep Mon–Sat 9–12.30, 2–7, Sun 10–1; mid-Sep to mid-Jun Mon–Sat 9–12, 2–6

www.forcalquier.com
An unpretentious website in English and French, with local information including plenty about the surrounding countryside

TIPS

● Breathe deeply—Forcalquier is said to have the cleanest air in France.
● There's a big market on Mondays.
● The tourist office organizes tours of the old town, citadel, cathedral and town hall.

Grand Canyon du Verdon

The plunging ravine of the river Verdon, 21km (13 miles) long and edged on each side by narrow clifftop roads, is one of the most dramatic natural sights in Europe.

THE SIGHTS

RATINGS	
Outdoor activities	●●●○
Photo stops	●●●●●
Walkability	●●●○

BASICS
✚ 287 K10
ℹ Hôtel-Dieu, rue de la Bourgade, 04360 Moustiers-Sainte-Marie (western edge of canyon), tel 04 92 74 67 84; Apr–end Sep 9.30–12.30, 2–7.30; Oct–end Mar 10–12, 2–5

www.ville-moustiers-sainte-marie.fr
www.castellane.org

TIPS
● Even a short drive along the Corniche Sublime is enough to be very impressive.
● For a drive alongside the canyon ▷ 221–223.
● On the canyon's south side, Balcons de la Mescla on the Corniche Sublime gives the best view.
● On the north bank, the Route des Crêtes drive and the *Point Sublime* are highlights.

Climbing the cliffs high above the Lac de Sainte-Croix (right).
Taking to the water (right, below)

SEEING THE GRAND CANYON DU VERDON

One of the most spectacular natural phenomena in Europe is the gorge of the river Verdon, in inland Provence, in recent years promoted by tourist offices as the 'Grand Canyon' of the Verdon. The town of Moustiers-Sainte-Marie (▷ 145) is at the western end of the gorge and Castellane (▷ 139) is near the eastern end. From both these towns, winding, difficult roads—little more than country lanes—run along the top of each side of the ravine, sometimes close to the edge. These reach a succession of breathtaking viewpoints giving fantastic vistas along the ravine and across the rocky terrain. Try to avoid July and August, when there is nose-to-tail traffic.

A fantastic way to see the canyon is on foot—a path runs the full length, although be ready for narrow ledges and dark tunnels. Always take a torch (flashlight), sweater, water and food, and beware of sudden changes in water levels due to upstream power stations. Wear suitable footwear and use bridges to cross the river. The paths are not suitable for children or for dogs. Before you set out, ask for the walking routes from the tourist offices at Moustiers-Sainte-Marie or Castellane. Kayaking and canoeing are other adventurous options, but you should try them only if you have an official guide and are proficient. You can rent kayaks from Castellane and Belvédère de Galetas.

HIGHLIGHTS

SOUTH BANK
The south side, called the Corniche Sublime, has the grander scenery and a string of better viewpoints. Along the winding road at the top of the canyon, several of these pull-offs and *points sublimes* allow you to linger over the view. One reason why this is more rewarding on the south side of the river is that the road is closer to the cliff edge for more of the distance. The best stretch here is called the Balcons de la Mescla, at the east end of the Corniche Sublime.

NORTH BANK
The north side is also extremely impressive, but the road is more hair-raising and there are fewer viewpoints, although the north bank's *Point Sublime* is perhaps the very best location on either side. What you see is rock face dropping sometimes more-or-less vertically several hundred metres down to the slender river at the bottom.

BACKGROUND

Rising just above La Foux d'Allos in the Mont des Trois Evêchés, the Verdon river flows south before looping west above Castellane to carve its way through the limestone plateau of Haute-Provence on its way to the river Durance. Between Castellane and Moustiers-Sainte-Marie the river has hewn the spectacular Grand Canyon into the plateau. From sheer cliffs some 700m (2,300ft) above the flowing river there are panoramic views down the length of this rocky corridor.

The first inhabitants of the gorges were the Ligurians, followed centuries later by shepherds fleeing the Saracens. 'Wild men' were said to live in the caves in the Middle Ages. The eminent speleologist E. A. Martel carried out the first scientific expedition to the gorges in 1905—it took him more than three days to travel the length, armed with a canoe, climbing rope and cameras. The first paths and viewpoints were constructed shortly after, and in 1947 the Corniche Sublime road was built on the south side. In 1997 the Gorges du Verdon became a Parc Naturel Régional but the theoretical protection this gives is sometimes hard to appreciate amid the heavy traffic that crawls along the road in summer.

The medieval village of Mane, watched over by its fortress

Pulpit carvings in Notre-Dame de Romigier, Manosque

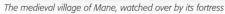

THE SIGHTS

GAP

✚ 281 J5 🛈 2a cours Frédéric Mistral, 05000 Gap, tel 04 92 52 56 56; Jul, Aug Mon–Sat 9–7; Sun 9.30–12.30; Sep–end Jun Mon–Sat 8.30–12.30, 2–6 🚆 Gap
www.ville-gap.fr

At an altitude of 750m (2,500ft), Gap is the highest *département* capital in France. The town, capital of the Hautes-Alpes, enjoys a climate that gives excellent skiing conditions in winter and Provençal warmth in summer.

The Romans established Gap in the first century AD, and 18 centuries later Napoleon Bonaparte spent a night here on his route back to Paris from Elba. For reminders of the town's history, head to rue Jean Eymar, now one of the main shopping streets, which has houses built along the ramparts, the town's oldest window, a small sundial and a washhouse.

Just outside town is the 220ha (500-acre) Charance Botanical Garden (mid-Apr to end May, Sep, Oct Wed–Mon 2–5; Jun–end Aug Wed–Mon 10–12, 2–6.30). It grows more than 3,000 species of wild mountain flowers and houses the world's largest collection of old roses. Its terraced gardens were listed as a historic monument in 1988.

Extending northeast of Gap is the Parc National des Écrins, one of France's largest but lesser-known parks, where hiking, rafting and hang-gliding are just three of the activities available.

GRAND CANYON DU VERDON

See pages 142–143.

GRÉOUX-LES-BAINS

✚ 286 J10 🛈 5 avenue des Marronniers, 04800 Gréoux-les-Bains, tel 04 92 78 01 08; Jul, Aug Mon–Sat 9–12, 2–6.30, Sun 9–12, 4–6; Apr–end Jun, Sep, Oct Mon–Sat 9–12, 2–6, Sun 9–12; Nov–end Mar Mon–Fri 9–12, 2–6, Sat 9–12, 2–5
www.greoux-les-bains.com

Around 3 million litres (660,000 gallons) a day emerge from the Gréoux springs, at an average temperature of 36°C (97°F). The Romans built spa baths here in the second century AD. They were reopened in the 17th century and were fashionable in the 19th after a stay by Napoleon Bonaparte's sister. They were entirely rebuilt in 1962 (▷ 200).

Gréoux is dominated by its ruined 12th-century castle of the Knights Templar. The pleasant old streets of the village have many art galleries and craft shops. See vivid stained glass and mosaics at the Atelier Musée du Vitrail et de la Mosaïque, in Grande Rue. In the same road is the Maison de Pauline, a typical Provençal house with traditional furnishings. The Crèche de Haute-Provence, outside Gréoux on the avenue des Alpes, is a miniature village with *santons*.

LURS

✚ 286 J9 🛈 Place de la Fontaine, 04700 Lurs, tel 04 92 79 10 20; Apr, Jun–end Sep; rest of year tel 04 92 79 95 24

Lurs, high above the west bank of the Durance, owes its survival to a group of graphic designers and printers. In the Middle Ages the village was summer home to the Bishops of Sisteron, but by the 20th century its fortunes had plummeted and local people had abandoned it because of its lack of electricity and water. It was saved from oblivion by the designers and printers, led by typographer Maximilian Vox, who moved in after World War II. The whole village, with its neatly kept streets and attractive houses, is now classified as a historic site.

In the last two weeks of August, Lurs hosts the prestigious Rencontre Internationale de Lure, aimed at graphic designers, photographers and printers.

MANE

✚ 286 H9

This medieval village, on a hill 4km (2.5 miles) south of Forcalquier, is dominated by its 12th- to 15th-century fortress. There's also a 16th-century church and a well-preserved old quarter, but the highlight is the Romanesque Prieuré de Salagon, a remarkable medieval priory outside the village on the N100. It has a lovely medicinal herb garden and also houses the Musée-Conservatoire Ethnologique de Haute-Provence (May–end Sep daily 10–12, 2–7; Oct–end Apr Sat, Sun 2–6), dedicated to the preservation of local tradition. Farther along the same road, the palatial Château de Sauvan, built in 1720 in Classical style, has lavish interiors and extensive gardens.

MANOSQUE

✚ 286 H10 🛈 Place du Docteur Joubert, 04100 Manosque, tel 04 92 72 16 00; mid-Jun to mid-Sep Mon–Sat 9–1, 2–7, Sun 10–12; mid-Sep to mid-Jun Mon–Sat 9–12.15, 1.30–6 🚆 Manosque.
www.manosque-tourisme.com

Penetrate the industrial periphery of this large town, on the banks of the Durance, to reach the appealing old quarter at its heart, entered via the 14th-century Porte Saunerie. The pedestrian-only rue Grande is the main street, lined with shops. It hosts a market on Monday, Wednesday, Friday and Saturday mornings. **Don't miss** Église Notre-Dame de Romigier has a sixth-century black wood Virgin (▷ 25) and a Renaissance carved doorway.

MOUSTIERS-SAINTE-MARIE

An exceptional village in a striking location, Moustiers clings to a river gorge in wild rocky hills.

Moustiers is one of the main access points for driving along the Grand Canyon du Verdon (▷ 142–143) and stands at the edge of a large lake, Lac de Sainte-Croix, an attractive and popular holiday area with trails, bicycle rental, horseback riding and water sports. But this sun-basking village makes a phenomenal sight in its own right. It is in rugged landscape beside a gorge, watched over by a chapel standing prominently on a rocky ledge. Most remarkable of all, a long chain strung across the gorge suspends a gilded star high above the village.

FAÏENCE
The village has long been famous for its high-quality glazed ceramics, known as faïences. The faïence industry dates from 1668, when, according to legend, a local potter learned the secrets of glazed ceramics from an Italian monk. Faïence manufacturing died out at the Revolution, but was revived in the 1920s. To see precious 17th- and 18th-century Moustiers work, as well as modern faïence, visit the Musée de la Faïence, in the town hall (Jul, Aug 9–12, 2–7; Apr–end Jun, Sep, Oct 9–12, 2–6). The village also has many shops selling pottery and workshops where you can buy straight from the producer.

CHAPEL AND STAR
The village came into being after monks from the Îles de Lérins (▷ 108) settled here in the fifth century AD. The monastic site was replaced in the 12th century by a chapel, Notre-Dame de Beauvoir, subsequently altered. The present building, a pleasant 20-minute walk from the heart of the village, dates mainly from the 12th and 16th centuries and has a Renaissance doorway and Romanesque and Gothic interior. There are two annual pilgrimages to the chapel. The famous star was originally an offering by a 12th-century seigneur of the Blacas family to Notre-Dame de Beauvoir in thanks for his free-dom from captivity. The star (and its chain) have been replaced several times and the tradition of keeping it there is now sacrosanct.

THE VILLAGE
Red-tiled old houses huddle along a tangle of vaulted alleys, narrow lanes and stairways arranged up the ravine's steep slopes. There's an attractive church with a landmark Italianate bell tower; originally 12th century, reworked in the 14th and 16th centuries, the church has a Romanesque porch, Romanesque nave and Gothic choir.

Moustiers is known for its vividly decorated faïences (above)

Notre-Dame de Beauvoir chapel, high above the village (top)

RATINGS	
Outdoor activities	●●●○
Photo stops	●●●○
Specialist shopping	●●●○
Walkability	●●●○

BASICS
⊞ 287 K10
🛈 Hôtel-Dieu, rue de la Bourgade, 04360 Moustiers-Sainte-Marie, tel 04 92 74 67 84; Apr–end Sep daily 9.30–12.30, 2–7.30; Oct–end Mar daily 10–12, 2–5

www.ville-moustiers-sainte-marie.fr
A straightforward, informative site in English and French about the village and its attractions.

TIPS
● Highlight of the year is the week-long Diana festival in September, ending with the *Fête de la Nativité* procession to the chapel on 8 September.
● It's worth walking up to the chapel, if only to see the fantastic view.

The capital of a Roman column in Riez-la-Romaine

RIEZ-LA-ROMAINE

➕ 286 K10 ℹ️ 4 allée Louis Gardiol, 04500 Riez, tel 04 92 77 99 09; Mon–Sat 9–1, 3–7, Sun 9–1
www.ville-riez.fr

Riez, on the road from Gréoux to Moustiers (D952) as it crosses the high Valensole plateau, was originally a Roman trading town. Four Corinthian marble columns of a temple to Apollo, standing incongruously in a field on the edge of town, are the sole visible remnant of that era. In the fifth century AD, the Roman baths were used as the foundation for a baptistery (ask at the tourist office if you would like to visit), one of a handful of Merovingian structures surviving in France. Inside is a small museum and alongside are early Christian ruins. To see more than 2,000 fossils and rocks, head to the Musée Nature en Provence, in the tourist office.

There are Renaissance houses in Grand Rue, while the side streets have workshops making *santons* (figurines) and pottery. The village hosts a truffle market on Wednesdays in winter.

SIMIANE-LA-ROTONDE

➕ 285 G9 ℹ️ Mairie, 04150 Simiane-la-Rotonde, tel 04 92 75 91 40
www.simiane.free.fr

Picturesque Simiane-la-Rotonde takes its name from a curious, truncated rotunda at the summit of the village. The 12th-century Rotonde is one of the few pieces of non-religious Romanesque architecture left in Provence.

The village winds around a little hill on the edge of the plateau separating Haute-Provence and the Vaucluse. Farmland and scenic lavender fields surround it.
Don't miss The Rotonde has a wonderful domed ceiling and carvings on the columns.

SISTERON

Here is an intriguing old town, a remarkable setting and an impressive hilltop Citadel with a wonderful view.

➕ 286 J8 ℹ️ Place de la République, 04200 Sisteron, tel 04 92 61 36 50; Jul, Aug Mon–Sat 9–7, Sun 10–1; Sep–end Jun Mon–Sat 9–12, 2–6
www.sisteron.com

RATINGS				
Historic interest	●	●	●	●
Photo stops	●	●	●	●	●
Walkability	●	●	●	

Sisteron, on the Route Napoléon (N85), stands at the frontier of Haute-Provence in a stupendous setting. The Alpine-Italianate town straddles the river Bévéra, in a narrow valley edged by cliffs, known as a *clue*. The cliffs are high, almost vertical and dramatically scored with the hues of various geological strata. The *clue* is fortified and watched over by the citadel because it once marked the border between Provence and Dauphiné. An 11th-century bridge connects the two sides of the town and was once a tollgate. From the road bridge farther down the river there is a lovely view of the tollgate bridge and the mountains behind it.

THE OLD TOWN
The fortified *vieille ville*, or old town, with five towers surviving from what was once a complete ring of defences, occupies a vantage point overlooking the rocky ravine. Inside the old quarter is a tangle of stepped alleys, narrow streets and covered passageways, known locally as *androns*. There's an attractive and interesting Romanesque church—the 12th-century Notre-Dame des Pommiers—a strong, simple building with later additions.

THE CITADEL
Sisteron's gaunt citadel (mid-Mar to mid-Nov daily 10–6) stands on a high ridge overlooking the town, its walls narrowing as they follow the rocky ledge. What remains—gates, towers, bastions—is very impressive. Napoleon Bonaparte stopped here on his march back to Paris in 1815. The citadel survived until World War II, when the Nazis used it as a garrison, strategic base and prison. Destroyed by Allied bombers on 15 August 1944, all that remains are the outer walls and the stupendous view.

Don't miss The citadel is well worth the climb.

Napoleon Bonaparte was among the visitors to Sisteron's citadel

THE SIGHTS

VAUCLUSE

Vaucluse is the Provence of old villages under russet roofs and dazzling purple lavender under sheer blue sky. There are good country restaurants, numerous Roman ruins and hills cloaked in fragrant wilderness.
The vibrant city of Avignon, the popes' residence in the 14th century, still dominates the region culturally, economically and spiritually.

Rémuzat
D94
Valréas
Nyons
D994
Suze-la-Rousse
St-Auban-sur-l'Ouvèze
Bollène
Vaison-la-Romaine
Sérignan-du-Comtat
Malaucène
Sèderon
D542
Bagnols-sur-Cèze
Orange
Mont Vento
Sault
Noyers-sur-Jabron
Carpentras
Mazan
D950
Châteauneuf-du-Pape
Pernes-les-Fontaines
Simiane-la-Rotonde
Lurs
Remoulins
Avignon
Abbaye de Sénanque
St-Saturnin-les-Apt
Fontaine-de-Vaucluse
Roussillon
Mane
Barbentane
Gordes
Apt
Manosque
Tarascon
N100
Saignon
St-Rémy-de-Provence
Cadenet
Ansouis
Les Baux-de-Provence
Sénas
Pertuis
Arles
Salon-de-Provence
Barben
Moyrargues
E80 A54
Miramas-le-Vieux
E80 Aix-en Provence
A8

The Abbaye de Sénanque is surrounded by lavender fields

ABBAYE DE SÉNANQUE

One of the 'Three Sisters' of the Cistercians in Provence, this abbey has a pure and simple beauty.

The Abbaye de Sénanque stands in the quiet, attractively wooded little valley of the Senancole, 4km (2.5 miles) upstream from Gordes (▷ 157) at the foot of the Plateau of Vaucluse. Lavender is cultivated beside it, beautiful with bright purple blooms in early summer. The honeyed stone abbey was built in the 12th century by the Cistercian Order, as the third—and last—of their monasteries in Provence. The three monasteries were known as the 'Three Cistercian Sisters of Provence'. The other two were Silvacane (▷ 55) and Le Thoronet (▷ 89). The sturdy, unadorned Romanesque main building is a perfect example of the Cistercian style.

AN ENDURING COMMUNITY

The community dedicated itself to austerity and hard work, received many gifts and prospered for a period. It went into decline after being attacked by the local sect known as the Vaudois in 1544. However, the damaged buildings were repaired at the beginning of the 18th century, and the monastery survived. It has remained in continuous occupation throughout its history, except for 60 years following the anti-religious violence of the French Revolution and also in the years 1969–88.

MONASTIC LIFE

The abbey buildings at Sénanque today are still partly occupied by a Cistercian monastery, with a pious atmosphere and a rule of silence—which visitors too are requested to respect. Notices advise that Sénanque abbey is not a tourist site but a place of monastic life. At present, all visitors must join a guided tour (in French only). Off the central courtyard extends a long, cool stone dormitory block under a barrel vault: Here 30 monks would sleep—fully clothed—on straw mattresses on the floor. This leads into the abbey church, its extremely plain appearance slightly softened by the rounded lines of the Romanesque pillars and arches. There is some modern stained glass, in a suitably simple style, added in 1994. The church is almost unique in facing north instead of east. Outside, the cloisters are at the heart of the abbey. The cloister pillars are decorated with carved capitals with simplified motifs of flowers and foliage.

RATINGS		
Historic interest	● ● ●	
Photo stops	● ● ● ●	
Walkability	● ● ●	

BASICS

✚ 285 F9 • Abbaye Notre-Dame de Sénanque, 84220 Gordes

☎ 04 90 72 05 72

◉ Mar–end Oct Mon–Sat 10–12, 2–6, Sun 2–6; Nov–end Feb Mon–Fri 2–5, Sat, Sun 2–6

💶 Adult €6, child (6–18) €2.50, under 6 free

🅿

🎫 All visitors must join a guided tour (in French)

🏛

🚻

www.senanque.fr

A simple, unpretentious multilingual website, with plenty of information for visitors.

TIPS

● After your visit, take the opportunity to buy lavender oils and soaps, handmade by the monks.

● Closure at 12 and 5 or 6 is very prompt.

● Dress modestly.

A golden saint watches over the Cathédrale Sainte-Anne, Apt

APT

➕ 285 G9 ℹ️ 20 avenue Philippe de Girard, 84400 Apt, tel 04 90 74 03 18; Jul, Aug Mon–Sat 9–7, Sun 9.30–12.30; May, Jun, Sep Mon–Sat 9–12, 2–6, Sun 9.30–12.30; Oct–end Apr Mon–Fri 9–12, 2–6
www.ot-apt.fr

Apt is a busy, lightly industrial country town, with tree-shaded squares, fountains and a vibrant street market every Saturday. It's the main town for the Lubéron area and has Roman origins. Its prosperity is partly thanks to agriculture, although ochre-processing is also important to the town—the ochre quarries are nearby.

The heart of Apt has the typical appearance of a busy Provençal inland town, with stone houses, red-tile roofs, narrow old streets and pretty squares. The main square is place de la Bouquerie.

Apt's main sight is the former cathedral church of Sainte-Anne, whose two crypts date from the 4th and 11th centuries. Two 14th-century stained-glass windows at the end of the apse depict St. Anne. Next door to the church is the 16th-century Tour de l'Horloge, straddling the rue des Marchands.

Apt was once noted for faïence with a distinctive marbled design, and examples of this fine workmanship can be seen, along with other items, in the modest Musée de l'Aventure Industrielle, in place du Pestel (Jun–end Sep Mon, Wed–Sat 10–12, 3–6.30; Oct–end May Mon, Wed–Sat 10–12, 2–5.30).

Place Jean Jaurès is home to the Maison du Parc du Lubéron, an information point for the Lubéron Regional Park.
Don't miss Apt is especially known for its crystallized fruit and fruit preserves.

A flag flies at the palatial chateau

ANSOUIS

This village lies prettily at the foot of one of the three great Renaissance chateaux of the Lubéron.

➕ 292 G10 ℹ️ Place du Château, 84240 Ansouis, tel 04 90 09 86 98; Feb–end Dec daily 10–12, 2–6. Closed every second Monday
www.ansouis.fr

RATINGS			
Historic interest	●	●	●
Photo stops	●	●	●
Walkability	●	●	●

Ansouis is well off the beaten track, 5km (3 miles) from the D973 midway between the small towns of Cadenet and Pertuis. The village is on the south facing side of a rocky crest on the summit of which stands a palatial chateau (Jul–end Sep daily 2–6; Easter–end Jun, Sep, Oct Wed–Mon 2–6; Nov–Easter Sun 2–6) Originally a 12th-century fortress, it was modernized and made more elegant during the Renaissance, and has remained the private home of the Sabran-Pontevès family for several centuries. More of a large country house than a castle, it has impressive halls and rooms, a large kitchen and superb formal gardens arranged on terraces (closed to visitors).

DUAL-IDENTITY CHATEAU
Viewing the chateau from the north, you're faced with an impenetrable fortress, part of the original building. But as you move round the exterior, the scene changes to an 18th-century mansion, with gardens and terraces shaded with chestnut trees. The interior, too, reflects this dual identity. There are reminders of the chateau's fortress days on the ground floor, with its weapons and armour. Upstairs, there are Flemish tapestries and elegant pieces of Italian-Renaissance furniture. The Provençal kitchen dates from the 18th century and is still in use today. Visitors are not allowed access to the exquisite garden, but you can get a lovely view of it from the upstairs gallery.

A CELIBATE COUPLE
St-Martin's church, next to the chateau, contains busts of two 13th-century saints, St. Delphine and St. Elzéar. Delpine, the daughter of an aristocratic family, took a vow of chastity as a young woman and nothing—not even marriage—pursuaded her to break it. She accepted a politically arranged marriage with Elzéar, son of the Sabran family, in a deal intended to unite support for Charles II of Naples, but she kept her chastity pledge. Elzéar also made a pledge, and the pious pair lived together in celibacy, although Elzéar soon died. Delphine lived another 37 years, patiently enduring poverty and carrying out good works.

Avignon

Romantic, riverside Avignon, with its massive stone fortifications, nursery-rhyme bridge and towering fortress of the medieval popes, has a long tradition of vivacity, art, culture and joie de vivre.

The Pont St-Bénézet reaches only part-way across the river

A tree-shaded outdoor café

See wonderful medieval art in the Petit Palais

RATINGS

Cultural interest	●●●●○
Historic interest	●●●●○
Photo stops	●●●●○
Walkability	●●●●○

BASICS

✚ 284 D9

🛈 41 cours Jean-Jaurès 84004 Avignon, tel 04 32 74 32 74; Apr–end Sep Mon–Sat 9–6, Sun 10–5; Oct–end Mar Mon–Fri 9–6, Sat 9–5, Sun 10–12

🚉 Main station in boulevard St-Rochand; TGV station 5km (3 miles) from the middle of the city

www.ot-avignon.fr
In English and French, with information on shopping, river cruises, hotels and museums.

SEEING AVIGNON

Several things give Avignon terrific appeal. It is easily accessible, with excellent road and rail connections. Impressive ramparts enclose the whole of the old city, creating a clearly defined area of manageable, walkable size—visitors don't have to grapple with the rest of this industrial city at all, but can generally spend their entire stay in the historic central area. The main entrance to the walled town is Porte de la République, opposite the rail station. A central shopping avenue (cours Jean-Jaurès and rue de la République) makes its way from the city gate to the main square, place de l'Hôtel de Ville, with its hundreds of outdoor tables. Most of the narrow backstreets either side have been attractively restored, and there is good shopping. At festival time in July, hundreds of thousands of visitors arrive from across Europe.

HIGHLIGHTS

PALAIS DES PAPES

✚ 153 B1 • Place du Palais, 84008 Avignon ☎ 04 90 27 50 00 🕐 Jul daily 9–9; Aug, Sep daily 9–8; mid-Mar to end Jun, Oct daily 9–7; Nov to mid-Mar 9.30–5.45. Last tickets sold one hour before closing 💶 Nov to mid-Mar: adult €7.50, child €6; joint ticket including Pont St-Bénézet: adult €9, child €7. Mid-Mar to end Oct: adult €9.50, child €7.50; joint ticket including Pont St-Bénézet: adult €11.50, child €9 🅿 Palais des Papes, underneath place du Palais 🚩 Guided tours several times a day; audioguides (included in entry price) are available in 8 languages 📷 👥
The 14th-century fortress of the popes of Avignon is a vast, forbidding building soaring above the rest of central Avignon. It stands on one side of a huge piazza, and was the home of the popes from 1309 to 1403. Inside is a maze of passageways, galleries, rooms and chapels. You may visit independently or join a guided tour in English. The main things to see are the Large Audience Hall and the Papal Bedroom, its walls decorated with birds and golden vines on a blue background. The Grand Tinel banquet hall, 45m (150ft) long, has fine Gobelin tapestries and beautifully restored panelling in the shape of a ship's keel on the ceiling. There's a good view from the Terrasses des Grands Dignitaires.

Jets of water spout from a fountain on the Rocher des Doms

PALAIS DES PAPES FLOORPLAN

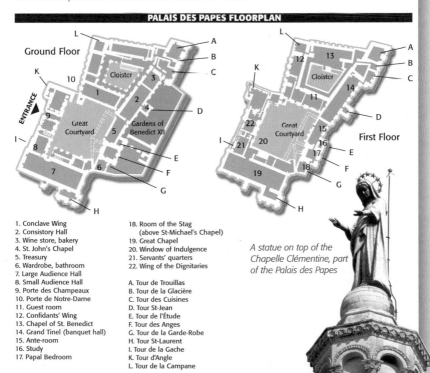

Ground Floor

L — A
B
C
K
10
Cloister
1
3
9
2
4 — D
Great
Courtyard
5
Gardens of
Benedict XII
I
8
E
7
6
F
G
H

First Floor

L — A
B
12
13
C
K
Cloister
14
11
22
Great
Courtyard
15
D
21
20
16
E
I
17
18
F
19
G
H

1. Conclave Wing
2. Consistory Hall
3. Wine store, bakery
4. St. John's Chapel
5. Treasury
6. Wardrobe, bathroom
7. Large Audience Hall
8. Small Audience Hall
9. Porte des Champeaux
10. Porte de Notre-Dame
11. Guest room
12. Confidants' Wing
13. Chapel of St. Benedict
14. Grand Tinel (banquet hall)
15. Ante-room
16. Study
17. Papal Bedroom

18. Room of the Stag
    (above St-Michael's Chapel)
19. Great Chapel
20. Window of Indulgence
21. Servants' quarters
22. Wing of the Dignitaries

A. Tour de Trouillas
B. Tour de la Glacière
C. Tour des Cuisines
D. Tour St-Jean
E. Tour de l'Étude
F. Tour des Anges
G. Tour de la Garde-Robe
H. Tour St-Laurent
I. Tour de la Gache
K. Tour d'Angle
L. Tour de la Campane

A statue on top of the Chapelle Clémentine, part of the Palais des Papes

- The *Avignon Passport* gives reductions on entry tickets to the main sights. You can buy it at the tourist office or at the participating sights.
- Two little sightseeing land trains set off frequently throughout the day from place du Palais (Apr–end Oct).
- The Festival d'Avignon (Avignon International Festival of Theatre), for three weeks in July, offers top-name entertainment, plus many fringe shows (www.festival-avignon.com).
- For a walk in Avignon ▷ 228–229.

ROCHER DES DOMS

✚ 153 B1

Leading off the place du Palais next to the papal palace, a steep path climbs up onto the peaceful Rocher des Doms public garden, which covers a rocky outcrop. The summit of the park gives dramatic views of the river and the countryside of western Provence.

MUSÉE CALVET

✚ 153 B2 • Hôtel Villeneuve-Martignan, 65 rue Joseph Vernet, 84000 ☎ 04 90 86 33 84 🕐 Wed–Mon 10–1, 2–6 💶 Adult €6, child (12–18) €3.50, under 12 free

Inside one of the town's many grand old mansions, the Calvet Museum has rooms around a courtyard displaying important collections of 15th- to 20th-century paintings and sculptures, period furniture, faïence and large amounts of fine gold and silver work. Among the modern painters on display are Soutine, Manet and Sisley.

VILLENEUVE-LÈS-AVIGNON

✚ Off map at 153 A1

One of the best vantage points to gain a sense of Avignon's medieval grandeur is the 13th-century Fort St-André at Villeneuve-lès-Avignon, on the other side of the river. The view is especially stirring at sunset, as the golden southern light bathes the town. When the popes moved to Avignon, the cardinals made their base at Villeneuve. It remains the perfect excursion from Avignon, and is very popular for an evening out.

Église St-Pierre (top)

PETIT PALAIS

✚ 153 B1 • 21 place du Palais, 84000 Avignon ☎ 04 90 86 44 58 🕐 Jun–end Sep Wed–Mon 10–1, 2–6; Oct–end May Wed–Mon 9.30–1, 2–5.30 💶 Adult €6, child €3.50 🅿 Palais des Papes, underneath place du Palais

The Petit Palais is an art museum with a remarkable collection of medieval works. It is noted for Italian Primitives, but there are also works of the Sienese, Venetian, Florentine and Avignon schools, as well as Romanesque and Gothic sculpture and frescoes. The palace dates from the 14th century. In the 16th century it was the luxurious palace of Cardinal Rovere, the future Pope Julius II. It is his acclaimed personal art collection that forms the nucleus of the art museum.

PONT ST-BÉNÉZET

✚ Off map at 153 B1 • Rue Ferruce, 84000 Avignon ☎ 04 90 85 60 16 🕐 Apr until start of Festival (1st week in Jul) daily 9–7; during Festival daily 9–9; Aug, Sep daily 9–8; Nov to mid-Mar daily 9.30–5.45; mid-Mar to end Mar daily 9.30–6.30. Last tickets sold 30 min before closing time 💶 Nov to mid-Mar: adult €3, child €2.50; joint ticket including Palais des Papes: adult €9, child €7; mid-Mar to end Oct: adult €3.50, child €3; joint ticket including Palais des Papes: adult €11.50, child €9 📷 Guided tours are available; audioguides (included in entry price) are available in 8 languages 🅿 Palais des Papes, underneath Place du Palais

A ramparts walkway gives access to what survives of the narrow cobbled bridge of St-Bénézet. This is the *pont d'Avignon* on which *on y danse* in the nursery rhyme *Sur le Pont d'Avignon*. Built in 1177 under the inspiration of a shepherd boy called Bénézet, the bridge originally went all the way across the Rhône to Villeneuve-lès-Avignon. In 1668 the Rhône flooded and washed away a large part of the bridge, leaving only what can be seen today. The surviving arches reach about halfway to Île de la Barthelasse, the island in midstream. The endearing little chapel of St-Nicolas, standing on the bridge, has two levels—simple Romaneque down below and Gothic on top.

FONDATION ANGLADON DUBRUJEAUD

⊞ 153 B2 • Hôtel de Massilian, 5 rue Laboureur, 84000 ☎ 04 90 82 29 03
⊙ Wed–Sun 1–6 (and Tue in high season) 💰 Adult €6, child €4 ▭ Guided visit
with art historians by appointment; language and price depends on demand
🅿 Street parking nearby

This modern art museum, founded in 1995, has become one of
Avignon's most important sights. Fondation Angladon Dubrujeaud
is the remarkable personal collection of artists Jean and Paulette
Angladon-Dubrujeaud. Housed in the Angladon-Dubrujeaud's
backstreet mansion, it focuses on 19th- and 20th-century art, with
works by Cézanne, Picasso and many leading Impressionists. There
is also a piece by Van Gogh.

BACKGROUND

Prehistoric Avignon sat on the Rocher des Doms, which, in
about 500BC, was developed by Greek settlers into the town of
Avenio. The Romans enlarged Avenio and laid out a Forum on
what is now the place de l'Hôtel de Ville, although the town was
eclipsed by Arles and Nîmes. In 1309 the papal court moved to
Avignon from Rome (▷ 27) and the city grew in size and
importance. The area remained in papal hands for centuries, only
becoming part of France again in 1791. During its time under
papal control, the city attracted a large wealthy clerical class, but
also political refugees and outcasts on the run from their own
communities, who were given refuge. Something of that
dichotomy survives today—there are many luxury shops and
well-to-do inhabitants but also people begging.

Avignon has a long history as a hub of entertainment. Its
cultural influence was confirmed in 1947, when the annual
Theatre Festival was launched.

A trompe-
l'oeil on
place de
l'Horloge
(above)

A woman in courtly costume

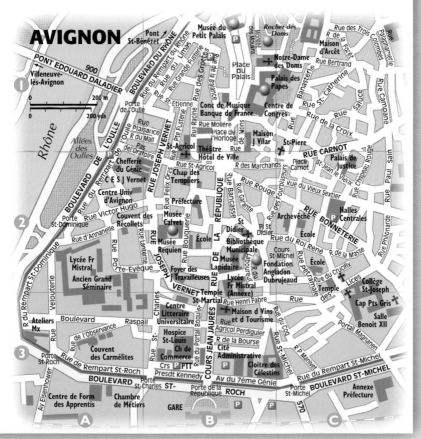

A cave dwelling in the troglodyte village of Barry

A church spire rises up over the rooftops of Bonnieux

BARRY

✚ 284 D7

In wild and rocky hills 5km (3 miles) from Bollène (▷ this page), the extraordinary troglodyte village of Barry is one of the best preserved in Provence. Known locally as Le Village Troglodyte, the site was inhabited continuously for thousands of years—possibly from as long ago as the Ligurian period (around 6000BC). The *bories* (drystone huts) were abandoned as recently as 1925 after some fatal rockslides.

From the parking area a track leads past a series of 'houses' consisting only of handsome stone façades placed across caves. Behind the façades, the caves have been carved into rooms to suit the needs of the occupants, and some have a surprising level of home comfort.

BEAUMES-DE-VENISE

✚ 284 E8 🚹 Maison des Dentelles, place du Marché, 84190 Beaumes-de-Venise, tel 04 90 62 94 39; summer daily 9–12, 2–7; winter Mon–Sat 9–12, 2–5.30

A noted wine village on the steep, rocky southern flank of the Dentelles de Montmirail in northern Vaucluse, Beaumes-de-Venise has for many centuries been known for its rich muscat dessert wine. The village produces other good wines too, and is also known for its high-quality olive oil and fruits, including melons, apricots and cherries. The Avignon popes owned a vineyard here in the 14th century, while Anne of Austria visited in 1660 to present a set of liturgical vestments in recognition of the village's wine-making skills.

Venise refers to the papal territory, the Comtat Venaissin, while *Beaumes* comes from

Baume, Provençal for grotto. The rocky terrain above the village is dotted with caves where the area's original inhabitants lived. Rising above them are the ruins of a 12th-century chateau.

BOLLÈNE

✚ 284 D7 🚹 Place Reynaud de la Gardette, 84500 Bollène, tel 04 90 40 51 45; mid-Apr to mid-Oct Mon–Sat 8.30–12, 2–7.30; mid-Oct to mid-Apr Mon–Sat 8.30–12, 2–5.30
🚇 Bollène
www.bollenetourisme.com

The highly industrialized Canal de Donzère-Mondragon runs parallel to the Rhône river between Montélimar and Orange, at the foot of pretty hills on the northwestern edge of Vaucluse. Standing beside the canal, the unassuming, long-established commercial and market town of Bollène is on the Roman Via Agrippa route and has become the main economic hub of the industrial zone. It is dominated by a vast nuclear plant just north of the town.

Traces of the historic Bollène survive, and there are some fine old houses with beautifully decorated doors in the old town around the church. A house in avenue Pasteur is where Louis Pasteur was staying in 1882 when he discovered an inoculation against swine fever. From the upper town, the view looks out onto the Cévennes hills across the Rhône.
Don't miss The cave-village of Barry (▷ this page) is nearby.

BONNIEUX

✚ 292 F10 🚹 7 place Carnot, Bonnieux, tel 04 90 75 91 90; Mon 2–6, Tue–Fri 9.30–12.30, 2–6
www.bonnieux.com

This lofty village on the north side of the Lubéron hills climbs up a hillside with a church at the

top and a church at the bottom. Steep lanes and cobbled steps lead up to the 12th-century church, now disused. A 17th-century building in rue de la République houses the Musée de la Boulangerie, a museum about bread making (May–end Oct Wed–Mon 10–12, 3–6.30). There are also a few remnants of fortifications dating from the time this was a Templar stronghold. The church at the bottom of the village, built in 1870, displays four 15th-century painted wooden panels.

The Pont Julien, a Roman bridge dating from around AD300, stands on the D149 just north of Bonnieux.
Don't miss There are lovely views of the valley and nearby *villages perchés* from the terrace near the 12th-century church.

CARPENTRAS

✚ 284 E8 🚹 Hôtel-Dieu, place Aristide Briand, 84200 Carpentras, tel 04 90 63 00 78; mid-Jun to mid-Sep Mon–Sat 9–7, Sun 9.30–1; mid-Sep to mid-Jun Mon–Sat 9.30–12.30, 2–6, Sun 9.30–1
www.ville-carpentras.fr

Intriguing reminders of times past can be seen in this country town, on the fertile plain northeast of Avignon. Originally a Roman settlement, it became an important religious town under papal rule. The historic old quarter is a tangled mass of lanes and narrow streets, once ringed with 14th-century ramparts but now enclosed by a circle of boulevards. Its Porte d'Orange gateway survives, and a first-century AD Roman Triumphal Arch stands behind the town's main sight, the 15th-century Ancienne Cathédral, in place du Général-de-Gaulle (daily 9–5). The cathedral has a superb Gothic doorway called Porte Juive (Jewish Door)

Fruit and vegetables at the Friday market in Carpentras

A vineyard at Châteauneuf-du-Pape

supposedly because Jewish converts to Christianity came in through this door. There was a big Jewish community here from Roman times onwards and the 14th-century synagogue, in place Maurice-Charretier (Mon–Thu 10–12, 3–5, Fri 10–12, 3–4) is said to be the oldest in France that is still in use, though having been extensively modernized in the 20th century, it does not give much indication of its age.
Don't miss If you're here on a Friday, visit the large market in the old town.

CAVAILLON

➕ 284 E10 ℹ️ Place François-Tourel, 84305 Cavaillon, tel 04 90 71 32 01; Jul, Aug Mon–Sat 9–12.30, 2–6.30, Sun 10–12; mid-Mar to end Jun, Sep, Oct Mon–Sat 9–12.30, 2–6.30; mid-Oct to mid-Mar Mon–Fri 9–12, 2–6, Sat 9–12 🚉 Cavaillon
www.cavaillon-luberon.com

Known as the 'Melon Capital of France', this prosperous town, irrigated by the Durance and Coulon rivers, grows a vast quantity of prime fruit and vegetables. Surrounded by lush market gardens, Cavaillon is one of the most productive agricultural hubs in France. Its high-quality produce has been praised since Roman times.

The only relic of the Roman era is a small first-century AD triumphal arch, moved stone by stone from next to the Cathédrale St-Véran to its present position in 1880. The Cathédrale St-Véran is an elegant 12th-century Romanesque structure with charming cloisters. Nearby on rue Hebraïque is the old synagogue, sole remnant of a once populous Jewish district. The ornate interior is impressive, while the small bakery beneath the main prayer hall is now a museum of the Jewish life of the Comtat Venaissin.

CHÂTEAUNEUF-DU-PAPE

This picturesque old fortified village among immaculate vineyards is dedicated to the production of its world-famous red wines.

🏠 284 D8 ℹ️ Place du Portail, Châteauneuf-du-Pape, tel 04 90 83 71 08; Jun–end Sep Mon–Sat 9.30 7, Sun 10–1, 2–6; Oct–end May Mon–Sat 9.30–12.30, 2–6, Sun 10 1, 2–6

RATINGS					
Good for wine	●	●	●	●	●
Historic interest	●	●	●		
Photo stops	●	●	●		
Walkability	●	●	●		

Châteauneuf is a picture-book medieval fortified village by a little river, not far from the Rhône. Old stone houses and lanes have been perfectly restored. The village is surrounded by its famous vineyards, all neatly tended. It is a popular visitor destination, with people coming not just to see the village but, more importantly, to taste the wines.

WINE TASTING

The tourist office can arrange visits to vineyards and wineries. In Cave Brotte at the bottom of the village, the Musée Père Anselme (mid-Jun to mid-Sep daily 9–12, 2–6; mid-Sep to mid-Jun daily 9–1, 2–7) explains about winemaking in the past, in addition to offering wine tasting and the chance to buy. Among the best-known vineyards in the town are Château Rayas, Château Le Nerthe, Château de Beaucastel, Château de la Gardine and the Château des Fines Roches. The *Fête de la Véraison* (▷ 204), in early August, is a good time to come and try the wine.

WINEMAKING

Winegrowers here choose from 13 types of grapes. The vineyard soil is covered with pebbles, to magnify the sun's heat during the day and seal it in at night. This, and the wide spacing between vines, results in a wine with a high alcohol content (12.5 per cent or higher). Most of the 13 million bottles of wine made here are a full-bodied red, although it's worth trying one of the 700,000 bottles of white. An authentic bottle of Châteauneuf-du-Pape has the crossed keys of the chateau embossed on the bottle.

POPES' SUMMER GETAWAY

The village, whose name means 'the Pope's new castle', was a summer hideaway of the 14th-century Avignon popes. It was they who ordered the first vineyards to be laid out. Little survives of the papal fortress at the summit of the village, blown up by the Germans in 1944. The ruins give good views of the Rhône valley.

Jagged Dentelles de Montmirail

Water from the powerful Fontaine de Vaucluse flows through the village and becomes the river Sorgue

CRESTET

➕ 284 E7

Quiet, charming and completely uncommercialized, this little village stands south of Vaison-la-Romaine on a crest of the Dentelles de Montmirail (▷ below). Cobbled alleyways climb through the village. To either side, the old houses have ancient wooden doorways. The tiny main square has a bubbling fountain and a 12th-century church. A pathway makes its way up to the former chateau (closed to the public).

The modern art exhibition space of the Centre International d'Art et de Sculpture (Mon–Fri 9–12, 2–6) stands above the village, in the Chemin de la Verrière.

DENTELLES DE MONTMIRAIL

➕ 284 E8 ℹ️ Maison des Dentelles, place du Marché, 84190 Beaumes-de-Venise, tel 04 90 62 94 39; summer daily 9–12, 2–7; winter Mon–Sat 9–12, 2–5.30

The Dentelles are an intriguing small range of jagged hills with limestone pinnacles rising from an important little wine area in northern Vaucluse. The higher part of the slopes is all wild wooded country, but most of the lower slopes are covered with vines producing Côte du Rhône red wines. A number of wine villages lie on the slopes of the Dentelles: Séguret (▷ 164) and Gigondas are among the prettiest and most evocative. Others include Vacqueyras and Beaumes-de-Venise (▷ 154). There is wine tasting at all the villages. At the foot of the north slope of the Dentelles is the town of Vaison-la-Romaine (▷ 166–168), with its intriguing Roman ruins and Romanesque cathedral of Notre-Dame-de-Nazareth.

FONTAINE-DE-VAUCLUSE

From this pretty village, a pleasant riverside path leads to one of the world's most powerful natural springs.

➕ 284 E9 ℹ️ Chemin du Gouffre, 84800, tel 04 90 20 32 22; Jul, Aug Mon–Sat 9–1, 2.30–6.30, Sun 9.30–1; Sep–end Jun Mon–Sat 9–12.30, 2.30–6, Sun 9.30–12.30 ❓ For a drive in the area ▷ 224–225

RATINGS	
Historic interest	●●●●
Photo stops	●●●
Walkability	●●●●

This pretty little riverside village is named after the nearby spring that has long fascinated both visitors and locals because the actual source of the water has never been located. Water gushes from beneath a sheer cliff into a strange, still and very deep pool, surrounded by rocks and vegetation and often by a dense, dripping spray. At its height, the Fontaine de Vaucluse is among the world's most powerful natural flows of fresh water: 630 million cubic metres (22,260 million cubic feet) of water emerge from it each year, flowing down the narrow valley to become the river Sorgue. For maximum effect, come in March or April.

CHEMIN DE LA FONTAINE

To reach the spring, you have to walk for some 15 minutes along the traffic-free Chemin de la Fontaine beside the Sorgue. In this enclosed valley now so full of visitors, the 14th-century poet Petrarch lived as a hermit for 16 years in the total isolation described in *De Vita Solitaria*. In the village, in quai du Château Vieux, there is a museum and library about Petrarch (Wed–Mon 10–6), in what is said to be his own house. Along the *chemin* are several other interesting attractions focusing on local history. The Musée d'Histoire 1939–1945 (daily 9.30–7.30) is mainly about daily life under the Nazi occupation and the Resistance, but also deals with the art and literature of the 'spirit of liberation'. A little farther on, Le Monde Souterrain de Norbert Casteret (Apr–end Aug daily 10–12, 2–6; Feb, Mar, Sep to mid-Nov Wed–Sun 10–12, 2–5) has collections of rocks and minerals but also deals vividly with efforts to discover the source of the water flowing from the Fontaine. A few paces farther along the *chemin*, Moulin à Papier Vallis Clausa (Mon–Sat 9–12.30, 2–6.30, Sun 10–12.30, 2–6.30) is a fascinating traditional water-powered paper mill.

THE SIGHTS

Admiring the view (above).
Exploring the narrow cobbled streets of medieval Gordes

GORDES

An exceptionally pretty and unusual village, medieval Gordes is a chic, arty hideaway noted for its curious *bories*.

The houses appear to be built one on top of the other as they climb the steep hill on which this picturesque old village stands. Medieval Gordes, in the southern part of the Vaucluse plateau, was abandoned during the early 20th century, but was quickly rediscovered and restored by artists and well-to-do visitors. Now a rather chic place to have a second home, it is popular with media people. As a result, it is well served with shops and restaurants at the expensive end of the scale. Narrow stairways and covered passages wind steeply around the hill, which is topped by a Renaissance chateau fancifully restored by modern artist Victor Vasarely. It now contains a gallery of the work of another modern artist, Pol Mara (Wed–Mon 10–12, 2–6). The tourist office is on the first floor of the chateau. The Grande Salle, which is part of the Mairie, has a Renaissance fireplace wonderfully ornamented with shells and flowers.

BORIES

Around the village are numerous *bories*, windowless dome-shaped drystone dwellings, many of them centuries old. They were used as shepherds' huts, storage sheds, animal shelters and seasonal or even permanent residences; some were inhabited until the 19th century. Provence has up to 6,000 *bories*, some dating back to prehistoric times and others built only a few hundred years ago. Vaucluse has a particularly high concentration. Their ingenious construction does not involve mortar—instead, each layer of flat stone slightly overlaps the next. To see a restored museum-village of these structures, follow the signs to the *Village des Bories,* which is off the D2, 4km (2.5 miles) from Gordes (Jun–end Sep daily 9–8, Oct–end May 9–5). The *bories* here are between 200 and 500 years old.

RATINGS

Good for kids	●●●
Historic interest	●●●●
Photo stops	●●●
Walkability	●●●●

BASICS

⊞ 285 F9

🈁 Le Château, 84220 Gordes, tel 04 90 72 02 75; summer Mon–Sat 9–12.30, 2–6.30, Sun 10–12, 2–6; winter Mon–Sat 9–12, 2–6, Sun 10–12, 2–6

www.gordes-village.com
This is a very attractive, interesting, useful website about the village and its sights.

TIP

● The village has a lively two-week music festival in August.

One of the drystone bories

Enjoying a drink in L'Isle-sur-la-Sorgue

A vineyard in the Lubéron hills

Bicycling along an avenue of plane trees near Malaucène

L'ISLE-SUR-LA-SORGUE

✚ 284 E9 ℹ Place de la Liberté, 84800 L'Isle-sur-la-Sorgue, tel 04 90 38 04 78; Jul, Aug Mon–Sat 9–1, 2.30–6.30, Sun 9.30–1; Sep–end Jun Mon–Sat 9–12.30, 2.30–6, Sun 9.30–12.30 www.ot-islesurlasorgue.fr

This curious old town stands on a large island in the river Sorgue and is enclosed by water channels, with several large, mossy water-wheels. The town's rich architecture is a legacy of once thriving silk and leather industries. Today it has several art galleries and antiques shops, and is the main town for buying and selling Provençal antiques, with a Sunday antiques market.

At the town's heart is a 17th-century church, Notre-Dame-des-Anges (Tue–Sun 10–12, 3–5) with a highly decorated baroque interior. There is also an 18th-century Hôtel-Dieu, in rue J. Théophile, preserving its original pharmacy (30-min guided tours Mon–Fri 9–12, 2–5; reserve ahead).

LACOSTE

✚ 285 F10

Little lanes stepping up towards a huge ruined chateau, and glorious rural views, have made this Lubéron hilltop village popular with second-homers. Remnants of the ramparts survive, with two gateways. The chateau (▷ 11) that dominates the village was the family home of the notorious Marquis de Sade (1740–1814), who in fact spent very little time here—the family owned several other fine houses in the area. Built in the 11th century, it used to be one of the grandest in the region.

LUBÉRON

✚ 292 F–G10 ℹ Maison du Parc Naturel du Lubéron, 60 place Jean Jaurès, 84404 Apt, tel 04 90 04 42 00; summer Mon–Fri 8.30–12, 1.30–7, Sat 8.30–12, 1.30–5; winter Mon–Fri 8.30–12, 1.30–6 www.parcduluberon.fr

The exceptionally picturesque and varied landscapes of the Lubéron hills are the epitome of the Provence heartland. Extending roughly from Cavaillon (Vaucluse) to Villeneuve (Alpes-de-Haute-Provence) the hills reach their highest point at Mourre Nègre (1,125m/3,690ft). Typical of the region are gaunt medieval hilltop villages with terraced fields and drystone *bories* (▷ 157), interspersed with expanses of dense wild heath. Many of the village houses have been restored as holiday homes or arty getaways. The fortified village of Ménerbes is the setting for British writer Peter Mayle's bestseller *A Year in Provence* (1989), while Lourmarin was the home of writer Albert Camus (1913–60), who is buried in the cemetery.

Much of the region is protected as a Parc Naturel Régional, ensuring its character and culture are preserved. The hills are rich in flora and fauna, with numerous species of wild flowers and colonies of rare birds such as Bonelli's Eagle, Egyptian Vulture and the Eagle Owl.

MALAUCÈNE

✚ 284 E8 ℹ Place de la Mairie, 84340 Malaucène, tel 04 90 65 22 59; daily 9–12.30, 2–6.30

This small town has become a popular base for hiking, horseback riding and bicycling on the steep slopes of the nearby Mont Ventoux (▷ 159) and Dentelles de Montmirail (▷ 156). Four fortified gates mark the entrances into the evocative central medieval quarter. Next to Porte Soubeyran is a fortified church noted for its wood carving and 18th-century organ loft. Rue St-Étienne and rue du Château climb past the crumbling old clock tower (a lookout during the Wars of Religion), reaching a high belvedere created from the ruins of the old chateau.

MAZAN

✚ 284 E8 ℹ 83 place du 8 Mai, 84380 Mazan, tel 04 90 69 74 27; summer Mon–Sat 9–12, 2–7, Sun 9.30–12.30; winter Mon–Fri 9–12, 2–6

Little Mazan lies beside the minor road that follows the Auzon river into the countryside east of Carpentras. Solid gateways lead into the mainly 16th- and 17th-century central part of town, rich with statues in niches, fountains and ancient doorways. The Chapelle des Pénitents Blancs, opposite the church, now houses the Musée de Mazan (Jun–Sep, Wed–Mon afternoons). Its most remarkable exhibit is the skeleton of a young fourth-century woman, supposedly killed by a stone from a catapult, which has left a gaping hole in the front of her skull.

MONT VENTOUX

See page 159.

OPPÈDE-LE-VIEUX

✚ 292 F10

Oppède-le-Vieux was once a bustling village with its own castle, but now is partly in ruins, with evocative overgrown pathways and old archways. The castle was ransacked during the Revolution and the village fell into decline when the Comtat Venaissin became part of France in 1791. But the village's fortunes began to look up in the 1940s, when a colony of artists moved in. You can walk up to the summit of the village, passing an old church, but take care as there are many unprotected drops.

Taking in the view from high on the Mont Ventoux (above).
A memorial to a Tour de France cyclist who died here in 1967 (right)

MONT VENTOUX

Rising high above the rest of the region, the neatly conical summit of Ventoux is one of the most distinctive sights in western Provence.

The awesome peak of Mont Ventoux, rising to 1,909m (6,261ft), dominates a wide area. Most of western Provence can see its huge pyramid shape. The mountain has been declared a World Biosphere Reserve. A paved road makes Ventoux accessible for fine-weather walks and drives. Even in winter, there are plenty of visitors, who come to Ventoux's own ski resort, Mont Serein. The snow lasts well into spring. In summer, the peak is often shrouded in cloud while the rest of Provence basks in sunshine. The 14th-century poet Petrarch was the first person to write about his ascent of the mountain—it took him two days. Today, some walks and excursions, including night visits, are organized from Bedoin Tourist Office (tel 04 90 65 63 95) and Malaucène Tourist Office (tel 04 90 65 22 59).

TO THE SUMMIT
Around the foot of the mountain is wooded hill country with a few simple villages. The road to the top climbs steeply, with sharp hairpins, its surface painted with graffiti and advertising most of the way. Provence seems to end as you continue the climb to the summit in summer, and another land is entered—bleak, cold, stony, unearthly, with howling winds. Yet there is plenty of low, tenacious vegetation, and in April or May there can be blankets of flowers even at the very top. Surprisingly, the road actually goes all the way to the summit of the mountain, where high-tech observation and communications equipment is installed. From here you look across another world, of distant crests and peaks and mountain ranges: It has been described as one of the best views in Europe. The vista takes in the Alps, the Rhône Valley, the Vaucluse Plateau, the Cévennes and the Mediterranean.

WINDY MOUNTAIN
The winds near the summit are rarely light, and reach more than 160km/h (100mph) when the *mistral* is blowing. Legend has it that the mountain owes its name to these winds—*ventour* is Provençal for windy. From November to the end of May sudden heavy snowfalls are possible at any time.

RATINGS				
Outdoor activities	●	●	●	●
Photo stops	●	●	●	● ●
Walkability	●	●	●	

BASICS

➕ 285 F8

🛈 Chalet d'Accueil du Mont Ventoux, tel 04 90 63 42 02

TIPS

● Check the weather forecast, and do not ascend Mont Ventoux in windy weather or when storms or snow are expected.
● Be prepared for low temperatures at the summit, averaging 11°C (52°F) colder than at the foot of the mountain.
● *Epeautre*, the wild barley that grows on the mountain, has become something of a local special—look for it on menus.

Orange

A vibrant, attractive and ancient town at the gateway to Provence, Orange is noted for some remarkable reminders of Roman times.

The Théâtre Antique hosts the Chorégies choral music festival

There are wonderful views from the Colline St-Eutrope

The Musée Municipal

➕ 284 D8
ℹ️ Cours Aristide Briand, 84100 Orange, tel 04 90 34 70 88; Apr–end Sep Mon–Sat 9.30–7, Sun and public hols 10–12.30, 2.30–6; Oct–end Mar Mon–Sat 10–1, 2–5
🚉 Orange

www.provence-orange.com
There are English pages but the links revert to French pages.

TIPS

• There is parking alongside cours A. Briand and in cours Pourtoules near the Théâtre Antique.
• *Chorégies* (the International Festival of Music and Theatre) is held in July and early August at the Théâtre Antique and other venues.

Part of the Arc de Triomphe (top), built in the first century BC

SEEING ORANGE

Well placed at the entrance to Provence for visitors coming down the Rhône valley highways, the attractive provincial town of Orange makes an enjoyable pause. It has impressive Roman structures, with two World Heritage Sites, one of which is the Roman theatre, whose huge backdrop wall was famously described by Louis XIV as 'the finest wall in my kingdom.' The central district of town dates from medieval times and is lively and bustling, with picturesque lanes and squares. It is small and easily explored on foot and the tourist office organizes guided tours. Orange is also the place to take stock of alternative routes and destinations: Here the roads diverge for access to Nîmes and western Provence; Avignon and the heart of Provence; or Carpentras, Mont Ventoux and the wine towns of Vaucluse. If you are driving into Orange, be aware that navigating your way around the outer boulevards can be tricky.

HIGHLIGHTS

THÉÂTRE ANTIQUE

• Rue Madeleine Roch, 84100 Orange ☎ 04 90 51 17 60 🕐 Jun–end Aug daily 9–8; Apr, May, Sep daily 9–7; Jan, Feb, Nov, Dec daily 9–5; Mar, Oct daily 9–6 🎫 Adult €7.50, child (7–17) €5.50, under 7 free. Ticket includes entry to the Musée Municipal 🎧 Audioguide included in entry price

The remarkable Roman theatre at the heart of Orange is one of the most important Roman structures surviving anywhere. The semi-circular auditorium, built into the slope of St-Eutrope hill, could hold 10,000 spectators and staged anything from circus acts to Greek tragedies. Still very much in use, its stage hosts many performances, including the annual *Chorégies* choral music festival. But the main focus is the stage wall. Standing 36m (119ft) high and measuring 103m (338ft) from end to end, the grandeur of the wall, decorated with columns, marbles, statues and mosaics, testifies to the important role the theatre played in the life of the Roman town. Actors and stagehands moved about unseen through hidden passageways within the wall. The statue of Augustus above the central royal door dates from the first century AD and was pieced together from fragments.

MUSÉE MUNICIPAL

• Rue Madeleine Roch, 84100 Orange ☎ 04 90 51 17 60 🕓 Jun–end Aug daily 9–8; Apr, May, Sep daily 9–7; Jan, Feb, Nov, Dec daily 9–5; Mar, Oct daily 9–6 🎫 Adult €7.50, child (7–17) €5.50, under 7 free. Ticket includes entry to the Théâtre Antique

The light and airy rooms of the first-rate municipal museum trace the history of the town and display some of the town's more important Roman and medieval relics, notably the Romans' remarkable Land Survey of Orange carved on marble. Old engravings and prints show the neglected state of the Roman theatre before it was restored.

ARC DE TRIOMPHE

• Avenue de l'Arc de Triomphe, 84100 Orange

The Arc de Triomphe is the grandiose three-arched monument erected to mark the defeat of the local tribes. Roman forces were defeated here by the local tribes in 105BC and it became an urgent priority for the Romans to conquer the area decisively. The triumphal arch was erected in 20BC to celebrate their eventual victory. It survives in astonishingly good condition, and is one of the oldest in existence. Rich carvings tell the story of other victories, including naval battles. The Arc is on a roundabout surrounded by traffic from the busy N7.

BACKGROUND

Originally a Celtic settlement called Arausio, Orange was conquered, with difficulty, by the Romans in 102BC. The town stood on the Via Agrippa highway and became a prosperous city. The Romans were driven out by Visigoths in the fifth century AD. Orange was an independent principality in medieval times. In 1622 the Dutch Prince of Nassau, later to become Prince of Orange, took possession of the city and it became a refuge for dissenters from Catholicism. To protect its small territory in southern France, the Dutch royal house enclosed Orange with ramparts, largely constructed with masonry from Roman buildings. Orange did not become part of France until the 1713 Treaty of Utrecht. In the 19th and 20th centuries, the town's position beside the Rhône and at the gateway to the south encouraged commercial and industrial development.

Admiring the view from the ruins of the fortress

MORE TO SEE
COLLINE ST-EUTROPE

The hill rising behind the theatre is called Colline St-Eutrope, and here many of the Roman items were found. There are great views from in front of the ruined foundations of a fortress here.

The Arc de Triomphe was built to celebrate Rome's triumph over the local tribes

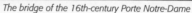

The bridge of the 16th-century Porte Notre-Dame

One of the many fountains that have given Pernes-les-Fontaines its name

PERNES-LES-FONTAINES

It's delightful to stroll in the narrow streets and squares of this aptly named little town, discovering the many fountains.

Medieval Pernes, in the papal territory of the Comtat Venaissin, was enclosed by its ramparts in the 14th century, and a great deal survives from those days. Pernes (*les Fontaines* was added to the name only in 1936) is a delightful, evocative historic town, with impressive gateways and fortifications, towers, lovely old squares and narrow streets, Renaissance houses and a cluster of old chapels. Its particular charm, though, derives from harnessing the waters of a river, the otherwise unremarkable Nesque, into numerous fountains. Just south of Carpentras, and 25km (16 miles) east of Avignon, it is well placed to be visited on a tour of the Vaucluse area.

THE FOUNTAINS

From the 15th century onwards, the Nesque was channelled into fountains in the village. More have been added over time, even in recent years, bringing the total to 36, along with 4 *lavoirs* (public washing areas). They range from the oldest, La Fontaine Reboul, more than 400 years old, to the modern, La Fontaine Villeneuve, added in 1952 and reputedly so awful that no one wishes to remove the moss that now obscures it. Among the most beautiful is La Fontaine de Cormoran, added in 1761.

BUT NOT JUST FOUNTAINS

The Tour Ferrande, in rue Barbes, shelters a remarkable series of 13th-century frescoes depicting religious and historical scenes in cartoon-strip style. The lovely 16th-century Porte Notre-Dame has a small chapel—Notre-Dame-des-Graces—built onto one of the piles of the river bridge. The 13th-century Tour de l'Horloge, or clock tower, is a last remnant of the chateau of the Counts of Toulouse. Rainy-day museums in the town include the Musée du Costume Comtadinone (open Sat and school hols), devoted to 19th-century local costume and housed in the Magasin Drapier, a fascinating preserved former drapers' shop in rue de la République. The Musée des Traditions Provençales (Sat and school hols), focusing on Provençal tradition and culture, is in the 17th-century Maison Fléchier, in place Fléchier.

Don't miss The walkway beside the Nesque gives an exquisite view of the bridge, the chapel, the keep and the town's clock tower.

RATINGS

Historic interest	●●●
Photo stops	●●●●
Walkability	●●●●

BASICS

➕ 284 E9

🛈 Place Gabriel Moutte, 84210 Pernes-les-Fontaines, tel 04 90 61 31 04/04 90 66 47 27; Jun–end Sep Mon–Sat 9–12.30, 2–7, Sun 9.30–12.30; Oct–end May Mon, Sat 10–12, Tue–Fri 10–12, 2–7

www.ville-pernes-les-fontaines.fr
An attractive, well-constructed website, in French only, including details of the lively *Fête du Patrimoine*

TIPS

● Visit in mid-September for the *Fête du Patrimoine*.
● Contact the tourist office to arrange a visit to the Tour Ferrande.

The strange landscape of Roussillon's ochre quarries (above).
Many of Roussillon's houses are tinted with shades of ochre (right)

ROUSSILLON

The vast ochre quarries next to this prettily pastel-tinted village are an astonishing sight.

You'll often see artists sketching or painting in this village high in the Lubéron hills. Roussillon is a curiosity, and a very attractive one. For centuries housing a community of ochre miners, the streets are edged by pretty homes tinted with 17 different shades of ochre across a warm spectrum from golden yellow to blood red. This beauty happened entirely by chance, as ochre miners over the centuries built cottages from the most conveniently available material, ochre rocks.

VISIT THE QUARRIES
The extensive area of former ochre quarries, extending like a bizarre dazzling wilderness next to the village, makes an unforgettable outing. The underground galleries are now closed but you can visit the disused quarries following the Ochre Path or *Sentier des Ocres* (Mar to mid-Nov daily 9–6; mid-Nov to end Feb daily 10–5.30). To enjoy it fully, you'll need to be able to walk well in difficult terrain.

LOCAL INDUSTRY
Ochre mining was an important industry here for hundreds of years. Indeed, Provençal ochre is thought to have been in use since prehistoric times. The Romans first developed the quarries into a major enterprise. After a decline in the medieval period, the ochre industry was restarted on a large scale in the 18th century, when ochre powders were shipped from Marseille to countries all over the world. At the beginning of the 20th century, nearly every adult in Roussillon was employed by the mine owners. Ochre was mined either in tall, underground galleries or in the open air. A new decline began in the 1920s, when synthetic dyes were first manufactured, and within a decade the mining of natural ochre was no longer viable. But artists and visitors continue to give life to this exceptional place.

RED ROOTS
The scientific explanation for the striking red hue of Roussillon's ochre is the combination of oxides. But legend blames it on the bloody death of a medieval lady called Seremonde, wife to Raymond of Avignon, who threw herself from the cliffs after her affair with a troubadour was discovered.

RATINGS				
Historic interest	● ● ●			
Photo stops	● ● ● ● ●			
Walkability	● ●			

BASICS
✚ 285 F9
ℹ Place de la Poste, 84220 Roussillon, tel 04 90 05 60 25; Mon–Sat 10–12, 2–5.30
💶 €2 to enter the quarries

www.roussillon-provence.com
A simple website, in French only, that successfully shows the impact of ochre on the village.

TIPS
● The simplest place to leave your car is in one of the parking areas close to the entrance to the quarries.
● For a walk in the quarries, wear something that you don't mind having stained with ochre.
● The rough terrain of the quarries could be difficult for young children. Even for others, there are some areas where it is necessary to take extra care.

The pretty rooftops of medieval Saignon

Lavender sachets and other crafts for sale in Sault

SAIGNON

✠ 285 G10 ℹ Mairie (town hall), tel 04 90 74 16 30 or 04 90 74 39 09

In an unspoiled area of the eastern Lubéron, the ancient hilltop fortress village of Saignon rises high above the Calavon valley. It is stretched along a ledge with its medieval castle at one end and the 12th-century Romanesque church of Notre-Dame-de-Pitié at the other. Approaching Saignon from Apt, it becomes clear why the village has been a natural fortress since Celto-Ligurian times—the towering rocks on which it stands would be enough to deter any attacker. At the same time, Saignon is open, bright and approachable, a typical Provençal village of picturesque streets, fountains, fine doorways on grand old houses and a clock tower and tree-shaded square. **Don't miss** Walkers can climb to the top of the high Saignon rock for an immense panorama with views reaching Mont Ventoux (▷ 159) and the Montagne de Lure.

ST-DIDIER

✠ 284 E9

Between Pernes-les-Fontaines (▷ 162) and Venasque (▷ 165), this peaceful little village, 6km (4 miles) from Carpentras (▷ 154–155), is known for its waters and enjoys an impressive setting in the Vaucluse upland. The tree-lined main street leads to a medieval gateway and church, behind which stands the Château de Thézan (closed to the public). This 15th-century building was converted in 1863 into a hydrotherapy venue still in use for the treatment of nervous disorders. Peek into the courtyard to see its fine Renaissance doorways and windows.

ST-SATURNIN-LES-APT

✠ 285 G9 ℹ Mairie (town hall), tel 04 90 75 43 12

The extensive fortified village of St-Saturnin looks towards the Lubéron from the southern slopes of the Vaucluse plateau. It is a richly productive agricultural village, surrounded by pleasing vineyards and cherry orchards, olives and lavender. It is known too for asparagus, honey and truffles. There are many holiday villas around the village, standing among the orchards.

Despite St-Saturnin's peaceful setting, a more turbulent past is recalled by the ruined defences: the gateways Portail Ayguier, Porte de Rome and Porte de Roque, the Tour du Portalet tower and vestiges of an 11th-century chateau. Remnants of a small Romanesque chapel at the top provide stirring views far across the region.

SAULT

✠ 285 G8 ℹ Avenue de la Promenade, 84390 Sault, tel 04 90 64 01 21; Apr–end Jun, Sep Mon–Sat 9–12, 2–6; Sun 9.30–12.30; Jul, Aug daily 9–1, 2–7; Oct–Mar Mon–Sat 10–12, 2–5 (closed Sat and Sun in Dec) www.saultenprovence.com

The airy little town of Sault is on a rock spur on the edge of the Vaucluse plateau, close to the towering presence of Mont Ventoux (▷ 159). The vivid upland landscape is decorated in early summer with fields of wheat and bright lavender. The main attraction is as a base for excursions, by car or on foot or bicycle, into the mountains. Little remains of the town's old chateau, but the central old quarter has several medieval and Renaissance houses. The church is remarkable for its barrel-vaulted nave supported by slender columns. The Musée de

Sault (Jul, Aug 3–6) displays local prehistoric and Gallo-Roman finds, as well as an incongruous Egyptian mummy. The Maison de la Chasse et de l'Environment (Jul, Aug Tue–Sun 10–12, 3–7; mid-Feb to mid-Dec Mon–Fri 10–12, 2–6) looks at the area's wildlife and the role of hunting in local culture.

SÉGURET

✠ 284 E8 ℹ Mairie, 84110 Séguret

This delightful village high on the slopes of the Dentelles de Montmirail (▷ 156) had fallen largely into ruins by the mid-20th century, when it was saved by the enthusiastic *Amis de Séguret* (Friends of Séguret), who restored its houses and monuments and instigated customs like the *Pegouado* torchlight procession at Christmas and the Provençal Folklore Fair in August. The village has a 15th-century fountain and a 12th-century church and is something of a local hub for crafts and culture. It also makes a good starting point for walks in the Dentelles woods. **Don't miss** Séguret's greatest attraction is the view from the main square, of vineyards below and rocky summits above.

SÉRIGNAN-DU-COMTAT

✠ 284 D8 ℹ L'Harmas de Fabre, route d'Orange, 84830 Sérignan-du-Comtat, tel 04 90 70 15 61; closed for renovation until 2005 www.museum-paca.org/harmas-collections.htm

A remarkable man, Jean-Henri Fabre, put this village on the map. Born to a poor family in 1823, Fabre rose to become a leading scientist and scholar. Acclaimed for his work in many fields outside of his specialism, the study of insects, Fabre became known too as an author

Séguret makes a good base for walks in the Dentelles de Montmirail

A short spire crowns the 6th-century baptistry, in Venasque

of school textbooks on many subjects. In March 1879, he purchased the house and land outside Sérignan that was to become his *harmas*, from a Provençal word meaning a secure enclosure. He cultivated this site as a haven for insect life, enabling him to pursue his studies. After Fabre's death in 1915, the Paris-based Musée National d'Histoire Naturelle purchased the *harmas*. Work to restore the house and garden began in 2000, with reopening of the site due in stages between 2005 and 2006.

LE THOR

🔲 284 E9 🔳 Place du 11 Novembre, 84250 Le Thor, tel 04 90 33 92 31; Mon 2–6, Tue–Fri 10–12, 2–6, Sat 10–12. Closed for a month in winter

One of the most impressive churches in the Vaucluse is Notre-Dame-du-Lac (daily 9.30–11.30), on the banks of the Sorgue river at the market town of Le Thor. Completed at the end of the 12th century, it marks the first transitional steps from Romanesque to Gothic. The Gothic vaulting in the nave is one of the earliest examples in Provence. The finely decorated west portal shelters a wooden statue of the Virgin.

Don't miss See stalactites and small pools in the beautiful caves called Grotte de Thouzon, around 3km (2 miles) north of Le Thor (Jul, Aug daily 10–7; Apr–end Jun, Sep–end Nov daily 10–12, 2–6; Mar Sun guided tours at 2.15, 3.20, 4.20, 5.30).

VAISON-LA-ROMAINE

See pages 166–168.

VALRÉAS

🔲 284 E7 🔳 Avenue Maréchal Leclerc, 84601 Valréas, tel 04 90 35 04 71; Nov–end Feb Mon–Sat 9.15–12.15, 2–5; Mar–22 Jun, Sep, Oct Mon–Sat

9.15–12.15, 2–6; 23 Jun–end Aug Mon–Sat 9.15–12.15, 2–7, Sun 9.15–12.15 ❓ The town celebrates *La Nuit du Petit-St-Jean* on 23 Jun with a spectacular torchlight procession www.ot-valreas.info

Valréas is a pleasant town whose economy is based on the cardboard industry, winemaking and lavender products. Administratively it is a curiosity: Officially in the Vaucluse *département*, physically it seems to have come adrift and finds itself surrounded by the Drôme *département*. This arrangement dates back to the 14th century, when the popes in Avignon wished to expand their Comtat Venaissin territory by purchasing land on the French side of the border. When King Charles VII heard that Valréas had been acquired by the popes, he ordered no more land to be sold to them—leaving Valréas and the surrounding villages isolated. When the *départements* of France were created in the 18th century, Valréas opted to remain part of the Vaucluse (and hence part of Provence). This is why Valréas likes to add the soubriquet *L'Enclave des Papes* to its name.

The historic heart of town has many fine old houses, the Romanesque church of Notre-Dame-de-Nazareth and the imposing 18th-century Château de Simiane, now housing the town hall and hosting temporary art exhibitions in summer. The town's cardboard manufacturing has flourished here since the 19th century, giving rise to an unexpectedly fascinating museum on packaging and printing, the Musée du Cartonnage et de l'Imprimerie, in avenue Maréchal Foch (Apr–end Oct Mon, Wed–Sat 10–12, 3–6, Sun 10–12).

Don't miss Travel to the nearby

village of Richerenches, 7km (4.5 miles) southeast, to see the famous truffle market every Saturday from November to the end of March.

VENASQUE

🔲 284 E9 🔳 Office de Tourisme du Pays de Venasque et des Monts-de-Vaucluse, Grand 'Rue, 84210 Venasque, tel 04 90 66 11 66; mid-Mar to end Oct Mon–Thu, Sat 9–12, 2–5, Fri, Sun 2–5 www.venasque.fr

The cherry orchards around Venasque look magnificent in spring, with their snow-like blossom. The town is on a high point in the Vaucluse hills, with a commanding view of the Carpentras plain. Its wild and lonely position has been of strategic importance for millennia, since the original Ligurian settlement of Vindasca was founded here. Dominating the route from Carpentras to Apt, Venasque became a refuge for the bishops of Carpentras after the Roman withdrawal in the third to fifth centuries AD.

The town's baptistery (May–end Sep daily 9.15–12, 1–6.30; Oct–end Apr daily 9.15–12, 1–5; closed over Christmas), beside the church, dates from the sixth century AD and is said to stand on the remains of a Roman temple. It is one of the oldest surviving religious buildings in France. Inside are fragments of a fifth-century sarcophagus and there is an octagonal font set in the floor. The strange holes in the wall of the north apse were intended to improve the acoustics.

At the other end of Venasque is the medieval rampart wall with three turrets, which once blocked the approach to this fortress village. Venasque was so important in the Middle Ages that it gave its name to the papal territories, the Comtat Venaissin.

THE SIGHTS

Vaison-la-Romaine

The largest archaeological site in France is also a pleasing little market town set among Provençal hills.

The Pont Romain, crossing the Ouvèze river

A Roman mosaic

The Théâtre Antique could hold 6,000 people in Roman times

SEEING VAISON-LA-ROMAINE

Vaison rises from the narrow gorge of the Ouvèze river in an attractive setting on the north side of the Dentelles de Montmirail (▷ 156), near where the hills meet the plain. The town's great attraction is its two connected archaeological sites, totalling 15ha (37 acres), where exceptional ruins of the Roman period have been uncovered. On the other side of the Ouvèze, reached by crossing a Roman bridge that is still in daily use, the town's medieval quarter, or Haute Ville (upper town), stands high on a hill. Apart from its impressive historical sights, Vaison is a thriving and appealing little market town. The Roman sites, archaeological museum and other sights may be visited on a single ticket, *Billet Tous Monuments*, available from the ticket office adjacent to the Roman sites.

HIGHLIGHTS

QUARTIER DU PUYMIN
• Avenue Général-de-Gaulle, 84110 Vaison-la-Romaine ☎ 04 90 36 02 11 ◉ Jul, Aug daily 9.30–6.30; Jun, Sep daily 9.30–6; Mar–end May, Oct daily 10–12.30, 2–6; Nov–end Feb daily 10–12, 2–4 ▣ *Billet Tous Monuments*: Adult €7, child (12–18) €3.50, under 12 free ▣
The Puymin quarter is the higher, larger of the two Roman sites. It has a visible street layout, some surviving walls and even some patches of frescoes and mosaic floors. The highlight is the Roman theatre (▷ below). Other points of interest include the extensive House of Apollon Lauré, named for a white marble head of Apollo; the even larger Tonnelle House; the public space known as the Sanctuary, decorated with statuary and probably with some religious connection; and an area of smaller houses and workshops.

THÉÂTRE ANTIQUE
• Within the Quartier du Puymin, same ticket and opening hours
Cut into the Puymin hill is first-century AD Roman Vaison's fine theatre, which was restored in the 20th century and is now the venue for a range of events. Its tiered rows of seating, joined by stairs and topped with a portico, could accommodate 6,000 spectators.

RATINGS
Cultural interest	●●●●
Historic interest	●●●●●
Photo stops	●●●●
Walkability	●●●

BASICS
✚ 284 E7
🛈 Place du Chanoine-Sautel, 84110 Vaison-la-Romaine, tel 04 90 36 02 11; Jun–end Sep daily 9–12.30, 2–6.30; Mar–end May daily 9.30–12, 2–6; Oct–end Feb daily 10–12, 2–5

www.vaison-la-romaine.com
In French and English; packed with photos and information about the town.

TIPS
• There's a large, lively street market every Tuesday morning.
• There are large parking areas next to the two Roman sites.
• A summer festival of drama, music and dance is held at the Roman theatre from early July to mid-August. Every three years, there is also a Festival of Choral Music.

Cheery sunflowers are among the blooms for sale in the market (left)

NOTRE-DAME DE NAZARETH

• Avenue Général-de-Gaulle, 84110 Vaison-la-Romaine 🌐 Nov–end Feb daily 10–12, 2–4; Mar–end May, Oct daily 10–12.30, 2–6; Jun, Sep daily 9.30–12.30, 2–6; Jul, Aug daily 9.30–12.30, 2–6.45 🅑 *Billet Tous Monuments*: Adult €7, child (12–18) €3, under 12 free 🅿

About 10 minutes' walk from the Quartier de la Villasse site, the Romanesque cathedral, Notre-Dame de Nazareth, has lovely 12th-century cloisters.

QUARTIER DE LA VILLASSE

• Avenue Général-de-Gaulle, 84110 Vaison-la-Romaine ☎ 04 90 36 02 11 🌐 Jul, Aug 9.30–12.30, 2–6.45; Jun, Sep 9.30–12.30, 2–6; Mar–end May, Oct 10–12.30, 2–6; Nov–end Feb 10–12, 2–4 🅑 *Billet Tous Monuments*: Adult €7, child (12–18) €3.50, under 12 free 🅿

A modern road separates the Villasse and Puymin sites. The lower site, called Quartier de la Villasse, is smaller but has a remarkable street of small shops, workshops and villas with mosaic floors. One notable structure is the ruins of the House of the Silver Bust, the largest house excavated in Vaison. The street's large paving stones are still in place, and there are sewers and other plumbing works beneath. On one side it is clear that the walkway was arcaded as the supporting columns survive. On the east side of the site are baths. The Théo Desplans Musée Archéologique (Theo Desplans Archaeology Museum: included in entry ticket for Villasse) on the site displays a collection of sculpture unearthed there.

Exploring reminders of Vaison's Roman days (above)

Decorated columns in the Cathédrale Notre-Dame de Nazareth (above right)

A Roman warrior

HAUTE VILLE

The medieval quarter (Haute Ville) stands apart from modern Vaison, rising on a hill on the other side of the river. A short walk leads up to this attractive district of lanes and alleys. At the top stand the ruins of the castle built in the 12th century by the Counts of Toulouse, and partly reconstructed in the 15th century. From here you can enjoy views down to the town and across to Mont Ventoux (▷ 159).

PONT ROMAIN

Vaison's main street, Grande Rue, runs down between old houses to the Roman bridge, which crosses the Ouvèze river. A single arch with a single-track cobbled roadway on top, it has not been widened or hardly even repaired in 2,000 years, although the parapet on top is modern. The present parapet was put in place in 1993, replacing the 17th-century parapet that was swept away in the catastrophic floods of 22 September 1992.

BACKGROUND

Vaison started out as a Gaulish settlement called Vasio. Colonized by the Romans in the second century BC, it became a prosperous town named Vasio Vocontiorum, linked to the other side of the Ouvèze by the Pont Romain, still in use today. After invasion by Visigoths and the fall of the Roman Empire, the town was re-established on the better protected hillside on the other side of the Ouvèze.

In the 18th century the town spread back across the river, and was built largely on top of the Roman ruins. In the 20th century excavations saved what was left of the ruins of the Roman town. The popularity of the Roman site with visitors led Vaison to develop other attractions, including hotels, restaurants and a summer festival of drama, music and dance.

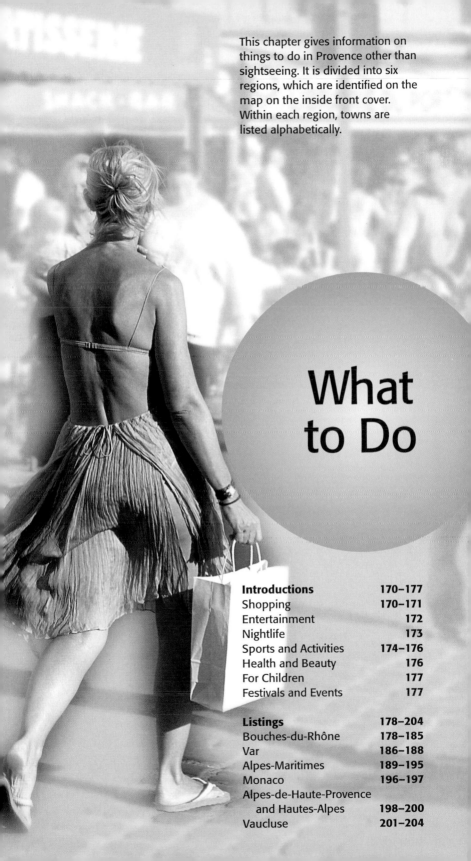

This chapter gives information on things to do in Provence other than sightseeing. It is divided into six regions, which are identified on the map on the inside front cover. Within each region, towns are listed alphabetically.

What to Do

SHOPPING

Provence is a seductive shopping destination, whether you're after local produce at the lively markets or chic Riviera fashion at a Cannes boutique. Herbs, soaps, perfumes, pottery, olive oil and wine are among the best buys of the region.

FOOD
Calisson sweets (candies), dried wild herbs, virgin olive oil and strings of garlic are the musts for any market shopping trip. The west coast of France may be more famous for its truffles, but the vast majority selected by top chefs come from Provence. For sensational jam, try the Les Merveilles range, and for other sugary treats sample candied fruits in Apt, *berlingots* (fruit humbugs) in Carpentras, nougat in Vence and *marrons glacés* (glazed chestnuts) in Collobrières.

Food is taken very seriously in France, with quality and freshness high on every shopper's list of priorities.

Most food stores, except supermarkets, specialize and usually only sell one type of product. The ones you are most likely to see are the *boulangerie* (bakery), *pâtisserie* (pastry/cake shop), *fromagerie* (cheese shop), *boucherie* (butcher's shop), *charcuterie* (delicatessen) and *poissonnerie* (fishmonger's).

WINES AND SPIRITS
Hypermarchés sell an excellent range of French wines and British visitors in particular will find prices less expensive than back home. It is also fun to buy from the vineyards (*domaines*) themselves. The Rhône and Lubéron have specialist wine routes.

REGIONAL SPECIAL BUYS
The air in the south is heavy with the scent of flowers, particularly around Grasse, famous for its perfumes. *Savon* (soap) *de Marseille* is known for its quality, and is often made with a base of olive oil. Nothing of the olive tree is wasted: The wood is carved into items from salad bowls to coasters.

Terracotta pottery is also widespread and you'll find bright ceramics in any market square. Ceramics in the shape of crickets and special garlic-scraper saucers are among the more unusual buys. For faïences (fine glazed ceramics) head to Moustiers-Sainte-Marie and for glassware try Biot.

INDIVIDUAL BOUTIQUES
Chain stores are finding their way into larger Provence towns, but there are many more individual boutiques

CHAIN STORES

NAME	Menswear	Womenswear	For children	Shoes	Cosmetics and toiletries	Sports equipment and clothes	Accessories	Household items	Books, music and DVDs	Perfume	CONTACT NUMBER
Alain Manoukian	✔	✔		✔			✔				04 96 17 63 50
André			✔	✔			✔				04 96 15 71 97
Bata			✔	✔			✔				04 91 54 25 96
Caroll		✔		✔			✔				04 96 11 24 04
Celio	✔						✔				04 91 90 25 39
Courir			✔	✔			✔				04 91 44 69 48
Du Pareil au Même			✔	✔			✔				04 91 54 43 50
Etam		✔		✔			✔				04 91 90 15 78
FNAC									✔		04 91 39 94 00
Go Sport	✔	✔	✔	✔		✔	✔				04 96 20 81 90
Mango		✔		✔			✔				04 91 60 11 45
Marionnaud										✔	04 91 90 62 70
Minelli				✔			✔				04 91 45 08 17
Monoprix	✔	✔	✔	✔	✔		✔	✔		✔	04 91 32 00 50
Morgan		✔					✔				04 91 09 84 55
Naf Naf	✔	✔	✔	✔			✔				04 91 54 19 67
Pimkie		✔	✔	✔			✔				04 91 45 07 16
Zara	✔	✔		✔			✔				04 91 00 33 69

selling fashion (prêt-à-porter), lingerie, shoes and items such as kitchenware. In larger cities the department store *(grand magasin)* brings all these specialists under one roof.

MARKETS

The *marché* (market) is a French institution. Large cities hold at least one daily market and smaller towns have a weekly one. They usually start around 7am and finish at noon. Discover the freshest seasonal produce, including fruit, vegetables and cheeses, and other products, from basketware to pottery. Buy *herbes de Provence* at Aix's sprawling market and flowers in old Nice. Other types of market advertise in the local paper or on posters in the area. *Foires artisanales* bring together potters, sculptors and other artists, and are held during the holiday season. A summer treat is the *marché nocturne*, a craft market that gets going after sunset, away from the sweltering afternoon sunshine. One of the best is at St-Rémy-de-Provence every Tuesday from June to the end of September. At Christmas there are wonderful Yuletide markets selling the famous *santons* (figurines) often based on local and well-known characters.

Marchés aux puces (flea markets) can be found in many cities. They are a bargain hunter's delight, with a mix of genuine antiques and flea-market goods—anything from furniture to china. Look out for genuine art nouveau glassware and top-quality hand-embroidered bed linens.

MODERN STORES

Supermarkets and hyper-markets *(hypermarchés* or *grandes-surfaces)* have sprung up on the outskirts of every big town or city. The main names include Carrefour, Auchan, Champion and E. Leclerc. Here you will find the *boulangerie*, *boucherie* and *charcuterie* under one roof. Often the *hypermarchés* are surrounded by other stores, such as DIY stores, in a *centre commercial* (shopping mall). The larger malls have restaurants.

CLOTHES

You'll find designer labels in the chic Riviera resorts and a good range of fashion stores in all the main towns. You can buy traditional Provençal cotton prints, known as *indiennes*, either by the length or ready-made into scarves, tops and skirts. Souléiado and Les Olivades stores are good places to look.

PRACTICALITIES

Some shops close from noon until mid afternoon. Hypermarkets usually remain open over lunch.
Non-EU visitors can reclaim VAT on certain purchases (▷ 265).

WHAT TO DO

In addition to countless individual boutiques and specialist shops, Provence has some chain stores, including well-known American, Spanish and British names. The chart below gives details of some of them, stating the number of branches each chain has in Provence and the telephone number of the Marseille store.

NUMBER OF SHOPS	DESCRIPTION	WEBSITE
16	Stylish clothes and accessories for women and men	www.alain-manoukian.com
12	Footwear for men, women and children	www.vivarte.fr
18	Smart and sporty shoes and boots for men, women and children	www.bata.com
22	Elegant clothes and accessories for women	www.caroll.com
15	Popular clothing and accessories for men	www.celio.com
27	Sports footwear and accessories (watches and bags) for the whole family	www.courir.com
8	Clothes, toys, pushchairs (strollers) and equipment for babies/children	www.dpam.com
12	Inexpensive fashion, lingerie and accessories for women	www.etam.com
8	Books, music, DVDs, computer equipment and concert tickets	www.fnac.com
11	Sports clothing, shoes, equipment and accessories for all	www.gosport.fr
10	Fashion and accessories for women	www.mango.es
39	Perfume stores	www.marionnaud.com
9	Funky shoes and boots	www.vivarte.fr
19	Department store selling food, household items, clothes and cosmetics	www.monoprix.fr
16	Fashions for women	www.morgandetoi.com
19	Clothes for women and children (Naf Naf) and men (Chevignon)	www.nafnaf.com
21	Clothes and accessories at rock-bottom prices for women and girls	www.pimkie.fr
10	Smart clothes and accessories for men and women	www.zara.es

ENTERTAINMENT

Quality performances combine with amazing venues on the Provence arts scene. Enjoy epic opera in Orange's Roman theatre, jazz in Nice's Cimiez gardens or major theatrical performances at the Avignon festival. For more intimate productions, try a fringe show in a café-theatre or chamber music in the cloisters of a church. Magazines in hotel foyers and tourist offices are a good source of information.

THEATRE
Every major city has a theatre. Seasons usually run from October until late spring. The fringe scene, with café-theatres and alternative productions, is usually more lively and has a year-round schedule.

In Avignon in July the famous festival (▷ 204) attracts troupes from around the world

Monte-Carlo Philharmonic Orchestra in concert

and you can often see Shakespeare in any of five or six languages. During the festival, Avignon stages many French premieres featuring top stars. Expect to see plays by Molière, Ibsen and Chekhov in venues ranging from the Papal Palace to side-street cafés. Fringe theatres in Marseille and the Théâtre des Ateliers in Aix-en-Provence specialize in works by local playwrights. Huge auditoriums in exhibition venues on the outskirts of major towns host touring productions of French rock musicals such as *Starmania* and *The Hunchback of Notre-Dame*.

DANCE
Contemporary dance festivals in Aix and Marseille draw crowds in summer, and Avignon's festival attracts international companies. The Centre Chorégraphique National is based at the Cité du Livre in Aix, where the Ballet Preljocaj hosts performances throughout the year. For information on the Ballet National de Marseille, look up www.ballet-de-marseille.com.

OPERA
In summer, Provence hosts many operatic productions, usually in historic settings. Most famous is the *Chorégies* (▷ 204) in Orange, when the Roman theatre hosts a couple of large-scale pageant productions of popular pieces such as *Carmen* and *La Traviata*. In Aix-en-Provence the *Festival d'Art Lyrique* (▷ 185) sees a temporary opera house erected in the courtyard of the Archbishop's Palace. This festival, with an emphasis on the works of Mozart and Benjamin Britten, is famous for discovering international opera stars of tomorrow.

CLASSICAL MUSIC
Aix and Orange's summer music festivals have orchestral concerts alongside the more famous opera. In Nice, you can enjoy sacred music in churches and summer concerts at the Cimiez monastery. Chamber music is celebrated with annual seasons featuring international performers in Menton (www.villedementon.com).

JAZZ
The Riviera is a beacon to the world's leading jazz musicians. Its two main events overlap, giving you the chance to overindulge in the most potent music. The pine groves of Antibes–Juan-Les-Pins have hosted the legends of jazz and swing for decades, with stars from both sides of the Atlantic (▷ 195). Rival performers line up in Nice's Cimiez gardens for the Nice Jazz Festival (▷ 195).

BOOKING TICKETS
Most box offices will accept telephone bookings with payment by credit card. FNAC

Two members of the Ballet National de Marseille perform

stores (www.fnac.com) and Virgin Megastores (www.virgin mega.fr) have ticket agencies selling seats for high-profile events and tourist offices often sell tickets for smaller festivals. Matinées are often less expensive than evening shows.

ETIQUETTE
Events in concert halls and opera houses require smart but not necessarily formal clothing—although you can dress up if you wish without feeling overdressed. Festivals have no dress code, although turning up in beachwear or shirtless may cause offence. Smoking is banned in auditoriums.

NIGHTLIFE

Don't expect great nightlife in the heart of the Provençal countryside—the serious clubbing takes place in town. University towns are best, so party animals should consider checking out the bars of Marseille for flyers announcing the next big event. During winter, clubs in the Côte d'Azur resorts appear deceptively sleepy. But from carnival time in spring right up until New Year the chic club scene comes alive, with minor royals and major celebs regularly on the guest list.

Rural Provence gets a slice of the action on 21 June, when midsummer balls in village squares give many city parties a run for their money.

THE CAFÉ-BAR
The inextricably linked café-bar is the lifeblood of French nightlife. Even the most humble village will have at

The Riviera has a lively club scene

least one place to hang out over a few drinks. In country areas French bars have multiple personalities—they are a place for teenagers to hang out over a game of pool, and somewhere for farmers to meet to discuss the latest subsidy controversy. In the cities, and especially in the resorts, bars are more sophisticated—diners drop in for an aperitif before dinner or a coffee and digestif afterwards.

Every bar worth its salt will have tables outside during the summer, and the most popular are those where the clientele can watch the world go by as

evening turns to night.

A PMU bar is a branch of the French tote system where you can bet on horse races and often watch races live on TV. However, these venues can be smoky and are not always used to welcoming visitors. In cities, bars open as early as 7am to serve breakfast and stay open until the early hours of the morning. Out of season and out of the cities, bars may close as early as 9pm.

Unaccompanied children under 16 are not allowed into bars and the legal age for drinking is 16, although children aged 14 to 16 may drink wine or beer if accompanied by an adult.

CABARET
Although the movie *La Cage aux Folles* (1978) was set in the south of France, revues are a peculiarly Parisian form of entertainment, and in Provence the closest thing you'll find will be floor shows at the casinos of Nice and Cannes (▷ 190), featuring the requisite showgirls in sequins and feathers.

CLUBS
Major cities and resorts have a lively club scene. Find flyers at tourist offices, music stores or trendy cafés. Clubs may open from 10pm but don't get started until midnight, then partying continues until dawn.

Smart dress is usually the rule. There is an admission charge on weekends and some week nights, but this usually includes your first drink.

CASINOS
Not necessarily just for James Bond types, a night at a casino is part entertainment, part spectator sport and, provided you don't go totally over the top and lose your shirt, a great place to mix with European high rollers. Dress well to avoid doormen's sneers. Tables open around 10pm and close around 4am. The doyenne has to be

Enjoying a drink outside on a summer's evening

Monte-Carlo's Casino (▷ 196). Money from the gaming tables is Monaco's principal income. Only foreigners are allowed to play, so you'll need your passport. Locals, even the royals, are barred from gambling.

GAY AND LESBIAN
Nice and St-Tropez have a lively gay bar and club scene (www.gay-provence.org). Inland, Aix-en-Provence and Avignon have a choice of venues. Marseille's gay community is student-led and tends to be more political, with its own Gay Pride march in late June or early July.

SPORTS AND ACTIVITIES

Provence has plenty to offer when it comes to outdoor activities—whether it's skiing in the Hautes-Alpes, windsurfing near Hyères or horseback riding through the Camargue. The French have a great enthusiasm for sports. If you can climb it, jump from it, ski down it, sail on it, swim under it, ride on it or slither through it, the French do it—and there will be an association to organize and publicize the activity. There are also plenty of spectator sports to enjoy, attracting sportsmen and women from across the world.

GENERAL INFORMATION

Each district has some form of sporting facility, be it a boules pitch, sports hall, swimming pool (*piscine*), tennis court or golf course. Information about these facilities appears in tourist publications under

Parachuting is an adventurous way to view the countryside

loisirs (leisure). Most tourist offices publish separate booklets focusing on their leisure facilities. The French Government Tourist Office (FGTO) also produces some excellent brochures on leisure and sporting activities.

AIR SPORTS

Local aerodromes host clubs specializing in flying (*vol*), gliding (*vol à voile*) or launching themselves out of planes (*parachutisme*). These are privately run members' clubs that generally welcome foreign members (although the price, at around €200, may be prohibitive for short-term visitors).

They also offer introductions (*baptêmes*) to the sport, with prices of around €75 for a flight, €400 for parachute training and €230 for a tandem parachute jump.
Fédération Française de Vol Libre: www.ffvl.com
Fédération Française de Vol à Voile: www.ffvv.com

BICYCLING

Bicycling (*cyclisme*), either off or on road, is a popular pastime, as well as a serious sport. It is easy to rent bicycles in towns and at major railway stations. Most tourist offices can offer itineraries for riders with mountain bikes (*vélo tous terrains—VTT*).
Fédération Française de Cyclisme: www.ffc.fr

The Tour de France is arguably the most important sporting event in France (www.letour.fr). The three-week event crosses the country in July, with its own carnival-style roadshow following in its wake. It often includes a stretch in Provence. You don't need a ticket, just find a suitable spot along the route on any stage. You'll need to arrive early as the roads are closed at least a couple of hours before the race is due to pass by.

CLIMBING

The Lubéron area attracts climbers from all over the world, and the Dentelles de Montmirail have been popular year-round since the 1940s.

The Club Alpin de Français (www.clubalpin.com) has information about climbing lessons or equipment rental for experienced climbers. Local tourist offices can put you in touch with caving groups.

FISHING

While fish farming is now one of the region's biggest growth industries, thousands of kilometres of waterways in Provence offer more tranquil angling and fly-fishing. Vaucluse alone has almost 3,000km (1,800 miles) of river banks. On rivers and lakes, some of which are private, you

Bicycling in the Vallée des Merveilles

will need a licence (available from fishing shops) to cast your line.

GOLF

Golfers have plenty of courses to choose from in Provence, especially on the coast. In some resorts, such as Nice, the golf course is seen as an extension of the four-star luxury experience.

Tourist offices have details of special offers on green fees for visitors, including passes allowing holidaymakers to visit a selection of courses, and can organize combined golfing and dining breaks. Choose from 18-hole courses, such as the

Golf Club d'Aix-Marseille (www.golfpass-provence.com), or smaller 9-hole options with fabulous views, such as the Chemin des Granet (www.opengolfclub.com). Fédération Française de Golf: www.ffg.org

HORSE RACING
Horse racing is a popular sport in France and there are hippodromes—race courses—in some of Provence's coastal towns and resorts. The Riviera's main venue is at Cagnes-sur-Mer (www.hippodrome-cotedazur.com) and Marseille has a choice of tracks (www.hippodrome-borely.com).

There are plenty of opportunities for sailing on the Mediterranean

HORSEBACK RIDING
The flat marshes of the Camargue offer some of the most spectacular yet undemanding routes for horseback riding *(équitation/randonée équestre)*. You'll also find riding clubs close to major towns and cities, including Les Milles, near Aix. Fédération Française d'Équitation: www.ffe.com

KAYAKING
Many of Provence's rivers are excellent for kayaking and canoeing, including the Sorgue and the Durance. The most spectacular settings are the Grand Canyon du Verdon (go

with a trained guide) and the Ubbaye Valley in the Alpes-de-Haute-Provence. You can rent equipment on site by the hour, the day or longer, or you can take an escorted kayak trip. The fast-flowing waters in the region are linked to hydro-electric power stations, so currents alter suddenly as barrages are raised or lowered. Do get up-to-the-minute local advice before venturing out. Fédération Française de Canöe-Kayak: www.ffck.org

MOTOR SPORTS
There is only one destination for Formula 1 fans: The most glamorous race on the circuit is at Monte-Carlo, where the cars twist and turn through the narrow streets rather than a specially built race track. Seeing legends of racing speeding past famous buildings and the magnificent views is breathtaking stuff. The presence of the jet set turns Monaco into much more than a Grand Prix, but if you simply want to watch the racing, prices for hillside viewing start at €115, with stand seats costing from €250 to €800. Racing under far more hazardous conditions, the Trophy Andros is the classic alpine ice-driving championship, one of the main events of Provence's winter resorts.

PARAPENTE
The *parapente* is a little like a parachute but more controllable, and you don't need to take a plane ride—a running jump from any high point launches you into the air. Pioneered in France, it is a popular sport. Fédération Française de Vol Libre: www.ffvl.com

RUGBY
There is a strong rugby following in France and the season (Sep–end May) culminates in the international Six Nations

Tournament, when France takes on England, Scotland, Wales, Ireland and Italy in a bid to be the best in Europe. While the most passionate rugby fans and the big money are in southwestern France, the southeast has two leagues: Provence and Côte d'Azur. There is loyal local support for teams such as RC Arlésien and Le Mourillon in Toulon. Firemen from the Marseille area form the team known as Sapeurs-Pompiers. Nice also has a top club.

SAILING
Most of Provence's 125 ports and marinas have sailing schools and boats for rent

Inland, white-water rafting is a popular activity

(www.voilecotedazur.com). For a change from Mediterranean scenery, head to the mountain lakes of the Alpes-de-Haute-Provence, such as Lac de Quinson and Lac du Castillon, where sailing is also popular.

SKIING/SNOWBOARDING
These are the principal sports of the winter season, and the Alpine resorts, including Isola 2000 and Val d'Allos, have a wide range of activities and training packages. Equipment rental and ski-school classes can vary in price according to the time of year. It is worth checking dates of the French school holidays, since outside

these periods excellent bargains may be had with discounts on hotels as well. Contact the École du Ski Français: www.esf.net or Club Alpin Français: www.clubalpin.com and www.skifrance.com

SOCCER
Soccer is one of the premier sports in France. Olympique de Marseille, wearing white, are among the south's sporting heroes. A.S. Monaco were top of the league in 2003. The season runs from August to the end of May and tickets for matches are like gold. A.S. Monaco plays at Stade Louis II (tel 377 92 05 40 00;

Saintes-Maries-de-la-Mer is one of the top places for windsurfing

www.asm-foot.mc); Olympique de Marseille at Velodrome 3, boulevard Michelet (tel 04 91 55 93 56; www.olympiquede marseille.com).

TENNIS
The mild winter climate means that the tennis stars come out in Provence as early as February, for the tournament in Nice. Monte-Carlo is another of the early meetings on the ATP Masters tour.

WALKING AND HIKING
Provence is criss-crossed by trails, with a series of *Sentiers de Grandes Randonnées* (long-distance trails) and *Petites Randonnées* (shorter walking routes) that are included on maps published by Institut Géographique National (IGN, Éspace IGN, rue La Boétie, 75008 Paris; www.ign.fr). Topographical guides are sold at tourist offices and park bookstores.

To supplement this network, every *département* and even local *communes* have shorter walks, including marked trails around lakes, along river banks or linking historical monuments. Most tourist offices have information about trails and walks in their area,

and town halls usually have free maps of local walks. An alternative option is the *Randonnée avec Âne*, where hikers travel with donkeys who carry baggage and picnics in their panniers (www.bourricot.com).

WINDSURFING
The happiest side effect of Provence's notorious *mistral* wind is that it produces champion windsurfers. When the weather is less stormy, gentler but effective winds are harnessed by experts at Saintes-Maries-de-la-Mer and at l'Almanarre, near Hyères. There are windsurfing schools all along the coast.

Resting on a rock during a walk in the Alpilles

HEALTH AND BEAUTY ♥

What the rest of the world has discovered in the last 10 years the French have known for centuries—that a little pampering is good for everyone.

SPAS AND THALASSOTHERAPY
France discovered the thera-peutic value of its natural water sources soon after it began to enjoy the taste of the waters themselves. One of the oldest is at Aix-en-Provence, where, long before the Romans built their spa resorts, Celtic women used to take to the 35°C (95°F) waters for their alleged fertility

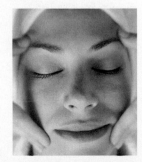

benefits. Today's Thermes Sextius Hydrotherapy Complex (▷ 180) uses those same hot waters and adds mud treatments and gym toning to the recipe. The most luxurious hotels on the Riviera now boast health spas and pamper-ing suites. The French invented thalassotherapy—the use of seawater in a variety of therapies—and thalassotherapy venues are dotted along the Mediterranean coast.

Save some time for a little pampering during your stay

FOR CHILDREN

There is plenty to entertain children in Provence, whether they prefer splashing in the warm waters of the Mediterranean, visiting an adventure park or waving at a parade during one of the region's many festivals. Museums are usually child-friendly and often have activity packs or worksheets for younger visitors. The region's Roman ruins have their own attraction for youngsters, bringing to life school history lessons.

BEACHES
There are excellent beaches along the Mediterranean coast, although some of the more exclusive addresses tend to frown on children being children. The best option is to find a less upscale stretch of beach, close to a water park, and sacrifice parental calm in preference for family harmony. Good family beaches include Le Lavandou, Bandol, La Ciotat, La Couronne (near Martigues) and Sausset-les-Pins.

FESTIVALS AND FAIRS
These are held throughout the year (▷ below) and are perfect for children. There are marching bands, merry-go-rounds, costumed minstrels, clowns and face painting. The Carnival parades often have child-friendly themes. Menton's *Fête du Citron* (▷ 195), in late February, regularly turns to children's books for its themes, and floats in recent years have evoked Disney, Asterix and Alice in Wonderland.

FOOD
Food tasting is always popular, with many a baker ready to share a slice of chocolate bread or sweetmaker some home-made candies. There are lots of olives and cheeses to sample on a trip to the weekly market.

ADVENTURE PARKS
More than 30 adventure parks and water parks provide a useful bribe to guarantee good behaviour on longer drives. Zoos and animal parks are also popular.

SPORTS
France has a comprehensive range of sports (▷ 174–176). The level of training and supervision is usually very high, so children can try a new sport or simply enjoy one in which they are already proficient—from horseback riding to bicycling, or windsurfing to snowboarding. Ski resorts have kids' clubs where youngsters can enjoy supervised training and entertainment while the adults play at their own pace.

WHAT TO DO

FESTIVALS AND EVENTS

You are unlikely to go hungry or thirsty at one of Provence's 500-or-so festivals. Whatever the theme, glasses and plates are filled and refilled. In addition to food and free-flowing wine, festivals often involve a lively procession in traditional costume. The events give you a glimpse into the history and character of the town or village, and of Provence itself. For France's national holidays ▷ 270.

RELIGIOUS
Provence is famous for its Nativity scenes: Craftsmen make *santons* for Nativity displays and shepherds lead their flocks to church on Christmas Eve for a life-size re-creation. Saintes-Maries-de-la-Mer brings together Christian and folk traditions with its gypsy pilgrimage (▷ 185). Saints days are celebrated with gusto: St. Eloi festivities in summer see fabulous processions, with garlanded horses pulling wagons piled with wheat.

ARTS
The Cannes Film Festival in May has the highest profile, but summer nights are filled with the sound of sopranos in open-air operas across Provence. Avignon has a lively fringe where you can enjoy the off-beat on a budget. Jazz is France's adopted art form, with top artists appearing along the Côte d'Azur in the summer.

FOOD AND DRINK
In October, France has a week of food festivals, street fairs and cookery contests. This pleasure is prolonged in Provence with an extra week of gastronomy in Vaison-la-Romaine, but the eating continues year-round. Wine country produces some excellent festivals, with chestnuts, roasted, puréed and baked, served with local wines along the Rhône, and olives complementing the wines of the Lubéron.

TRADITIONAL
May Day is the *Fête des Gardians*, when the cowboys of the Camargue display their rodeo skills and race in the Roman theatre at Arles. St-Tropez's noisy and ebullient *bravades* are nominally a celebration of the town's patron saint, but in reality a commemoration of the rout of a Spanish armada.

BOUCHES-DU-RHÔNE

With its long coastline, Bouches-du-Rhône is good for water sports, especially windsurfing at Saintes-Maries-de-la-Mer. The wetlands of the Camargue entice horseback riders, bicyclists, walkers and birdwatchers. Arles, Aix-en-Provence and St-Rémy-de-Provence are good shopping destinations, while culture-lovers should time their visit to coincide with one of the many events, including the festivals of Aix and Avignon in July.

KEY TO SYMBOLS	
🏛	Shopping
🎭	Entertainment
🍸	Nightlife
🏃	Sports
✪	Activities
♡	Health and Beauty
✿	For Children

AIX-EN-PROVENCE

🏛 CHOCOLATERIE DE PUYRICARD

7 rue Rifle-Rafle, 13100 Aix-en-Provence
Tel 04 42 21 13 26
www.puyricard.fr
This local chocolatier is renowned internationally for the quality of its products (there is no vegetable fat, cocoa butter only). A popular chocolate is Cézanne's Nail, which reproduces the copper paving stones in Aix that indicate a circuit dedicated to the local painter. You can see where the chocolates are made out in the countryside near the village of Puyricard.
🕐 Mon–Sat 9–7

🏛 CONFISERIE ENTRECASTEAUX

2 rue Entrecasteaux, 13100 Aix-en-Provence
Tel 04 42 27 15 02
This is *the* place to buy *calissons,* an Aix specialty. Made according to a family recipe for four generations, they come in a diamond-shaped box, reproducing the original shape of the *calisson.* Other treats include glacé fruit, nougat and chocolate.
🕐 Mon–Sat 8–12, 2–7

🏛 MARCHÉ AUX ANTIQUAIRES

Place du Palais de Justice, 13100 Aix-en-Provence
Browse this antiques market for period furniture, old books and decorative items. Credit cards are not accepted.
🕐 Tue, Thu, Sat 7–1

🏛 MARCHÉ AUX HERBES

Place Richelme, 13100 Aix-en-Provence
Local farmers arrive early to display their cheeses, fruit and vegetables under the shade of plane trees. The produce is fresh, smells good and tastes great. Credit cards are not accepted.
🕐 Tue, Thu, Sat 7–1

🎭 LE CÉZANNE

1 rue Marcel-Guillaume, 13100 Aix-en-Provence
Tel 08 36 68 72 70
www.lecezanne.com
This nine-screen cinema complex focuses on Hollywood blockbusters and major hits at the French box office. Some film premieres also take place here. The films are rarely shown in their original language.
🕐 Screenings daily 11am–10pm 🎟 €8

🎭 LA FONDERIE

14 cours St-Louis, 13100 Aix-en-Provence
Tel 04 42 63 10 11
Concerts at this former foundry range from rock to reggae. There are also plays. The two auditoriums have capacity for 300 and 100 people and there is also a bar. Credit cards are not accepted.
🕐 Varies 🎟 €2–€12

HOT BRASS
Quartier Celony, route d'Eguilles, 13090
Aix-en-Provence
Tel 04 42 21 05 57
For more than 20 years, this
has been the haunt of jazz
lovers and, sometimes, of
great names on the musical
scene—the numerous
pictures adorning the walls
testify to this.
🕐 Fri, Sat 11.30pm–5am 💶 €16

THÉÂTRE ET CHANSONS
1 rue Émile Tavan, 13100
Aix-en-Provence
Tel 04 42 27 37 39
http://theatre.et.chansons.free.fr
This 70-seat auditorium is
entirely dedicated to songs:
old-fashioned tunes, sung
poetry or original performances by founder Isabelle
Bloch-Delahaie. Singing
workshops are also arranged.
🕐 Shows often take place at 8.30pm
💶 Around €12

CASINO DE AIX
Avenue de l'Europe, 13601
Aix-en-Provence
Tel 04 42 59 69 00
A blue glass pyramid is in
the core of this 21st-century
building and light plays on its
façade every evening. You'll
find slot machines by the
hundreds and a games room,
but also four restaurants and
a concert hall.
🕐 Daily 9.45am–3am (until 4am
Fri–Sun) 💶 Entry to the games room:
€11 ❓ You must be over 18 to enter
the games room

BISTROT AIXOIS
37 cours Sextius, 13100 Aix-en-Provence
Tel 04 42 27 50 10
This is the place to see and be
seen for Aix's beautiful young
people. It's so packed on
weekends that it can be
difficult to find dancing space.
Luckily, there's more room—
and air—upstairs.
🕐 Mon–Sat 7pm–2am

LES DEUX GARÇONS
53 cours Mirabeau, 13100
Aix-en-Provence
Tel 04 42 26 00 51
www.les2garcons.com
This 17th-century café has
been registered as a historic
monument. There's a terrace
facing the city's main street, a
large dining room on the
ground floor and a piano bar
(after 7pm) on the first floor.
🕐 Daily 6am–2am

LE DIVINO
Mas des Aubères, route de Venelles
13100 Aix-en-Provence
Tel 04 42 21 28 28
www.divino.fr
Mauve tones dominate the

*If you don't fancy the traditional
calisson sweets, there are plenty
of chocolates (above) to enjoy*

interior of this temple of
techno, with its talented DJs
and restaurant upstairs.
🕐 Fri–Sun 11pm–5am 💶 €16, free
for women on Fri

HAPPY DAYS
Place Richelme, 13100 Aix-en-Provence
Tel 04 42 21 02 35
On the liveliest square in town,
this bar is popular with the
fashionable crowd. The funky
interior has yellow and
burgundy walls and furniture.
🕐 Mon–Sat 8am–2am (food is served
12–4)

KEY NIGHTS
1 route des Milles, 13100
Aix-en-Provence
Tel 04 42 27 40 90
Disco rhythms, foam parties
and theme nights featuring
prizes create a fun atmosphere
enjoyed by a young crowd.
🕐 Fri–Sun midnight–6am 💶 Free for
women; €16 for men on Sat, €10–€15
on other nights

QUEEN'S HEAD
11 Petite Rue St-Jean, 13100
Aix-en-Provence
Tel 04 42 26 26 13
A little piece of England, with
a large wooden bar where
beer on tap is served in a
convivial atmosphere. For a
more intimate setting, head to
the comfortable saloon bar,
with its fabulous club
armchairs.
🕐 Mon–Sat 6pm–2am

BOWLING DU BRAS D'OR
23 boulevard Charrier, 13100
Aix-en-Provence
Tel 04 42 27 69 92
www.bowlingdubrasdor.com
These ten-pin bowling alleys
are popular with students at
the nearby university. Table
football, billiards, arcade
games and a large screen
showing sport are also on site.
🕐 Daily 2pm–2.30am 💶 €4–€6 per
game, plus €1.50 for shoe rental

KART'IN AIX
Zone d'Activité des Milles, 820 rue
André Ampère, 13100 Aix-en-Provence
Tel 04 42 97 79 99
www.kart-in.fr
Test your skills on the longest
indoor karting track in the
south of France (more than
550m/600 yards long). As with
Formula 1 circuits, your time is
displayed on an electronic
clock. After the race, enjoy a
drink in the panoramic bar.
🕐 Tue–Thu 6pm–midnight, Fri
6pm–1am, Sat 3pm–1am, Sun
3pm–9pm 💶 €18 for a 10-min session

WHAT TO DO

☻ THERMES SEXTIUS
55 cours Sextius, 13100
Aix-en-Provence
Tel 04 42 23 81 82
www.thermes-sextius.com
The spa uses naturally warm mineralized water (35°C/95°F), which has flowed from the nearby Montagne Sainte-Victoire for centuries. It opened in 1999, in an 18th-century building close to the ancient Roman pool founded by the Roman general Caius Sextius. The hydro-therapeutic treatments focus on reducing stress and toxins.
⏰ Mon–Fri 8.30–7.30, Sat 8.30–6.30
💆 Full facial Zen re-energizing treatment €95, mud application €35

ARLES

⛫ BIJOUX DUMONT
3 rue du Palais, 13200 Arles
Tel 04 90 96 05 66
This family business has been making reproductions of original Provençal jewellery since 1967. Most use 18-carat gold, silver or semi-precious stones and they incorporate emblems of the region. Choose from cicada brooches, Provençal crosses or Saintes-Maries-de-la-Mer cross pendants.
⏰ Tue–Sat 9–12, 2.30–7

⛫ CHRISTIAN LACROIX
52 rue République, 13200 Arles
Tel 04 90 96 11 16
www.christianlacroix.com
The celebrated haute-couture designer was born in Arles and his vibrant collections certainly capture the spirit of the south. His gilded embroideries are reminiscent of toreador costumes and use only the finest fabrics.
⏰ Mon 2.30–7, Tue–Sat 9–12, 2–7

♫ THÉÂTRE D'ARLES
Boulevard Clemenceau, 13200
Arles
Tel 04 90 52 51 55,
ticket line 04 90 52 51 51
This theatre presents a mixture of contemporary drama and ballet from companies

around France and beyond. There are also regular children's shows.
⏰ Ticket office: Mon–Fri 11–3, 5–6.30
💶 Adult €17, child €8

♫ CARGO DE NUIT
7 avenue Sadi Carnot, 13200 Arles
Tel 04 90 49 55 99
www.cargodenuit.com
You'll find an eclectic mix here, from jazz fusion and salsa to reggae. The venue is a springboard for young talents every Thursday. The concert hall has a capacity of 300 and there is also a restaurant piano bar.
⏰ Concerts Thu–Sat evening
💶 Free–€10 for the concerts

Fashion designer Christian Lacroix was born in Arles

♫ EL PATIO
Le Patio de Camargue, 13200 Arles
Tel 04 90 49 51 76
www.chico.fr
Here you'll be entertained by Chico, leader of the celebrated band the Gypsy Kings. At this hacienda on the banks of the Rhône, he organizes gypsy evenings with flamenco and rumba.
⏰ Sat 8pm 💶 Adult €45, child €22.50
❓ Reserve ahead

☻ LE KRYSTAL
Hameau de Moulès, 13280 Arles
Tel 04 90 98 32 40
www.lekrystal.com
Enjoy theme nights at this venue, with its modern steel

and pink decor and blue neon lights. The choice includes zouk, go-go dancers and Latin. Dance to an orchestra every Sunday and Monday.
⏰ Club: Fri, Sat 10pm–6am. Dancing: Sun, Mon 2.30–8 💶 €10–€18

✪ LA CABANO DIS EGO
Le Sambuc, 13200 Arles
Tel 04 90 97 20 62
www.cabano-dis-ego.com
Horses and bulls are bred here and the owners organize activities including traditional horseback riding, French cowboy games and even hot-air balloon flights.
⏰ Open all year 💶 Varies

✪ CAMARGUE SAFARIS GALLON ORGANISATION
36 avenue Edouard Herriot, 13200 Arles
Tel 04 90 93 60 31
www.camargue.fr/safari4x4.html
Get off the beaten track and discover the Camargue's wildlife on a four-wheel drive safari. See the inland waters, horses, bulls and flamingos. Some deals also include biking and horseback riding. Credit cards are not accepted.
⏰ All year long by appointment
💶 €19 per person for 1 hour 30 min, €46 for 3 hour 30 min

✪ EUROPBIKE PROVENCE
1 rue Philippe Lebon, 13200 Arles
Tel 04 90 49 54 69
www.europbike-provence.com
Explore the area around Arles on two wheels. Europbike has been renting bicycles since 1978, and they can offer you a number of suggested routes. They also rent in-line skates.
⏰ Open all year 💶 Bicycle rental €16 for one day, €58 for one week

AUBAGNE

⛫ SANTONS MARCEL CARBONEL
6 promenade du Jeune Anacharsis, 13400 Aubagne
Tel 04 42 03 17 45
www.santonsmarcelcarbonel.com
A Provençal tradition, the *santons* are clay figures that

represent biblical characters and craftsmen. This family business sells 700 different figures; full Provençal *crêches* are also available. Marcel Carbonal was elected best craftsman of France in 1961.

Tue–Sat 9.30–12.30, 2.30–6.30

CABRIÈS

🎭 LE FOLIE'S

Zone commerciale de Plan-de-Campagne, 13480 Cabriès
Tel 04 42 02 87 20
www.le-joggingrose.com

This venue offers a show true to French music-hall tradition: sequins and feathers for the scantily clad dancers who sing, tap and cancan dance. Dinner is served during the show.

🕐 Fri, Sat 9pm 💶 €48 or €60 for show and meal (depending on which menu); drinks are included

LA CIOTAT

🤿 PLONGÉE 2000

35 quai Mitterrand, 13600 La Ciotat
Tel 04 42 71 93 02
www.plongee-2000.com

Scuba dives take place in areas with a high concentration of grouper; one site also boasts a statue of the Virgin Mary, another a Roman pool. There are also special dives for children (8 years and over) and for people with disabilities. Credit cards are not accepted.

🕐 Daily 9–12, 2–7 💶 €30 for a first dive, then starts at €20 per dive

FONTVIEILLE

🏠 DOMAINE OLIVIER D'AUGE

Auge, 13990 Fontvieille
Tel 04 90 54 62 95
www.olivier-d-auge.com

Olivier d'Auge keeps alive one of the traditions of the Baux valley by producing both wine and olive oil. Among the products available are some Provençal hampers containing wine, olive oil and other local specials, including tapenade and pesto.

🕐 By appointment only

MALLEMORT

⛳ GOLF DE PONT ROYAL

Domaine de Pont-Royal, 13370 Mallemort
Tel 04 90 57 40 79

Severiano Ballesteros designed this 18-hole course. The restaurant is called Esbeulavie—'life is beautiful' in Provençal.

🕐 Daily 9–5.30 (7am–7.30pm Jul, Aug); closed some Wed during low season 💶 Green fee: €42–€56

MARSEILLE

🏢 BOUTIQUE OFFICIELLE DE L'OLYMPIQUE DE MARSEILLE

44 boulevard de la Canebière, 13003 Marseille
Tel 04 91 33 20 01
www.madeinsport.com

Marseille is known for its soap (savon), often made with a base of olive oil

People from Marseille are passionate about their soccer team, the Olympique de Marseille or OM. This shop is entirely dedicated to it and its TV screen broadcasts videos in praise of the team. OM's official jersey is a popular item, but you may also be tempted by a soft toy or board game.

🕐 Mon–Sat 10–7 🚇 Noailles

🏢 LA COMPAGNIE DE PROVENCE

1 rue Caisserie, 13001 Marseille
Tel 04 91 56 20 94
www.lcdp-marseille.com

Marseille soap is known all over the world. Just moments from the old port, this store

offers variations on the traditional cube—it comes enriched with clay, essential oils and honey. The soap is attractively packaged with brown wrapping paper and a piece of string.

🕐 Mon–Sat 10–7 🚇 Vieux-Port

🏢 FOUR DES NAVETTES

136 rue Sainte, 13007 Marseille
Tel 04 91 33 32 12
www.fourdesnavettes.com

The city's oldest bakery, established in 1781, is the place to get *navettes*, boat-shaped biscuits scented with orange flower water, one of Marseille's specialties. Following tradition, the bread oven, which features prominently inside the shop and dates back to 1781, is blessed on 2 February by Marseille's archbishop. Credit cards are not accepted.

🕐 Mon–Sat 7am–8pm; Sun 9–1, 3–7.30 🚌 55, 61, 81

🏢 MADAME ZAZA OF MARSEILLE

73 cours Julien, 13006 Marseille
Tel 04 91 48 05 57

Zaza is the name of the local designer behind this collection, which betrays Mediterranean influences: Shirts and skirts are made of beautiful fabrics and are sometimes embroidered with gold. The store's pleasant interior has beamed ceilings and a terracotta-tiled floor typical of Provence.

🕐 Mon–Fri 10–1.30, 2–7, Sat 10–7

🏢 MARCHÉ AUX POISSONS

Vieux-Port, 13001 Marseille

This vibrant market, emblematic of the city, is a must see. Fish is extremely fresh, and gutted and scaled on the spot. Credit cards are not accepted.

🕐 Daily 8–1 🚇 Vieux-Port

🏛 MARCHÉ DES CAPUCINS

Place des Capucins, 13001 Marseille
At this market you'll find spices, fruit and vegetables from all over the world (with much from Northern Africa). Alongside these exotic offerings, are some discounted household goods. Credit cards are not accepted.
🕐 Mon–Sat 8.30–7 🚇 Noailles

🏛 LA ROUTE DES VINS

486 rue Paradis, 13008 Marseille
Tel 04 91 22 84 00
In every one of France's wine regions, a circuit known as 'la route des vins' (the wine road) encourages the discovery of local vineyards. There is good representation of most at this shop, including those typical of Provence, in a pleasant interior with barrels and wooden wine boxes.
🕐 Mon–Sat 9.30–1, 3.30–8 🚇 Rond-Point du Prado

🎭 LA BALEINE QUI DIT VAGUES

48 rue Barbaroux, 13001 Marseille
Tel 04 91 48 95 60
www.labaleinequiditvagues.com
The name of this venue means 'the whale who says waves', in reference to the traditional Native American tale in which a whale symbolizes the memory of the world. It hosts storytelling performances, many for children.
🕐 Fri–Sat 8pm, Wed 2.30pm, children's performances Oct–end Jun
🚇 Réformes 🎟 €2

🎭 LE CÉSAR

4 place Castellane, 13006 Marseille
Tel 04 91 37 12 80
High-quality arts films and the screening of films in their original language are the attraction of this three-screen repertoire cinema. Short films and previews followed by debates with the director or the actors complete the picture. Credit cards are not accepted.
🕐 Screenings: daily 1pm–10pm
🎟 Ticket around €7 🚇 Castellane

🎭 CHOCOLAT THÉÂTRE

59 cours Julien, 13006 Marseille
Tel 04 91 42 19 29
www.chocolattheatre.com
This 100-seat café-theatre saw the rise of many comedians and is now an institution in Marseille. There are some show-plus-dinner deals or you can eat at the adjoining tapas bar. Credit cards are not accepted.
🕐 Tue–Sat 8pm–2am 🎟 €14–€18 (with dinner €34–€39) 🚇 Cours Julien

🎭 CINÉMA LES VARIÉTÉS

37 rue Vincent Soppo, 13001 Marseille
Tel 04 96 11 61 61
This former grand old theatre, inaugurated in 1956, now has

Shopping for fruit at the Marché des Capucins, Marseille

four auditoriums. It shows mainly arty films, in their original language. There is also exhibition space and a café. Credit cards are not accepted.
🕐 Daily 1pm–10pm 🎟 €7
🚇 Noailles

🎭 DOCK DES SUDS

12 rue Urbain V, 13002 Marseille
Tel 04 91 99 00 00
www.dock-des-suds.org
These dockland warehouses are home to a 2,500-seat auditorium and an 800-seat cabaret, and also many restaurants. Cabaret, concerts and exhibitions are staged.
🕐 Tue–Fri 9–12, 2–5 🎟 Varies
🚇 National

🎭 LE DÔME

48 avenue St-Just, 13004 Marseille
Tel 04 91 12 21 21
www.le-dome.com
A green arch stands on top of the metal dome of this imposing concert hall, which seats 8,500 people. Productions include concerts, musicals, one-man shows and plays.
🕐 8.30pm 🎟 €30–€70 🚇 St-Just

🎭 ESPACE JULIEN

39 cours Julien, 13006 Marseille
Tel 04 91 24 34 10
www.espace-julien.com
Enjoy an eclectic selection of music here, including jazz and rock. The popular venue, on a pedestrian-only street packed with bars and cafés, holds 1,000 people. Credit cards are not accepted.
🕐 7.30pm–2am when there is a concert 🎟 Varies 🚇 Cours Julien

🎭 FRICHE DE LA BELLE DE MAI

23 rue Guibal, 13003 Marseille
Tel 04 95 04 95 04
www.lafriche.org
This former warehouse is home to the Système Friche theatre, the alternative Grenouille (Frog) radio station and venue for many concerts and exhibitions; rap group IAM have regularly appeared. There is a bar on site. Credit cards are not accepted.
🕐 Daily 9am–7pm 🎟 Varies 🚌 49

🎭 OPÉRA DE MARSEILLE

Place Ernest Reyer, 13001 Marseille
Tel 04 91 55 11 10
www.mairie-marseille.fr
Built in 1685, this 1,800-seat auditorium has a profusion of frescoes and candelabras. Home to the Philharmonic Orchestra of Marseille, it also hosts operas. Credit cards are not accepted.
🕐 Varies 🎟 €8–€55 🚇 Vieux-Port

WHAT TO DO

LE PELLE-MÊLE
8 place aux Huiles, 13100 Marseille
Tel 04 91 54 85 26
France's greatest jazz musicians have played here on the small stage. The leather and wood interior creates a warm atmosphere and an intimate setting for gigs.
Tue–Sat 6pm–2am Varies

THÉÂTRE NATIONAL DE MARSEILLE—LA CRIÉE
30 quai de Rive Neuve, 13007 Marseille
Tel 04 91 54 70 54
www.theatre-lacriee.com
This building was erected in 1981 in place of the fish market. There are two auditoriums with 782 and 260 seats. Productions range from the classics to contemporary plays, and some musicals.
Varies €20 Vieux Port

LES TROIS PALMES
2 boulevard Léon-Bancal, 13011 Marseille
Tel 04 91 87 91 87
www.les3palmes.com
Named after the palm trees at its entrance, this cinema has 11 auditoriums and a bar. It shows major box office hits.
Daily 1.30pm–10pm Adult €9, child (under 12) €6

20,000 LIEUES
Les Goudes, 13008 Marseille
Tel 04 91 25 05 24
http://20000lieues.free.fr
This venue, with its beautiful wooden interior, regularly welcomes pop, rock and funk bands. It's a good place to have a drink in a convivial atmosphere. Steaming bowls of pasta are served at all hours.
Daily 11am–2am No cover charge 19, 20

BAR DE LA MARINE
15 quai de Rive Neuve, 13007 Marseille
Tel 04 91 54 95 42
Facing the old port, this fashionable bar has a cool atmosphere and a soundtrack of acid jazz.
Daily 7am–2am

BAR DE LA SAMARITAINE
2 quai du Port, 13002 Marseille
Tel 04 91 90 31 41
This 1930s bar is a local institution. Its terrace, facing the picturesque old port, becomes a piano bar from Thursday to Saturday.
Daily 6am–10pm (til 11.30pm Jul, Aug)

CASTING MODE CAFÉ
148 avenue Pierre Mendès-France, 13008 Marseille
Tel 04 91 71 24 12
www.casting-mode-cafe.com
A fashionable venue that regularly turns into a catwalk for showcasing the work of local designers. The rest of the

Try Pelle-Mêle, in Marseille, if jazz is your thing

time you can enjoy the sea view from the terrace. Innovative Mediterranean cuisine is on the menu.
Daily 9am–2am (food served until 11.30pm) 19

EL COCHINO
11 rue des Trois-Mages, 13006 Marseille
Tel 04 91 47 29 66
Pigs really do fly here, or at least hang from the ceiling. You'll also find some on a plate of cold-cut meats, along with cheese, as a suggested accompaniment to a glass of wine.
Tue–Sat 6pm–2am Notre-Dame-du-Mont

MÉTAL CAFÉ
20 rue Fortia, 13001 Marseille
Tel 04 91 54 03 03
The club's decor has mixed influences: an Eastern theme for one of its mezzanines, fleur-de-lis for the second. Dance, house and disco rhythms are enjoyed by the happy few who manage to get in.
Thu–Sat 10.30pm–dawn Vieux Port

O'BRADY'S IRISH PUB
378 avenue de Mazargues, 13008 Marseille
Tel 04 91 71 53 71
www.obradys.com
Named after its owner, Jean-Luc Brady, this pub has a sports theme, with hanging flags and jerseys, and a big screen for those all-important games. You can enjoy live music on Mondays.
Daily 11am–1.30am 23, 45

L'OM CAFÉ
25 quai des Belges, 13001 Marseille
Tel 04 91 33 80 33
Named after the city's soccer team, Olympique de Marseille or OM, this café broadcasts soccer games. Sit out on the terrace facing the port.
Mon–Sat 8am–midnight, Sun 8am–10pm Vieux Port

LA BOULE FLORIAN
La Boule Florian, 36 avenue de Florian, 13010 Marseille
Tel 04 91 44 85 36
This bar-restaurant is home to the region's largest pétanque club and boasts a pitch that can welcome up to 35 games at a time. Competitions take place every weekend, weather permitting. Credit cards are not accepted.
Daily Free
15, stop at Florian

🅚 CENTRE DE LOISIRS DES GOUDES

2 boulevard Alexandre Delabre, 13008 Marseille
Tel 04 91 25 13 16
www.goudes-plongee.com
This company will take you diving in the Bay of Marseille, around the Rioux archipelago, where caves and old wrecks host extraordinary marine life. Some packages include meals, use of kayaks and mountain bikes.
🕒 Daily 8am–10pm 🅤 €45 for first dive, €173 for a weekend 🚍 19

🅚 STADE VÉLODROME

3 boulevard Michelet, 13008 Marseille
Tel 04 91 76 91 76
www.olympiquedemarseille.com
A 60,000-seat stadium that is home to Olympique de Marseille, the city's soccer team. The locals are passionate about the sport and every game is a big event.
🕒 8pm–11pm on match nights
🅤 Adult around €30 🅡 Rond-Point du Prado

🅞 CENTRE DE BIEN-ÊTRE CHÂTEAU BERGER

281 Corniche J.F Kennedy, 13007 Marseille
Tel 04 91 52 61 61
www.chateauberger.com
A castle overlooking the Mediterranean is the classy setting for this well-being venue. It is hard not to feel relaxed in such surroundings, and the treatments also help. You can combine workouts with the benefits of sea water.
🕒 Mon–Sat 9.30–6.30

NÎMES

🅔 LA CURE GOURMANDE

24 boulevard Victor Hugo, 30000 Nîmes
Tel 04 66 23 45 72
This store, part of a small chain, has handmade chocolates, cookies, lollipops, calissons and chocolate olives. It is an ideal place to buy gift-wrapped goodies as souvenirs and presents.
🕒 Summer daily 1.30–6.30

LE PARADOU

🅧 LA PETITE PROVENCE DU PARADOU

See page 70.

ST-CANNAT

🅧 VILLAGE DES AUTOMATES

Route Nationale 7, 13760 St-Cannat
Tel 04 42 57 30 30
www.villagedesautomates.com
This is a model village with a difference—A succession of little wooden houses are home to robots that reproduce scenes from fairy tales, including Jonathan Swift's *Gulliver* and La Fontaine's *Fox and Crow*. There is also a 'farm' with miniature

Get into the festival spirit at Maria Maria

animals, a snack bar and amusement park.
🕒 Apr–end Sep daily 10–6; Oct–end Mar Wed, Sat, Sun 10–5
🅤 Adult €8, child (3–14) €5

SAINTES-MARIES-DE-LA-MER

🅔 BOUTIQUE DU GARDIAN

9 rue Victor Hugo, 13460 Saintes-Maries-de-la-Mer
Tel 04 90 97 85 34
www.legardian.com/boutique
A *gardian* is a cowboy in the Camargue, and this is where you'll find the clothes to get outfitted like one: felt hat, broad belt and *gardian* boots (tall and made of soft leather). You'll also find a range of

outdoor brands. Totems and *gardian* saddles decorate the boutique's wooden interior.
🕒 Summer daily 9.30–8; winter daily 9.30–12, 2–6

🅔 MARIA MARIA

7 place des Remparts, 13460 Saintes-Maries-de-la-Mer
Tel 04 90 97 71 60
www.mariamaria.camargue.fr
There's a *feria* (festival) atmosphere at this boutique, which, in an ochre-walled and Spanish blue-tiled interior, showcases clothes emblematic of the exuberance of the south: Andalusian costumes, embroidered shirts, *gardian* clothes. You'll find some big names (Christian Lacroix, Tomar Artesania), but the shop is also the sole authorized distributor of some local designers.
🕒 Daily 10–12.30, 2–6 (9–9 in summer and during special events)

🅞 A.C.T. TIKI III

Le Grau d'Orguon–D38, 13460 Saintes-Maries-de-la-Mer
Tel 04 90 97 81 68/04 90 97 81 22
www.tiki3.fr
During this 90-minute boat excursion on the Petit Rhône river, you'll get close to the pastures and the *manade* (herds of bulls and horses), a landscape typical of Camargue. Credit cards are not accepted.
🕒 Mar–end Nov 🅤 €10 per person
❓ Reservations advised

🅞 PROMENADE DES RIÈGES

Route de Cacharel, 13460 Saintes-Maries-de-la-Mer
Tel 04 90 97 91 38
www.promenadedesrieges.com
These horseback-riding excursions let you discover the scenery of the Camargue's inland waters, beaches and wildlife (including flamingos). The stables have the white horses for which the Camargue is famous and use locally made saddles. Credit cards are not accepted.
🕒 By appointment 🅤 2-hour excursion €26.50, full-day from €61

WHAT TO DO

THALACAP CAMARGUE
Rue du Docteur Cambon, 13460
Saintes-Maries-de-la-Mer
Tel 04 90 99 22 22
www.thalacap.fr
This thalassotherapy spa offers a wide range of treatments where you can benefit from the therapeutic values of sea water, including seaweed and mud wrap and hydromassage. It's coupled with a hotel to allow week-long treatments. Facilities include a gym, hammam (Turkish bath), sauna and two sea-water pools (indoor and outdoor).
Daily 9–12, 2–8; closed mid-Nov to mid-Dec One night plus 4 thalasso-therapy treatments, breakfast and dinner €163; half-day plus 3 treatments €73

ST-RÉMY-DE-PROVENCE

CHOCOLATERIE JOËL DURAND
3 boulevard Victor Hugo, 13210
St-Rémy-de-Provence
Tel 04 90 92 38 25
Chocolate-maker Joël Durand, a Breton, fell in love with Provence and has since been combining chocolate with this region's local produce. Nothing is too audacious for someone who once associated chocolate with foie gras; his latest creation mixes chocolate with black olives.
Tue–Sat 9.30–12, 2.30–7.30, Sun 10–1

LILAMAND
5 avenue Albert Schweitzer, 13210
St-Rémy-de-Provence
Tel 04 90 92 11 08
www.lilamand.com
Glacé fruit has been the house specialty here since 1866. For generation after generation, working to recipes passed from father to son, Lilamand has been preserving in sugar many of the fruits that are emblematic of Provence. Try the Orangettes (glazed pieces of orange meant to be dunked in chocolate), the glacé chest-nuts or the glacé fruit jam.
Mon–Fri 8–12, 2–6

TERRE È PROVENCE
1 rue Lafayette, 13210
St-Rémy-de-Provence
Tel 04 90 92 28 52
This family business specializes in traditional pottery, including hand-painted plates, carafes and other dishes. The octagonal plates decorated with flowers or olives are beautiful.
Daily 9.30–1, 2–7 (closed Sun, Mon Jan–end Mar)

FESTIVALS AND EVENTS

MAY

FÊTE DES GARDIANS
Arles
Tel 04 90 18 41 20
Camargue cowboys parade on horseback.
May 1

FÊTE DE LA TRANSHUMANCE
St-Rémy-de-Provence
Local people celebrate the sheep migrations between the mountains and the plains.
Whit Monday (late May or early Jun)

THE GYPSY PILGRIMAGE
Saintes-Maries-de-la-Mer
Tourist Office: avenue Van Gogh
Tel 04 90 97 82 55
www.saintes-maries.carmargue.fr
Gypsy families gather for the pilgrimage to the church at the southern tip of the Carmargue, marking the traditional landing point of saints Marie-Salomé and Marie-Jacobé when they sailed from the Holy Land. Sarah, the Maries' servant, is the patron saint of the gypsy community and this is France's largest gypsy gathering.
24–25 May (there is a second pilgrimage on Sun closest to 22 Oct)

JUNE

FERIA DE PENTECÔTE
Nîmes
Tel 04 66 58 38 00 (tourist office)
www.ot-nimes.fr
It's said to be the biggest festival in Europe after Munich's *Oktoberfest*. Five days of celebration include

DISCOTHEQUE LA HAUTE GALINE
Chemin Cante Perdrix et Galine, 13210
St-Rémy-de-Provence
Tel 04 90 92 00 03
One of the few late-night options in this part of Provence, La Haute Galine offers various musical styles.
Fri and Sat from 9pm
€18

parades, street parties and, not to everyone's taste, bull chasing and fighting.
Usually 2nd weekend in Jun
Free

FÊTE DE LA TARASQUE
Tarascon
Tel 04 90 91 03 52
A dragon-like *tarasque* is led through the streets.
Last Sun

Aix's Théâtre de l'Archevêché

JULY

FESTIVAL D'AIX
Aix-en-Provence
Tel 04 42 17 34 34
www.festival-aix.com
This opera festival, also known as the *Festival International d'Art Lyrique et de la Musique*, lasts about three weeks.

RENCONTRES DES SUDS
Théâtre Antique and other venues
Dance, drama, music and opera.
12–18 Jul

VAR

Var has more than 150km (90 miles) of beaches, making it ideal for water sports or simply relaxing on the shore. Inland, you can walk in the Massif des Maures or the Massif de l'Esterel. For chic shopping head to St-Tropez, or for something more unusual try Cogolin, with its pipes, or Collobrières, with its candied chestnuts.

KEY TO SYMBOLS

- 🛍 Shopping
- 🎭 Entertainment
- 🍸 Nightlife
- 🏃 Sports
- ✪ Activities
- ♥ Health and Beauty
- ✹ For Children

AIGUINES

✪ LES GUIDES DES CALANQUES ET DU VERDON
Le Galetas, 83630 Aiguines
Tel 04 94 84 22 55
www.les-guides.net
Explore the caves of Rampins, Néoules and Castelette or raft and rock climb above ground. Credit cards are not accepted.
 €46–€58 for a caving expedition

BORMES-LES-MIMOSAS

🛍 PÉPINIÈRES CAVATORE
488 Chemin de Bénat, 83230 Bormes-les-Mimosas
Tel 04 94 00 40 23
www.pepinierescavatore.com
Mimosa trees are the specialty at this nursery—visit in February to see the trees in full bloom. Credit cards are not accepted.
✪ Jun–end Sep Mon–Fri 9–12; Oct–end May Mon–Fri 9–12, 1.30–5

COGOLIN

🛍 PIPES COURRIEU
58–60 avenue Georges Clemenceau, 83310 Cogolin
Tel 04 94 54 63 82
www.courrieupipes.fr
Since 1802, and following methods passed from father to son, the same family has been making pipes out of briar from the nearby Maures mountains. These are marked with a silver cockerel, emblem of Cogolin village. A wide range of accessories for pipes and cigars are also available.
✪ Mon–Sat 9–12, 2–6

COLLOBRIÈRES

🛍 MARCHÉ COLLOBRIÈROIS
Place de la Libération, 83610 Collobrières
Collobrières is surrounded by chestnut groves and its vibrant farmers' market has a wide selection of chestnut products. These range from *marrons glacés* and chestnut jam to chestnut-wood wickerwork. There are also cork products and other regional specialties such as olives and honey. Credit cards are not accepted.
✪ Thu, Sun 8–1

DRAGUIGNAN

🛍 DOMAINE RABIEGA
Clos Dière, 83300 Draguignan
Tel 04 94 68 44 22
www.rabiega.com
This vineyard is owned by the company that produces Absolut Vodka. It has been planted with Cabernet Sauvignon, Syrah, Cinsaut, Grenache and Carignan, which are used for rosé and red wines, and Chardonnay, Sauvignon Blanc and Viognier, for the whites.
✪ Apr–end Oct Mon–Sat 9–12, 2–5; Nov–end Mar by appointment

FRÉJUS

🏃 CENTRE INTERNATIONAL DE PLONGÉE DE FRÉJUS
Aire de Carénage, Port Fréjus, 83606 Fréjus
Tel 04 94 52 34 99
www.cip-frejus.com
A diving organization that arranges excursions to sites on the Bay of Cannes, including Cap Dramont. There are wreck dives in the area between Dramont and St-Tropez and night dives.
✪ All year long by appointment
 First dive: €38

○ HÔTEL THALASSOTHÉRAPIE

Port-Fréjus Ouest, 83606 Fréjus
Tel 04 94 52 55 00
www.hotelthalasso-portfrejus.fr
This spa is part of a modern three-star hotel that faces the sea. Choose from eight types of treatment using sea water: Tonic Treatment, Back Clinic, Leg Circulation, Well-being, Shape and Balance, Mother and Baby, Harmony, World and massages. Facilities include an indoor sea-water pool, a Turkish bath and an outdoor swimming pool.
◉ All year long 🏷 Tonic treatment/leg circulation: €87 per day. Invigorating weekend (2 nights, with breakfast and evening meal): €300 ❓ Reservations required

✪ PARC ZOOLOGIQUE DE FRÉJUS

Le Capitou, 83600 Fréjus
Tel 04 98 11 37 37
www.zoo-frejus.com
Elephants, kangaroos and hippopotamuses are among the creatures living in this safari park, covering 20ha (50 acres). Three islands are home to chimps. Don't miss the sea lion and tiger choreography.
◉ Jun–end Aug daily 10–6; Sep–end May 10–5 🏷 Adult €10, child (4–10) €6, under 4 free

✪ AQUATICA

Route Nationale 98, 83600 Fréjus
Tel 04 94 51 82 51
www.parc-aquatica.com
This is the Riviera's biggest water park, covering 8ha (20 acres). Choose from a profusion of pools and water slides, including Europe's largest wave pool, the Twin-Twister (four interlaced slides) and the 'Grand Canyon' river. There are theme restaurants and souvenir shops on site.
◉ Jun to mid-Sep daily 10–6 (till 7 Aug) 🏷 Adult €22, child (under 12 years and over 1m/3.2ft tall) €18, free for children under 1m

GASSIN

⊞ LA MAISON DES CONFITURES

Chemin Bourrian, 83580 Gassin
Tel 04 94 43 41 58
You'll find every conceivable type of jam at this store, which is nestled between vineyards in a small village near St-Tropez that offers wonderful views. There are more than 500 varieties of jam, including some typically regional ones (thyme, lavender, fig and nut) and savoury jams (such as onion).
◉ Summer Mon–Sat 9–8; winter Mon–Sat 9–7

Explore Provence's underwater landscape on a diving expedition

GONFARON

✪ VILLAGE DES TORTUES

83590 Gonfaron
Tel 04 94 78 26 41
www.tortues.com
A venue for the study of tortoises that is coupled with a park where you can see rare species in their natural habitat. Spring is the best time to visit, when the tortoises are more active. A tortoise clinic, nursery and information points help you learn more about these endangered species.
◉ Mar–end Nov daily 9–7 🏷 Adult €8, child (4–16) €5, under 4 free

LORGUES

⊞ DOMAINE DE L'ESTELLO

Route de Garce, 83510 Lorgues
Tel 04 94 73 22 22
www.lestello.com
This vineyard, of 32ha (79 acres), produces an 'adventure wine', a name that echoes the owner's personal history: Roger Tordjman left his successful business one day to go sailing for 15 years, before anchoring in Provence.
◉ Mon–Fri 9–12.30, 2–6, Sat 3–6

MONTMEYAN

✪ LOCATION NAUTIC

Montmeyan Plage, 83670 Montmeyan
Tel 04 92 74 40 76
www.locationnautic.fr
This boat rental company offers you the chance to discover the Esparron de Verdon lake by kayak, pedal-boat or motorboat. Credit cards are not accepted.
◉ Apr–end Oct daily 🏷 1-hour pedal-boat rental starts at €12; electric boat rental starts at €22

PIERREFEU-DU-VAR

⊞ DOMAINE DU POURRET

Route de Hyères, 83390 Pierrefeu du Var
Tel 04 94 48 20 57
www.domaine-du-pourret.com
Stretching over 8ha (20 acres), this vineyard produces red and rosé 'Côtes de Provence' wines bearing the AOC label. Vinegars and Provençal delicacies are also offered.
◉ By appointment

PORQUEROLLES

✪ PORQUEROLLES PLONGÉE

Zone Artisanale 7, 83400 Porquerolles
Tel 04 98 04 62 22
www.porquerolles-plongee.com
Porquerolles Plongée, based on one of the Îles d'Hyères, organizes dives, some onto wrecks, including cargo ships and even a submarine.
◉ Apr to mid-Nov daily dawn–dusk; by appointment rest of year 🏷 €43 for the first dive

ST-CYR-SUR-MER

🎭 LES FOLIES TERRIBLES
904 route Port d'Alon, 83470
St-Cyr-sur-Mer
Tel 04 94 26 15 62
www.foliesterribles.com
This two-hour Moulin Rouge-style spectacular, with cancan dancers and other entertainers, is the largest in the area.
🕐 Ticket office: 2pm–midnight. Shows mid-Jul to end Aug daily; Sep–end Feb, Apr to mid-Jul Fri, Sat 8.30pm, Sun 1.30pm 💶 Show and dinner from €38; show €25 (evening), €20 (afternoon)

SANARY-SUR-MER

🎭 THEATRE GALLI
Rue Raoul Henry, 83110 Sanary-sur-Mer
Tel 04 94 88 53 90
www.sanarysurmer.com
This small theatre hosts plays and concerts. It is also a community venue for dances, tastings and amateur shows.
🕐 Ticket office: Mon–Fri 10–12, 3–6 and 1 hour before performances

ST-TROPEZ

🏬 MARCHÉ AUX POISSONS
Place aux Herbes, 83990 St-Tropez
This picturesque fish market provides an endearing snapshot of life in St-Tropez; it's also the best place to get Mediterranean fish such as red mullet, scorpion fish and rainbow wrasse. Credit cards are not accepted.
🕐 Daily 7am–1pm

🏬 MARCHÉ PROVENÇAL
Place des Lices, 83990 St-Tropez
You'll find all the typical food of Provence at this market. There's also an antiques corner and some local crafts. Credit cards are not accepted.
🕐 Tue, Sat 8–1

🏬 RONDINI
16 rue Clemenceau, 83990 St-Tropez
Tel 04 94 97 19 55
www.nova.fr/rondini
Since 1927, this family business has been making the *Tropézienne*, a Roman-style sandal worn by many celebrities, including Picasso.
🕐 Daily 9.30–12, 3–7

🏬 LA TARTE TROPÉZIENNE
36 rue Clemenceau, 83990
St-Tropez
Tel 04 94 97 71 42
www.tarte-tropezienne.com
In 1955, while he was catering for the actors of the film *And God Created Woman*, confectioner Alexandre Micka created the cake filled with cream that gives this shop its name. It was a great success and one of the film's stars, Brigitte Bardot, christened it *tarte tropézienne*.
🕐 Feb–end Oct daily 8–8

🍸 BAR ANGLAIS
Hôtel Sube, 15 quai Suffren 83990
Tel 04 94 97 30 04

The Rondini store has been making Tropézienne *sandals since 1927*

The 'English Bar' is on the first floor of the prestigious Hotel Sube. Its wooden interior has a marine theme and there's a good choice of draught beers.
🕐 Daily 7.30am–1am (till 3am May–end Oct)

🍸 LES CAVES DU ROY
Avenue Foch, 83990 St-Tropez
Tel 04 94 56 68 00
www.lescavesduroy.com
Part of luxury Hôtel Byblos, this club is the haunt of the rich and famous. The interior has Eastern influences, with pillars and tones of red.
🕐 Mid-Apr to end Oct: Fri, Sat 11.30pm–5am; daily in Jul, Aug

🍸 VIP ROOM
Résidences du Nouveau Port, 83990
St-Tropez
Tel 04 94 97 14 70
www.viproom.fr
The VIP Room has a classy club interior, with white wall seats, contemporary art and video projections. This is definitely the haunt of a VIP clientele. As a funky touch, the staff wear white Stetsons. There is a restaurant on site.
🕐 May–end Sep daily 9pm–5am; mid-Oct to end Apr daily 9pm–3am

SALERNES

🏬 POTERIE DU CHÂTEAU
Route de Draguignan, Quartier St-Romain, 83690 Salernes
Tel 04 94 70 63 46
www.guideweb.com/poterie-du-chateau
Choose from brightly painted decorative items such as teapots, plates, cooking pots and bowls.
🕐 Mon–Sat 9–12.30, 2.30–7, Sun 3–7

TOULON

🎭 THÉÂTRE/OPÉRA DE TOULON
Boulevard de Strasbourg, 83000 Toulon
Tel 04 94 92 58 59
This superb 18th-century opera house hosts plays, opera and concerts by local, national and international companies.
🕐 Ticket office: Mon–Sat 10–12.30, 3.30–7 💶 Tickets start at €8

FESTIVALS AND EVENTS

FEBRUARY

CORSO DU MIMOSA
Bormes-les-Mimosas
This is a celebration of the yellow, vanilla-scented flower that gave the village its name.
🕐 21 Feb

MAY

BRAVADE DE ST-TORPES
St-Tropez
St-Tropez remembers its patron saint.
🕐 16 May

ALPES-MARITIMES

Cannes is the place to go for haute-couture boutiques, while Grasse, farther inland, is the world's perfume capital. Sporting options range from winter skiing at Isola 2000 to sailing on the shimmering waters of the Mediterranean. Film buffs may like to brave Cannes in May and jazz fans should catch the Nice Jazz Festival in the summer.

KEY TO SYMBOLS	
🛍	Shopping
🎭	Entertainment
🍸	Nightlife
⚽	Sports
★	Activities
♥	Health and Beauty
🧒	For Children

ANTIBES

🛍 ART-THÉ
3 place Mariejol, 06600 Antibes
Tel 04 93 34 44 41
This tiny gallery shows the work of local artists. A small café serves drinks and light snacks.
🕐 Apr–end Sep daily 10–7; Oct–end Mar Tue–Sat 10–7

🍸 LA SIESTA
Route du Bord de Mer, 06600 Antibes–Juan-les-Pins
Tel 04 93 33 31 31
This club is packed all summer thanks to a great variety of entertainment, including several dance floors, a swimming pool, restaurant, casino and access to the beach.
🕐 Mid-Jun to mid-Sep daily 11pm–5am; Mid-Sep to mid-Jun Fri, Sat 11pm–5am 💶 €15–€20

♥ THALAZUR ANTIBES
770 chemin Moyennes Bréguières, 06600 Antibes
Tel 04 92 91 82 00
www.thalazur.fr
This spa, part of a hotel, has indoor and outdoor swimming pools, a gym, sauna, hammam (Turkish bath), Jacuzzi, solarium, beauty institute and a day nursery. Four types of treatment are on offer: Vitality, Oriental, Weight loss and Leg circulation.
🕐 All year, upon reservation 💶 €162 for a full day

🧒 MARINELAND
Route Nationale 7, 306 avenue Mozart, 06600 Antibes
Tel 04 93 33 49 49
www.marineland.fr
Watch sharks from the safety of a glass tunnel, or Orcadia, choreography involving seals, killer whales and dolphins. Marineland is part of a complex of theme parks that also includes a farm, Butterfly Jungle, Aqua-Splash (summer only) and Adventure Golf.
🕐 Sep–end Jun daily 10–6; Jul, Aug daily 10am–midnight 💶 Adult €24, child (4–12) €16, under 4 free

BIOT

🛍 VERRERIE DE BIOT
5 chemin des Combes, 06410 Biot
Tel 04 93 65 03 00
www.verreriebiot.com
Biot is known as the glassblowers' capital. On this site, you'll find a gallery and museum dedicated to glass, a glass workshop, a showroom and an interior-design boutique. You can buy beautiful hand-blown bottles, decanters, jars, dishes and glasses and visit the workshop.
🕐 Mon–Sat 9.30–6; Sun 10.30–1, 2.30–6

CAGNES-SUR-MER

🎭 CASINO DE CAGNES-SUR-MER
116 boulevard de la Plage, 06800 Cagnes-sur-Mer
Tel 04 92 27 14 40
www.groupetranchant.com
There is a relaxed atmosphere at this modern casino. You'll find 50 slot machines, a games room with poker and blackjack and a restaurant. Formal dress isn't required.
🕐 Daily 10am–4am 💶 Entry to games room €10

CANNES

🏛 CANNES ENGLISH BOOKS

11 rue Bivouac-Napoléon, 06400
Cannes
Tel 04 93 99 40 08
The large collection of books in
English at this store should
meet all literary tastes: novels,
best-sellers, cookbooks, travel
guides. A friendly bilingual
welcome and a prime location
(right behind the Palais des
Festivals) also explain why it is
popular with the English-
speaking community.
🕐 Mon–Sat 10–1, 2–6

🏛 JACQUES LOUP

21 rue d'Antibes, 06400 Cannes
Tel 04 93 39 28 35
www.jacques-loup.com
In addition to its own
collection, this shoe shop
carries the hottest designs
from international shoemakers
such as Bottega Veneta,
Rossi, Church's and Tod's.
It also stocks clothes from
Prada, Marni and Miu Miu.
It's an institution for every
fashionista in Cannes.
🕐 Mon–Sat 9.30–8

🏛 MARCHÉ DE FORVILLE

Rue du Marché de Forville, 06400
Cannes
Even if you're not planning to
buy anything (but it's going
to be hard to resist), Cannes'
biggest market is worth seeing
for its bright displays of fruit,
vegetables, flowers and
cheeses. The venue is partially
covered. Credit cards are
not accepted.
🕐 Tue–Sun 7am–1pm (there is an
antiques market on Mon)

🎭 ALEXANDRE III

19 boulevard Alexandre, 06400
Cannes
Tel 04 93 94 33 44
This old cinema-turned-theatre
stages plays, ranging from
the classics to more modern
works.
🕐 Open all year

🎵 ÉGLISE RÉFORMÉE DE FRANCE

9 rue Croix, 06400 Cannes
Tel 04 93 39 35 55
With excellent acoustics, this
19th-century Protestant church
regularly hosts choral, classical
and chamber music concerts
and organ recitals.
🕐 Usually Sat or Sun at 5pm
💶 Donation

🎵 PALAIS DES FESTIVALS ET DES CONGRÈS

1 boulevard la Croisette, 06400 Cannes
Tel 04 93 39 01 01
www.cannes.fr
The Cannes Film Festival takes
place in this venue, built in
1982. At other times, the

A cheery flower stand in the Marché de Forville, Cannes

palais welcomes international
exhibitions, as well as staging
performances in its 2,300-seat
Lumière auditorium and plays,
ballets and concerts in the
1,000-seat Théâtre Debussy.

🎰 CASINO CROISETTE

1 Esplanade Lucien Barrière, 06406
Cannes
Tel 04 92 98 78 00
www.lucienbarriere.com
If you have money left to
burn after your visit to Cannes,
blow it (or win some more)
at this casino, with nearly
300 slot machines, roulette
and blackjack.
🕐 Daily 10am–5am (8pm for the
games room) 💶 Games room €10

🍸 CAT CORNER

22 rue Macé, 06400 Cannes
Tel 04 93 39 31 31
www.catcorner.com
The small dance floor here is
popular with a young and well-
off crowd that likes to party
until the wee hours of the
morning to funk, groove and
house rhythms.
🕐 Daily 11.30pm–5am 💶 €16

🍸 LE FESTIVAL

52 La Croisette, 06400 Cannes
Tel 04 93 38 04 81
www.lefestival.fr
Between two luxury hotels and
facing the sea, this bar's
terrace, open all year round, is
a popular place for people-
watching and admiring the
beautiful expanse of blue to
the horizon.
🕐 Daily 9am–midnight

🍸 MORRISON'S IRISH PUB

10 rue Teisseire, 06400 Cannes
Tel 04 92 98 16 17
www.morrisonspub.com
This pub, with its convivial
wooden interior, boasts a big
screen, beloved of sports fans.
There is live music every
Wednesday and Thursday
evening. Guinness and
Kilkenny are on tap, served by
friendly Irish staff.
🕐 Daily 7pm–2am

🍸 WHISKY À GOGO LADY BIRD

115 avenue de Lérins, 06400 Cannes
Tel 04 93 43 20 63
www.whiskyagogo.fr
An institution in Cannes, this
club is actually older than its
mid-20s, wealthy clientele.
There are two floors, with
peach walls, burgundy wall
seats and golden columns, as
well as a VIP lounge. Disco and
dance rhythms dominate.
🕐 Fri, Sat 11pm–5am (also Wed, Thu
in Jul, daily in Aug) 💶 €16 (including
one drink)

WHAT TO DO

ⓨ ZANZIBAR
85 rue Félix-Faure, 06400 Cannes
Tel 04 93 39 30 75
www.lezanzibar.com
Popular with the gay community, this club has a prime
location near the Palais des
Festivals, pleasant decor with a
marine theme and good
techno rhythms.
🕐 Daily 6pm–dawn

ⓞ PLAGE DE L'HÔTEL MARTINEZ
Hôtel Martinez, 73 boulevard
la Croisette, 06400 Cannes
Tel 04 92 98 74 22
www.hotel-martinez.com
The private beach of luxury
Hôtel Martinez isn't exclusively
reserved for its clients. Relax in
one of its comfortable lounge
chairs or take part in water
sports, including parasailing
and waterskiing.
🕐 Apr–end Oct daily 10–7 🎟 Lounge
chair rental in high season around €35
per day

CANNES LA BOCCA
ⓞ CANNES BOWLING
189 avenue Francis-Tonner, 06150
Cannes La Bocca
Tel 04 93 47 02 25
www.cannesbowling.com
There are 16 bowling lanes
and 21 pool tables here. A DJ
spices up the atmosphere on
weekends and there's a
restaurant on site with Formula
1-themed decor.
🕐 Sun–Thu 3pm–2.30am, Fri, Sat
3pm–4am 🎟 €6 per game; €2 for
shoe rental

ⓞ AÉROCLUB D'ANTIBES
Aérodrome de Cannes Mandelieu, 245
avenue Francis Tonner, 06150
Cannes La Bocca
Tel 04 93 47 64 43
www.aeroclub-antibes.com
This flying club, just west of
Cannes, will take you over the
Bay of St-Tropez, the Alps and
the cliffs of Bonifacio in the
south of Corsica.
🕐 By reservation 🎟 €45 for a first
flight of 20 min

LE CANNET ROCHEVILLE
ⓑ MARCHÉ BIOLOGIQUE
Quartier l'Aubarède, 06110 Le Cannet
Rocheville
Buy regional products that are
certified organic at this small
market. It's the true taste of
Provence. Credit cards are not
accepted.
🕐 Wed 7am–1pm

ÈZE
ⓑ L'HERMINETTE EZASQUE
1 rue Principale, Èze
Tel 04 93 41 13 59
This shop, in the walls of the
old gateway, sells wonderful
Christmas cribs and *santons*.
🕐 Summer daily 10–7; winter
daily 10–6

*Perfume from Fragonard makes
an ideal gift*

GRASSE
ⓑ FRAGONARD
20 boulevard Fragonard, 06130
Grasse
Tel 04 93 36 44 65
www.fragonard.com
World-renowned as a perfume
capital, Grasse is home to
many perfumeries. Fragonard,
dating back to the 18th
century, is one of the oldest
and the most prestigious. Visit
the perfume museum before
shopping for fragrances.
🕐 Factory daily 9–6.30, shop 9–6

ISOLA
ⓞ ISOLA 2000
Tourist office: Immeuble le Pélevos,
Isola 2000
Tel 04 93 23 15 15
www.isola2000.com
At an altitude of 2,000m
(6,500ft), this ski resort offers
50 tracks and one snow park
with heli-skiing, snow scooters
and an ice rink. In summer, the
outdoor activities continue with
hiking and horseback riding.
🎟 Ski pass €20–€23

JUAN-LES-PINS
ⓞ HYDRO ULM JUAN-LES-PINS
Ponton Hollywood, 06160 Juan-les-Pins
Tel 04 93 67 05 11
www.hydro-ulm.com
Touring the Rade du Golfe on
a hybrid of a super-light plane
and a boat gives you a wonder
ful bird's-eye view of islands
and lighthouses. Juan-les-Pins
is on the Golfe Juan, west
of Antibes.
🕐 Daily by appointment; closed Jan
🎟 €60 for a 25-min flight

MENTON
ⓑ LES IMAGES DE PROVENCE
21 rue St-Michel, 06500 Menton
Tel 04 93 57 09 98
This company designs and
prints its own beautiful
Provençal fabrics, which it sells
by the metre or transformed
into finished items, from tablecloths, napkins and bed linens
to other soft furnishings.
🕐 Mon–Sat 9–12, 3–7

ⓕ CASINO DE MENTON
2 avenue Félix Faure, 06500 Menton
Tel 04 93 35 78 38
www.lucienbarriere.com
Behind a Moorish-style façade,
you'll find 150 slot machines,
some games rooms, two
bars, a restaurant and club
Le Brummell. Formal dress
is required.
🕐 Daily 10am–3am (until 4am Fri,
Sat); table game room opens at 8pm
🎟 Entry to the games room €10

MOUGINS

🏃 BUGGY CROSS
909 chemin Font-de-Currault, 06250 Mougins
Tel 04 93 69 02 74
Next to the Automobile Museum, you can experience the thrill of speed on one of three tracks in a quad bike, kart or mini-motorcycle. There are also vehicles for children aged four and over.
🕐 Summer Wed, Sat, Sun 11–8; winter Wed, Sat, Sun 11–6 💶 Adult €14.50 for 10 min, child €7 for 10 min

💗 SPA SHISEIDO AU MAS CANDILLE
Boulevard Clément-Rebuffel, 06250 Mougins
Tel 04 92 28 43 43
www.lemascandille.com
East meets West at this spa, which offers massages combining body sculpting with the ancient Japanese arts of shiatsu and chi. These come complete with aromatherapy products, aimed at both the skin and the mind. Shiseido products are used in all the treatments.
🕐 Daily 10–7 💶 75-min facial €88; 30-min massage €55

NICE

📖 THE CAT'S WHISKERS
30 rue Lamartine, 06000 Nice
Tel 04 93 80 02 66
Browse through books in English, including detective novels, best-sellers, children's stories and classics. Some are secondhand.
🕐 Mon–Fri 9.30–12, 2–6.30; Sat 9.30–12, 5–6.30

📖 LA CHAPELLERIE
36 cours Saleya, 06300 Nice
Tel 04 93 62 52 54
www.chapellerie.com
Here you'll find hats for every occasion: from the panama to the beanie, and wedding hats. A custom-made service is also available. This popular shop often provides accessories to the entertainment industry.
🕐 Mon–Sat 9.30–12.30, 2–7

📖 GLACIER FENOCCHIO
2 place Rossetti, 06300 Nice
Tel 04 93 80 72 52
Quite simply Nice's best ice cream maker. The key to its success? Big servings and truly original tastes: Alongside the traditional peach melba and café liegeois, you may want to try the tomato or chewing-gum sorbet. The pretty location, facing Sainte-Réparate Cathedral, comes as a bonus.
🕐 Mar–end Jun, Sep to mid-Nov Tue–Sun 8–12, 2–4; Jul, Aug daily 8–5.30

📖 JEAN-LOUIS MARTINETTI
17 rue de la Préfecture, 06300 Nice
Tel 04 93 85 61 30
www.webstore.fr/couleurs-de-nice/

Find your perfect hat at La Chapellerie, Nice

Jean-Louis Martinetti's photography is an ode to Nice. He uses simple compositions (for example, a palm tree framed by the sea) in bold tones.
🕐 Tue–Sat 10–12.30, 3–7

📖 LOCAVENTURE
13 rue Fontaine-de-la-Ville, 06300 Nice
Tel 04 93 56 14 67
www.locaventure.com
Snowboarding, scuba diving, rock climbing, caving, inline skating and much more: This shop rents out all the equipment you'll need for an outdoor adventure. Its staff also offer advice on activities.
🕐 Mon–Sat 8–12, 3–7; Sun 8–12, 6–8

📖 MARCHÉ À LA BROCANTE
Cours Saleya, 06300 Nice
This antiques market mostly welcomes professionals, and the items on display are often highly collectable. Among the possibilities are genuine Gallé glasswork, old postcards, jewellery and ethnic artwork. Credit cards are not accepted.
🕐 Mon 8–5

📖 MARCHÉ AUX FLEURS
Cours Saleya, 06300 Nice
This flower market is in the animated cours Saleya, with its many shops and cafés. As the weather is so pleasant, exotic plants and trees are offered, including orange and lemon trees and cacti. In February, mimosa is in full blossom. Credit cards are not accepted.
🕐 Tue–Sat 6.30–5.30, Sun 6.30–1.30

📖 MARCHÉ SALEYA
Cours Saleya, 06300 Nice
This fruit and vegetable market keeps the spirit of Provence alive. You'll find lots of locally grown produce, including olives, tomatoes and basil. Credit cards are not accepted.
🕐 Tue–Sun 7am–1pm

📖 MARCHÉ SALEYA D'ARTISANAT D'ART
Cours Saleya, 06300 Nice
Take a stroll through Nice's evening arts and crafts market after a drink at a nearby bar. You'll find Provençal handicrafts, plus crafts from other regions of the world.
🕐 Jun–end Sep Tue–Sun 6pm–midnight

📖 MARTIN FLEURS
28 rue Hôtel-des-Postes, 06000 Nice
Tel 04 93 85 28 63
www.martin-fleurs.com
This florist offers an impressive range of bouquets—some could even qualify as floral sculpture. Exotic flowers are widely used.
🕐 Mon–Sat 8.30–7.30

🏛 MOULIN À HUILE ALZIARI

4 rue St-François-de-Paule, 06300 Nice
Tel 04 93 85 76 92

The olive oil on sale in this shop comes from a mill in Nice's northwest corner, which you can visit by appointment.
🕐 Tue–Sat 8.30–12.30, 2.15–7

🎭 AUDITORIUM DU CONSERVATOIRE NATIONAL DE RÉGION

24 boulevard de Cimiez, 06100 Nice
Tel 04 92 26 72 20

The students at the Regional Academy of Music open their rehearsals every Monday. The event, known as *Les Lundis Kosmas,* was established more than 20 years ago and named after the composer Kosma.
🕐 Mon 6pm (except school hols)
💷 Free

🎭 BAR DES OISEAUX

5 rue St-Vincent, 06300 Nice
Tel 04 93 80 27 33

Comedy shows, concerts and philosophical debates are staged at this café-theatre. Local comedian Noëlle Perna put the venue on the map with her show that plays with the local dialect.
🕐 Mon–Fri 12–3, 7pm–1am; Sat 7pm–1am 💷 €13 for a theatre show (otherwise varies)

🎭 BOUFF' SCÈNE

2 rue Caissotti, 06300 Nice
Tel 04 93 16 90 13
www.lebouffscene.com

This warm and inviting little theatre puts budding and more well-known comedians on stage. Reserve ahead. Credit cards are not accepted.
🕐 Thu–Sun 9pm–midnight
💷 €10–€20

🎬 CINEMA RIALTO

4 rue de Rivoli, 06000 Nice
Tel 0836 680 041

This five-screen venue is one of the few cinemas in Nice to show films in their original language. You can see the latest releases, but also some alternative films.
🕐 Daily 11–11 💷 €7

🎬 CINÉMATHÈQUE

Acropolis 3, esplanade Kennedy, 06300 Nice
Tel 04 92 04 06 66
www.cinematheque-nice.com

Henri Langlois created this impressive film archive more than 20 years ago. Every month, theme-based retrospectives and festivals put the great classics on the bill. Credit cards are not accepted.
🕐 Oct–end Jun Tue–Sat 2–10, Sun 3–5 💷 €3

🎭 OPÉRA DE NICE

4–6 rue St-François-de-Paule, 06300 Nice
Tel 04 93 13 98 53
www.ville-nice.fr

Wacky sculpture outside the Théâtre National de Nice

Majestic frescoes and a massive chandelier decorate this Italianate theatre, inaugurated in 1885, which stages opera, classical music and ballet.
🕐 Tue–Sat, shows at 4pm and 8pm
💷 Opera €16–€82

🎬 PATHÉ MASSÉNA

31 avenue Jean-Médecin, 06000 Nice
Tel 08 92 68 22 88
www.pathe.fr

The 12 screens at this cinema show Hollywood blockbusters and the latest French releases.
🕐 Daily 10–10 💷 €8

🎭 THÉÂTRE DE LA TRAVERSE

2 rue François-Guisol, 06300 Nice
Tel 04 93 55 67 46
www.la-traverse.com

Adjoining La Traverse publishing house and its bookstore, this 45-seat theatre likes to experiment. The plays vary from one-person shows and comedy to drama and historical works.
🕐 Oct–end Jun: shows on Fri and Sat at 8.30pm and Sun at 4pm 💷 €13

🎭 THÉÂTRE NATIONAL DE NICE

Promenade des Arts, 06300 Nice
Tel 04 93 13 90 90

Both classic and contemporary plays are on the bill at this theatre, with its marble tower. You can also see some dance.
🕐 Big auditorium: Mon–Sat 8.30pm, Sun 3pm. Small auditorium: Mon–Sat 9pm, Sun 3.30pm 💷 €10–€30

🍷 CASA DEL SOL

12 Cité du Parc, 06300 Nice
Tel 04 93 62 87 28

Latin America and Morocco inspire the interior of this tapas bar, which has wrought-iron decorations, warm hues and table-top mosaics. There's lounge music during dinner and a disco after midnight.
🕐 Tue–Sat 6pm–2.30am

🍷 LE CHAT PERCHÉ

4 place Garibaldi, 06000 Nice
Tel 04 93 89 20 80
www.averse.com/catsound/

This vibrant venue regularly organizes exhibitions and has a DJ every Friday night. Otherwise sporting events are shown on a big screen; table football and a dartboard are also available.
🕐 Mon–Sat 8am–10.30pm

🍷 CHERRY'S CAFÉ

36 rue des Ponchettes, 06300 Nice
Tel 04 93 13 85 45

This gay- and lesbian-friendly bar-restaurant is in a former fisherman's house. There are sea views from the terrace.
🕐 Wed–Mon 12 noon–12.30am

CHEZ WAYNE'S
15 rue de la Préfecture, 06000 Nice
Tel 04 93 13 46 99
www.waynes.fr
Food, drink and live music are available at this English-American bar and restaurant. There is a sunny terrace and an interior that pays tribute to rock music with guitars and concert posters on the walls.
Daily noon–1am

L'F
6 place Charles-Félix, 06300 Nice
Tel 04 93 85 74 10
www.l-f2000.com
On the liveliest street in town, this café has one of Nice's best terraces, heated during colder spells. Inside is a 1930s and 1940s interior, with a black-and-white chequered floor.
Daily 8am–3am

GHOST HOUSE
3 rue Barillerie, 06300 Nice
Tel 04 93 92 93 37
This fashionable bar has comfortable sofas, gleaming mirrors and a well-stocked library. The place gets packed when the resident DJ plays techno, hip hop or soul on theme nights.
Daily 7pm–2.30am

GRAND CAFÉ DE LYON
33 avenue Jean Médecin, 06000 Nice
Tel 04 93 88 13 17
www.cafedelyon.fr
This art nouveau-style bistro, established in 1900, is an institution in Nice. It's a brasserie at lunchtime, a tea room in the afternoon and later, a good place for a drink.
Daily 7am–midnight

LE LAFAYETTE
64 rue Gioffrédo, 06000 Nice
Tel 04 93 85 44 67
A piece of railway track lies behind the bar and a repro-duction of the underwater world adorns the ceiling. Such original decor gives a funky twist to this centrally located venue.
Mon–Sat 6.30am–2.30am

MASTER HOME
11 rue de la Préfecture, 06300 Nice
Tel 04 93 80 33 82
www.master-home.com
There's a large choice of beers and whiskies at this Scottish-theme pub, which doubles as an internet café. There's a DJ in the evenings.
Mon–Fri 10am–2.30am; Sat, Sun 2pm–2.30am

THOR
32 cours Saleya, 06300 Nice
Tel 04 93 62 49 90
www.thor-pub.com
This Scandinavian pub is very popular with students and is one of the liveliest venues in town. There is a large choice of

There are plenty of opportunities to play golf on the Côte d'Azur

beers on tap and live music every night. The concert hall upstairs has a vaulted ceiling.
Daily 6pm–2.30am

PATINOIRE JEAN BOUIN
Esplanade Maréchal-de-Lattre-de-Tassigny, 06600 Nice
Tel 04 93 80 80 80
www.carilis.fr
During the day, this Olympic-size skating rink welcomes those looking for a little icy adventure. The atmosphere changes in the evening, when disco takes over.
Tue, Thu 9pm–11.30pm, Wed 2–6, 9–11.30, Fri 8pm–1am, Sat 2–6, 9pm–2am, Sun 9am–11.45am, 2.30–6.30   Entry €4; skate rental €3

STADE MUNICIPAL DU RAY (LÉO LAGRANGE)
25 avenue du Ray, 06100 Nice
Tel 0892 785 757/04 92 07 79 42
www.ogcnice.com
This 17,000-seat stadium has staged some memorable soccer matches. It's home to the OGC Nice soccer club, better known as *Les Aiglons* (The Eaglets).
Matches usually start around 8pm
€7–€35

LE CENTRE
1 promenade des Anglais, 06000 Nice
Tel 04 93 87 82 14
www.accueil-beaute.com
On the ninth floor of the luxury Meridien hotel, this beauty venue will pamper you from top to toe. Why not start with the 'New Skin' body treatment or a Dead Sea mud wrap, continue with a massage with essential oils, and finish with a French manicure? Facilities include a sauna, hammam (Turkish bath), Jacuzzi, fitness equipment and tanning beds.
Mon–Sat 9–8   Regenerating facial €60; Dead Sea mud wrap €35

OPIO

GOLF OPIO VALBONNE
Route de Roquefort, 06650 Opio
Tel 04 93 12 00 08
www.opengolfclub.com
English architect Donald Harradine designed this 18-hole golf course, in a 220ha (545-acre) park. Training sessions and competitions are regularly organized and there is a restaurant on site.
Daily 8–5.30   Green fee €65

ST-ÉTIENNE DE TINÉE

🅡 AURON ST-ÉTIENNE DE TINÉE

Tourist Office: 1 rue Communes de France, 06660 St-Étienne de Tinée
Tel 04 93 02 41 96
www.auron.com

This ski resort, at an altitude of between 1,600m (5,250ft) and 2,400m (7,900ft), has 39 runs and 27 ski lifts. Ski, snowboard or choose from hang-gliding, sleigh tours, ice-skating and snow scooters.
🕐 Ski resort open Dec–end Apr, depending on snowfall 🎟 Ski pass €20–€23 per day

ST-JEAN-CAP-FERRAT

🅧 ZOO DU CAP-FERRAT

117 boulevard Général-de-Gaulle, 06230 St-Jean-Cap-Ferrat
Tel 04 93 76 07 60
www.zoocapferrat.com

Attempting to reproduce the natural habitat of more than 300 animals, including crocodiles, monkeys and tigers, this zoo has numerous pools and grottos. Visit it on foot, and watch the animals in their enclosed areas. You can get really close to the tigers, protected by a Plexiglas wall. There is a snack bar and playground on site.
🕐 Apr–end Oct daily 9.30–7; Nov–end Mar daily 9.30–5.30 🎟 Adult €10, child (4–10) €7, under 4 free

LA TURBIE

🅡 GOLF CLUB DE MONTE-CARLO

Route du Mont Agel, 06320 La Turbie
Tel 04 93 41 09 11

At an altitude of 900m (3,000ft), this 18-hole golf course has great views of the French and Italian mountains and the sandy coastline.
🕐 Mon 8–5, Tue–Sun 8–6 🎟 Round of golf €85–€100

FESTIVALS AND EVENTS

FEBRUARY

FÊTE DU CITRON

Menton
Jardin Biovès, Menton
www.feteducitron.com

This festival celebrates the main crop of the area—lemons. The highlight is a parade of floats decorated with thousands of lemons.
🕐 Late Feb 🎟 Entry to static displays €8; seat for start of parade €8; seat for finish of parade €14 (parade prices include entry to static displays)

Oranges and lemons in Menton

NICE CARNIVAL

Nice
Tel 0892 707 407 (tourist office)
www.nicecarnaval.com

The Riviera celebrates Mardi Gras with two weeks of parades. Huge papier-mâché floats proceed through the town to be set alight at sea on the final night. Pay to sit in the stands or look out of your hotel window for free.

APRIL

NICE TENNIS OPEN

Nice
Lawn Tennis Club, 5 avenue Suzanne Lenguen, Nice
Tel 04 92 15 58 00

This championship attracts top tennis players.

MAY

FILM FESTIVAL

Cannes
Tel 01 53 59 61 00
www.festival-cannes.fr/

May means Hollywood comes to the Riviera as stars are photographed along the Croisette and the steps of the Palais des Festivals. All the biggest screenings and parties are invitation only, but there are some public screenings.

MAY/JUNE

PROCESSION DAI LIMACA

Gorbio
Villagers celebrate the previous winter's olive harvest with a magical night-time procession.

JUNE

FESTIVAL DE MUSIQUE SACRÉE

Nice
2 place Masséna, 06364 Nice
Tel 04 97 13 23 95/04 97 13 36 89

The Festival of Sacred Music celebrated its 30th anniversary in 2004. Religious music is played in the chapels and churches of Vieux Nice.
🎟 €5–€23

JULY

JAZZ À JUAN

Juan-les-Pins
Pinède Gould, 06600
Antibes
Tourist office: 04 92 90 53 00
www.antibesjuanlespins.com

This is one of Europe's best jazz festivals. Expect some of the greatest names, such as Maceo Parker and Marcus Miller.
🕐 One week around mid-Jul
🎟 Adult €20–€40, child €10

NICE JAZZ FESTIVAL

Nice
Tel 04 93 87 16 28
www.nicejazzfest.com

Les Arènes de Cimiez is the venue for this lively event.
🕐 Two weeks in Jul

MONACO

Stylish boutiques, chic nightlife and a world-famous casino sum up the unique experience that is Monaco. If you can't afford to sail one of the luxury yachts, at least stroll along the quayside and soak up the extravagance. Alternatively, come face to face with a shark at the wonderful Musée Océanographique.

KEY TO SYMBOLS
- 🕮 **Shopping**
- 🎭 **Entertainment**
- ▼ **Nightlife**
- ⚽ **Sports**
- ✪ **Activities**
- ♡ **Health and Beauty**
- ✳ **For Children**

🕮 CENTRE COMMERCIAL LE MÉTROPOLE
17 avenue des Spélugues, 98000 Monaco
www.ccmetropole.com
A stone's throw from the casino, this shopping complex has majestic Belle-Époque decor, including marble alleys and Bohemian glass candelabras. There are three levels, with 80 boutiques specializing in top-notch fashion, beauty, household goods and leisure equipment.
🕒 Mon–Sat 10–7.30

🕮 CLOTHING FERRAGAMO
Hôtel Hermitage, place Beaumarchais
Monte-Carlo
Tel 377 93 25 12 21
The Ferragamo trademarks are elegant Italian shoes first made famous in Hollywood. Today

the empire has grown into a full couture house featuring simple elegant designs for men and women.
🕒 Mon–Sat 9.30–1, 2.30–7

🎭 LE SPORTING
Galerie du Sporting d'hiver, place du Casino, 98000 Monaco
Tel 377 93 25 36 81
www.cinemasporting.com
Most films are shown in their original language at this three-screen cinema.
🕒 Daily 2–9 🎟 €9

🎭 OPÉRA DE MONTE-CARLO
Place du Casino, 98000 Monaco
Tel 377 92 16 22 99
www.opera.mc
Since its inauguration by actress Sarah Bernhardt in 1879, this impressive Belle-Époque opera house has welcomed the world's greatest voices. The architect, Charles Garnier, also designed the Opéra Garnier in Paris.
🎟 From €17

▼ LE SPORTING D'ÉTÉ
Avenue Princesse Grace, 98000 Monaco
Tel 377 92 16 36 36
www.sportingmontecarlo.com
With a sunroof and large windows facing the sea, this concert hall has a majestic setting. It welcomes the biggest international stars. There is also a casino and club on site.
🕒 End Jun–early Sep show daily 11pm
🎟 Varies

▼ CASINO DE MONTE-CARLO
Place du Casino, 98000 Monaco
Tel 377 92 16 20 00
www.casino-monte-carlo.com
The rich and famous flock to this grand Belle-Époque gambling temple, decorated with frescoes and paintings and featured in several movies, including James Bond films. The dress code is smart and you must be over 18.
🕒 Café de Paris (slot machines) opens at 10am 🎟 Entry €10 and a further €10 to enter games room

🍸 LE JIMMY'Z

Sporting d'Été, avenue Princesse Grace, 98000 Monaco

Tel 377 92 16 22 77

You'll face highly selective entry here and even higher prices once you get in—entering the haunt of the jet set has its toll. The reward is partying with faces seen in magazines, in a luxurious interior with a Cuban smoking room and Japanese garden.

🕐 May–end Oct daily 11pm–5am; Nov–end Apr Wed–Sun 11.30pm–5am 💶 Entry is free

🍸 MCCARTHY'S

7 rue du Portier, 98000 Monaco

Tel 377 93 25 87 67

www.monte-carlo.mc/mccarthys

Convivial decor, with barrels and wooden stools, Guinness on tap, a big screen showing sports and live music on weekends: Welcome to a little piece of Ireland. Sit out on the terrace in fair weather.

🕐 Daily 6pm–5am

🏖 PLAGE DU LARVOTTO

Avenue Princesse Grace, 98000 Monaco

Tel 377 93 30 63 84

Lifeguards are on site during the high season at this sandy beach, making it a good place to swim. Changing rooms and showers are available and there are bars and restaurants nearby.

🎾 COUNTRY CLUB DE MONTE-CARLO

155 avenue Princesse Grace, 06190 Roquebrune (just outside Monaco)

Tel 04 93 41 30 15

www.mccc.mc

This club has 21 clay tennis courts, which all look out to the sea. A squash court, fitness club and pool come as a bonus. It is home every year to the prestigious ATP Masters Series (▷ this page).

🕐 Daily 8am–8.30pm 💶 €36 for a day pass

💧 THERMES MARINS DE MONTE-CARLO

2 avenue Monte-Carlo, 98000 Monaco

Tel 377 92 16 40 40

www.sbm.mc

The pools, solariums and gym here have large windows that look onto the sea. There are beautiful hammams (Turkish baths) whose decor obeys the Moresque tradition, with blue and white tiled mosaics and little fountains. Treatments include Eastern massages and the latest innovations in marine therapy.

🕐 Daily 8–8 💶 €125 for 4 thalasso-therapy treatments, entry to the pool and hammam; €90 for 1-hour facial

Monaco Grand Prix is a highlight of the Formula 1 calendar

🐠 MUSÉE OCÉANOGRAPHIQUE

Avenue St-Martin, 98000 Monaco

Tel 377 93 15 36 00

www.oceano.mc

Hundreds of tropical fish are protected from sharks by coral reef at this fascinating giant aquarium (▷ 133). Another attraction is the micro-aquarium: A magnifying glass is used with a camera to film microscopic aquatic animals. In the basement, discover the skeletons of sea animals, including a blue whale. There is a terrace bar-restaurant.

🕐 Jul, Aug daily 9.30–7.30; Apr–end Jun, Sep daily 9.30–7; Oct–end Mar daily 10–6 💶 Adult €11, child (6–18) €6

JANUARY

MONTE-CARLO RALLY

January

Automobile Club de Monaco

23 boulevard Albert Ier

98000 Monaco

Tel 377 93 15 26 00

www.acm.mc

This three-day trial tests the driving skills of participants as they follow a route through the snow- and ice-covered minor roads in the Alps behind Monaco.

🕐 Last week in Jan

JANUARY/FEBRUARY

FESTIVAL INTERNATIONAL DU CIRQUE

Espace Fontvieille, avenue des Ligures, 98000 Monaco

Tel 377 92 05 23 45 (ticket office)

www.montecarlofestivals.com

This circus festival, established in 1974, involves animal tamers, clowns and magicians. Trophies are awarded to the best acts, which are performed for a second time during the closing night's gala.

🕐 End Jan–early Feb 💶 Adult €75–€90, child (under 13) €9 (or adult price for good seats)

APRIL

ATP MASTERS TENNIS CHAMPIONSHIP

Country Club de Monte-Carlo, 155 avenue Princesse Grace, 06190 Roquebrune

Tel 04 93 41 30 15

www.mccc.mc

Top names in tennis gather for this championship.

MAY

GRAND PRIX

Automobile Club de Monaco, 23 boulevard Albert Ier, 98000 Monaco

Tel 377 93 15 26 00

www.acm.mc

Monte-Carlo's annual week-end in the spotlight, when the city becomes a race track.

💶 €40–€420

ALPES-DE-HAUTE-PROVENCE AND HAUTES-ALPES

WHAT TO DO

Most of the action here is in the great outdoors: sailing on mountain lakes, skiing at Allos, hang-gliding over wild valleys or simply walking in the Alpine scenery. If you're shopping, head to Moustiers-Sainte-Marie for faïences (fine glazed ceramics) and Digne-les-Bains for lavender products.

KEY TO SYMBOLS	
🌐	Shopping
🎭	Entertainment
🍸	Nightlife
🎿	Sports
✪	Activities
♡	Health and Beauty
✹	For Children

BARCELONNETTE

🎭 CINÉ UBAYE
Rue Mercier, 04400 Barcelonnette
Tel 04 92 81 37 26
This two-screen cinema shows general releases and occasionally other films. Credit cards are not accepted.
🕐 Tue–Sun 3–9pm 💶 €8

🎿 ÉCOLE DE PARAPENTE DE LA VALLÉE DE L'UBAYE
Le Pont Long, 04400 Barcelonnette
Tel 04 92 81 34 93
www.ubaye-parapente.com
Discover the beautiful Ubaye valley from the sky on a paraglide, accompanied by an instructor. In winter, you can wear your skis!
🕐 All year long by appointment
💶 Flight with instructor €150

🎿 RANDO PASSION
04400 Barcelonnette (start points vary)
Tel 04 92 81 43 34
http://rando.passion.free.fr/index.htm
Try a wide range of activities with Rando Passion. In winter there's cross-country skiing, snowshoeing and the possibility of spending the night in an igloo. In summer, you can hike and mountain bike. Credit cards are not accepted.
🕐 Varies 🎿 Cross-country skiing 2.5-hour class: €19; one-day mountain bike rental: €25

CASTELLANE

🎿 ABOARD RAFTING
8 place de l'Église, 04120 Castellane
Tel 04 92 83 76 11
www.aboard-rafting.com
Experience the thrill of white-water rafting through the gorges of Verdon or, if you prefer, see the waterfalls and natural pools by canoe. You can avoid getting wet by renting a mountain bike and seeing the area on two wheels.
🕐 Apr to mid-Oct daily 9–7
💶 Half-day's rafting €55; guided 90-min airboat trip €30

DIGNE-LES-BAINS

🌐 SAVEURS ET COULEURS
7 boulevard Gassendi, 04000 Digne-les-Bains
Tel 04 92 36 04 06
www.saveurs-et-couleurs.fr
The tastes (saveurs) and colours are those of Provence: fine oils, vinegars, prepared dishes, alcohol, perfumes, Marseille soap, plaids and tablecloths made from Provençal fabrics and other decorative items made of olive wood and terracotta. The store also stocks products from Hédiard, a world-famous Parisian épicerie.
🕐 Tue–Sat 8.30–12.30, 2.30–7.15

🎭 PALAIS DES EXPOSITIONS
1 place de la République, 04000 Digne-les-Bains
Tel 04 92 31 15 21
www.mairie-dignelesbains.fr
This venue hosts theatre and dance, but mostly concerts, including international singers. The modular auditorium holds up to 3,000 people.

GOLF DE DIGNE LES BAINS
4 route du Chaffaut, 04000
Digne-les-Bains
Tel 04 92 30 58 00
www.golfdigne.com
You'll get wonderful views from this 18-hole course, nestled between mountains. A restaurant, two-star hotel, swimming pool and tennis court are also on site.
Daily 9–6 (8–8 during the high season) Green fee €30–€45

ÉTABLISSEMENT THERMAL DE DIGNE-LES-BAINS
Eurothermes, BP163, 04000
Digne-les-Bains
Tel 04 92 32 32 92
This spa uses naturally warm and mineralized waters praised for centuries for their therapeutic benefits. Options include facials, mud wraps and an aquagym.
Mid-Feb to end Nov daily €285 for 5 days of treatments (excluding accommodation); mud wrap €30; aquagym session €10; 45-min facial €28

TRAIN DES PIGNES
1 avenue Pierre Sémard, 04000
Digne-les-Bains
Tel 04 92 31 01 58
www.trainprovence.com
Since 1891, a single steam-powered carriage has chugged along a track linking the Alps to Provence. The train, with old-fashioned wooden benches, is a stylish way to see Provence's mountain scenery.
May–Oct daily from 7am
From €13 (€35.30 to Nice and back)

RÉSERVE NATURELLE GÉOLOGIQUE DE HAUTE PROVENCE
Parc St-Benoît, 04005 Digne-les-Bains
Tel 04 92 36 70 70
www.resgeol04.org
Explore this nature reserve following one of the many trails, then learn more at the three museums: 'Earth and Time' in Sisteron, 'Fossils' in Castellane and the 'Walking Museum' in Digne-les-Bains. Credit cards are not accepted.

Museums: Apr–end Oct daily 9–12, 2–5.30; Nov–end Mar Mon–Fri 9–12, 2–5.30 (until 4.30 on Fri). Park: Apr–end Oct daily 8–7; Nov–end Mar: Mon–Fri 8–7 Adult €5, child (9–16) €3, under 9 free

FORCALQUIER
DISTILLERIES ET DOMAINES DE PROVENCE
Z.A. Les Chalus, 04300 Forcalquier
Tel 04 92 75 00 58
www.distilleries-provence.com
Since 1898, this distillery has been producing the 'Pastis Henri Bardouin', a local specialty. Other Provençal spirits and liqueurs are also available. These include Le Bau (sparkling Muscat), L'Absente

Soothe your aches and pains at Digne-les-Bains' renowned spa

(a variation on absinthe) and M. P. Roux Elixir (an alcoholic infusion of regional herbs).
Apr–end Jan Mon, Wed–Sat 9–12, 2–6

OLIVIERS ET CO
3 rue Cordeliers, 04300 Forcalquier
Tel 04 92 75 00 75
www.oliviers-co.com
This boutique is dedicated to olive products. You can buy oils from all over Provence. Preserved olives and Provençal dishes made with this ingredient (such as tapenade) are also for sale, alongside olive-wood salad bowls and utensils.
Mon, Wed–Sat 9.30–1, 3–7

PIANO BAR LE SAXO
13 boulevard Latourette, 04300
Forcalquier
Tel 04 92 75 00 30
The piano bar, bar and restaurant here each have a rustic wood interior. In winter, there's live music and pizza, in summer themed party nights.
Apr–end Oct daily 8pm–2am; Nov–end Mar Fri, Sat 8pm–2am

LE PAYS DE FORCALQUIER ET LA MONTAGNE DE LURE EN VÉLO
Tourist office: 13 place du Bourguet, 04300 Forcalquier
Tel 04 92 75 10 02
www.velopaysforcalquier.com
A 60km (37-mile) bicycling route winds through the villages surrounding Forcalquier and the Montagne de Lure. You can stay at guesthouses and eat at roadside restaurants en route.

GAP
CAFÉ MUSIQUE
1 rue de la Cathédrale, 05000 Gap
Tel 04 92 52 34 17
This unusual live music café hosts local jazz, rock and blues bands each Friday night but also stages an eclectic mixture of small theatre productions and one-person shows.
Thu–Sat 10pm–2am No entry fee on non-performance nights; on other nights, entry starts at €8

GRÉOUX-LES-BAINS
GRAND CASINO DE GRÉOUX LES BAINS
Avenue des Thermes, 04800
Gréoux-les-Bains
Tel 04 92 78 00 00
Alongside the casino and its games room and 30 slot machines, you'll find a bar and restaurant. There is a tea dance every Wednesday 4–7pm, and numerous theme evenings. The interior follows a Venetian theme, with masks and candelabras.
Daily 10am–4am

♥ ETABLISSEMENT THERMAL DE GRÉOUX-LES-BAINS

Quai des Hautes Plaines, 04800 Gréoux-les-Bains
Tel 04 92 70 40 00
www.sante-eau.com
'Troglodyte, Celtic, Gallo-Roman': The note on the façade reminds you that hydrotherapy has been practised here for centuries. There are many energizing and relaxing treatments and some 'Hydrotherapy-plus-golf' deals.
🕙 Mar to mid-Dec Mon–Sat 🎫 €60 for discovery package (4 treatments)

♣ CRÈCHE DE HAUTE-PROVENCE

See page 144.

MANOSQUE

⊕ MOULIN DE L'OLIVETTE

Place de l'Olivette, 04000 Manosque
Tel 04 92 72 00 99
http://perso.wanadoo.fr/moulinolivette/
Buy produce from many of the region's olive groves from this agricultural cooperative. Pressing and bottling takes place on site and you can visit the mill in November and December, when it is in operation just after the harvest. The oil produced here bears the 'AOC' label and won the prestigious 2002 Concours Général Agricole de Paris.
🕙 Mon–Sat 8–12, 2–6.30

⊕ LA REMISE DU PAYSAN

Avenue Georges Pompidou, 04100 Manosque
Tel 04 92 87 33 37
You'll find a great selection of local produce at this grocery, including fruit and vegetables, vintages of olive oil, fine vinegar and fruit juices.
🕙 Mon–Sat 8–12.30, 3–7.30, Sun 8–1

🎭 THÉÂTRE JEAN LE BLEU

Allée Provence, 04100 Manosque
Tel 04 92 87 37 28
This 700-seat theatre is named after writer Jean Gionot (Jean Le Bleu) and sometimes stages his plays. Other productions include dance, one-person shows, comedy and films. Credit cards are not accepted.
🕙 Varies 🎫 Around €13

LE MONETIER-LES-BAINS

⊕ LA FERME DES BOUSSARDES

Le Lauzet, 05220 Le Monetier-les-Bains
Tel 04 92 24 42 13
www.lafermedesboussardes.com
This farm shop sells home-

The village of Moustiers-Sainte-Marie is known for its faïences

produced foie gras, charcuterie and meats, plus pre-cooked stews. The farm also has a restaurant, rooms and *gîtes*.
🕙 Daily 9–12, 2–7

MOUSTIERS-SAINTE-MARIE

⊕ ATELIER SOLEIL

Chemin Marcel Provence, 04360 Moustiers-Sainte-Marie
04 92 74 63 05
www.soleil-deux.fr
In a former oil mill, this studio produces faïence. You can browse the beautiful collection of vases, plates and pitchers.
🕙 Daily 10–7

PRA-LOUP

🎿 STATION DE PRA-LOUP

Tourist office: Maison de Pra-Loup, 04400 Pra-Loup
Tel 04 92 84 10 04
www.praloup.com
In winter, 53 ski lifts take you up the slopes, at an altitude of up to 2,500m (8,200ft). In summer, activities include paragliding, rafting, canyoning and mountain biking.
🎫 Ski pass: €25 per day

ST-JACQUES

⊕ FERME AUBERGE DU DOMAINE D'AIGUINES

Le Village, 04330 St-Jacques
Tel 04 92 34 25 72
This farm specializes in ducks. Products for sale include foie gras, paté, gizzard, breast and rillettes. You can sample some on the spot, as the farm is coupled with an inn offering duck dishes.
🕙 Opening hours vary; call before you visit

FESTIVALS AND EVENTS

APRIL

SPEED SKIING WORLD CUP EVENT
Vars
Contact details: ODT Vars, 05560 Vars
Tel 04 92 46 51 31
www.vars-ski.com
Speed skiing is the most extreme of the downhill winter events, with skiers reaching speeds of over 200km/h (125mph) as they plummet straight down a glassy piste.
🕙 Dates vary each ski season

AUGUST

CORSO DE LA LAVANDE
Digne-les-Bains
The spa town celebrates its other main industry—lavender.
🕙 Five days around the 1st weekend in Aug

WHAT TO DO

VAUCLUSE

The Avignon Festival and *Chorégles* opera festival at Orange are highlights of the cultural calendar. If you're shopping for edible treats to take home, try candied fruits in Apt and *berlingots* (boiled sweets) in Carpentras. Many sporting activities take place on the slopes of the towering Mont Ventoux, including paragliding and mountain biking.

WHAT TO DO

KEY TO SYMBOLS
- 🌐 Shopping
- 🎭 Entertainment
- 🍸 Nightlife
- ⚽ Sports
- ✪ Activities
- 💧 Health and Beauty
- ✷ For Children

APT

🌐 APT UNION
Quartier Salignan, BP 137, 84405 Apt
Tel 04 90 76 31 31
www.kerryaptunion.com
Renowned for its glacé fruit, this confectioner is a world leader when it comes to the glacé cherry. Beautiful wooden boxes contain the fruits. To visit the factory, reserve ahead.
🕐 Mon–Sat 9–12, 2–6

AVIGNON

🌐 BOULANGERIE TROUILLAS
14 place des Châtaignes, 84000 Avignon
Tel 04 90 86 10 84
One of the best Provençal snacks is *fougasse* bread. You'll find a variety of *fougasses* here: with olives, nuts and *grattelons* (bacon).
🕐 Mon–Sat 6am–8pm

🌐 CHAPELIER MOURET
20 rue des Marchands, 84000 Avignon
Tel 04 90 85 39 38
The same family has been making hats here since 1860, following methods passed from father to son. There's a great collection of panamas and *capelines* (wide-brimmed hats typical of the region).
🕐 Tue–Sat 10–12.30, 2–7

🌐 MARCHÉ DES HALLES
Place Pie, 84000 Avignon
Sample or purchase a wide range of local produce at this market. If you don't feel like buying, simply stroll along the aisles lined with stands. Credit cards are not accepted.
🕐 Tue–Sun 6am–1.30pm

🌐 MARCHÉ AUX PUCES
Place des Carmes, 84000 Avignon
Antiques dealers mix with locals who have emptied their cellars at this large bazaar. Arrive early to have the best chance of finding a bargain. After you have finished browsing, you can enjoy a drink in one of the nearby cafés. Credit cards are not accepted.
🕐 Sun 7–1

🌐 MARCHÉ DES REMPARTS ST-MICHEL
Porte St-Michel, 84000 Avignon
Avignon's biggest market takes you to the other side of the Mediterranean, with North African spices, vegetables and fruit. Credit cards are not accepted.
🕐 Sat, Sun 6am–1pm

🌐 SHAKESPEARE LIBRAIRIE
155 rue Carreterie, 84000 Avignon
Tel 04 90 27 38 50
There are many secondhand books in English at this store, which is coupled with a tea room. No visit is complete without some tea and cake.
🕐 Tue–Sat 9.30–12.30, 2–6.30

🌐 LA TROPÉZIENNE
22 rue St-Agricole, 84000 Avignon
Tel 04 90 86 24 72
www.la-tropezienne.fr st
This shop is famous for its *papalines*—black chocolates filled with Origan du Comtat, a liqueur scented with 60 regional spices. Other products include glacé fruit, jams and the house special, *tropézienne*, a cake filled with cream.
🕐 Tue–Sun 8–8 (daily in Jul)

🎭 BIG BANG THÉÂTRE
18 rue Guillaume-Puy, 84000 Avignon
Tel 04 90 27 12 71
This popular little theatre likes to experiment. The eclectic schedule includes dance, music and drama.
🕐 Open all year round 🍴 From €13

🎭 LE ROUGE GORGE
Place de la Mirande, 84000 Avignon
Tel 04 90 14 02 54
www.lerougegorge.fr
On Fridays and Saturdays this former printing works hosts cabaret-style dinner theatre, with dancers and fine food. The rest of the week sees jazz, rock, samba and flamenco.
🕐 Sep–end Jul Fri, Sat (and other show nights) 8pm–3am 🍴 Dinner/cabaret €40–€45, concert €5–€15

🎭 OPÉRA-THÉÂTRE D'AVIGNON ET DES PAYS DE VAUCLUSE
1 rue Racine, 84000 Avignon
Tel 04 90 82 42 42
There is lavish decor at this Italian-style theatre, with gilded panels, painted ceilings and statues of playwrights Molière and Racine.
🕐 Tue–Sat 8.30pm, Sun 2.30pm

🎭 THÉÂTRE DU CHIEN QUI FUME
75 rue des Teinturiers, 84000 Avignon
Tel 04 90 85 25 87
www.chienquifume.com
Enjoy theatre, songs and dance by celebrated or budding actors here. Entry is free on the last Friday of the month for the 'open-mike' event. Credit cards are not accepted.
🕐 Performances at 8.30pm
🍴 €10–€22

🍷 BAR DE L'HÔTEL D'EUROPE
12 place Crillon, 84000 Avignon
Tel 04 90 14 76 76
www.hotel-d-europe.fr
This elegant bar is part of a four-star hotel in a 16th-century building. Sit out in the pleasant shady courtyard in fair weather.
🕐 Daily noon–1am

🍷 LE BLUES
25 rue Carnot, 84000 Avignon
Tel 04 90 85 79 71
Choose from two bars and two dance floors at this venue, which hosts karaoke nights, disco, live rock, jazz and blues.
🕐 Daily 11pm–5am

🍷 LE CID
11 place de l'Horloge, 84000 Avignon
Tel 04 90 82 30 38
www.lecidcafe.com
Seventies pop decor and house and lounge rhythms are the key elements of this bar, popular with the gay and lesbian community. Brasserie fare is served at lunchtime.
🕐 Daily 7am–1.30am (until 3am Jul)

Avignon-based Chapelier Mouret has been making hats for around 150 years

🍷 CADILLAC CAFÉ
11 bis route de Lyon, 84000 Avignon
Tel 04 90 86 99 57
Go back to 1950s Americana at this venue, with its frescoes of Marilyn and Elvis, pool tables and video games. There are plenty of theme nights and barbecues in summer.
🕐 Daily 2pm–1am

🍷 CUBANITO'S CAFÉ
51 rue Carnot, 84000 Avignon
Tel 04 90 27 90 59
Che Guevara posters adorn the walls at this Cuban den where you can enjoy a rum cocktail. Try a free salsa class any evening at 9pm.
🕐 Tue–Fri 8am–1am, Sat 10am–1am

🍷 OPÉRA CAFÉ
24 place de l'Horloge, 84000 Avignon
Tel 04 90 86 17 43
This contemporary chic bar-restaurant, on Avignon's busiest square, has been a hit with the trendy crowd since it opened in 2001. There is a DJ every evening.
🕐 Daily 9am–1am (til 3am Jul)

🍷 RED ZONE BAR
25 rue Carnot, 84000 Avignon
Tel 04 90 27 02 44
www.redzonebar.com
Here you'll find salsa on Tuesday night, live music on Wednesday, student night on Thursday and dancing on Friday and Saturday.
🕐 Daily 9pm–3am

🍷 TAPALOCAS
15 rue Galante, 84000 Avignon
Tel 04 90 82 56 84
www.tapalocas.com
Always bustling, this former warehouse turned bodega, with long wooden tables and a mosaic-adorned bar, offers a large choice of tapas, including spicy potatoes and fried fish.
🕐 Daily 11.45am–1am

✈ AÉROCLUB D'AVIGNON
Aéroport d'Avignon-Caumont, 84000 Avignon
Tel 04 90 84 17 17
These small planes are a fun and quick way to discover Avignon and its surroundings. In 15 minutes you'll tour the city, in 30 you'll see the Pont du Gard and in 45 you'll reach Mont Ventoux.
🍴 €45 for a 15-min flight (€60 for 2 people)

🎳 BOWLING
Avenue Paul-Claudel, 84000 Avignon
Tel 04 90 88 50 11
Test your skills on one of the 16 computerized bowling alleys here. Drinks and sandwiches are available.
🕐 Daily 3pm–2am (until 4am Fri, Sat)
🍴 €4–€6 per game (including shoe rental)

WHAT TO DO

PATINOIRE D'AVIGNON
2483 chemin de l'Amandier, 84000 Avignon
Tel 04 90 88 54 32
The local ice-hockey team, the Castors (the Beavers), are based at this ice rink. Credit cards are not accepted.
🕐 Mon–Fri 9.30–12, 3–5.30 (also 9–11.30pm Fri), Sat 3–5.30, 9–11.30, Sun 3–6 💶 Entry and skate rental €8

BONNIEUX
ÉTABLISSEMENT VERNIN
RN 100, 84480 Bonnieux
Tel 04 90 04 63 04
www.carreaux-d-apt.com
This factory has been using Apt clay to make tiles since 1870. Traditional methods are still used today: The clay is hand-worked, then dries in the sun before it's fired. Choose from a wide range of tiles, either plain or decorated.
🕐 Mon–Sat 9–12, 2–6

CARPENTRAS
CONFISERIE BONO
280 allée Jean Jaurès, 84200 Carpentras
Tel 04 90 63 04 99
www.confiseriebono.fr
Glacé fruits, a specialty in Provence, have been prepared at this store since 1925. The traditional methods that made its reputation are still used: Carefully chosen fruits are slowly cooked about a dozen times. Various assortments fill baskets, boxes and china. Credit cards are not accepted.
🕐 Mon–Fri 9–12, 2.30–7, Sat 10–12

LES OLIVADES
102 rue Moricelly, 84200 Carpentras
Tel 04 90 63 33 50
www.les-olivades.com
Les Olivades has been manufacturing printed fabrics since 1818, first seeking its inspiration in the *indiennes* (fabrics imported from India during the 17th century), then establishing the product as a tradition of Provence. Their beautiful collection includes some tableware and clothing.
🕐 Mon–Sat 9.30–12, 2–6

MARCHÉ DE LA TRUFFE
Place Aristide Briand, 84200 Carpentras
Black truffle is cultivated in the Vaucluse and collected during winter with the help of dogs. This market displays their regional specialty. Credit cards are not accepted.
🕐 Mid-Nov to mid-Mar Fri 9am–11am

CAVAILLON
LE GRENIER À SONS
157 avenue du Général-de-Gaulle, 84301 Cavaillon
Tel 04 90 06 44 20
www.grenier-a-sons.org
This dynamic 350-seat concert hall stages jazz, rock, blues, reggae and more, by established musicians and

L'Occitane, in L'Isle-sur-la-Sorgue, sells a range of scented products

budding talents. There's also a bar and gallery.
🕐 Sep–end Jul daily 9–12, 2–7 (till 12 on concert nights) 💶 Around €10

COUSTELLET
GARE DE COUSTELLET
Quai Entreprises, 84660 Coustellet
Tel 04 90 76 84 38
avec.lagare.free.fr
Formerly a railway station, this is now a 280-seat venue hosting gigs by groups performing anything from jazz to rock. Painting and photography exhibitions are held in what was previously the concourse. Credit cards are not accepted.
🕐 Fri–Sat 9pm–2am 💶 Concerts €5–€15

GORDES
HOT AIR BALLOON PROVENCE
Le Mas Fourniguière Joucas, 84220 Gordes
Tel 04 90 05 76 77
www.avignon-et-provence.com/ballooning/fr/infos.htm
These hot-air balloons fly over the picturesque villages of the Lubéron, including Gordes, Roussillon and Lacoste. The tour lasts between 60 and 90 minutes. Enjoy a Provence-style picnic and champagne after landing.
🕐 By appointment 💶 €230 per person or €145 for 40-min flight

L'ISLE-SUR-LA-SORGUE
L'OCCITANE
30 rue République, 84800 L'Isle-sur-la-Sorgue
Tel 04 90 20 71 47
www.loccitane.com
The scents of Provence have been captured in a wide range of products for the body, face and home: lavender-scented creams and incense, soap from Marseille enriched with olive oil or honey, and home fragrances. Perfect for re-creating a Provençal atmosphere on your return.
🕐 Tue–Sat 10–1, 2–7

LAURIS
CAP RANDO
Mas de Recaute, 84360 Lauris
Tel 04 90 08 41 44
www.caprando.com
This equestrian venue organizes various routes for discovering Provence on horseback. These include exploring the Parc Naturel Régional du Lubéron, following the lavender route (from the Lubéron to Verdon and then Nice) and crossing the Provencal Alps. Some carriage tours are also available.
🕐 All year long by appointment 💶 €800–€1,000 for a full week (all meals included)

LUBÉRON

🚴 VÉLO LOISIR EN LUBÉRON

BP14, 04280 Céreste
04 92 79 05 82
www.veloloisirluberon.com
This bicycling club organizes tours in the Parc Naturel Régional du Lubéron: from Cavaillon to Forcalquier via Apt, for example. The club has a mine of information on renting a bike, finding a bed for the night and getting your luggage to your next stop.
🕐 Mon–Fri 9–12.30, 2–6

MORIÈRES-LÈS-AVIGNON

🚴 GOLF DE CHÂTEAUBLANC

Les Plans, 84310 Morières-lès-Avignon
Tel 04 90 33 39 08
www.golfchateaublanc.com
There are two courses here: one 9-hole and one 18-hole. After your game, have a bite to eat at the restaurant.
🕐 Daily 8am–7pm 💶 18 holes: Mon–Fri €34, Sat, Sun €44 (€23 and €26 for 9 holes)

ORANGE

🍷 CHÂTEAU DE BEAUCASTEL

84100 Orange
Tel 04 90 70 41 00
www.beaucastel.com
This vineyard is on land that has been owned by the Beaucastel family since 1549. Wine is made according to traditional organic methods. Varieties include Grenache, Syrah and Muscardin.
🕐 By appointment

PIERRELATTE

🐊 LA FERME AUX CROCODILES

Les Blanchettes, 26700 Pierrelatte
Tel 04 75 04 33 73
www.lafermeauxcrocodiles.com
On the Vaucluse/Drôme border, La Ferme aux Crocodiles lets children see crocodiles, alligators and other reptiles. The whole farm is under cover, with a huge dome ceiling. There's a playground and snack bar.
🕐 Apr–end Oct daily 9.30–7; Nov–end Mar daily 9.30–5 💶 Adult €8.30, child (3–12) €6

ST-MARTIN-DE-CASTILLON

🐴 LOU CALEU

Madame et Monsieur Rondard, RN100, 84750 St-Martin-de-Castillon
Tel 04 90 75 28 88
www.loucaleu.com
The owners of this hotel and restaurant also run stables. Go on a short ride or a trek of several days. The trails take you through the beautiful Lubéron.
🕐 Phone to reserve 💶 1-hour ride €17, full day (including meal) €77

LE THOR

🎵 AUDITORIUM DE VAUCLUSE

Chemin des Estourans, 84250 Le Thor
Tel 04 90 33 97 32

Soaking up the atmosphere at the Théâtre Antique, Orange

This venue welcomes all sorts of high quality shows. Renowned French singers are regularly on the bill (Adamo, Nougaro), but also international performers such as the Russian army choir.
🕐 Mon–Sat 10–12, 4–6

VAISON-LA-ROMAINE

🏛 SOULÉIADO

2 cours Henri Fabre, 84110 Vaison-la-Romaine
Tel 04 90 36 38 33
The vibrancy of Provence is beautifully expressed in the fabrics for sale in this store, from tablecloths and drapes to shirts and skirts.
🕐 Mon–Sat 9.30–1, 2–7

FESTIVALS AND EVENTS

JULY

AVIGNON FESTIVAL
Avignon
Tel 04 90 14 14 14
www.festival-avignon.com
Provence becomes the world capital of culture in July when the biggest names in theatre, dance and music flock to Avignon for a season of spectacular performances against a stunning backdrop. There's also plenty of free street entertainment.
🕐 Three weeks in Jul

CHORÉGIES
Orange
Tel 04 90 34 24 24
www.choregies.asso.fr
Orange's world-famous opera and classical music festival.
🕐 Mid-Jul to early Aug

AUGUST

FÊTE DE LA LAVANDE
Sault
Jardin des Lavandes
Tel 04 90 64 14 97
Sweet-smelling festivities in a town surrounded by lavender.

FÊTE DE LA VÉRAISON
Châteauneuf-du-Pape
Medieval pageantry celebrates the maturing of the grapes. Wine producers set up stalls in the village, where you can taste their produce.
🕐 Early August

WHAT TO DO

Go out and about in Provence with these five driving tours, six walks and a bicycle ride. They explore Provence's varied attractions, from a city walk in Avignon to a drive along the Côte d'Azur. The locations of the walks and tours are marked on the map on page 206. It is advisable to buy a detailed map of the area before you set out.

Out and About

KEY TO THIS MAP

❷ Drive ■ City

❹ Walk ● Town

OUT AND ABOUT

KEY TO ROUTE MAPS IN THIS CHAPTER

★ Start point

▬ Route

▪▪ Alternative route

▶ Route direction

❷ Walk start point on drive

❻ Featured sight along route

● Place of interest in Sights section

● Other place of interest

☀ Viewpoint

621 ▲ Height in metres

BARRAGE DE BIMONT

This walk gives you excellent views to the imposing Montagne Sainte-Victoire, the mountain that captivated the painter Paul Cézanne and appeared in many of his greatest works. It begins from the Bimont Dam (Barrage de Bimont) then takes you to a low ridge, where you can enjoy views of the Massif de la Sainte-Baume. For a drive that takes in the Barrage de Bimont ▷ 208–209.

THE WALK

Length: 3.5km (2 miles)

Allow: 1 hour

Start/end: the parking area at the Barrage de Bimont

HOW TO GET THERE

The Barrage de Bimont is around 7km (4 miles) east of Aix-en-Provence

The Barrage de Bimont dams the Infernet river to form an artificial lake, the Lac du Bimont. This lake provides water to the local towns.

★ Start from the parking area at the Barrage de Bimont. Leave through the gates at the left end of the parking area, go along the road and cross the dam. Look to the right here to see a collection lake feeding a system of canals that go through the mountains. On the left, the Montagne Sainte-Victoire is topped by a commemorative cross.

❶ The Victory Mountain (▷ 79) was so called after the Romans defeated the Teutonic barbarians at a battle that took place nearby in around 102BC. The cross on its summit, called the Croix de Provence, is 18m (59ft) high and is the third to be placed there.

At the end of the path, go through a car barrier, passing a notice that warns of the risk of forest fires. The wide track continues uphill then flattens out to reach a fork. Take the left fork to reach a viewpoint that looks over the Sainte-Victoire ridge and trees to the Massif de la Sainte-Baume.

❷ The Sainte-Baume massif is home to one of the most unusual forests in Provence, now a biological reserve. It is one of the few woodlands in the area where trees native to northern Europe grow. There is also a cave that has become a shrine to St. Mary Magdalene.

Continue walking another few hundred metres in the direction of the Croix de Provence, on the summit, through country that opens out to reach another clump of trees. Here, the trail bears right, with a smaller trail going straight ahead. Go up this smaller trail through a very pretty stretch of mixed woodland, where you can see many different flowers.

As the trail flattens out and then begins to go downhill, a smaller trail merges from the left. Soon there is a more definite left fork. Turn left down this trail, where you may be lucky enough to see green lizards among the flowers.

At a T-junction of tracks, take the smaller one, which goes left. This leads to the lake. At the lake, turn left up a rougher, narrower trail that leads back to the dam. Go over the dam to return to the parking area.

A view across the Massif de la Sainte-Baume

OUT AND ABOUT

WHEN TO GO

This is a short walk and can be done at any time of year. Access from the parking area is through a gate that is locked at 10pm in high season and dusk the rest of the year.

WHERE TO EAT

Take a picnic and water with you, as there is nowhere along the route where you can buy food. There are picnic tables and benches under the shade of pine trees just after crossing the dam.

BASICS

Tourist information

There is a Maison de Sainte-Victoire information office at St-Antonin-sur-Bayon.

☎ 04 42 66 84 40

❓ Don't smoke on this walk, as you may risk starting a forest fire.

THE HEART OF PROVENCE

This tour starts in Aix-en-Provence and takes in the Montagne Sainte-Victoire, which inspired the painter Paul Cézanne, before turning south towards the Massif de la Sainte-Baume, where you'll have a view to Marseille. The roads are narrow in places and hilly in others, but this makes the drive interesting rather than arduous.

THE DRIVE

Length: 135km (84 miles)

Allow: 1 day

Start/end: Aix-en-Provence

The heart of Aix-en-Provence (▷ 58–61) is the cours Mirabeau, a wide boulevard planted with a double row of plane trees that provide welcome shade from the summer sun. North of here lies Vieil Aix, the oldest and most charming section of the city.

★ Leave Aix-en-Provence on the D10, towards St-Marc-Jaumegarde and Vauvenargues, to reach the Barrage de Bimont after about 7km (4 miles).

❶ The lake behind the Barrage de Bimont dam provides water for local towns. For a walk here ▷ 207.

Continue on the D10 to Vauvenargues.

❷ The pretty village of Vauvenargues is famous for its Renaissance chateau, inherited by Pablo Picasso in 1958. The artist died here in 1973 and is buried within the extensive grounds. The park and chateau are not open to the public.

Rejoin the D10 by driving straight through the village (there is only one road). The D10, now signed for Jouques and Rians, runs along the northern flank of the Montagne Sainte-Victoire.

❸ The Victory Mountain (▷ 79) was a great inspiration to the artist Paul Cézanne.

Bear right shortly, following the D223 signed for Rians. The road narrows and climbs, but offers good views all the way. At the next intersection, take a left turn (no sign). This is the D23 towards Rians, which ends at a T-junction with the D3. Take a right turn, signed for Ollières and St-Maximin-la-Sainte-Baume.

Approaching St-Maximin, turn left at the traffic lights, then right and left again as you cross St-Maximin.

❹ St-Maximin-la-Sainte-Baume has a wonderful basilica that is the best example of Gothic architecture in Provence. It was built on the site of a sixth-century church that was, according to local legend, the resting place for the remains of St. Mary Magdalene. Construction of the new basilica started in 1295 and continued until the 16th century, although no belfry was ever built and the west front was unfinished.

At a roundabout, go straight over to take the N560 signposted Nans-les-Pins. Bear right as the main road bears left. This smaller road goes under a railway bridge and is signed for Aubagne, Marseille and St-Zacharie. Continue for 100m (110 yards), then turn left at traffic lights. Go straight over at the next traffic lights on to the D64 signed Mazaugues. Follow the D64 until it reaches the D1 and turn right towards Rougiers. Turn left off the D1 into the village at the sign for Rougiers *centre*, and left again at the café/*tabac* up the rue Ste-Anne. This goes uphill towards a ruin and a church that you'll see on top of the hill ahead. It then bears sharp left and goes through an open barrier, before continuing up the valley. Go over a crest and down to an intersection. Turn right onto the D95 (only the back of the sign is visible, so to check that you are on the right road make sure the wrong side indicates Plan-d'Aups). Go past signs warning of deer, and continue to the Hôtellerie at La Sainte-Baume.

❺ The Hôtellerie is a 19th-century restoration of a Dominican friars' pilgrim hostel, dating from medieval times. It has now become an international base for spiritual studies.

Continue on the D80 through Plan-d'Aups, after which the road widens. At the next intersection, bear right onto a road signed for Auriol, which joins the D45A to make a long, twisty descent around many hairpin bends. When you reach the N560 at a roundabout, take the first exit signed St-Zacharie. When you reach the village, continue until a road on the left, the D85, is signed Trets and Col du Petit Galibier. Stay on this road, later the D12, which climbs providing fine views, to reach Trets.

❻ Trets was originally Roman, but much of the current town dates from the Middle Ages. You can see the remains of medieval walls, as well as square 14th-century towers and a castle and church that date from the 15th-century.

Approaching Trets, turn left at a roundabout, go straight over a mini-roundabout, and bear left at the next intersection to approach a roundabout with a fountain. Bear left here too onto the D908 signed Peynier.

❼ The village of Peynier has a pleasant Romanesque church.

Pass Peynier to the south and climb through wooded hills. After 4km (2.5 miles) take the D46C to the right, signed for Belcodène, and go through the village following signs for Fuveau. At a fork in the road, keep right, go over the *autoroute* and enter Fuveau. Turn left and right into the main square, then, almost immediately, take the first street on the left, which is the road to Aix-en-Provence and Gardanne. At a roundabout with a central fountain, take the exit signed for Aix and continue to the N96. Turn right and follow this road and the N7 to Aix.

Cézanne's inspiration,
Montagne Sainte-Victoire

Pablo Picasso lived and died in this chateau at Vauvenargues. He is
buried in the grounds

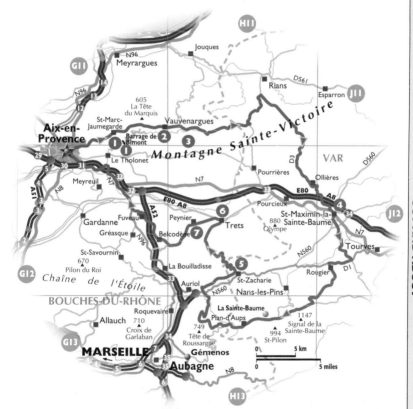

Jouques

H11

G11

N96
Meyrargues

Rians

D561

Esparron

J11

605
La Tête
du Marquis

St-Marc-
Jaumegarde

Vauvenargues

14

13

12

**Aix-en-
Provence**

N96

Barrage de
Bimont

1

2

3

Montagne Sainte-Victoire

Le Tholonet

VAR

D560

29

Meyreuil

31

N7

5

30

A51

N8

37

37

Pourrières

D3

Ollières

E80 A8

N7

E80

A8

33

4

34

J12

Pourcieux

6

St-Maximin-la-
Sainte-Baume

880
Olympe

A52

Peynier

Gardanne

Fuveau

Trets

N560

Gréasque

N96

Belcodène

7

Tourves

St-Savournin

670
Pilon du Roi

La Bouilladisse

5

Rougier

D1

G12

Chaîne de l'Étoile

33

Auriol

St-Zacharie

N560

Nans-les-Pins

BOUCHES-DU-RHÔNE

Roquevaire

La Sainte-Baume
Plan-d'Aups

1147
Signal de la
Sainte-Baume

Allauch

710
Croix de
Garlaban

749
Tête de
Roussargue

994
St-Pilon

0   5 km

34

G13

MARSEILLE

35

35

Gémenos

0   5 miles

5

6

35

Aubagne

N8

6

H13

*A café on cours Mirabeau, in
Aix-en-Provence*

WHERE TO EAT

There are many restaurants and
brasseries in St-Maximin-la-
Sainte-Baume.

BASICS

Hôtellerie la Sainte-Baume
Outside the village of Plan-d'Aups
☎ 04 42 04 54 84

BOUCHES-DU-RHÔNE THE HEART OF PROVENCE   **20**

THE CAMARGUE BY CAR

The Camargue—the Rhône delta—is huge, and comparatively few roads penetrate its marshy secrets. To see herds of grazing Camargue bulls watched over by their cowboy *gardians,* and far more birds than can be seen from the roads, consider supplementing the drive by taking a boat trip from a town such as Saintes-Maries-de-la-Mer. As with many driving tours of the Camargue, this one begins in Arles, famous for its Roman legacies and as the haunt of artist Vincent Van Gogh.

THE DRIVE

Length:	95km (59 miles)
Allow:	1 day
Start/end:	Arles

★ Arles (▷ 62–65), on the Rhône and north of the Camargue, has exceptionally well-preserved Roman remnants and some good art museums containing works by Pablo Picasso and Paul Gauguin.

Head west from Arles and cross the Grand Rhône. Take the D570 (signed for Saintes-Maries-de-la-Mer) to Albaron, once a powerful stronghold but now fighting off the sea with pumping stations rather then repelling human invaders. From here take the D37 to Méjanes.

❶ Méjanes is a small lakeside resort with a narrow-gauge railway, a bullring and ponies and horses for rent.

From here, follow the D37 as it runs past the Étang de Vaccarès, the largest of the Camargue's lagoons.

❷ The Étang de Vaccarès (▷ 69) is part of a nature reserve called the Réserve Nationale de Camargue, which has its visitor office and headquarters at La Capelière. On this stretch, stop the car at any of the laybys (turnouts) and the distinctive smell of marsh immediately becomes apparent—a combination of salt, rotting vegetation and growing plants.

At Villeneuve, turn south towards La Capelière.

It's easy to miss the excellent visitor centre—keep a lookout for the sign and be ready to turn off the road on the left. There are marked nature trails, and the 1.5km (1-mile) path around the building has signs giving details about the area's plants and animals.

Continue south past Salin-de-Badon, noted for its birds, to Salin-de-Giraud.

❸ Salin-de-Giraud is the best known of the region's salt-producing towns. The tree-lined avenues are dominated by the Solvay refinery, where glittering piles of salt can be glimpsed through the railings.

Now take the D36 north as it slices through the marshy land to the west of the sluggish Grand Rhône. Eventually it joins the D570, which leads back to Arles.

WILDLIFE OF THE CAMARGUE

The Camargue is famous for its dazzling white horses and unique black bulls, but this wilderness is also home to countless birds, including ducks, waders and geese. The wide, shallow lagoons provide excellent feeding grounds for swans, avocets and egrets, while the freshwater reed beds are used as nesting sites by bitterns, herons and warblers. Surveys have also recorded 24,000 pink flamingos here, a truly spectacular sight. Perhaps the most remarkable of the creatures that thrive here is the brine shrimp, a crustacean just over 1.5cm (0.6in) long. It has evolved in such a way that it can live in virtually fresh or very salty water with equal ease, and so is able to survive both floods and droughts.

One of the Camargue's famous white horses (right).
Calm waters of the Étang de Vaccarès (below)

OUT AND ABOUT

The Roman arena at Arles (left).
Camargue cattle (below)

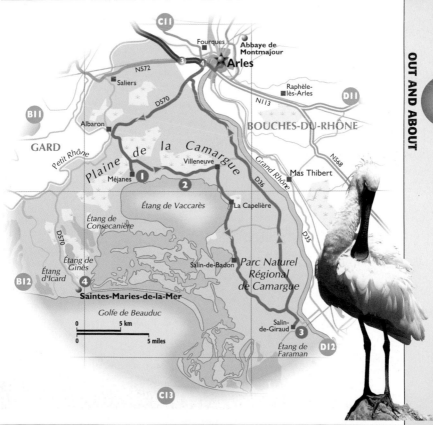

THE CAMARGUE BY BICYCLE

Bicycling is a good way to explore the flat, sometimes blustery, distances of the Camargue. This circular route is 20km (12.5 miles) and makes an excellent bicycle tour. It begins in Saintes-Maries-de-la-Mer, where you'll find several places that rent bicycles. The tourist office on avenue Van Gogh has a list. The route takes in the Parc Ornithologique du Pont de Gau, perfect for birdwatching.

THE TOUR

Length: 20km (12.5 miles)

Allow: 1.5 hours to 4 hours, depending on how long you spend at the bird reserve and if you do the extra 10km (6-mile) detour to the Château d'Avignon.

Start/end: Saintes-Maries-de-la-Mer

★ Saintes-Maries-de-la-Mer (▷ 83) is named after Mary Magdalene, Marie-Salomé (the mother of James and John the Apostles) and Marie-Jacobé (the sister or sister-in-law of the Virgin Mary), who were said to have landed here by boat from the Holy Land with Sarah, their servant. Sarah is the patron saint of gypsies and there is a large festival in her memory every May. In the crypt of the fortified Romanesque church is the black statue of Sarah, often draped in chiffon.

Leave Saintes-Maries on the D85A, a minor road that runs between the Réserve

Départementale des Impériaux et du Malagroy on your right and the Étang de Ginès on the left. After 4km (2.5 miles) the road bears left (there's a good view east here near the Mas de Cacharel), while an alternative route branches off right to Méjanes. After 6km (4 miles) the D85A joins the D570, the main road, at Pioch-Badet. For a longer trip, turn

right and cycle 5km (3 miles) to the Château d'Avignon (closed on Tuesdays), with its collection of 19th-century furniture. Heading south back towards Saintes-Maries will bring you past the Maison du Parc Naturel Régional de Camargue and the Parc Ornithologique du Pont de Gau (▷ 69).

❶ The Parc Ornithologique du Pont de Gau is a great place for birdwatching. The Camargue is a haven for birds, including pink flamingos, ducks, egrets, herons, cranes, geese and swans. Large aviaries at the park show the rarer species.

To return along the Petit-Rhône after the Parc Ornithologique du Pont de Gau, turn right onto the D85 just before the Musée de Cire (wax museum) and then left onto the D38, which loops back into Saintes-Maries-de-la-Mer around the Étang des Launes.

OUT AND ABOUT

Stately Château d'Avignon (above) is worth a detour.
The bell tower of the fortified Notre-Dame-de-la-Mer, at Saintes-Maries-de-la-Mer (top)

Take a boat trip on the water (left) or a leisurely horseback ride beside it (below) to explore the area

Hostellerie du Pont de Gau
Avenue Arles, 13460 Saintes-Maries-de-la-Mer
☎ 04 90 97 81 53
Small hotel with a good, moderately priced restaurant

BII

GARD

Méjanes

Le Ménage

Parc Naturel Régional de Camargue

Pioch Badet

BOUCHES-DU-RHÔNE

Étang de Consecanière

Étang des Fourneaux

Petit Rhône

D570

Pont du Gau

Ginès

Étang de Ginès
Parc ornithologique

Étang de Malagroy

Étang dit l'Impérial

I

B12

Étang du Cabri

Étang d'Icard

C12

0   3 km
0   3 miles

Saintes-Maries-de-la-Mer

Golfe de Beauduc

OUT AND ABOUT

Tourist information
5 avenue Van Gogh, 13460
Saintes-Maries-de-la-Mer
☎ 04 90 97 82 55
⏰ Jul, Aug daily 9–8; Apr–end Jun, Sep daily 9–7; Mar, Oct daily 9–6; Nov–end Feb daily 9–5
www.saintesmaries.com

Château d'Avignon
☎ 04 90 97 58 58
⏰ Guided tours only: Wed–Mon 10–5
💷 Adult €3, under 16 free
🎫 Tours every hour

Parc Ornithologique du Pont de Gau
☎ 04 90 97 82 62
⏰ Apr–end Sep daily 9–dusk; Oct–end Mar 10–dusk
www.parcornithologique.com

AROUND ST-TROPEZ

This walk tempts you with high-class shopping, then takes you to the marina crammed with sleek motor yachts. Equilibrium is restored with a visit to an exceptional museum of art. Then you leave the glitz behind to enter the oldest part of town, followed by an easy climb to the Citadelle, where you can enjoy views of the town and bay.

THE WALK

Length: 2km (1.4 miles)
Allow: 2 hours, plus time for visits
Start/end: Place des Lices (there is parking at the nearby parking des Lices)

HOW TO GET THERE

If you are driving, take the D98 along the shore of the Bay of St-Tropez and follow signs for parking des Lices.

★ Place des Lices is a large open area where markets, town gatherings and games of pétanque take place in the shade of the plane trees. The northern edge is defined by boulevard Louis Blanc; here you'll find La Tarte Tropezienne, a pastry and coffee shop, whose success (there are now several in the area) has been built on a single irresistible brioche, orange blossom and cream confection, the recipe for which is protected by patent.

Descend some steps, cross the *place* and enter the pedestrian-only rue Georges Clemenceau. This is lined with high-quality boutiques; at the other end is an arcade called le Grand Passage—a misnomer as it is small, unless the name refers to the size of the wallet necessary to shop here. Cross rue Allard to the quay and bear left. Where the quay turns right, the Musée de l'Annonciade is on the left.

❶ The Musée de l'Annonciade (▷ 99) is a must for enthusiasts of post-Impressionist art. Cubism, Expressionism, the Fauves and the Nabis group are all represented.

Retrace your steps along the quay, admiring the luxury boats on your left and the statue of Pierre-André de Suffen, an 18th-century admiral and founding father of St-Tropez, on the right. Pick up a town map at the tourist office next on the right, behind the resort's most famous café-terrace, Sénéquier.

❷ Sénéquier, right on the waterfront, is the place to enjoy an expresso or an ice cream while watching the well-heeled stroll by or play on their yachts just feet away.

Continue along the waterfront to reach the Môle Jean Reveille, the jetty enclosing the port, which rewards you with a wonderful view of the town on one side and views out over the Bay of St-Tropez on the other. Descend from the Môle by the Tour du Portalet and enter an alley, rue Portalet. Go left into rue St-Esprit and first-right into rue du Puits. Turn left into place de l'Hôtel de Ville and second-right into rue St-Jean to reach the parish church, Notre-Dame de l'Assomption.

❸ Notre-Dame de l'Assomption's bright steeple is a town landmark, and the sound of its bells is delightful. Inside you can see the painted bust of St-Tropez (Torpes), the figurehead of processions during the town's *Bravades* festivals (▷ 188).

Return to place de l'Hôtel de Ville and turn right to go through the Porte du Revelen; the small cove on the left is the original fishermen's port. Walk up rue des Remparts, bear left across place des Remparts and climb steps up to a road. Turn right down the road for 25m (23 yards), then go left between two anchors and climb more steps up to the Citadelle (▷ 98).

❹ The Citadelle dates from the 16th century and is now a museum. The emphasis is on seafaring traditions and the fearless fighting by the locals in defence of their town in previous years. The grounds around the Citadelle are often used for temporary exhibitions, especially sculpture.

Retrace your path down the steps, enjoying views through oleanders and sweet-smelling eucalyptus to the town and the bay. Cross the road to enter the pedestrian-only rue de la Citadelle. At a tiny crossroads, turn right into rue des Commerçants and pause for a coffee at Chez Fuchs, where a *cave à cigares* holds more than 10,000 cigars and a small spiral staircase leads to a popular Provençal restaurant. Opposite the bar is a small alley leading down to place aux Herbes.

❺ Place aux Herbes is tiny but exquisitely pretty. Here daily market stalls offer fresh fruit, vegetables and flowers. On the left, an arch leads into the shade of the fish market, where the night's catch is sold by the fishermen's wives.

Pass through the fish market and emerge at the other end next to the tourist office. Cross over into rue François Sibilli, walk up to place de la Garonne, and continue to place des Lices.

La Tarte Tropezienne coffee shop, where you can try the eponymous cake

OUT AND ABOUT

After walking around the port, stop for lunch or a drink at Sénéquier

WHERE TO EAT

Sénéquier
Quai Jean-Jaurès, St-Tropez
☎ 04 94 97 00 90
🕐 Summer daily 8–8; winter daily 8–7

Chez Fuchs
7 rue des Commerçants, St-Tropez
☎ 04 94 97 01 25
🕐 Summer daily 7am–midnight; winter hours vary

BASICS

Tourist Information Office,
Quai Jean-Jaurès, St-Tropez
☎ 04 94 97 45 21
🕐 Jul, Aug daily 9.30–8; Apr–end Jun, Sep, Oct daily 9.30–12.30, 2–7; Nov–end Mar daily 9.30–12.30, 2–6
www.saint-tropez.st

WHEN TO GO

The walk can be done at any time of year. If you are driving to St-Tropez in summer, start early to avoid the heavy traffic.

The boats moored at St-Tropez come in only one size—extra large

VALLÉE DES MERVEILLES

The Valley of Marvels is in the Parc National du Mercantour, a vast scenic area of peaks, valleys and lakes spanning the Alpes-Maritimes and Alpes-de-Haute-Provence *départements* and joined to the Parco Naturale dell'Argentera in Italy. The park shelters Alpine and Mediterranean flora and fauna. At least 25 of its plant species are not found anywhere else in the world and at least half of all France's flower species are represented. Protected animals include ibex, wild sheep and wolves. This hike takes you past glacial boulders with images of figures and tools carved by ancient Ligurians.

BE PREPARED

The only way to reach the Vallée des Merveilles is on foot—not only are there no real roads, but private vehicles are generally banned from this section of the park because it is a protected zone. (Some four-wheel-drive visitor vehicles are allowed on the first section to the Refuge des Merveilles.) You need to allow at least a day for this hike and start early in the morning. If you want to stay in the area overnight, options include the *refuges* (Refuge des Merveilles at Lac Long or Refuge de Valmasque at Lac Vert) or one of the hotels at the winter ski resort of Castérino, although not all are open year round. Camping is not allowed. Sudden storms are frequent and violent; plan your hike with the park office in Tende and take your map with you, wear suitable hiking boots and take food and drinks. The final part of this walk involves a taxi ride, so have cash available.

THE WALK

Length: 30km (18.5 miles)
Allow: 1 day
Start/end: Parking area at Lac des Mesches

HOW TO GET THERE

St-Dalmas-de-Tende is in the far southeast of France near the Italian border, off the E74 south of Tende.

★ St-Dalmas-de-Tende, a small village, is the gateway to the Vallée des Merveilles. To reach the start of the walk, drive up the D91 towards Lac des Mesches, passing through peaceful woods with the rocky heights of Cime de la Nauque to the left. At the lake there is a spacious parking area.

Follow the footpath towards Lac Long, which will take several hours. At first the walking is pleasant and easy, winding through wooded slopes, but then the path begins to rise steeply.

❶ Lac Long's chilly shores are surrounded by pines and in spring the area is a wonderful sight as wild flowers bloom. All around is the stony mass of mountains, with Mont Bégo looming to the north.

This is the southern end of the Vallée des Merveilles and here is the ❷ Refuge des Merveilles. The valley can be sinister in dull light, with the rocks a threatening dark shade.

At this point you join the GR52 *Grandes Randonnées* trail. Climb until you reach Mont des Merveilles, at which point you can start to look for the carvings. As there are few obvious landmarks to describe where they are, refer to the maps from the park offices.

Peace, tranquillity and wonderful views in the Vallée des Merveilles

❸ These ancient carvings number more than 100,000. Yet it is easy to miss them, especially in winter when many are covered in snow. It is thought that the oldest date from about 1800BC, with others added in Roman times. No one knows why these intriguing images were carved, although one theory is that Mont Bégo (sometimes called the Magic Mountain) was a sacred site, and the images were etched into the rocks as votive offerings by prehistoric pilgrims. The drawings were not properly studied until the 1890s, when naturalist Clarence Bicknell excavated and catalogued them. He showed how the diagrams of hunting weapons, daggers, animals and mysterious symbols provide a unique insight into the Ligurian culture.

The trail continues past a string of lakes through the valley towards Lac du Basto. Although difficult to find, engravings are littered along the path, some of them close and others towards the slopes of the mountains. Before Lac du Basto, GR52 heads off to the left, while your path continues towards Valmasque.

❹ There is a *refuge* at Valmasque, near Lac Vert, a lovely place where Mont Sainte-Marie looks down from a height of 2,738m (8,981ft).

Here the path turns northeast for the home stretch. After Mont Peracouerte farther on, turn right and head south to Castérino.

❺ The tiny resort of Castérino is in an attractive setting on the D91.

Take a taxi from Castérino for the final 3km (2 miles) to the parking area at Lac des Mesches.

WHEN TO GO

Spring is the best time to come for the wild flowers. Always reserve ahead if you are planning to stay or eat in one of the *refuges*. Bear in mind that they are not always open.

WHERE TO EAT

You can have meals at the *refuges* if you reserve ahead. There are seasonal cafés and *auberges* at Castérino; some have terraces with good views.

Refuge des Merveilles
☎ 04 93 04 64 64 (evenings only)
🕐 Jun to mid-Oct; weekends and French school hols rest of year
www.tendemerveilles.com/merveilles

Refuge de Valmasque
☎ No phone; write to Refuge de Valmasque, 06430 Tende
🕐 Jun–end Sep

BASICS

Maison du Parc National
103 avenue du 16 Sept 1947, 06430 Tende
☎ 04 93 04 67 00
www.parc-mercantour.fr

📷 For guided tours in the Vallée des Merveilles, ▷ 230

This representation of a chieftain (above) is one of thousands of ancient rock engravings in the Vallée des Merveilles

CÔTE D'AZUR AND THE PARC NATIONAL DU MERCANTOUR

There could hardly be a greater contrast than that between the Côte d'Azur coast and the Parc National du Mercantour. One is glitter and bustle, the other peace and unspoiled beauty. This driving tour combines the two, starting in Menton, one of the most pleasant of the Côte d'Azur towns, and then heading north into the hills. Be aware that the roads to the north of the Côte d'Azur tend to be winding and slow.

THE DRIVE

Length: 150km (93 miles)
Allow: 1 day
Start/end: Menton

★ **Menton** (▷ 114–115) describes itself as the warmest town on the Côte d'Azur, and the citrus orchards seem to reinforce this claim. It is a picture-postcard Italian town that finds itself on the French side of the border.

From the middle of town, take the road signed *Autoroute (Nice, Italia)* and *Sospel*. Follow signs for Sospel on the D2566, going under the A8 and passing through Castillon-Neuf, until you reach Sospel.

① The pretty village of **Sospel** (▷ 125) has an 11th-century bridge, rebuilt in 1947 after it was damaged during the war.

At Sospel, go over the rail crossing and then turn left, following signs for Moulinet and Col de Turini. Bear left at a bend onto the D2204 and climb up to Col St-Jean, from where there are superb views down to Sospel. Go over Col de Braus (1,002m/ 3,287ft) and descend around hairpin bends almost into l'Escarène. Just after a rail bridge take a right turn, signed for Lucéram and Peïra-Cava. Drive through the village of Lucéram.

② **Lucéram** is a haphazard collection of medieval alleys.

At the next junction, isolated and on a steep hill, bear left, following signs for Turini. The road climbs around 16 hairpin turns and passes through Peïra-Cava.

③ **Peïra-Cava** is one of the best viewpoints on the route, with a superb panorama to the Parc National du Mercantour (▷ 122–123).

Continue to the Col de Turini.

④ The **Col de Turini**, at an altitude of 1,607m (5,271ft), has fine views. There is a hotel, café and restaurant.

Turn left onto the D70, signed for La Bollène-Vésubie and Nice, carefully descending the long, winding road from the pass. After about 10km (6 miles), look for a chapel on the left (on a bend) just after the Chapelle-St-Honorat tunnel.

⑤ There is a parking place at this chapel and superb views over La Bollène-Vésubie.

Continue through La Bollène. At a T-junction turn left onto the D2565, signed for Nice and St-Martin-Vésubie, to reach a valley bottom. There, follow signs for Lantosque and Nice, going straight on at first, then turning left along the main road. After 1km (0.6 miles) you can either go right and drive through Lantosque village, or take the bypass. The road through the village rejoins the main road; if you go that way turn right (signed for Nice).
   Continue through St-Jean-de-la-Rivière. About 1km (0.6 miles) beyond St-Jean, take the

left fork, the D19, signed *Nice par Levens*—be sure to follow this sign since both directions are signed for Nice. The road narrows and climbs up the side of the Vésubie valley. After you leave the tunnel just before Duranus, there is a viewpoint to the right, the Saut des Français, above sheer cliffs. Continue along the road into Levens

⑥ **Levens** (▷ 113) has a pretty main square with shady gardens and good views.

Leave Levens on the D19, signed for Nice. Continue for about 16km (10 miles), passing Tourrette-Levens. Just after St-André you'll go under the A8. Take a left turn at the traffic lights here, signed for Sospel, cross a river and go straight over at the next set of traffic lights to go back under the A8. Take the next right turn, signed for Route de Turin, crossing the river and a level crossing (rail crossing). Take a left turn at the traffic lights, signed for La Trinité and Drap, and at a roundabout take the road signed for La Turbie and Laghet. Follow the D2204A up a winding valley to the sanctuary at Laghet. There, a hairpin turn takes the road sharply to the right. Pass under the A8 again, and turn left at the

Sospel's evocative toll gate, on a bridge over the river Bévéra

OUT AND ABOUT

next intersection (an *autoroute* access road, signed for Menton). Turn left again at the next intersection onto a road signed for La Turbie and Monaco. Continue to La Turbie.

7 La Turbie (▷ 126) is an ancient village on the Via Julia, a road built by Julius Caesar to link Genoa with Cimiez, on the northern outskirts of Nice. Its triumphal arch, the Trophée des Alpes, was built by Augustus Caesar in about 6BC.

Drive through La Turbie and bear left past a hotel, following signs for Roquebrune and Menton, and then go downhill. At the bottom, take a right turn at the traffic lights, signed for Nice and Beausoleil. Take a left turn at the next set of traffic lights, signed for Cap Martin. As it leaves the heart of the village, the road veers sharply left. Go straight ahead here, on the road signed for Mayerling and Cap Martin. This road soon reaches the sea. Park here for the start of the walk on page 220.

Follow the coast road back to Menton.

The Trophée des Alpes, in La Turbie

WHERE TO EAT

Les Trois Vallées Hotel-Restaurant
Col de Turini
☎ 04 93 04 23 23

There are several bars and restaurants in Sospel.

Wild flowers and mountain scenery in the Vallée des Merveilles

OUT AND ABOUT

CAP MARTIN COAST

This coastal walk visits what many consider to be the most attractive section of the Côte d'Azur. A long linear walk (you return by train), it is best done in the afternoon, after the heat of the day has passed and the sun is at the best angle for the views. The walk takes you past rhododendrons, cascades of honeysuckle and huge cactus plants to the right, with the turquoise sea to the left and coastal towns ahead. You can extend the walk by continuing into Monaco.

THE WALK

Length: 6km (4 miles)
Allow: 1.5 hours (longer if you continue to Monte-Carlo)
Start: Cap Martin
End: Cabbé or Monte-Carlo
❓ The journey back to the start point involves a train ride

HOW TO GET THERE

Cap Martin is east of Monaco, close to the Italian border.

★ Cap Martin's thrusting headland has long been a lookout point—the ruined tower at its heart was once a fortified medieval watchtower. At the base of the tower are the remains of an 11th-century priory. Legend has it that the prior had an agreement with the local folk that if the tower's bell rang, they would all hurry to the site to defend the monks. One night, just to test the system, the prior rang the bell and was very pleased with the speedy response. The local people were less

pleased and a few nights later, when the bell rang again, they did not bother to turn out. But this time it was no trial run, and the priory was sacked by pirates and all the monks killed. Today Cap Martin is a rich suburb of Menton (▷ 114–115), its mansions set among sweet-smelling mimosa and olive trees.

Start from the parking area at the seaward end of avenue Winston Churchill on Cap Martin. Go back in the direction in which you drove, then pass to the left of the hotel entrance, along a wide path at the edge of the sea. The path is marked at its start by a sign for Ville de Roquebrune-Cap Martin, and a list of times for walks. Follow the path as it skirts the edge of private gardens and smart hotels. The path heads west along the edge of Cap Martin. There is a superb view of Monaco ahead and the sea to the left.

❶ The path is named Promenade Le Corbusier after the highly influential architect of the 1920s, who is connected with this stretch of coast through his association with artist and designer Eileen Gray. Her imaginative house above the shore was designated a historic monument in 1998. The house, hidden from view, lies below the path that continues up the western side of the Cap. Here the path is very close to the rail line.

In several places, steps lead up to the Cap, but the best route continues to Cabbé, from where trains run back into Carnolès. From Carnolès station, head seaward and follow the coastal path back to the parking area.

Alternatively, to extend the walk, continue from Cabbé along the path into Monte-Carlo.

❷ Monte-Carlo (▷ 134–136) is part of the principality of Monaco.

Trains from Monaco also serve Carnolès. This longer walk has the advantage of a glorious entrance to Monaco, but the disadvantage is that the route occasionally strays onto roads.

WHERE TO EAT

There are expensive, high-quality restaurants in Cap Martin and less expensive places in Cabbé.

WHEN TO GO

Before you set off, check there is a suitably timed train from Cabbé to take you back to Carnolès.

A member of the Royal Guard, Monaco (far left)

The harbour and town of Menton (left)

OUT AND ABOUT

GRAND CANYON DU VERDON

This drive offers dramatic views of the Grand Canyon du Verdon, as you follow the river west from Castellane to the vast Lac de Sainte-Croix. After refreshment in the pretty village of Moustiers-Sainte-Marie, you return by following the Verdon's south bank—a slightly easier drive, with equally superb views.

THE DRIVE

Length: 137 km (85 miles)
Allow: one day (excluding walks)
Start/end: Castellane

BE PREPARED

If you intend to leave your car and do any walking, it's a good idea to ask for the walking routes from the tourist office at Castellane or Moustiers-Sainte-Marie before you set out. Always check weather conditions and take a torch (flashlight), water and food (▷ 142).

★ The hill town of Castellane (▷ 139) is a popular base for walkers and climbers, sitting at an altitude of 730m (2,372ft). The Chapelle Notre-Dame du Roc watches over the town from a rock 184m (603ft) farther up. Castellane has two small museums and a soap- and perfume-making factory— but its main attraction is as the starting point for one of Europe's most exciting drives, along the Gorges du Verdon.

Leave Castellane from the round-about by the Grand Hôtel du Levant, where the D952 is signed for Moustiers-Sainte-Marie. Soon you'll see the striking rock formation—the Cadières de Brands—reach for the sky above the picturesque village of Chasteuil. The road splits at the Pont de Soleils; this is the bridge you'll reach on the return route to Castellane. Bear right to stay on the D952 signed Moustiers; soon you'll enter a short tunnel. Immediately at the tunnel exit a sign on the left indicates the D23B to the Belvédère du Couloir Samson. A short, dead-end road takes you to this viewpoint, at the bottom of the Verdon valley.

❶ The Belvédère du Couloir Samson has parking spaces. From here you can follow part of a seven-hour walk to a summit called La Maline at 1,460m (4,745ft).

Noticeboards emphasize the need for careful preparation, professional equipment and careful attention to the rapidly changing water level of the river.

Back in your car, return to the D952 and turn left. Bear left in the village of Rougon and about 1km (less than a mile) before reaching the small village of La Palud-sur-Verdon, a sign left indicates the Route des Crêtes.

❷ The Route des Crêtes offers unforgettable views of the canyon. It climbs to the highest points of the north bank of the river, with numerous *belvédères* where you can stop and enjoy the view.

A sign indicates whether the Route des Crêtes is *ouvert* (open) or closed because of snow. If it is closed, skip to point 3 (▷ 222). Otherwise, turn off onto the dramatic road. When you reach the Pas de la Baou, at an altitude of 1,285m (4,176ft), the river is 715m (2,313ft) below. From these heights, the road starts to descend and there are expansive views to the west, with frequent sightings of the route on the south bank that you will follow later. But don't take your eyes from the road: There are few safety barriers or walls around these hair-pinned descents. You are likely to encounter walkers along this stretch until the road returns you to La Palud-sur-Verdon, where you can pause for coffee.

The wild scenery of the Grand Canyon du Verdon

OUT AND ABOUT

❸ La Palud-sur-Verdon is a good place to visit if you enjoy outdoor activities. You can rent mountain bicycles or find a guided walk or climb. The town hall, in a small chateau, has an exhibition explaining the geology, flora and fauna of the area.

Turn left on the D952, signed for Moustiers. As the road reaches the end of the Grand Canyon, there are tremendous views to the Lac de Sainte-Croix, which on a sunny day glows an almost luminous blue. At a roundabout, bear right to Moustiers-Sainte-Marie—an ideal place to eat lunch beneath the shade of the plane trees.

❹ Moustiers-Sainte-Marie (▷ 145) is known for its faïence (fine glazed ceramics) and for a silver star suspended on a chain between two rock faces. Legend tells that it was first erected by a knight grateful for his return to the village after being held prisoner by the Saracens. The chain measures 227m (737ft) and the star is replaced whenever the chain breaks—about twice every century. The current star measures nearly 1.15m (4ft) across.

Leave Moustiers by retracing your route back to the roundabout, going straight over on the D957 and following the sign for Aiguines. The road crosses a bridge where the Verdon river flows into the lake. You can rent kayaks and electric boats here and take them for a short distance beneath the steep canyon walls. Shortly, take a left turn onto the D19 to Aiguines.

❺ Aiguines has a privately-owned chateau with tiled turrets, which is a pretty sight as you approach the village from below. Park in the road in the heart of the village and go by foot down steps on the right to a small arcade of artisanal shops. One of these specializes in wood-turning, once the village's single but prosperous industry. Look for wooden boules covered in nails—much in demand before solid metal boules were developed.

Continue along the D19 as it climbs out of Aiguines and stop at the orientation table about 1km (less than a mile) farther on. The river and views are now mainly on your left, with numerous stopping places and well-signed viewing points. Care should be taken on these sometimes narrow corners, and especially at a short series of mini-tunnels cut into the rock face—the Tunnel de Fayet. The last of the viewing opportunities is at the Balcons de la Mescla.

❻ The Balcons de la Mescla has a bar-restaurant where you can stop for refreshments and enjoy more superb views.

After several kilometres, watch for signs to Trigance and a Maison de l'Information. Turn left onto the recently-surfaced stretch of road and descend to the village.

❼ Trigance has small shops, a well, an art gallery and the last working water-powered flour mill in Provence, all dominated by a sombre chateau (closed to the public).

The tourist office is a farther 5km (3 miles) out of the heart of the village. Follow the road as it skirts Trigance to the south. At a T-junction with the D955, turn right; the tourist office is on the right after 500m (545 yards).

❽ The tourist office has excellent displays about local geology and you can also buy local produce there, including wonderful Provençal soap.

Head back along the D955 until you reach the Pont de Soleils; turn right on the D952 to return to Castellane.

Looking out over the Lac de Sainte-Croix

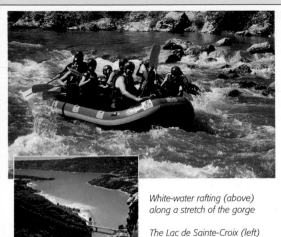

WHERE TO EAT

Ma Petite Auberge
Boulevard de la République, Castellane
☎ 04 92 83 62 06
🕐 Mar–early Nov daily 12–2.30,
7–10.30.

La Treille Muscate
Place de l'Église, Moustiers-Sainte-Marie
☎ 04 92 74 64 31
🕐 Mon 12–2, Wed–Sun 12–2, 7–10;
closed Jan and last two weeks of Nov

*White-water rafting (above)
along a stretch of the gorge*

The Lac de Sainte-Croix (left)

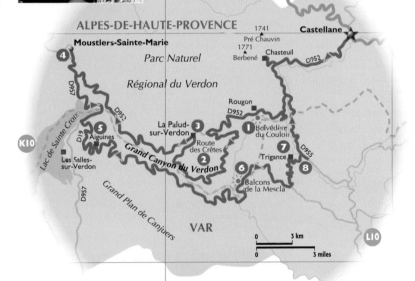

OUT AND ABOUT

WHEN TO GO

July and August are best avoided,
as the roads will be busy with
traffic. The Route des Crêtes
may be closed because of snow
between November and April.

*The privately owned chateau on
the approach to Aiguines*

BASICS

Castellane Tourist Information
34 rue Nationale, Castellane
☎ 04 92 83 61 14 🕐 Jul, Aug
Mon–Sat 9–12.30, 2–7, Sun 9–12.30;
Sep–end Jun Mon–Sat 9.15–12, 2–6

Moustiers Tourist Information
Rue de la Bourgade, Moustiers-Sainte-
Marie
☎ 04 92 74 67 84 🕐 Apr–end Sep
9.30–12.30, 2–7.30; Oct–end Mar
10–12, 2–5

FONTAINE-DE-VAUCLUSE

The Fontaine de Vaucluse is one of the most powerful resurgent springs in the world, and visitors flock to the village that bears its name to see the water flow. An early admirer was Petrarch, who lived here in the 14th century. This tour begins in the village, before heading out to explore the surrounding area. It takes in L'Isle-sur-la-Sorgue, with its canals and waterfalls, L'Abbaye de Sénanque, famous for its lavender, and the hill village of Gordes.

THE DRIVE

Length: 65km (40 miles)
Allow: 1 day
Start/end: Fontaine-de-Vaucluse

★ The Fontaine de Vaucluse (▷ 156) is at its most powerful in spring, when water levels are boosted by melting snow and up to 200 cubic metres (7,000 cubic feet) of water per second thunder out. It is here that the river Sorgue begins. The spring is around 2km (1.2 miles) from the heart of the village. There are several attractions on the way, including a history museum.

Park in the village and walk to place de la Colonne, with its statue of Petrarch. Follow the woodland path to the spring.

Walk back to your car and start the drive by heading for L'Isle-sur-la-Sorgue.

❶ L'Isle-sur-la-Sorgue (▷ 158), as its name suggests, is on an island in the river Sorgue. Stroll past the soothing canals and watermills or visit the magnificent baroque Notre-Dame-des-Anges. The town is also the antiques capital of Provence.

Take the D938 north to Pernes-les-Fontaines, 11km (7 miles) away.

❷ Pernes-les-Fontaines (▷ 162) has no fewer than 36 fountains, many dating from the 18th century. Book a guided tour around the Tour Ferrande to see some of the oldest frescoes in France, dating from the 13th century. Notre-Dame-des-Graces and the 16th-century Porte Notre-Dame are also worth seeing.

Leave Pernes-les-Fontaines and follow signs for St-Didier, and then Le Beaucet.

❸ At Le Beaucet you'll find a ruined castle, cave dwellings and a pilgrimage site dedicated to rainmaker St. Gens. A monument to French Resistance fighters was added to the parking area in 1995.

Take the D247 to Venasque, a beautiful cliff-top village that was once the seat of bishops.

❹ Venasque (▷ 165) was once a formidable stronghold and gave shelter to the bishops of Carpentras during the barbarian invasions. The baptistery, founded in the sixth century AD, is one of the oldest religious buildings in France.

The D4 winds its way through a sea of vines until it meets the D177, where it enters the Forêt de Murs and then plunges through a steep and mysterious gorge, with towering limestone walls on either side. The Abbaye de Sénanque waits at the other end.

❺ The Abbaye de Sénanque (▷ 148) is a Cistercian monastery dating from the mid-12th century and is surrounded by lavender fields. At dusk, listen for the clank of bells as sheep are rounded up for the night.

After Sénanque, you reach the picturesque hill village of Gordes, whose houses seem to cling precariously to the terraces.

❻ Gordes (▷ 157) is dominated by a Renaissance chateau made of honey-hued stone and restored by Hungarian artist Victor Vasarely. An art gallery displays pop art works by Pol Mara. The Grande Salle, on the first floor, has a wonderful Renaissance fireplace.

Leave Gordes on the D2 and follow signs to the Village des Bories, 4km (2.5 miles) away.

❼ The Village des Bories (▷ 157) is intriguing as no one knows why the stone huts (bories) were built here. This style of dwellings was first used in megalithic times.

The D2 ends with signs to Fontaine-de-Vaucluse pointing in opposite directions. Take the tourist route, which is more scenic, to return to the village.

The hillside village of Gordes

OUT AND ABOUT

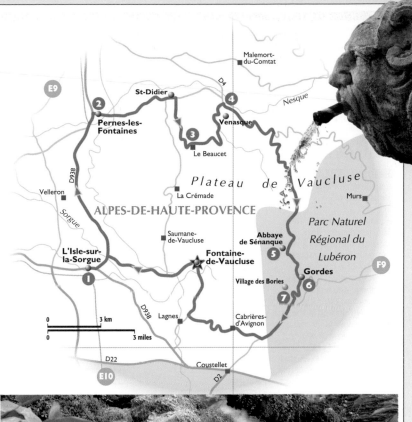

WHERE TO EAT

All the towns and villages on the route have brasseries and cafés and there are several good restaurants in Gordes and Pernes-les-Fontaines.

Au Fil de Temps
✉ Place Giraud, Pernes-les-Fontaines
☎ 04 90 66 48 61
🕐 Closed Tue, Wed

BASICS

Tourist Information
✉ Chemin du Gouffre, 84800 Fontaine-de-Vaucluse
☎ 04 90 20 32 22
🕐 Jul, Aug Mon–Sat 9–1, 2.30–6.30, Sun 9.30–1; Sep–end Jun Mon–Sat 9–12.30, 2.30–6, Sun 9.30–12.30

The Village des Bories

WHEN TO GO

The Fontaine de Vaucluse is in full flow in spring. In summer, it can be less impressive.

A street in L'Isle-sur-la-Sorgue

VAISON-LA-ROMAINE

The legacy of the Romans lives on in Vaison-la-Romaine, where you can see ruins dating back around 2,000 years. This walk takes you past the town's Roman bridge, medieval gateway and 12th-century cathedral.

THE WALK

Length: 3.5km (2 miles)
Allow: 1.5 hours
Start/end: Vaison-la-Romaine's main parking area, avenue Général-de-Gaulle

HOW TO GET THERE

Vaison-la-Romaine is 30km (19 miles) northeast of Orange

Vaison-la-Romaine (▷ 166–168) straddles the river Ouvèze and over the centuries its inhabitants have moved back and forth from one bank to the other. The Celts were the first to build a settlement on the hill here. The Romans arrived in the second century BC, choosing to set up *Vasio Vocontiorum* on the other side of the river. Today, you can see excavated Roman ruins in the lower half of town, while the upper part has reminders of its late-medieval heyday.

★ Start from the main parking area, next to the Roman sites on avenue Général-de-Gaulle. Walk through the busy and appealing heart of town down to the ancient Pont Romain.

❶ The Pont Romain is a Roman bridge, 17m (56ft) long. Note the level of the Ouvèze river below the bridge: Usually a trickle at the bottom

of the deep valley, in the disastrous floods of September 1992 the river flowed over the top of the Pont Romain.

Take the road opposite the bridge, which leads up to the Haute Ville. Go through the arched gateway, a remnant of the medieval ramparts.

❷ Upper Vaison is an almost complete medieval town, with attractive alleys of houses dating from the 13th and 14th centuries. The fortifications were constructed in part with stones from the ruins of the Roman town.

Turn sharply left, backtracking a little, up the narrow rue de l'Horloge. Continue climbing, looking towards the clock tower that gives the road its name. Follow the road around to the right, and turn left at a T-junction onto rue de l'Église, following signs for the chateau. There is a viewpoint to the left, near the church. Pass the church and continue uphill to Plan Pascal and on again, up some steps, to the rue de la Charité. This road narrows into a rough track. At the end of the stone wall on the left, turn left and climb to the ruins of the chateau.

❸ The chateau gives you wonderful views of the Roman ruins and the lower town. A Celtic fortress once stood here. The current chateau was built

by Count Raymond of Toulouse in the 12th century. It now stands in ruins and is closed to the public.

Return to the stone wall. Turn right and then left under an arch and go down the rough-hewn steps. These lead to a beautiful square with a fountain and the Hôtel de Prévôt.

Leave the square to the left and go down rue des Fours, one of the prettiest streets in old Vaison. When a road leads off to the right, keep straight ahead. Turn right at the next junction to reach a T-junction. Turn left, then take the next turn on the right, which opens up to a view of the lower town. Descend the steps on the left and then more steps to the right, to reach rue du Château. Turn left and follow the road to a main road junction. Bear right and cross the River Ouvèze by the Pont Neuf. Take the first right into avenue Jules Ferry and then go left to reach the cathedral.

❹ The Romanesque Cathédrale Notre-Dame de Nazareth was built in the 12th century, on the site of a sixth-century Merovingian church. The old bishop's throne sits behind the altar and on the north side of the cathedral there are lovely 12th-century cloisters.

Return to avenue Jules Ferry and walk the 500m (545 yards) or so along it to avenue Général-de-Gaulle and the entrance to the Quartier du Puymin.

❺ The Quartier du Puymin has some fascinating Roman ruins, including several villas and a theatre that held around 6,000 people.

After visiting this extensive Roman site, cross the road to enter the other major area, the Quartier de la Villasse, where you'll find the Roman baths. The parking area is nearby.

Diadumenos flexes his muscles in Vaison-la-Romaine

OUT AND ABOUT

A Vaison-la-Romaine fountain in a pleasantly shaded spot

WHEN TO GO

You can do this walk at any time of year. On cool, clear days there are good views of Mont Ventoux (▷ 159) from the chateau ruins.

BASICS

Tourist Information

✉ Place du Chanoine-Sautel, 84110 Vaison-la-Romaine

☎ 04 90 36 02 11

🕐 Jun–end Sep daily 9–12.30, 2–6.30; Mar–end May daily 9.30–12, 2–6; Oct–end Feb daily 10–12, 2–5

www.vaison-la-romaine.com

❓ The walk has some steep climbs.

WHERE TO EAT

There are plenty of restaurants on and around the Grande Rue and place Chanoine-Sautel, near the Roman sites.

Some of the sights at Vaison-la-Romaine: Roman ruins, a 12th-century castle and narrow, flower-lined streets.

OUT AND ABOUT

AVIGNON

Avignon offers a winning combination: culture, history, cafés and shops. This walk includes some of Avignon's most well-known sights, including the famous bridge and the mighty Palais des Papes, but also leads you down quieter cobbled streets and to small shady squares.

THE WALK

Length: 3km (2 miles)
Allow: half a day
Start/end: Place du Palais, Avignon

HOW TO GET THERE

Avignon is just off the A7 *autoroute*

★ The formidable Palais des Papes was created for the popes in the 14th century. Inside, vivid frescoes help you imagine the sumptuous conditions that once existed here. Several other interesting buildings sit around the place du Palais, including the 17th-century Hôtel des Monnaies, the 14th-century Petit Palais at the far end and the 12th-century cathedral, Notre-Dames-des-Doms, right beside the palace.

Start from the place du Palais. Take the ramp rising from the square beside the cathedral, to the park and gardens of the Rocher des Doms.

❶ The Rocher des Doms is a high point overlooking the Rhône river. From one side it offers a fine view of Pont St-Bénézet, the legendary medieval Pont d'Avignon.

From April to the end of September, you can reach the bridge from the park. The rest of the year, follow the signs down narrow streets and worn steps to the river. This is the Quartier de la Balance, a renowned gypsy area in the 19th century. Visit the Pont St-Bénézet and its chapel.

❷ Pont St-Bénézet owes its fame to the children's rhyme *Sur le Pont d'Avignon* and was built in the 12th century, legend has it, by a shepherd called Bénézet, who was acting on the orders of an angel. A terrible flood in the 17th century caused it to lose all but four of its 22 arches.

Leave the bridge through the small shop and walk back alongside the remains of the papal fortifications to the Porte du Rhône. Pass through and turn immediately right to walk in their shadow until you come to place Crillon, with its shady trees and pretty paved square. Pass the Hôtel d'Europe, then turn right and walk for some 400m (430 yards) along rue Joseph Vernet to the Musée Calvet.

❸ The Musée Calvet is the city's main museum, with beautiful collections of French, Italian, Flemish and Dutch paintings, sculptures, porcelain and furniture from the last five centuries. Nearby is the Musée Requien, with a small natural history collection.

At the end of rue Joseph Vernet, turn left into the hectic rue de la République, Avignon's main thoroughfare. Almost immediately, on the right side of the road, is the Musée Lapidaire.

❹ The Lapidaire museum is an annex of the Musée Calvet, housing local architectural finds. It is in a 17th-century Jesuit college.

Turn left out of the museum and left again down rue F. Mistral. Turn left into rue Laboureur. Number five is the Fondation Angladon Debrujeaud.

❺ Fondation Angladon Debrujeaud is a wonderful art museum that opened in the mid-1990s in the Hôtel de Massilian. Highlights include paintings by Cézanne, Picasso and Degas, as well as personal works by the two founders.

Continue along rue Laboureur to the pretty place St-Didier.

❻ Place St-Didier is home to the lovely Provençal-style church of St-Didier and the striking tower of the Livrée de Ceccano.

Return to the rue de la République along the small rue du Prevôt, then turn right and continue until you reach place de l'Horloge.

❼ Place de l'Horloge is a large, shady square with a medieval clock tower and plenty of cafés. Enjoy a drink and watch the antics of street musicians, jugglers and painters.

Take the pedestrian-only rue des Marchands to the Église St-Pierre, with its Renaissance carvings; then cross place St-Pierre and follow signs to the Palais des Papes. The route weaves through narrow alleys to reach a rear entrance to the shop in the Palais. Keep left to follow the lane back to the place du Palais.

The 12th-century Pont St-Bénézet

OUT AND ABOUT

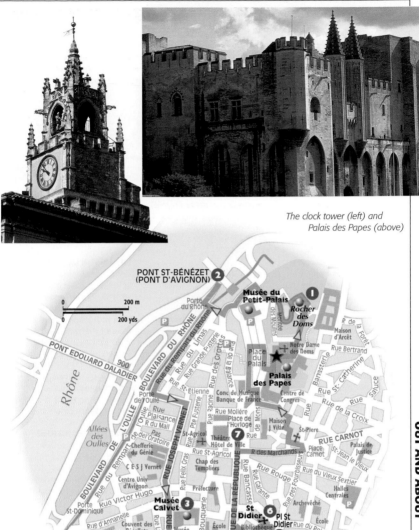

The clock tower (left) and
Palais des Papes (above)

OUT AND ABOUT

WHEN TO GO
You can enjoy this walk any
time of year. The shrubs in the
gardens of Rocher des Doms
are at their best in April, and
the views early in the morning
are stunning.

BASICS
Tourist Information
✉ 41 cours Jean-Jaurès 84004
☎ 04 32 74 32 74
🕐 Apr–end Sep Mon–Sat 9–6, Sun
10–5; Oct–end Mar Mon–Fri 9–6, Sat
9–5, Sun 10–12

WHERE TO EAT
There are many restaurants and
cafés on the route, especially in
place de l'Horloge.

ORGANIZED TOURS

Guided excursions can help you explore Provence with the added bonus of local knowledge. The trips below include outdoor sports such as horseback riding, white-water rafting, kayaking and bicycling, as well as cooking courses, walking tours and photography trips.

AQUA VIVA EST
12 boulevard de la République, 04120 Castellane
Tel 04 92 83 75 74 (France)
www.aquavivaest.com
Guided full- and half-day white-water rafting, canoeing and kayaking trips along the Gorges du Verdon and the Vésubie and Tinée rivers.
🕒 Apr–late Sep 🚶 Full day (5 hours) €61, half day (2.5 hours) €40

THE CHAIN GANG CYCLE TOURS LTD
30 Prospect Park, Exeter EX4 6NA, UK
Tel 01392 662262 (UK);
011 44 1392 662262 (from US)
www.thechaingang.co.uk
Excellent guided bicycle tours, with luggage transfer from hotel to hotel. Itineraries to suit all abilities.
🕒 Jun–end Sep 🚶 7-day packages from £740/$1,345, including bicycles, accommodation, breakfast and dinner

DESTINATION MERVEILLES
10 rue des Mesures, 06270 Villeneuve-Loubet
Tel 04 93 73 09 07 (France)
www.destination-merveilles.com
The rocks of the Vallée des Merveilles are decorated with thousands of prehistoric hieroglyphs but the best are not open to the public without a guide. Destination Merveilles offers three-day walking tours of the region or two-day 4X4 trips to the Vallée des Merveilles or the Roya Valley.
🕒 Jun–end Sep 🚶 3 days hiking €188, 2 days 4X4 trip €154

DESTINATION PROVENCE
49 Stonegate, York, YO1 8AW, UK
Tel 01904 622220 (UK);
011 44 1904 622220 (from US)
www.destinationprovence.co.uk
Destination Provence offers various tours, with themes

including fine cuisine (cooking courses and gorgeous meals), painting or wine. There are also language courses.
🕒 Apr–end Sep 🚶 Week-long courses from £469/$852

KAYAK VERT
Mas de Sylvéréal, 30600 Sylvéréal
Tel 04 66 73 57 17 (France)
www.canoe.france.com
These kayak excursions take place in the beautiful Camargue. Small groups are taken by an instructor. Credit cards are not accepted.
🕒 All year 🚶 €10 per hour; half-day excursions start at €20 ❓ Reservations required

---
TIP
● If your French isn't strong, check whether your guide speaks English before you reserve a tour.

LIGHT AND LAND
Rowley Cottage, Westhope, Hereford HR4 8BU, UK
Tel 01432 839111 (UK);
011 44 1432 839111 (from US)
www.lightandland.co.uk
Photographic tours led by landscape and wildlife photographers. All ability levels are welcome.
🕒 Jun 🚶 1-week packages, including accommodation and meals, are around £1,395/$2,540

LES LAURONS
84750 Caseneuve
Tel 04 90 75 23 97 (France)
www.laurons.com
A horseback riding 'hamlet' of several different-sized stone *gîtes* (cottages), welcoming 3–19 people. You can rent a horse for the week and ride every day. The price includes a meal on

the first night and breakfast the first morning.
🚶 Gîte rental from €400 per week, horse rental €100 per week, day trek with picnic €90

LA MAISON DU GUIDE
Meeting point: bar-restaurant La Ceinture, 30600 Montcalm
Tel 04 66 73 52 30 (France)
www.maisonduguide.camargue.fr
Take your place aboard a trailer towed by a tractor and get close to the animals of the Camargue. Themes include nature, bird life and local traditions. Credit cards are not accepted.
🕒 Apr–end Sep 🚶 €18 for a half-day excursion ❓ Reservations required

SHERPA EXPEDITIONS
131a Heston Road, Hounslow TW5 0RF, UK
Tel 020 8577 2717 (UK);
011 44 20 8577 2717 (from US)
www.sherpa-walking-holidays.co.uk
This organization specializes in guided, self-guiding and themed walking tours around Provence, including inn-to-inn walks with luggage transfer. There are itineraries to suit all ability levels, as well as self-guiding bicycle tours.
🕒 Apr–end Oct 🚶 Prices for UK visitors start at £718 for 8 days, including flights; prices for US visitors start at around $1,175, excluding flights

VISIOBULLE
Ponton Courbet, boulevard d'Aguillon, 06600 Antibes (ticket office)
Tel 04 93 74 85 42 (France)
www.visiobulle.com
Take a glass-bottom boat trip from Juan-les-Pins and enjoy views of the seabed.
🕒 4 departures daily Apr–end Jun and Sep; 7 times daily Jul, Aug 🚶 Adult €11, child (5–12) €5

OUT AND ABOUT

This chapter lists places to eat and stay, broken down by region, then alphabetically by town.

Eating and Staying

EATING OUT IN PROVENCE AND THE CÔTE D'AZUR

Provençal cuisine is as much a reflection of the region as the landscape and architecture. The sultry climate encourages wonderful fresh produce, bursting with aromatic, sun-drenched tastes. The staples of dishes *à la provençale* include virgin olive oil, garlic, tomatoes and wild herbs. Fish is in plentiful supply, fresh from the Mediterranean ports.

BRASSERIES AND BISTROS

Brasseries and bistros are good places to enjoy local dishes, such as bouillabaisse, in a friendly, informal setting. Brasseries were once brewery bars that served meals. They open longer hours than restaurants and bistros. Bistros are often small, independent or family-run restaurants serving traditional cooking, with a modest wine list.

RESTAURANTS

Celebrity chefs are the standard-bearers of haute cuisine, and their dining rooms in Provence are regarded as the equal of any Parisian establishment. Alain Ducasse and Jacques and Laurent Pourcel are among those who dictate the food fads of tomorrow. Every town has its respected restaurants, where you'll find starched linen, polished glass and silverware and a sense of hushed reverence for the gastronomic offerings to come. Remember to dress well and reserve in advance. The dining rooms of Logis de France hotels (▷ 246) offer quality regional food.

The *menu dégustation*, found in only the finest restaurants, is a *prix-fixe* menu with a sample of the top dishes and a choice of appropriate wines. The best value are the weekday set lunchtime menus, bringing a meal at even the most stellar establishments down to a realistic price.

CAFÉS AND BARS

Cafés and bars serve coffee, soft drinks, alcohol, snacks and often herbal and traditional teas too. They open from breakfast until late in the evening and you can expect to pay a little more for your drink if you sit at a table or on the outdoor terrace. You'll notice the locals tend to stand at the bar. Bars often have newspapers and you can linger over your cup of coffee.

CUTTING COSTS

If you are on a budget, have your main meal at lunchtime, when most restaurants serve a *menu du jour* of two or three courses with a glass of wine for around 50 per cent of the evening cost. Many restaurants also have *prix-fixe* meals in the evening too, with three, four or more courses, the best of which is the *menu gastronomique*.

OPENING TIMES

Most restaurants and bistros keep strict serving times. Restaurants open at 12, close at 2.30, then reopen at 7.30. Except in the bustling heart of a lively city, restaurants stop taking orders between 10pm and 11pm, although in summer people tend to dine later. Many restaurants are closed for lunch on Saturday and Monday and for dinner on Sunday evenings. Some on the coast close completely between November and Easter.

ETIQUETTE

Only the very top restaurants have a dress code, but it is usual to dress up when dining in a more formal venue. Most restaurants include the tip in the price of dishes, indicated by *service compris* or *s.c.* You may want to leave an extra tip if you are especially impressed with the service. By law restaurants must provide a non-smoking section, although this may be a token table by the toilets. Address staff as *Monsieur*, *Madame* or *Mademoiselle*.

VEGETARIAN AND WORLD CUISINE

In recent years, a move to lighter dishes and simpler techniques has, belatedly, acknowledged vegetarian tastes, although France's concept of vegetarianism is a little hazy, sometimes involving beef stock, chicken and bacon. Larger towns have North African, Lebanese and Vietnamese restaurants and Italian restaurants are also popular.

PROVENÇAL CUISINE

STYLES
...**provençale:** with olive oil, garlic, tomatoes, onion and herbs.
...**niçoise:** with olive oil, garlic, tomatoes, onion, herbs, olives, capers, anchovies and tarragon.

MEAT
Agneau de Sisteron: this lamb has grazed on mountain pastures and is lean and tasty.
Boeuf gardiane: the Camargue's version of beef braised in red wine.

Soupe de poisson: this is a classic, inexpensive soup of puréed mixed fish.
Truite: trout, often fresh from mountain streams.
...**à la meunière:** a method of serving fish, fried in butter then presented with lemon juice, butter and parsley.

CHEESE
Be sure to try some local cheeses made from the milk of goats (*chèvres*) or ewes (*brebis*).

Daube: meat stewed in wine.
Lapin: rabbit often comes simmered in wine and herbs, as does hare (*lièvre*).

SALADS AND OTHER DISHES
Aïoli: a delicious garlic mayonnaise, often served with raw vegetables as an hors d'oeuvre.
Cargolade: stew of snails in wine.
Pissaladière: a tasty flan containing olives, onions and anchovies.
Pistou: sauce made of ground garlic, basil and cheese bound with olive oil.
Ratatouille: tomatoes, onions, courgettes (zucchini) and aubergines (eggplant) slow cooked in garlic and olive oil.
Rouille: a spicy mayonnaise made with garlic and chilli.
Salade niçoise: the traditional Nice salad includes tomatoes, French beans, anchovies, olives, peppers and boiled egg.
Socca: this tasty pancake, made from chick pea flour, is a Nice specialty and is sure to satisfy hunger pangs.

FISH
Bouillabaisse: fish stew served with *aïoli* or *rouille*.
Bourride: fish soup-cum-stew.
Brandade de morue: paste of salt cod mixed with milk, garlic and olive oil.
Crabe: crab.
Gambas: giant prawns.
Homard: lobster.
Loup de mer: sea bass—this tastes best grilled with vine shoots or fennel.
Rouget: red mullet.
Merlan: hake.
Moules: mussels.
Oursins: sea urchins.
Palourdes: clams.

Banon: creamy sheep's cheese.
Petits chèvres: these small roundels of goat's cheese have often been rolled in herbs.
Poivre d'âne: there's a peppery taste to this goat's cheese.

FRENCH SAUCES
Béchamel: a classic sauce of flour, butter and milk. Often a base of other sauces such as Mornay, with cheese.
Béarnaise: egg yolk, vinegar, butter, white wine, shallots and tarragon.
Diane: cream and pepper sauce.
Chasseur: hunter style, with wine, mushrooms, shallots and herbs.
Demi-glace: brown sauce of stock with sherry or Madeira wine.

HOW TO ORDER STEAK
The French like their meat lightly cooked. Lamb will come rare unless you demand otherwise. If you order steak, you will be asked how you would like it cooked. The options are:
Bleu: blue, the rarest steak, warm on the outside but uncooked and cool in the middle.
Saignant: bloody, or rare, the steak is cooked until it starts to bleed and is warm in the middle.
À point: literally 'at the point'. The meat is cooked until it just stops bleeding. Many restaurants serve steak *à point* with some blood in the middle. If you want a warm pink middle but no visible blood, ask for steak *plus à point*. It's not an official French term, but good restaurants should oblige.
Bien cuit: 'well cooked', with only a narrow pink middle. If you want no pink to remain, ask for it *bien bien cuit*, although your waiter may not be impressed.

For more French food terms ▷ 277.

EATING

BOUCHES-DU-RHÔNE

AIX-EN-PROVENCE

L'AIXQUIS
22 rue Victor Leydet, 13100
Aix-en-Provence
Tel 04 42 27 76 16
www.aixquis.com

The setting here, with elegantly
laid tables and subtle lighting,
is perfect for a romantic
dinner. Fresh flowers and
a tile floor give the place a
Provençal feel. The food is

fine Mediterranean cuisine:
Warm lobster salad with
coral vinaigrette is the
signature dish.
🕐 Tue–Sat 12–1.30, 7.30–9.30;
closed Aug
🍷 L €82, D €106, Wine €18

LE P'TIT PUITS
14 rue des Bernardines, 13100
Aix-en-Provence
Tel 04 42 91 42 77

Le P'tit Puits refers to the little
well that sits in the vaulted
basement here. The dining
room is warm and welcoming:
The dark-orange tablecloths
complement the tawny walls,
and the soft lighting keeps the
mood relaxed. A long menu
includes fondues, hearty
stuffed baked potatoes, salads
and Provence-style fish.
🕐 Mon–Fri 12–2.30, 7.30–10;
Sat 7.30–10
🍷 L €27, D €30, Wine €10

ARLES

CORAZON
1 bis rue Réattu, 13200
Arles
Tel 04 90 96 32 53

Corazon is in a wonderful
16th-century town house with
a courtyard and fountain. The
succession of small dining
rooms creates a tranquil,
intimate mood and the tones
of white and soft brown match
the exposed stone. The menu
has fine regional cuisine, with
some Camargue specialties
such as beef served with a
pepper and anchovy sauce.
🕐 Tue–Sat 12–2.30, 7.30–10; closed
Nov and 1–15 Jan
🍷 L €36, D €108, Wine €20

LA GUEULE DU LOUP
39 rue des Arènes, 13200
Arles
Tel 04 90 96 96 69

The beige walls hung with
pictures contrast perfectly with
the exposed stone in this
restaurant. Though the cuisine
is true to the traditions of the
Camargue and Provence, it is
also influenced by owner/chef
Jean-Jacques Allard. A sample
dish is eels from the Camargue
served with a leek and chicory
fondue in red-wine sauce.
🕐 Mar–end Sep Tue–Sat 12–1.30,
7.30–9.30, Sun 12–1.30, Mon 7–9.30;
Oct–end Dec, Feb Tue–Sat 12–1.30,
7.30–9.30, Sun 12–1.30; closed Jan
🍷 L €24, D €50, Wine €15

LOU MARQUÈS
9 boulevard des Lices, 13631
Arles
Tel 04 90 52 52 52
www.hotel-julescesar.fr

There's a regal columned
entrance to this restaurant, in
a 12th-century former convent.
The refined dining room has
large wood panels and drapes
in shades of the south—blues
subtly punctuated with
touches of yellow. The fine and
inventive cuisine betrays its
local influences: sea bass and
a citrus fruit fondue scented
with local olive oil, gingerbread
millefeuille and caramel ice
cream. The restaurant is part of
a four-star hotel.
🕐 Tue–Fri, Sun 12–1.30, 7.30–9.30,
Mon 7.30–9.30
🍷 L €64, D €98, Wine €20

LA MAMMA
20 rue de l'Amphithéâtre, 13200
Arles
Tel 04 90 96 11 60
www.lamammaarles.com

This restaurant, near the
amphitheatre, has a rustic feel,
with a tile floor, wicker chairs,
decorative agricultural items
and a pizza oven. Expect Italian
and regional cuisine such as
sautéed beef with olives,
crudités with anchovy sauce
and, of course, pizzas.
🕐 Tue–Sat 12–2.30, 7–10.30,
Sun 12–2.30
🍷 L €22, D €32, Wine €12

LES BAUX-DE-PROVENCE

LA REINE JEANNE
Grande Rue, 13520
Les Baux-de-Provence
Tel 04 90 54 32 06
www.la-reinejeanne.com

The large windows of this
small restaurant are perfect for

enjoying views of the valley.
The restaurant, in the heart of
Les Baux, has pleasant decor.
The regional cuisine available
includes peppers marinated in
olive oil, leg of lamb with garlic
pickles and Provençal platter
with olive tapenade. A cod and
poached vegetable *aïoli* is
served every Friday.
🕐 Daily 12–2, 7.30–9.30
🍷 L €32, D €52, Wine €15

EATING

OUSTAU DE BAUMANIÈRE

13520 Les Baux-de-Provence
Tel 04 90 54 33 07
www.oustaudebaumaniere.com

This restaurant, in a 16th-century Provençal country house, is part of a four-star

hotel. Dine on the terrace to enjoy views of the forest of cypresses and rocky outcrops or in the elegant dining room. The exquisite dishes include truffle and leek ravioli and 'blue' lobster with a herb salad.

🕐 Apr–end Dec Fri–Tue 12–2, 7–9, Wed, Thu 7–9; closed Jan–end Mar
🍴 L €168, D €220, Wine €40

BEAURECUEIL

RELAIS SAINTE-VICTOIRE

13100 Beaurecueil
Tel 04 42 66 94 98
www.relais-sainte-victoire.com

This pink country house lies in the countryside of Aix, near the Montagne Sainte-Victoire. Of the three dining rooms, one is on the veranda—evocative of an Italian patio with its bright tiled floor and wrought iron. The two other rooms are Provençal in style. Fine Mediterranean cuisine includes a lot of fish and other local produce. Recommended dishes include confit of lamb with olive oil and poached eggs with creamy truffle sauce. An excellent rosemary sorbet is served between courses.

🕐 Tue–Sat 12–1.30, 7.30–9.30, Sun 12–1.30; closed first week of Jan
🍴 L €80, D €120, Wine €18

CARNOUX

LE COLOMBIER

2 avenue Claude Debussy, 13470 Carnoux
Tel 04 42 73 62 82

Large frescoes depicting the seaside decorate this restaurant. The chef prepares classic dishes such as stuffed mutton tripe and beef slowly cooked in red wine. With cheese and dessert included in all menus, Le Colombier is good value for the money.

🕐 Tue–Sun 12–2.30, 7.30–10
🍴 L €40, D €70, Wine €8

CASSIS

LE ROMARIN

5 rue Séverin Icard, 13260 Cassis
Tel 04 42 01 09 93
www.leromarin.com

Rosemary (*romarin*) is of course used in the cuisine here, alongside many of the scents and tastes of Provence: goat's cheese salad with pine nuts, grilled lamb on skewers, plus a lot of fish. The

pleasant dining room is inspired by the hues of the region.

🕐 Jun–end Aug daily 7.30–11pm; Sep–end Dec, Feb–end May Wed–Sun 12–2, 7.30–10.30
🍴 L €34, D €48, Wine €8.

LA CIOTAT

RIF

Calanque de Figuerolles, 13600 La Ciotat
Tel 04 42 08 41 71
www.figuerolles.com

RIF stands for 'Independent Republic of Figuerolles'. Descend the 87 steps to discover the small wooden house that's home to this restaurant, which looks out onto a secluded creek. The menu has a Mediterranean accent, with a hint of Russian.

🕐 May–end Nov daily 12–2, 7–10; Dec–end Apr Thu–Mon 12–2, 7–10
🍴 L €46, D €60, Wine €15

GRAVESON-EN-PROVENCE

AUBERGE DE LA CANDELIÈRE

2 avenue du Lieutenant Atger, 13690 Graveson-en-Provence
Tel 04 90 95 71 18
www.auberge-candeliere.com

A charming town house, with a yellow façade dotted with blue shutters, is home to this restaurant. The fine cuisine has a local accent: sea bass flambéed with pastis (a local aniseed aperitif), duck fillet with a red-wine sauce. In summer, dinner is served on the terrace. There is a tea room in the afternoon.

🕐 Mon, Tue, Thu–Sun 12–3, 8–9.30
🍴 L €32, D €52, Wine €7

MARSEILLE

LES ARCENAULX

25 cours Estienne d'Orves, 13001 Marseille
Tel 04 91 59 80 30
www.les-arcenaulx.com

Numerous books line the walls of Marseille's former arsenal, which has a beamed ceiling and long red banquettes. Sophisticated regional cuisine includes honey and lemon duck served with citron-scented courgette (zucchini) gratin. In the afternoon, Les Arcenaulx is a tea room.

🕐 Mon–Sat 12 noon–11pm
🍴 L €50, D €90, Wine €18

CHEZ FONFON

140 rue du Vallon des Auffes, 13007 Marseille
Tel 04 91 52 14 38

The lively fishing port is the place to try bouillabaisse, the fish soup that Marseille's restaurants excel in producing. Chez Fonfon is an institution in town and has been run by the same family for more than 50 years. Its elegant interior has green wicker chairs, a white-and-terracotta tile floor and Provençal fabrics.

🕐 Mon 7.30–10, Tue–Sat 12–2, 7.30–10
🍴 L €60, D €80, Wine €15

CHEZ LOURY

3 rue Fortia, 13001 Marseille
Tel 04 91 33 09 73
www.loury.com
This popular restaurant, close
to the old port, puts the best of
Mediterranean ingredients on
the menu. Try herb-roasted sea
urchin, home-smoked salmon
or bouillabaisse.

🕐 Mon–Sat 12–2, 7.30–9.30
🍽 L €32, D €44, Wine €14

MOURIES

LE VIEUX FOUR

5 cours Paul Revoil, 13890 Mouries
Tel 04 90 47 64 94
An imposing 18th-century
oven (*four*) is the focal point of
this rustic dining room, with
tile floors, beamed ceilings and
wicker chairs. Dinner is served
on the terrace under the shade
of plane trees when the
weather permits. The cuisine
uses olive oil produced in
Mouries. Fine regional cuisine
is offered and some pizzas are
served in the evening.
🕐 Jul, Aug daily 12–2, 7–10; Mar–end
Jun, Sep–end Dec Thu–Mon 12–2,
7–10, Tue, Wed 12–2; closed mid-Dec
to mid-Feb
🍽 L €22, D €34, Wine €14

NÎMES

LE BOUCHON ET L'ASSIETTE

5 rue de Sauve, 30000 Nîmes
Tel 04 66 62 02 93
A lovely old building next to
the Fontaine gardens houses
this restaurant. With *prix-fixe*
menus starting at €15, better
value would be hard to find.
The creative cooking is beautifully presented. Try the lightly
grilled foie gras with peppers
and grape caramel. In the
dining room, simple furnishings offset exposed beams
and stone walls.
🕐 Thu–Mon 12–1.30, 7.30–10; closed
1–15 Jan and 3 weeks Aug
🍽 L €40, D €55, Wine €15

LE VINTAGE CAFÉ

7 rue de Bernis, 30000 Nîmes
Tel 04 66 21 04 45
This delightful little bistro is in
a tiny square with a fountain,
between the arena and
La Maison Carrée. The dining
room doubles as a gallery for
local artists.
🕐 Tue–Fri 11–2.30, 7–11, Sat 7–11;
closed 2 weeks Aug
🍽 L €30, D €45, Wine €8

SAINTES-MARIES-DE-LA-MER

LES EMBRUNS

11 avenue de la Plage, 13460
Saintes-Maries-de-la-Mer
Tel 04 90 97 92 40
www.chez.com/embruns
Enjoy the best local ingredients
at this restaurant, with its rustic
yet refined interior. Freshly
caught seafood is served in a
variety of guises, including in
paella, one of the specialties.

🕐 Daily 12–2, 7.30–10
🍽 L €24, D €50, Wine €15

ST-RÉMY-DE-PROVENCE

LE BISTROT DES ALPILLES

15 boulevard Mirabeau, 13210
St-Rémy-de-Provence
Tel 04 90 92 09 17
www.bistrotdesalpilles.com
This popular bistro has large
paintings of toreadors on its
walls. The food has a southern
accent. For dessert, don't miss
the lavender, thyme and
rose sorbets.

🕐 Daily 12–2, 7.30–10
🍽 L €30, D €60, Wine €15

LA SERRE

8 rue de la Commune, 13210
St-Rémy-de-Provence
Tel 04 90 92 37 21
http://la.serre.free.fr
This restaurant deserves its
name, 'glasshouse': It comes
complete with a banana tree
and other exotic plants and a
little fountain. Chef Serge

Gille-Nave loves to experiment
with herbs, and when it
comes to desserts this
grandson of Gaston Lenôtre,
one of France's celebrated
cake-makers, is at his best:
Try the marvellous lavender-
scented gingerbread and
geranium sorbet. There is a
vegetarian menu.
🕐 Daily 5.30pm–midnight
🍽 D €44, Wine €20

TARASCON

ABBAYE ST-MICHEL DE FRIGOLET

Communauté des Prémontrés,
Abbaye St-Michel de Frigolet, 13150
Tarascon
Tel 04 90 90 52 70
www.frigolet.com
At the heart of a 12th-century
abbey, still occupied by a
monastic community, this
restaurant has an exceptional
setting. The two dining rooms
(one with a beamed ceiling)
are Provençal in style, with
tile floors and yellow and
burgundy tablecloths. In fine
weather, you can dine out on
the terrace and enjoy its
wonderful views of the
surrounding mountains. The
cuisine has a regional accent,
and many dishes incorporate
the local Frigolet liqueur.
Try the red mullet with basil
mayonnaise and Frigolet
liqueur crème brûlée.
🕐 Daily 12–1.30, 7–8.45; closed Jan
🍽 L €25, D €37, Wine €10

VAR

PRICES AND SYMBOLS

The prices given are for a two-course lunch (L) and a three-course dinner (D) for two people, without drinks. The wine price is for the least expensive bottle. The restaurants are listed alphabetically (excluding *Le*, *La* and *Les*). For a key to the symbols, ▷ 2.

LA CADIÈRE D'AZUR

HOSTELLERIE BÉRARD

6 rue Gabriel Peri, 83740
La Cadière d'Azur
Tel 04 94 90 11 43
www.hotel-berard.com

At this country inn at the heart of the Bandol vineyard, chef René Bérard creates dishes that reflect his love of local produce. The John Dory with a wine and shallot sauce, potato croquette and celery is wonderful. Elegantly set tables, beamed ceilings and a beautiful view complete the enjoyment.

🕐 Mon, Sat 7.30–9.30; Tue–Fri, Sun 12.30–1.30, 7.30–9.30

🍷 L €80, D €100, Wine €13

FRÉJUS

L'ABRI-COTIER

Quai Marc Antoine, 83600 Fréjus
Tel 04 94 51 11 33

There's a superb view of the port from this restaurant, with its heated terrace. Outstanding dishes such as sea bass in champagne sauce and bay prawns mingle happily on the menu with simple but tasty meals such as pizzas. There's a children's menu.

🕐 Thu–Mon 12–2.30, 7.30–10, Tue 12–2.30

🍷 L €36, D €48, Wine €15

GRIMAUD

LES SANTONS

Route National 558, 83310 Grimaud
Tel 04 94 43 21 02

The chef here uses the freshest local ingredients for his classic French and Mediterranean dishes. It's popular with the chic set from St-Tropez so make reservations in summer and at weekends.

🕐 Mon, Thu–Sun 12–2.30, 7–10; Tue, Wed 7–10

🍷 L €50, D €90, Wine €14

HYÈRES

LA COLOMBE

663 route de Toulon-La Bayorre, 83400 Hyères
Tel 04 94 35 35 16

Chef Pascal Bonamy likes to innovate, mixing the finest ingredients. His sea bass dish comes with asparagus and pearl onions, and he uses peppers from Espelette, in the Basque country. The restaurant's refined interior, with yellow and blue tones and cane chairs, has a regional influence.

🕐 Sep–end Jun Tue–Sat 12–1.30, 7.30–9.30, Sun 12–1.30; Jul, Aug Tue–Fri, Sun 12–1.30, 7.30–9.30, Sat 7.30–9.30

🍷 L €52, D €90, Wine €17

LORGUES

CHÂTEAU DE BERNE

Chemin de Berne, 83510 Lorgues
Tel 04 94 60 48 88
www.chateauberne.com

The castle that is home to this restaurant is at the heart of a 550ha (1,358-acre) domain and its vineyard. Food comes fresh from the inn's organic garden, or from the local markets. Wonderful combinations of regional foods include garlic- and thyme-grilled lamb from Sisteron. Eat on the terrace or in the beamed dining room. To accompany the meal, the chateau's own vintages are a must. The dining room is strictly non-smoking.

🕐 Mid-Feb to end Nov daily 12–2, 7–9

🍷 L €116, D €116 (wine is included)

ST-AYGULF

LA SOUPIÈRE

283 boulevard Honoré de Balzac, 83370 St-Aygulf
Tel 04 94 81 30 50
www.la-soupiere.com

Close to the beach and the town's main square, this unpretentious little restaurant is dedicated to local cuisine. There's lots of fish, notably the *soupière de la mer*, the house special, an original combination of fish soup and paella.

🕐 Feb–end Jun, Sep–end Dec Tue–Sun 12–2, 7.30–9.30; Jul, Aug daily 12–2, 7.30–9.30

🍷 L €22, D €44, Wine €12

SPECIAL IN ST-TROPEZ

CAFÉ DES ARTS

Place des Lices, 83990 St-Tropez
Tel 04 94 97 02 25

Some think the soul of the real St-Tropez lies within these four walls. The Café des Arts is on a square in the heart of town and has one of the best terraces. Enjoy a meal while watching the bustle of the market or locals playing a game of boules. It's definitely the place to be seen.

🕐 Food served daily 12–2.30, 7.30–11; café open 8am to midnight

🍷 L €62, D €84, Wine €18

ST-TROPEZ

MAISON LEÏ MOUSCARDINS

Tour de Portalet, port de St-Tropez, 83990 St-Tropez
Tel 04 94 97 29 00

Set in the heart of St-Tropez's famous port, surrounded by fantastic yachts and cruisers, the airy Maison Leï Mouscardins has a menu concentrating on exquisite fresh seafood. The *assiette de fruits de mer* is a delicious mixture of generous quantities of oysters, prawns, crayfish and whelks and is a must for a long lunch accompanied by a chilled bottle of white wine.

🕐 Wed–Mon 12–2.30, 6.30–10.30. Closed 12 Nov–5 Feb

🍷 L €60, D €120, Wine €18

TOURTOUR

LES CHÊNES VERT

Route de Villecroze, 83690 Tourtour
Tel 04 94 70 55 06

This restaurant's name (the green oaks) reflects its verdant surroundings, in high oak and pine forest perched above the surrounding Provençal plains. The restaurant is in a renovated villa with the ambiance of a family home. The menu is classic French, with generous use of the grandest ingredients, such as lobster, truffles and foie gras.

🕐 Thu–Mon 12–2.15, 7–9.30. Closed 1 Jul–8 Jul

🍷 L €50, D €90, Wine €15

ALPES-MARITIMES AND MONACO

ANTIBES

LE BRÛLOT
3 rue Frédéric Isnard, 06600 Antibes
Tel 04 93 34 17 76
www.brulot.com
Authenticity is key at this restaurant, with its exposed stone, beamed ceilings and

antique baker's oven. A second room in the vaulted basement dates back to the 12th century. The cuisine makes good use of the wood oven: grilled steak with Provençal herbs and grilled scampi flambéed with pastis (a local aniseed spirit). Specials include couscous on Thursdays and ham on the bone on Fridays.
🕐 Mon–Wed 7.30–10, Thu–Sat 12–2.30, 7.30–10
🍽 L €40, D €60, Wine €12

AURIBEAU-SUR-SIAGNE

LA VIGNETTE HAUTE
370 route du Village, 06810 Auribeau-sur-Siagne
Tel 04 93 42 20 01
www.vignettehaute.com
This inn, off the beaten track, has a dining room lit by oil lamps. There are beamed ceilings, exposed brick vaults and arches, and the restaurant looks onto the sheepfold and its flock. The traditional cuisine includes sea bass with red onions and violet artichoke or liquorice pigeon. Ask to visit the private museum, Le

Curiosa, displaying a collection entitled Love and Humour.
🕐 Daily 12–2, 7.30–10. Closed mid-Nov to mid-Dec
🍽 L €58, D €160 (wine is included)

CANNES

CAFFE ROMA
1 square Mérimée, 06400 Cannes
Tel 04 93 38 05 04
www.cafferoma.fr
Come to this Italian bar-restaurant for an ice cream, cocktail or one of the Italian specialties: ravioli stuffed with cheese and spinach, and veal with lemon sauce and pine nuts. Leave room for the home-made tiramisu. Eat on the terrace or in the elegant dining room (seats 80). The restaurant is always bustling.

🕐 Daily 7am–1am
🍽 L €30, D €42, Wine €12

CHEZ ASTOUX
27 rue Félix Faure, 06400 Cannes
Tel 04 93 39 21 87
www.astouxbrun.com
Seafood is the specialty at this popular bistro. The large shell-fish platters are a tasty option but you can also enjoy fish soup and poached or grilled fish, including saffron cod. There is a covered terrace and take-out service is available.

🕐 Daily 8am–midnight
🍽 L €46, D €80, Wine €15

CLARIDGE
2 place du Général de Gaulle, 06400 Cannes
Tel 04 93 39 05 86
Come here for a drink, ice cream or traditional brasserie fare until late into the night. There's a pub atmosphere, with sports shown on a large screen, although the decor sticks to the brasserie theme, with marble tables.
🕐 Daily 7am–2.30am
🍽 L €24, D €30, Wine €10

ESCALE DE CHINE
58 rue Jean Jaurès, 06400 Cannes
Tel 04 93 99 15 99
www.escaledechine.com
The ornate decoration in this Chinese restaurant includes a profusion of exotic wood,

mirrors, columns and gilded panels, yet it manages to avoid kitsch. The refined cuisine includes dishes such as Chinese fondue and Peking duck.
🕐 Wed–Sun 12–2.30, 7–11, Mon, Tue 7–11
🍽 L €22, D €38, Wine €11

LA POTINIÈRE DU PALAIS
13 square Mérimée, 06400 Cannes
Tel 04 93 39 02 82
www.lapotiniere.fr
The *palais* (palace) refers to the Palais des Festivals, where major events in Cannes take place. But there's more to this restaurant than a choice location. The cooking is exceptionally good and the menu has a lot of fish and classics such as grilled steak and roast chicken. The pleasant dining room, decorated in yellows and pale greens, is a bonus.
🕐 Mon–Sat 12–2.30, 7.30–10
🍽 L €43, D €60, Wine €16

EATING

LA VILLA DES LYS
10 boulevard La Croisette, 06400
Cannes
Tel 04 92 98 77 41
www.lucienbarriere.com
The best ingredients and
refined presentation come
together here to create
wonderful dishes such as
steamed turbot with sage,
grilled asparagus, grappa
tomatoes, fried cherries and
smoked bacon. To comple-
ment Chef Bruno Oger's
exquisite cuisine, an
exceptional cellar boasts rare
vintages such as the Château
Margaux 1914. You can
appreciate such delicacies on
the tranquil terrace, which
looks out to the sea, or in
the dining room, decorated
with period furniture, large
mirrors and ochre and
burgundy tones.

🕐 Tue–Sat 7.30–10
🍽 D €250, Wine €75

ÈZE
LA VOILE D'AZUR
Moyenne Corniche, rue du Barri, 06360
Èze
Tel 04 92 10 66 66
www.chevredor.com
The luxury Château de la
Chèvre d'Or hotel shelters this
restaurant, with its sumptuous
sea-inspired interior. The
restaurant has a wonderful
view of the sea and coastline,
while the kitchen offers
cosmopolitan cuisine: raw bass
sushi-style, tagine of chicken
with lemon grass, fillets of
bream à la plancha.
🕐 Daily 12–2, 7–11
🍽 L €210 (including wine), D €300,
Wine €50

GRASSE
LA BASTIDE ST-ANTOINE –JACQUES CHIBOIS
48 avenue Henri-Dunant, 06130 Grasse
Tel 04 93 70 94 94
www.jacques-chibois.com
An olive grove surrounds this
18th-century Provençal town
house. The elegant dining
room has period furniture and
fine tableware and makes
discreet use of materials from
the area: tile floor and fine
fabric for the curtains. The
Mediterranean cuisine includes
the finest ingredients:
lobster with a black olive
fondue, Provençal roast rabbit
with stuffed potato.
Reservations are essential.
🕐 Daily 12–1.30, 8–9.30
🍽 L €160, D €200, Wine €40

MOUGINS
LA FERME DE MOUGINS
10 avenue St-Basile, 06250 Mougins
Tel 04 93 90 03 74
www.lafermedemougins.fr
This elegant restaurant is in a
former farmhouse, with
beamed ceilings, rustic wicker
chairs and fine tableware.
The regional cuisine includes
ginger braised lobster,
seasonal vegetables with a
cardamom shellfish gratin,
gingerbread with pear
poached in red wine, and
cinnamon ice cream.
🕐 Tue–Sat 12.15–1.30, 7.30–9.30,
Sun 12.15–1.30
🍽 L €75, D €168, Wine €28

■ SPECIAL IN MOUGINS ■
LE MOULIN DE MOUGINS
Quartier Notre-Dame-de-Vie, 06250
Mougins
Tel 04 93 75 78 24
www.moulin-mougins.com
Surrounded by greenery
and decorated with
contemporary works of art,
this 16th-century former olive
mill provides a gastronomic
treat. The cuisine is a
sophisticated combination
of Mediterranean tastes
reinvented by the day. The
menu varies according to the
season. The excellent wine
cellar has more than 5,000
vintages. You can also take
cooking classes here.
🕐 Tue–Sun 12–2.30, 7.30–9.30;
closed in Dec and the first two weeks
of Jan
🍽 L €140, D €200, Wine €28

NICE
L'ÂNE ROUGE
7 quai des Deux-Emmanuel,
06300 Nice
Tel 04 93 89 49 63
www.anerougenice.com
Chef Michel Devilliers likes to
cook fish, and his creations are
tantalizing: succulent scallops
roasted with chorizo, fresh and
dried tomatoes and thyme
flower. The warm, elegant
interior has beamed ceilings
and a large fireplace. The
flower-filled terrace has a
view of the port.
🕐 Fri–Tue 12–2.30, 7.30–10,
Thu 7.30–10; closed Feb
🍽 L €64, D €102, Wine €18

CHÂTEAU DES OLLIÈRES
39 avenue des Baumettes, 06000
Nice
Tel 04 92 15 77 99
www.chateaudesollieres.com
This former villa was converted
into a chateau by the Russian
Prince Alexei Lobanov-
Rostowsky in 1885. Paintings,
drapes, candelabra and period
furniture all contribute to the
refined atmosphere. The
cuisine uses local ingredients
where possible and includes
lamb in an olive crust, crab
mousse on a bed of fresh
herbs with a tomato coulis,
and a citrus fruit gratin with
orange cookie.
🕐 Daily 12–2.30, 7.30–9.30;
closed Jan
🍽 L €84, D €128, Wine €15

CHEZ SIMON
St-Antoine-de-Ginestière, 06200
Nice
Tel 04 93 86 51 62
www.restaurantchezsimon.com
Five generations of the
same family have run this
restaurant, once an inn. The
traditional dining room has
beamed ceilings, wicker
chairs and a plough-wheel
candelabrum. In fine weather,
choose the terrace, where you
can dine while watching a
game of pétanque. The
Provençal cuisine includes
stuffed mutton tripe and hake.
🕐 Daily 12.30–2, 7.30–10
🍽 L €56, D €56, Wine €15

LA MAISON DE MARIE
5 rue Masséna, 06000 Nice
Tel 04 93 82 15 93
www.lamaisondemarie.com
This restaurant is sheltered from the hustle and bustle of rue Masséna by a peaceful paved courtyard. It is ideal for a romantic meal, with candlelit tables in the evening. In fair weather, a couple of tables are set out on the terrace. The Mediterranean cuisine includes sardines stuffed with pine nuts and lamb with a herb crust.
Ⓒ Daily 12–2, 7–11
Ⓕ L €36, D €36, Wine €13

RESTAURANT BOCCACCIO
7 rue Masséna, 06000 Nice
Tel 04 93 87 71 76
www.boccaccio-nice.com
There are no less than six dining rooms here, all of which have a marine theme. One has a large aquarium, another with a vaulted wooden ceiling is reminiscent of the interior of a caravel (a historic small ship), and model boats carry on the theme. The menu has Mediterranean seafood dishes such as bass in a salty crust, bouillabaisse and seafood platters.
Ⓒ Daily 12–2.30, 7–11
Ⓕ L €90, D €90, Wine €24

LE SAFARI
1 cours Saleya, 06300 Nice
Tel 04 93 80 18 44
www.restaurantsafari.com
This restaurant is on a lively street and its terrace bulges with people in good weather. The interior is bistro-style, complete with a little blackboard displaying the menu. On offer are Nice specialties (salad of chopped fresh artichokes with olive oil and lemon, crudités with warm anchovy sauce) and a great choice of freshly baked pizza.
Ⓒ Daily 12–2.30, 7–11
Ⓕ L €52, D €80, Wine €12

RAYOL-CANADEL
MAURIN DES MAURES
Avenue Mistral, 83820
Rayol-Canadel
Tel 04 94 05 60 11
www.maurin-des-maures.com
This brasserie is named after a legendary character who spent his life hunting in the Maures mountains. In the dining room, a painting depicts a piece of his story. The brasserie fare has a southern accent, with dishes including courgette (zucchini) and goat's cheese tart, vegetable lasagne and the house fried fish.
Ⓒ Daily 12–2, 7–10
Ⓕ L €40, D €54, Wine €13

TOURRETTES-SUR-LOUP
L'AUBERGE DE TOURRETTES
11 route de Grasse, 06140
Tourrettes-sur-Loup
Tel 04 93 59 30 05
www.aubergedetourrettes.fr
Behind the stoves of this Provençal inn is young chef Christophe Dufau, born and raised in the region before later deciding to travel the world. His cuisine reflects his origins and interests: A subtle combination of local and exotic ingredients is used in dishes such as sea bass marinated in passion fruit. The same refinement has been extended to the decor, which is discreetly Provençal. Dinner is served on the terrace, weather permitting. The restaurant won the 2000 Cuisine Provençal competition organized by the Chamber of Commerce and Industry of Var.
Ⓒ Mon, Thu–Sun 12–2.30, 7–10
Ⓕ L €48, D €84, Wine €29

LA ROSE DES VENTS
Plage du Larvotto, 98000 Monaco
Tel 377 97 70 46 96
www.larosedesventsmonaco.com
On its own private beach, La Rose des Vents combines formal dining with a day by the sea—interrupt your swimming simply to move to your table for an ample lunch under the shade of a parasol. The menu is a combination of French and Italian, with a good range of seafood. There is a buffet for Sunday lunch.
Ⓒ Daily 12–3.30, 7.30–10.30 (closed Mon in winter)
Ⓕ L €40, D €80, Wine €12

LE LOUIS XV
Hôtel de Paris, place du Casino, 98000 Monaco
Tel 377 92 16 29 76
www.alain-ducasse.com
The height of luxury, this restaurant is within the majestic Hôtel de Paris, built in 1864. The Mediterranean-

inspired menu changes with the seasons and is thematic. Topics include the kitchen garden, hunting, the farm, the sea and rivers. The sumptuous Louis XV-style interior provides a fitting backdrop for a feast fit for a king.
Ⓒ Thu–Mon 12–2, 7.30–9.30; Wed dinner in Jul and Aug; closed 3 weeks Dec and 2 weeks Mar
Ⓕ L €240, D €272, Wine €90

STARS N'BARS
6 quai Antoine I, La Condamine, 98000 Monaco
Tel 377 97 97 95 95
www.starsnbars.com
This popular American-style bar-restaurant, with a predominantly Tex-Mex menu, is the perfect place for families tired of more formal French restaurants. The bar has lots of games to keep kids occupied. In the evenings there's disco or live music.
Ⓒ Tue–Sun: Food is served 11.30am–midnight; the bar is open until 2am
Ⓕ L €25, D €50, Wine €10

EATING

ALPES-DE-HAUTE-PROVENCE AND HAUTES-ALPES

BRIANÇON

RESTAURANT LES ÉCRINS

11 place du Champ de Mars, 05100 Briançon
Tel 04 92 20 35 16
www.resto-les-ecrins.com

In the Serre Chevalier ski area just outside Briançon, this wooden-beamed restaurant focuses on hearty local mountain cuisine, including *raclette*, fondues and *tartiflette*. There's a terrace for summer dining.

🕐 Lunch Tue–Sun, dinner Tue–Sat
🍽 L €25, D €60, Wine €8.50

CHÂTEAU-ARNOUX

LA BONNE ÉTAPE

Chemin du Lac, 04160 Château-Arnoux
Tel 04 92 64 00 09
www.bonneetape.com

Enjoy the refined setting of an old country house, with high-back padded chairs, fine tableware and paintings. Lamb from Sisteron features on the sophisticated menu. Ask for the lavender-scented honey ice cream—the perfect dessert.

🕐 Mid-Apr to mid-Oct daily 12–1.30, 7.30–9.30; mid-Oct to mid-Apr Wed–Sun 12–1.30, 7.30–9.30
🍽 L €100, D €140, Wine €35

L'OUSTAOU DE LA FOUN

RN 85, 04160 Château-Arnoux
Tel 04 92 62 65 30

A house built of Durance stone, with an internal courtyard and fountain, is home to this restaurant. One dining room has exposed stone; the other is vaulted. The finest ingredients are used. The langoustines, lamb with ratatouille and truffle dishes (in season) are excellent.

🕐 Tue–Sat 12–1.30, 8–9.30, Sun 12–1.30; closed first week Jan and last week Jun
🍽 L €40, D €100, Wine €14

DABISSE

LE VIEUX COLOMBIER

D4, 04190 La Bastide Dabisse
Tel 04 92 34 32 32

This 19th-century *relais de poste* (coaching inn) on the banks of the Durance has a rustic dining room and tree-lined terrace. It serves classic French recipes.

🕐 Mon, Tue, Thu–Sat 12–2.30, 7–9.30; Sun 12–2.30. Closed 1 Jan–15 Jan
🍽 L €34, D €56, Wine €12

FORCALQUIER

LE LAPIN TANT PIS

Avenue St-Promasse 10, 04300 Forcalquier
Tel 04 92 75 38 88

There is a delicious *menu du jour* here. The dishes are prepared by Gérard Vivès using whatever is freshest in the local market—treats include green vegetables in curry with tomato chutney or lamb braised in *crème* of garlic.

🕐 Daily 7.30–9.30
🍽 D €90, Wine €14

FOUX D'ALLOS

LE VERDON

Galerie Commerciale, 04260 Foux d'Allos
Tel 04 92 83 83 77
www.restaurant-leverdon.com

This restaurant is in an imposing chalet in the Foux d'Allos ski resort. The rustic interior has wood and exposed bricks, while the sunny terrace gives wonderful mountain views. The place is famous for pizza, but you can also enjoy cheese fondue and other dishes.

🕐 Jun to mid-Sep, Dec–end Apr daily 12–2, 7–9.30
🍽 L €28, D €28, Wine €9

MANOSQUE

CAFÉ DE LA POSTE

Rue Reine-Jeanne, 04100 Manosque
Tel 04 92 72 69 02
www.cafedelaposte.com

This café and its terrace look onto the city's oldest public garden. Inside is contemporary green and orange decor. Enjoy salad and cold platters, or more elaborate dishes such as foie gras with fig marmalade. The menu also caters to vegetarians, with some dishes using organic tofu and wheat.

🕐 Mon–Sat 7am–1am
🍽 L €30, D €36, Wine €11

LE GAVROCHE

21 avenue Jean Giono, 04100 Manosque
Tel 04 92 72 03 36
http://perso.wanadoo.fr/gavroche1/

At the heart of Manosque, this brasserie is the image of an

old Parisian café with a long bar, bistro tables and chairs and some beautiful trompe l'oeil paintings. In addition to the main dining room, there's a vaulted basement and a terrace. Traditional brasserie fare includes seafood platters, grilled fish and a dish of the day. Local specialties include stuffed mutton tripe.

🕐 Mon 12–2, Tue–Sat 12–2, 7–midnight
🍽 L €34, D €34, Wine €13

RESTAURANT DOMINIQUE BUCAILLE

La Filature, 43 boulevard des Tilleuls, 04100 Manosque
Tel 04 92 77 32 28

In a 17th-century cotton mill, this elegant restaurant has attractive vaults, Parisian-style street lamps and a tile floor. Chef Dominique Bucaille uses local ingredients beautifully. Expect treats such as wild truffle or suckling lamb with vegetables.

🕐 Mon–Sat 12–2.30, 7.30–9.30. Closed mid-Jul to mid-Aug
🍽 L €84, D €120, Wine €30

EATING

MONETIER-LES-BAINS

LA FERME DES BOUSSARDES
Le Lauzet, 05220 Monetier-les-Bains
Tel 04 92 24 42 13
www.lafermedesboussardes.com
A farm *auberge* (inn) in the heart of the Serre Chevalier ski area, La Ferme des Boussardes grows its own produce. The dishes are typical of the region, with charcuterie, duck, simple salads, foie gras and cheeses predominating. This is an excellent place to try French mountain cuisine.
🕒 Lunch, dinner daily (by reservation)
🍽 L €30, D €60, Wine €9

MOUSTIERS-SAINTE-MARIE

FERME SAINTE-CÉCILE
Route des Gorges du Verdon, 04360 Moustiers-Sainte-Marie
Tel 04 92 74 64 18
www.ferme-ste-cecile.com
The restaurant is in a former 18th-century hillside farm.

The interior has beamed ceilings, white wooden chairs and cheerful blue and yellow tablecloths. The menu makes the most of local ingredients: lamb in a spicy crust, foie gras with a thyme courgette (zucchini) marmalade. In fine weather, opt for the terrace and enjoy views of the surrounding mountains.
🕒 Tue–Sun 12–2, 7–9; closed mid-Nov to end Dec and 2 weeks in Feb
🍽 L €40, D €60, Wine €14

LA BASTIDE DE MOUSTIERS
Chemin de Quinson, 04360 Moustiers-Sainte-Marie
Tel 04 92 70 47 47
www.bastide-moustiers.com
This gorgeous 17th-century Provençal *bastide* (country house) is owned by renowned master chef Alain Ducasse, who took personal charge of the renovations. The restaurant is managed with great aplomb by his personally chosen team. The menu changes daily, taking into account what is in season in the vast *bastide* gardens or at local markets, but every dish displays its haute-cuisine pedigree. The price remains reasonable for the quality. The restaurant is part of a four-star inn (▷ 255).
🕒 Mar–end Nov daily 12–2.30, 7–9.30; Jan, Feb Mon–Wed, Sat, Sun 12–2.30, 7–9.30; closed end Nov to mid-Dec
🍽 L €80, D €80, Wine €18

SISTERON

LE RATELIER
55 place Paul Arène, 04200 Sisteron
Tel 04 92 61 01 83
www.chez.com/ratelier/
You'll find traditional cuisine at this unpretentious, friendly eatery. Sisteron is famous for its lamb, and the house specialty has it grilled and served with a garlic sauce. For a real local experience, try the *pied paquets* (stuffed mutton tripe). There is an as-much-as-you-can-eat hors d'oeuvre buffet. The rustic interior has a tile floor and wicker chairs. Outside is a large terrace.

🕒 Feb–end Dec Mon–Sat 12–2, 7.30–9.30. Closed in Jan
🍽 L €24, D €52, Wine €15

LA CITADELLE
126 rue Saunerie, 04200 Sisteron
Tel 04 92 61 13 52
This is a great place to try local dishes, including stuffed mutton tripe, Sisteron lamb and frozen nougat. Chef Jean-François Destremont is a master at cooking fish the Provençal way. Dishes include sea bass with garlic mayonnaise and, in season, there's a game menu.
🕒 Jun–end Sep daily 12–2.30, 7.30–10; Oct–end May Thu–Tue 12–2.30, 7.30–10
🍽 L €30, D €56, Wine €7

LES BECS FINS
16 rue Saunerie, 04200 Sisteron
Tel 04 92 61 12 04
http://becsfins.free.fr/
Chef and owner Raphaël Videau masters rustic local specialties: lamb terrine with

thyme and mint, home-made foie gras and the inventive frog legs flambéed with pastis. A pleasant shaded terrace looks onto a pedestrian-only street.
🕒 Mon, Thu–Sat 12–1.30, 7–9.30, Tue, Sun 12–2.30 (daily in Jul, Aug)
🍽 L €30, D €60, Wine €11

VALENSOLE

HOSTELLERIE DE LA FUSTE
La Fuste, 04210 Valensole
Tel 04 92 72 05 95
www.lafuste.com
This elegant country residence houses a restaurant and four-star hotel. In summer, dinner is served in the garden. The menu follows the seasons: lamb roasted with thyme and served with a garlic cream in summer, variations involving mushrooms and truffles in winter.
🕒 Apr–end Sep daily 11.30–2, 7.30–9; Oct–end Mar Tue–Sat 11.30–2, 7.30–9, Sun 11.30–2
🍽 L €94, D €126, Wine €14

EATING

VAUCLUSE

APT

AUBERGE DU LUBÉRON

8 place du Faubourg du Ballet, 84400 Apt
Tel 04 90 74 12 50
www.auberge-luberon-peuzin.com
The interior of this inn is subtly elegant, with old furniture, beautiful drapes and pastel tones for the veranda dining room. There are wonderful

views of the Apt valley from the terrace. Lubéron regional cuisine dominates the menu in dishes such as pan-fried duck foie gras with regional glacé fruits, which is one of the chef's specialties. The dessert menu is extensive.
🕐 Mon, Tue 7.30–9.30, Wed–Sun 12–2, 7.30–9.30; closed 10 Nov–10 Dec, first 2 weeks of Jan
🍴 L, D €58–€136, Wine €18

AVIGNON

LA COMPAGNIE DES COMPTOIRS

83 rue Joseph Vernet, 84000 Avignon
Tel 04 90 85 99 04
www.lacompagniedescomptoirs.com
Dine in elegant surroundings at this top-quality restaurant, launched by Olivier Château and the Pourcel brothers. The delicious cuisine has a Provençal accent.
🕐 Tue–Sat 12–2.30, 7–11
🍴 L €140, D €230, Wine €45

SPECIAL IN AVIGNON

CHRISTIAN ÉTIENNE

10 rue de Mons, 84000 Avignon
Tel 04 90 86 16 50
www.christian-etienne.fr

This elegant restaurant is in a 14th-century palace and its dining room has beautiful painted ceilings and frescoes. The pretty terrace looks onto the Palais des Papes. Christian Étienne, former sous-chef at the luxury Ritz Hotel in Paris, creates exquisite regional dishes, with truffles and tomatoes his preferred ingredients—black truffle omelette is one of the house specialties.
🕐 Tue–Sat 12–1.15, 7.30–9.15
🍴 L €100, D €140, Wine €16

L'ENTRÉE DES ARTISTES

1 place des Carmes, 84000 Avignon
Tel 04 90 82 46 90
There's a retro bistro-style interior behind the red façade of this restaurant. Pictures of famous actresses and old opera posters hang on the walls. The pleasant terrace looks onto a lively square.

The chef accommodates market finds and the menu changes frequently. You may be lucky enough to sample the home-smoked salmon, the daube of duck (the meat is

slowly cooked in wine) or the crêpes Suzette (pancakes flambéed with bitter orange liqueur).
🕐 Mon–Fri 12–1.30, 7.30–10.30
🍴 L €32, D €42, Wine €11

LA FOURCHETTE

17 rue Racine, 84000 Avignon
Tel 04 90 85 20 93
Wood panels, wicker chairs and a multitude of forks (*fourchettes*) hanging on the wall give this restaurant a simple yet original feel. The menu offers innovative regional cuisine. Smoked haddock ravioli, sardines marinated in coriander and thyme custard showcase the interesting use of local food. The menu varies depending on what's available at the market each day.

🕐 Mon–Fri 12.15–1.45, 7.15–9.45; closed first 3 weeks of Aug
🍴 L €46, D €52, Wine €12

GRAND CAFÉ

Cour Maria-Casarès, 84000 Avignon
Tel 04 90 86 86 77
The Grand Café, next to Cinéma Utopia, is perfect for a drink or some regional cuisine before or after a film. The interior is impressive—the former warehouse has kept its red-brick vaulted ceiling and also has four huge mirrors.
🕐 Tue–Sat 12–12
🍴 L €32, D €60, Wine €15

EATING

LE SIMPLE SIMON

26 rue Petite-Fusterie, 84000 Avignon
Tel 04 90 86 62 70

This is a little piece of old England in the heart of Avignon. Inside there are beamed ceilings, plates hanging on the walls, a collection of teapots and a large round table in the middle of the room where the cakes and other desserts are displayed. During the afternoon it's a

great place to enjoy a cup of tea and a cake. At lunchtime, the dish of the day is often of British influence.

🕙 Mon–Sat 12–7; closed Aug
🍽 L €30 (lunch only)

LE VERNET

58 rue Joseph-Vernet, 84000 Avignon
Tel 04 90 86 64 53
www.levernet.fr

You'll find classic cuisine with a Provençal accent at this elegant restaurant, in an 18th-century town house. The house specialty is *l'agnolade d'Avignon*, sautéed lamb shoulder with olives, carrots and herbs.

🕙 Mon–Sat 11.30–2, 7–10; closed mid-Dec to mid-Jan
🍽 L €40, D €80, Wine €18

WOOLOOMOOLOO

16 rue des Teinturiers, 84000 Avignon
Tel 04 90 85 28 44
www.woolloo.com

A collection of African masks and other works of art, trinkets

and low tables with cushions as seats create an unusual

atmosphere. Order *mafé* (beef cooked slowly in a peanut butter sauce) or other tastes from around the world. The terrace looks onto one of Avignon's most picturesque streets.

🕙 Daily 12–2.30, 8–10.30
🍽 L €24, D €44, Wine €9

BONNIEUX

LA BASTIDE DE CAPELONGUE

Bastide de Capelongue, 84480 Bonnieux
Tel 04 90 75 89 78
www.edouardloubet.com/
Capelongue/

This restaurant is in a country-house hotel perched on a hill. The refined decor makes good use of local materials (tile floor, wrought-iron furniture for the terrace). Local specialties are served and there is a large choice of salads for lunch.

🕙 Mid-Mar to mid-Dec daily 12–2, 7–9
🍽 L €76, D €120, Wine €27

LE PONT JULIEN

Le Pont Julien: RN 100, 84480 Bonnieux
Tel 04 90 74 48 44
www.lepontjulien.com

At the heart of Lubéron's regional park, Le Pont Julien is in a traditional Provençal house. The unpretentious interior includes lamps and paintings. There are two dining rooms and a terrace, and the menu offers a tour of Mediterranean specialties, from bouillabaisse to Lubéron goat's cheese to roast leg of lamb typical of Haute-Provence.

🕙 Thu–Mon 12–1.45, 7.45–8.45, Wed 7.45–8.45
🍽 L €38, D €44, Wine €15

CAIRANNE

AUBERGE CASTEL MIREÏO

Route d'Orange, 84290 Cairanne
Tel 04 90 30 82 20
www.castelmireio.fr

There are fine views from the terrace of this welcoming restaurant, which is part of a hotel. The menu includes many local dishes: rabbit terrine marinated in wine from Cairanne served with an onion marmalade, poultry from the Drôme region, truffles (in season). Plus there is a good selection of local wines.

🕙 Sun, Mon, Wed 12–2.30, Tue, Thu–Sat 12–2.30, 7.30–9.30; closed Jan
🍽 L €38, D €48, Wine €15

CHEVAL-BLANC

L'AUBERGE DE CHEVAL BLANC

481 avenue de la Canebière, 84460 Cheval-Blanc
Tel 04 32 50 18 55

Chef Hervé Perrasse prepares the great classics of Provençal cuisine with obvious pleasure. The *escabèche millefeuille* (anchovies in puff pastry) or melt-in-your-mouth Provençal flan made with fresh, local herbs and white wine are excellent choices. There's a pleasant shaded terrace, which looks onto a garden, and the dining room has beamed ceilings, wicker chairs and displays of works by local artist Christine Darellis.

🕙 Mon, Sat 7.30–10, Thu, Fri and Sun 12–2, 7.30–10
🍽 L €32, D €78, Wine €19

LE CRESTET

LE MAS DE MAGALI

Quartier Chante Coucou, 84110 Le Crestet
Tel 04 90 36 39 91
www.masdemagali.com

There's a lovely setting in a country house in a park planted with oak trees for this restaurant. Eat on the terrace or in the elegant dining room, decorated in Provençal style with a romantic twist. Blue, yellow and white set the tone, with mirrors and subdued lighting. Dishes to try include terrine of foie gras, chicken with a mushroom sauce and zabaglione for dessert.

🕙 May–end Sep Thu–Tue 7.30–9
🍽 D €48, Wine €12

GIGONDAS

L'OUSTALET

Place Portail, 84190 Gigondas
Tel 04 90 65 85 30
www.oustalet-gigondas.com

This restaurant is at the heart of a small medieval town surrounded by olive groves and vineyards. Enjoy dinner on the terrace, under the shade

EATING

of plane trees, or in the rustic dining room, with beamed ceilings and exposed brick. Try warm duck foie gras with green tomato chutney, or roasted local pigeon. Seasonal dishes are available, including truffle in winter. The local Gigondas wine is worth sampling.

🕐 Mon 7.30–9.30, Tue–Sat 12–2, 7.30–9.30

🍴 L €64, D €130, Wine €20

GORDES

HOSTELLERIE LE PHEBUS

Route de Murs, 84220 Joucas-Gordes
Tel 04 90 05 78 83
www.lephebus.com

Le Phebus is both a restaurant and a four-star hotel. Chef Xavier Mathieu's sophisticated regional cuisine includes fillet of sole pan-fried in salt butter with tangy jasmine and vanilla and farmhouse duck foie gras. You can eat in the elegant dining room, which has beamed ceilings, or you may prefer the terrace and its fantastic views.

🕐 Mid-Mar to mid-Nov Mon, Fri, Sat 12–1.30, 7–9.30, Tue–Thu, Sun 7–9.30

🍴 L €100, D €100, Wine €28

LAURIS

LA TABLE DES MAMÉES

1 rue du Mûrier, 84360 Lauris
Tel 04 90 08 34 66

Exposed stone, vaulted ceilings, a large fireplace and soft lighting enhance this 14th-century country-house

restaurant. The cuisine is also full of character, with dishes

such as duck with olives, garlic and courgettes (zucchini) and traditional fish soup. The cellar contains plenty of local wines.

🕐 Tue–Sat 12–2.30, 7.30–10, Sun 12–2.30; closed Mar

🍴 L €40, D €45, Wine €18

LOURMARIN

LE MOULIN DE LOURMARIN

Rue du Temple, 84160 Lourmarin
Tel 04 90 68 06 69
www.moulindelourmarin.com

A former 18th-century oil mill is home to this restaurant. Under beautiful vaults, tables have been dressed with blue and yellow, and are lit by candles. Chef Edouard Loubet uses vegetables fresh from the restaurant's garden, and herbs and spices typical of the Lubéron region: wheat and clam risotto with spices from the Apt region and pigeon from the Alpilles with a reduction of rocket (arugula).

🕐 Mon, Thu–Sun 12–2, 7–9.30; closed mid-Jan to mid-Feb and last two weeks of Nov

🍴 L €182, D €182, Wine €25

ORANGE

RESTAURANT DES PRINCES

Hôtel des Princes, 86 avenue de l'Arc de Triomphe, 84100 Orange
Tel 04 90 51 87 87
www.amarys-orange.com

There has been a hotel/restaurant on this site in the heart of the old town since the 17th century. Today the Restaurant des Princes offers a light modern dining room with a menu of French dishes plus a few regional specialties. A buffet is also available.

🕐 Daily 12–2.30, 7–10.30

🍴 L €25, D €30, Wine €9

PIOLENC

L'ORANGERIE

4 rue de l'Ormeau, 84420 Piolenc
Tel 04 90 29 59 88
www.orangerie.net

Micky and Gérard Delarocque's 18th-century country house is full of originality. Micky likes to write, and punctuates the menu with her prose. Gérard paints and his works of art adorn the dining room's exposed brick walls. The cuisine is rustic but also uses exotic combinations such as spiced duck fillet served with figs. The menu changes seasonally. In summer, dinner is also served in the garden.

🕐 Mon 7.30–9.30; Tue–Sun 12–1.30, 7.30–9.30 (closed on Sun in winter)

🍴 L €34, D €70, Wine €15

ROCHEGUDE

CHÂTEAU DE ROCHEGUDE

26790 Rochegude
Tel 04 75 97 21 10

In a hamlet 10km (6 miles) north of Orange, this amazing 12th-century fortress, once the summer residence of the local Marquis, is now a beautifully presented hotel and restaurant. The menu is seasonal, using the best Provençal ingredients, including the famed truffle. In winter meals are served in the medieval armoury, in summer on the chateau terrace.

🕐 Daily 12–2, 7.30–9.30; closed mid-Nov to mid-Dec

🍴 L €38, D €76, Wine €14

VAISON-LA-ROMAINE

LA FONTAINE RESTAURANT

Le Beffroi, rue de l'Evêché, Cité Médiévale, 84110 Vaison-la-Romaine
Tel 04 90 36 04 71
www.le-beffroi.com

This hotel/restaurant, in a 16th- and 17th-century building in the old town, has an ornate dining room. The menu concentrates on traditional Provençal dishes and the wine cellar stocks predominantly local Côte du Rhône and Ventoux labels that complement the food.

🕐 Apr–end Oct Mon, Wed–Fri 7.30–9.30, Sat, Sun 12–2, 7.30–9.30 (also open Tue 7.30–9.30 in Jul)

🍴 L €50, D €80, Wine €15

STAYING IN PROVENCE AND THE CÔTE D'AZUR

Simplicity or luxury is the key choice for a stay in Provence, with the grand hotels of the Riviera contrasting with old stone buildings inland and homey chalets in the mountains. A new generation of boutique hotels combines the two, with minimalistic decor and high-tech luxuries.

Hotels are inspected regularly and classified into six categories: no star, 1*, 2*, 3*, 4* and 4*L (Luxury). They must display their rates (including tax) both outside the hotel and in the rooms, and charge per room and not per person. You generally have to pay extra for breakfast and for any additional beds you may want in your room. Aix-en-Provence, Avignon and Marseille take part in the *Bon Weekend en Ville* promotion. This runs from November until the end of March and offers two nights for the price of one at a range of hotels for stays beginning on a Friday or Saturday night (www.bon-week-end-en-villes.com).

LUXURY

Traditional haunts of the rich and famous include the fabulous Belle-Époque hotels on the Riviera, which offer the full luxury treatment. These have been joined by new designer hotels such as the Hi-Hôtel in Nice, where concept rooms involve rock pools and high-tech plasma screens. Smaller, but no less expensive, are the boutique hotels, with no more than a couple of dozen rooms styled by fashion gurus. For true luxury, find a top-of-the-range *mas* (country house) with a swimming pool or a first-class restaurant with rooms. Many restored country houses also offer plenty of pampering, and a chance to get back to basics by learning old country recipes from the chefs in the kitchens. In most of the luxury hotels on the coast, health and beauty treatments are provided in state-of-the-art spas.

ON A BUDGET

Independent city hotels are often surprisingly chic, although occasionally horribly dated and draughty. International chain hotels and motels are the easy option, and while these may be useful overnight stops on long *autoroute* journeys south, there are far more interesting options available at similar prices. Best of all are the Logis

de France—small, family-run inns and hotels offering good standards, from basic and comfortable to charming. Most have restaurants, serving traditional local dishes. All are regularly inspected and listed on the website www.logis-de-france.fr. Some offer themed packages which promote winter sports, fishing or hiking. In more remote areas, hotels offer deals including dinner or all meals. Budget beds are also offered at youth hostels *(Auberges de Jeunesse),* although you have to be a member of the International Youth Hostelling Federation or of the Youth Hostelling Federation of your home country. Look up the website www.fuaj.org for a list of youth hostels in the region.

BED-AND-BREAKFAST

The *chambre d'hôte* is France's answer to the traditional bed-and-breakfast, and tourist offices have lists of families who offer rooms to visitors. However, the best *chambres d'hôte* are affiliated with the Gîtes de France organization (▷ below). Often housed in converted farm buildings or restored watermills, they give you the opportunity to experience French life. Breakfast usually includes home-made treats, from fresh croissants to jams. Since many are run by farmers' wives and vineyard owners, it is worth taking the *table d'hôte* option and dining with the host family at least once.

SELF-CATERING

While plenty of companies sell package deals at self-contained holiday parks—with the obligatory kids' club, face painting and live entertainment in season—a popular alternative is to rent a *gîte*. These are self-contained cottages, houses and apartments, often with swimming pools, in small towns and country areas, and may be classified by the organization Gîtes de France (www.gites-de-france.fr). You can rent *gîtes* for one week or

The grand Carlton Hotel looks out onto the boulevard de la Croisette in glamorous Cannes; other famous hotels along the Côte d'Azur include the Negresco (far left), in Nice

two, and the accommodation is usually simple and decent (bring your own linen or rent on site), but with a certain rustic charm. Other self-catering options range from isolated farmhouses to grand villas or beach apartments on the Riviera.

CAMPING

Provence's warm, dry climate makes camping a popular choice for visitors from abroad and also from cooler parts of France. There are around 900 campsites in the region, the majority of which are in the Var *département*. Campsites, officially graded from 0 to 4*, are regularly inspected and rated as carefully as the nation's hotels. Most have excellent facilities, with mobile homes and pre-pitched tents. The best have swimming pools, supermarkets and

restaurants. Visitors with their own caravans (trailers) and tents can find inexpensive sites offering electricity, showers and bathrooms. From April to the end of October, it is important to reserve ahead.

Don't park your motorhome or put up your tent beside the beach or on the roadside. Police stations and tourist offices have addresses of local campsites in an emergency. The National Federation of Campsites can be contacted at 01 42 72 84 08 or www.campingfrance.com. Campsites can become extremely crowded on the Côte d'Azur during July and August. If you prefer *camping sauvage* (camping away from official campsites), check with the local town hall first as it is often forbidden, especially in areas at risk of forest fires.

BOUCHES-DU-RHÔNE

AIX-EN-PROVENCE

HÔTEL LE PIGONNET
5 avenue du Pigonnet, 13090 Aix
Tel 04 42 59 02 90
www.hotelpigonnet.com

Four-star Le Pigonnet is in the heart of town, at the end of a tree-lined street. There's a wonderful view of the Victory Mountain. Inside is refined elegance. There is a restaurant.
🏦 €160–€270, excluding breakfast
🛏 48
🏊 Outdoor

ARLES

GRAND HÔTEL NORD-PINUS
Place du Forum, 13200 Arles
Tel 04 90 93 44 44
www.nord-pinus.com
The style of this four-star hotel crosses places and times: Persian carpets, paintings, various objets d'arts and antique furniture. There is also a restaurant.
🏦 €125–€275, including breakfast
🛏 25
🌐

HÔTEL CALENDAL
5 rue Porte-de-Laure, 13200 Arles
Tel 04 90 96 11 89
www.lecalendal.com
Some of the bedrooms in this 17th-century building, now a two-star hotel, face the Roman arena. Others overlook the hotel's exquisite garden courtyard. Inside there are tile floors, wrought iron and warm tones. In fine weather, enjoy breakfast and light meals in the shade of palm trees.
🕐 Closed Jan
🏦 €45–€75, excluding breakfast
🛏 38
🌐

HÔTEL D'ARLATAN
26 rue Sauvage, 13631 Arles
Tel 04 90 93 56 66
www.hotel-arlatan.fr
There's quite a history to this three-star hotel: It was built on the site of Constantin Basilica and has many Roman relics, as well as a 16th-century vaulted ceiling. Take breakfast in the peaceful walled garden. There is private parking.

🏦 €85–€153, excluding breakfast
🛏 48
🌐

LE MAS DE PEINT
Le Sambuc, 13200 Arles
Tel 04 90 97 20 62
www.masdepeint.com
This was the house of 17th-

century Lyon draper, Antoine Peint. It became a farm in the

19th century: Rice is still grown on the estate and cattle are bred. The bedrooms are rustic yet refined. Some have beamed ceilings, others a Victorian bathroom. Enjoy farm-grown food in the evenings.
🕐 Closed mid-Jan to mid-Mar, mid-Nov to mid-Dec
🏦 €197–€254, excluding breakfast
🛏 8, plus 3 suites
🌐 🏊 Outdoor

BARBENTANE

HÔTEL CASTEL-MOUISSON
Quartier Castel-Mouisson, 13570 Barbentane
Tel 04 90 95 51 17
www.hotel-castelmouisson.com
This small hotel lies at the bottom of the hill in Barbentane, surrounded by greenery. The rooms are comfortably furnished; a large fireplace brings warmth to the living room. There is a breakfast room but no restaurant.
🕐 Closed Nov–end Mar
🏦 €56–€69, excluding breakfast
🛏 17
🏊 Outdoor

LES BAUX-DE-PROVENCE

HÔTEL LA BENVENGUDO
Vallon de l'Arcoule, 13520 Les Baux-de-Provence
Tel 04 90 54 32 54
www.benvengudo.com
This ivy-covered hotel, built in 1967, has a huge garden. Inside are beamed ceilings and antique furniture; white walls

give an airy feel. Some of the bedrooms are in adjoining buildings and some have a balcony or a terrace. Facilities include a tennis court and boules pitch. The restaurant serves local cuisine.
🕐 Closed Nov to mid-Dec
🏦 €134–€184, including breakfast
🛏 24
🌐 🏊 Outdoor

STAYING

LE MAS D'AIGRET
Col de la Vayède, 13520
Les Baux-de-Provence
Tel 04 90 54 20 00
www.masdaigret.com
Nestled against a cliff, this
three-star hotel has wonderful
views and some surprising
interiors—the breakfast room,

bar, lounge and some of the
guest rooms have been carved
out of the rock and you can
see the exposed rockface. The
simple, tasteful bedrooms
have floral bedspreads and
white furniture, and there is
a restaurant.
🖾 €95–€170, excluding breakfast (€12)
🛈 16
🅢 🏊 Outdoor

LE MAS DE L'OULIVIÉ
Les Arcoules, 13520
Les Baux-de-Provence
Tel 04 90 54 35 78
www.masdeloulivie.com
An olive grove surrounds this
hotel in a Provençal cottage.
The lounge has beamed ceilings and a large fireplace; the
bedrooms have beautiful
fabrics, tile floors and subtle
lighting. The pool has been

attractively landscaped with
rocks, a beach down to the
water and a spa. Breakfast is
served by the pool.
🕐 Closed mid-Nov to mid-Mar
🖾 €95–€230, excluding breakfast
🛈 25
🏊 Outdoor

CASSIS
AUBERGE DE JEUNESSE DE CASSIS
La Fontasse, 13260
Cassis
Tel 04 42 01 02 72
www.fuaj.org
This youth hostel is in the
heart of the Massif of
Calanques, so is well placed
for hikes. It is not for those
looking for comfort, although
the place may please the
environmentally friendly:
Waste is recycled, there's
solar energy for electricity
and a rainwater cistern. This
results in limited facilities—
there are no showers—but
cooking equipment is
available. You'll sleep in a
10-bed dormitory. Credit cards
are not accepted.
🕐 Closed end Dec to mid-Jan
🖾 €9 per person
🛈 60

SPECIAL IN CASSIS
LES ROCHES BLANCHES
Route des Calanques, 13714
Cassis
Tel 04 42 01 09 30
www.roches-blanches-cassis.com

Sitting on top of a cliff, with
gardens cascading down to
the sea, this four-star hotel
has breathtaking views: Its
pool seems to melt into the
Mediterranean, which fills the
horizon. Most of the bed-
rooms have a balcony or
terrace and all have been
tastefully decorated with fine
fabrics and pretty shades.
Enjoy dinner on the terrace or
in the dining room, with its
large bay windows.
🕐 Closed Nov to mid-Mar
🖾 €120–€185, excluding breakfast
🛈 24
🏊 Outdoor

GÉMENOS
LE RELAIS DE LA MAGDELEINE
Route d'Aix-en-Provence, 13420
Gémenos
Tel 04 42 32 20 16
www.relais-magdeleine.com
This hotel, in a pretty garden,
has an attractive 18th-century

façade. The interior is tastefully
decorated with antiques and
the bedrooms have period furniture, warm hues and tile
floors. The restaurant serves
fine Provençal cuisine. You can
eat dinner on the terrace.
🕐 Closed Dec to mid-Mar
🖾 €120–€165, excluding breakfast
🛈 24
🏊 Outdoor

MARSEILLE
HÔTEL LE CORBUSIER
280 boulevard Michelet, 3rd floor,
13008 Marseille
Tel 04 91 16 78 00
The hotel is in a block of 300
apartments designed by Le
Corbusier. For this monument
of modern architecture, he
devised a revolutionary
concept—to re-create a city
within a single building. As

such, it comes complete with
play areas, shops, a cinema, a
bar and a library. The delight-
fully simple bedrooms look to
the sea or the park and terrace.
There is private parking.
🖾 €45–€70, excluding breakfast
🛈 21
🚇 Rond-Point du Prado

HÔTEL HERMÈS

2 rue Bonneterie, 13002 Marseille
Tel 04 96 11 63 63
www.hotelmarseille.com

This two-star hotel is by the Vieux Port, a picturesque and animated spot packed with

restaurants and cafés. Although lacking the character of older hotels, bedrooms are light and have a TV and some have a balcony.

💶 €50–€100, excluding breakfast (€11)
🄯
🄰 Vieux Port

HÔTEL DE ROME ET ST-PIERRE

7 cours St-Louis, 13001 Marseille
Tel 04 91 54 19 52
www.hotelderome.com

This three-star hotel is in a 19th-century building near the Vieux Port. The refined interior (drapes and candelabra in the bedrooms) sometimes betrays art deco influences. You'll find comfortable armchairs in the reading room and wrought-iron furniture in the breakfast room. Bedrooms have a TV

and minibar and there is a safe and laundry service. Business facilities include a large meeting room with a telephone and VCR, and a photocopier.

💶 €74–€84, excluding breakfast
🄯 43
🄯
🄰 Vieux Port, Noailles

HÔTEL ST-LOUIS

2 rue des Récollettes, 13001 Marseille
Tel 04 91 54 02 74
www.hotel-st-louis.com

The Napoleonic façade of this two-star hotel, dotted with wrought-iron balconies, is

listed as a historic monument. The hotel is close to the animated Canebière and Old Port. The comfortable bedrooms have been simply decorated and they all have a TV. The reception area has more character, with terracotta hues and a tile floor. Facilities include internet access.

💶 €59–€83, excluding breakfast
🄯 22
🄰 Vieux Port, Noailles

LE PETIT NICE PASSÉDAT

Anse de Maldormé, Corniche J. F. Kennedy, 13007 Marseille
Tel 04 91 59 25 92
www.petitnice-passedat.com

Stay here for luxury, calm and the immensity of the Mediterranean for a backdrop. The contemporary interior of this four-star hotel exudes tranquillity. The owners

aim for a communion of the four elements: air (panorama and the scents of Provence), water (the Mediterranean), earth (the gardens) and fire (when the evening sun sets the place aglow). The restaurant is excellent.

💶 €250–€490, excluding breakfast
🄯 13
🄯 🚗 Outdoor 🄿

NÎMES

HÔTEL IMPERATOR CONCORDE

Quai de la Fontaine, 15 rue Gaston-Bossier, 30000 Nîmes
Tel 04 66 21 90 30
www.hotel-imperator.com

Although this hotel fronts onto the road, the magnificent gardens more than make up for that. Both Ernest Hemingway and Ava Gardner were lured to this wonderful place, overlooking the Jardin de la Fontaine and place Picasso, to relax in its extravagant rooms. Start your evening with cocktails on the terrace overlooking the fountain and finish it in one of the spacious, well-designed rooms.

💶 €99–€198, excluding breakfast (€16)
🄯 62
🄯

ST-CANNAT

MAS DE FAUCHON

Quartier Fauchon, 13760 St-Cannat
Tel 04 42 50 61 77
www.mas-de-fauchon.fr

Hidden in the countryside, this small hotel offers peace and relaxation. The bedrooms have been personalized: a four-poster bed in one, flowery curtains matching the cushions in another. Each has a private terrace. The adjoining restaurant serves regional cuisine and is in a former shepherd's house with beamed ceilings and a fireplace. This place has character.

💶 €140–€160, excluding breakfast
🄯 9
🄯 🚗 Outdoor

ST-RÉMY-DE-PROVENCE

CHÂTEAU DE ROUSSAN

Route de Tarascon, 13210 St-Rémy-de-Provence
Tel 04 90 92 11 63
www.chateau-de-roussan.com

This former residence of the Marquis de Gange was built on land owned by his famous ancestor, Nostradamus. A hotel since 1951, its rooms are beautifully decorated. The surrounding parkland, with its century-old trees and swans gliding on its ponds, adds romantic charm. There is a restaurant.

💶 €73–€99, excluding breakfast
🄯 21

STAYING

VAR

LES ARCS-SUR-ARGENS

LOGIS DU GUETTEUR
Place du Château, 83460
Les Arcs-sur-Argens
Tel 04 94 99 51 10
www.logisduguetteur.com
This three-star hotel is in a beautifully restored 11th-century castle. Dine in the vaulted basement, where a fire crackles in winter, or by the pool. Most bedrooms have panoramic mountain views.
🅖 Closed mid-Jan to mid-Mar
🅦 €120, excluding breakfast
🅘 12
🅢 🏊 Outdoor

SPECIAL IN LA CELLE
HOSTELLERIE DE L'ABBAYE DE LA CELLE
Place du Général-de-Gaulle, 83170
La Celle
Tel 04 98 05 14 14
www.abbaye-celle.com
Stay in a restored 18th-century abbey at the heart of a vineyard and decorated with antiques. The takeover in 2002 by celebrated chef Alain Ducasse added a new dimension to this four-star address: It's now coupled with an excellent restaurant.
🅖 Closed in Jan
🅦 €240–€290, excluding breakfast
🅘 10
🏊 Outdoor

LA CROIX-VALMER

CHÂTEAU DE VALMER
Route de Gigaro, 83420 La Croix-Valmer
Tel 04 94 55 15 15
www.chateau-valmer.com
The chateau has a private beach, tennis court and large swimming pool surrounded by palm trees. The bedrooms have Provençal furnishings and marble bathrooms. Some have a canopy bed and some suites can take up to four people. Sample Mediterranean cuisine

at La Pinède Plage restaurant by the beach. Private parking is available.
🅖 Closed Oct to mid-Apr
🅦 €200–€360, excluding breakfast
🅘 42
🅢 🏊 Outdoor

FRÉJUS

L'ARÉNA
145 rue Général de Gaulle, 83600 Fréjus
Tel 04 94 17 09 40
www.arena-hotel.com
In the heart of Fréjus, this three-star hotel has a terra-cotta façade, palm trees in the

garden, wooden furniture in the bedrooms and a restaurant. In summer, enjoy breakfast by the pool. Private parking is available.
🅖 Closed mid-Dec to mid-Jan
🅦 €95–€150, excluding breakfast (€10)
🅘 36
🅢 🏊 Outdoor

RAMATUELLE

CAMPING KON TIKI
Route des Plages, 83350 Ramatuelle
Tel 04 94 55 96 96
www.campazur.com
On the edge of Pampelonne beach, this high-class camping ground is very popular, so reserve ahead. The mobile homes come in four styles: Beach chalet, Penthouse, California and Mercure. Each has two bedrooms, a kitchenette, lounge area and bathroom. Alternatively, bring your own caravan (trailer) or mobile home and hook up to water and electricity. Facilities include a grocery, restaurant, bar, tennis court and hot showers.
🅖 Closed Nov–end Mar
🅦 €44–€160 per night to rent a mobile home

LA FERME D'AUGUSTIN
Tahiti, 83350 Ramatuelle
Tel 04 94 55 97 00
www.fermeaugustin.com
This three-star hotel combines rusticity with modern comfort—a spa bath in the bathroom, dressing rooms in the suite and a balneo pool (heated and with hydro massaging jets) in the garden. Inside there are beamed ceilings and a fireplace in the lounge. The beach is nearby.
🅖 Open mid-Mar to mid-Oct
🅦 €100–€260, excluding breakfast
🅘 46
🅢 🏊 Outside

SAINTE-MAXIME

HOSTELLERIE LA CROISETTE
2 boulevard des Romarins, 83120 Sainte-Maxime
Tel 04 94 96 17 75
www.hotel-la-croisette.com
An imposing villa with a pink façade and blue shutters houses this three-star hotel. Most of the simple, sunny bedrooms give beautiful views of the bay. The beach is nearby.
🅖 Open mid-Mar to mid-Oct
🅦 €110–€147, excluding breakfast
🅘 16
🅢

ST-TROPEZ

HÔTEL BYBLOS
Avenue Paul Signac, 83990 St-Tropez
Tel 04 94 56 68 00
www.byblos.com

This luxurious hotel is popular with the jet set. Behind an ochre and blue façade the sophisticated interior is decorated with local materials. There are antiques, pretty fabrics and ceramics.
🅖 Closed Nov to mid-Apr
🅦 €350–€740, excluding breakfast (€32)
🅘 52 rooms, 43 suites
🅢 🏊 Outdoor 🏋

STAYING

ALPES-MARITIMES AND MONACO

CANNES

CHALET DE L'ISÈRE

42 avenue de Grasse, 06400 Cannes
Tel 04 93 38 50 80

Breakfast is served in a pretty tiled garden at this two-star hotel. Bedrooms have been simply decorated, yet each has its own touch. There is a restaurant. The Palais des Festivals is a 10-minute walk away.
🛏 €51–€56, excluding breakfast
🛌 8

HÔTEL DE PARIS

34 boulevard d'Alsace, 06400 Cannes
Tel 04 93 38 30 89
www.hotel-de-paris.com
This three-star hotel has a pink 19th-century façade, which contrasts beautifully with the blue of the outdoor pool. Inside, there is antique furniture and even some medieval armour. Facilities include a private beach, swimming pool, Jacuzzi and hammam (Turkish bath). Bedrooms have satellite TV, a safe and connection point for laptops.
🛏 €105–€150, excluding breakfast
🛌 50
🏊 Outdoor

SPECIAL IN CANNES

HOTEL MARTINEZ

73 boulevard de la Croisette, 06400 Cannes
Tel 04 92 98 73 00
www.hotel-martinez.com
This mythical palace, popular with celebrities during the Film Festival, faces the Bay of Cannes. The luxurious decor betrays art deco influence: Dark woods and marble or deep carpets set the tone. Services include a bar, restaurants, business facilities and private beach.

🛏 €260–€800, excluding breakfast
🛌 386 rooms, 27 suites
🏊 Outdoor 📺

MENTON

CLARIDGE'S

39 avenue de Verdun, 06500 Menton
Tel 04 93 35 72 53
www.claridges-menton.com
This two-star hotel is just a couple of kilometres from chic Monaco and close to beaches. The simply decorated bedrooms are quite small but they

are comfortable and have satellite TV. There's a bar and lounge, and a terrace looks onto the street.
🛏 €47–€54, excluding breakfast
🛌 39
🛎 (In 24 rooms)

HÔTEL AIGLON

7 avenue de la Madone, 06500 Menton
Tel 04 93 57 55 55
www.hotelaiglon.net
Close to the sea, this prestigious three-star hotel is in a 20th-century town house. Cross its luxurious garden, climb its marble stairs and you'll discover an elegant interior, with fine furniture and objets d'art. The bedrooms have satellite TV, a safe and minibar. Other facilities include a kids' playground, table tennis and parking. The pool is

heated and there's a solarium. Le Riaumont restaurant serves fine Provençal cuisine. You can dine on the poolside terrace.
🛏 €112–€151, including breakfast
🛌 29
🏊 Outdoor 🛎

MOUGINS

LE MANOIR DE L'ETANG

66 allée du Manoir, 06250 Mougins
Tel 04 92 28 36 00
www.manoir-de-letang.com
In a park dotted with ponds, this three-star hotel is in an elegant, ivy-clad 19th-century residence. The interior is decorated with antique furniture.

The restaurant serves fine local cuisine by the pool or in the pretty dining room.
🔒 Closed Nov–end Mar
🛏 €160–€250, excluding breakfast
🛌 22
🏊 Outdoor

STAYING

LES MUSCADINS

18 boulevard Courteline, 06250
Mougins
Tel 04 92 28 28 28
www.lesmuscadins.com

Pablo Picasso once stayed at
this former guesthouse, now a
four-star hotel. The ochre

façade and tile floor are
inspired by the region and
antiques add to the elegance.
Each room has a personal
touch, such as a wrought-iron
four-poster bed or patterned
tile floors. Fine local cuisine
is served in the restaurant;
lobster is one of the specials.

🍴 €235–€260, excluding breakfast
🛏 10
📶

NICE

AUBERGE DE JEUNESSE DE NICE

Route Forestière du Mont-Alban, 06300
Nice
Tel 04 93 89 23 64
www.fuaj.org

This youth hostel is in the
wooded hills of Mont Boron, at
an altitude of 100m (328ft).
There are beautiful views of
Nice. Dormitories have six to
eight beds and there is a
communal room with a TV.
Facilities also include a kitchen,
laundry service and internet

access. The hostel is 10km
(6 miles) from the city and
the beach. Credit cards are
not accepted.

🍴 €17.50 per person, including
breakfast
🛏 56

HÔTEL ARMENONVILLE

20 avenue des Fleurs, 06000 Nice
Tel 04 93 96 86 00
www.hotel-armenonville.com

There's a pretty setting for this
two-star hotel, in a 20th-
century mansion surrounded
by a flower garden. Some of
the rooms have a terrace and
look onto this greenery. All are
bright and have been tastefully
decorated with antique
furniture and beautiful tiled
bathrooms. Breakfast can be
served in the garden.

🍴 €72–€96, excluding breakfast
🛏 12
📶

HÔTEL DE LA BUFFA

56 rue de la Buffa, 06000 Nice
Tel 04 93 88 77 35
www.hotel-buffa.com

This two-star hotel is in an
early 20th-century building,
close to the Promenade des
Anglais and the sea. The
unpretentious interior is
inviting and bedrooms have
Provençal fabrics. The street-
facing rooms have double
glazing. There's private parking.

🍴 €65–€69, excluding breakfast (€8)
🛏 14
📶

HÔTEL WINDSOR

11 rue Dalpozzo, 06300 Nice
Tel 04 93 88 59 35
www.hotelwindsornice.com

This is no ordinary hotel, rather
a sanctuary for the soul. A
protector Buddha sits
enthroned in the reception
area. Massages are available.
Contemporary artists have
personalized each of the
rooms, which are influenced
by Honegger, Ducorroy, Barry

and local artist Ben. The hotel
is a work of art.

🍴 €105–€155, excluding breakfast
🛏 57
📶 🏊 Outdoor 🎾

SPECIAL IN NICE

HÔTEL NEGRESCO

37 promenade des Anglais, 06000
Nice
Tel 04 93 16 64 00
www.hotel-negresco-nice.com

Built in 1912, this palace and
its signature dome have been

given landmark status. The
interior is an ode to fine
art, from the Renaissance to
the modern: In the Salon
Royal, Niki de Saint-Phalle's
Nana, an oversize sculpture
of a woman, sits happily
next to classical portraits.
The hotel has its own
private beach.

🍴 €280–€480, including breakfast
🛏 145 rooms, 12 suites
📶

ROQUEBRUNE-CAP-MARTIN

LES DEUX FRÈRES

Le Village, 06190
Roquebrune-Cap-Martin
Tel 04 93 28 99 00
www.lesdeuxfreres.com

Most of the rooms at this hotel
have wonderful views of the
Mediterranean and Monaco.
The rooms are refined and
original: The Moroccan room
has a leopard skin, the Marine
room has blue-and-white
striped bed linen and
the Medieval room has a
wrought-iron bench.
Gourmet cuisine is served in
the restaurant, on the terrace,
or by the fireplace in winter.

🍴 €91–€101, excluding breakfast
🛏 10

STAYING

ROQUEFORT-LES-PINS

AUBERGE DU COLOMBIER

06330 Roquefort-les-Pins
Tel 04 90 60 33 00
www.auberge-du-colombier.com
At an altitude of 200m (656ft),
this three-star inn and the
surrounding park overlook the
Bastidon valley. The rooms
have been simply decorated
and all have a TV. Regional
cuisine is served in the dining
room. Facilities include a
swimming pool, tennis court
and conference room, or you
could try a game of boules or
table tennis in the park.
🛏 €64–€104, excluding breakfast
🛏 18
🏊 Outdoor

ST-JEAN-CAP-FERRAT

HÔTEL BRISE MARINE

58 avenue Jean Mermoz, 06230
St-Jean-Cap-Ferrat
Tel 04 93 76 04 36
www.hotel-brisemarine.com

This three-star hotel is in an
Italian-style villa, built 1878.
The ochre façade has blue
shutters and faces the sea.
There are excellent views
from the garden, the patio
and terraces, and from some
of the simple, elegant bedrooms. Each room has a TV,
safe and minibar. There is
no restaurant on site. Parking
is available.
🕙 Closed Nov–end Jan
🛏 €130–€150, excluding breakfast
🛏 16
💲

ST-PAUL-DE-VENCE

HÔTEL LE HAMEAU

528 route de La Colle, 06570
St-Paul-de-Vence
Tel 04 93 32 80 24
www.le-hameau.com
Overlooking the village of
St-Paul-de-Vence and its valley,
this three-star hotel is in an

18th-century farm complex
with whitewashed walls,
arched entrances and tiled
roofs. Some bedrooms have a
private terrace. The garden has
fragrant jasmine, citrus trees
and honeysuckle.
🕙 Closed mid-Nov to mid-Feb
🛏 €120–€152, excluding breakfast
🛏 14
💲 🏊 Outdoor

VILLEFRANCHE-SUR-MER

HÔTEL WELCOME

1 quai Courbet, 06230
Villefranche-sur-Mer
Tel 04 93 76 27 62
www.welcomehotel.com
Hôtel Welcome is in a modern
building overlooking the bay.
All bedrooms have balconies—
their views seduced writer
and film director Jean Cocteau,

a former guest. The interior has
a contemporary elegance. The
bedrooms are bright, some
decorated with floral fabrics.
There is no restaurant.
🕙 Closed mid-Nov to Christmas
🛏 €155–€200, excluding breakfast
(€12)
🛏 37
💲

HOTEL ALEXANDRA

35 boulevard Princesse-Charlotte,
Monte-Carlo
Tel 377 93 50 63 13
www.monte-carlo.mc/alexandra
This recently refurbished hotel
is less than 500m (550 yards)
from the attractions of Monte-
Carlo—the casino, restaurants,
nightlife and elegant shops.
The exterior has classic Belle-
Époque features, while the
rooms are modern. All have
soundproofing, mini-bar and
TV. The hotel is a good-value
option for its location.
🛏 56 rooms
🛏 €106–€143, excluding breakfast
(€13)
💲

HÔTEL HERMITAGE

Square Beaumarchais,
98000 Monaco
Tel 377 92 16 40 00
www.montecarloresort.com

This Belle-Époque luxury
hotel faces the Mediterranean.
It has a panoramic restaurant,
Le Vistamar, and you can have
breakfast under a glass ceiling
designed by Gustave Eiffel.
The services are those you
would expect of a luxury
hotel, including a helicopter
shuttle service between
Monaco and Nice airports.
There is direct access to Les
Thermes Marins de Monaco
Spa and Health Resort.
🛏 €700–€900, excluding breakfast
(€32)
🛏 213, plus 18 suites
💲 🏊 Indoor 🏋

STAYING

Prices are for a double room for one night. All the hotels listed accept credit cards unless otherwise stated. Note that rates vary widely throughout the year. For a key to the symbols, ▷ 2.

BARCELONNETTE

AUBERGE DU CLOS SOREL
Les Molanès, Pra-Loup 1500, 04400 Barcelonnette
Tel 04 92 84 10 74
www.clos-sorel.com
This three-star inn, in a 17th-century farm, has beamed ceilings, exposed stonework and fireplaces. In winter, a chairlift just 200m (220 yards) from the hotel provides access to the ski slopes. A restaurant

serves dinner in winter only.
🔆 Closed May to mid-Jun, Sep to 20 Dec
💶 €86–€138, excluding breakfast
ⓘ 11
🏊 Outdoor

CHEZ ARLETTE SIGNORET
Domaine de Lara, St Pons, 04000 Barcelonnette
Tel 04 92 81 52 81
www.domainedelara.com
With only five bedrooms, there's an intimate atmosphere in this cottage, a couple of kilometres from Pra-Loup and Sauze ski resorts. Inside, there are beamed ceilings and antique furniture. You can dine with your hostess. Credit cards are not accepted.
💶 €59–€67, including breakfast
ⓘ 5

FORCALQUIER

AUBERGE CHAREMBEAU
Route de Niozelles, 04300 Forcalquier
Tel 04 92 70 91 70
www.charembeau.com
This two-star country inn, close to the picturesque village of Niozelles, is in an 18th-century farmhouse. Some rooms can take up to four people and have a kitchenette. There's a tennis court outside.
🔆 Closed mid-Nov to mid-Feb
💶 €54–€106, excluding breakfast
ⓘ 23
🏊 Outdoor

GAP

HOTEL LE CLOS
20ter, avenue Cdt Dumont, 05000 Gap
Tel 04 92 51 37 04
www.leclos.fr
A landscaped garden surrounds this comfortable two-star hotel. There is a large restaurant on site and the terrace is popular with diners in summer. Rooms are simple and comfortable.
🔆 Closed 25 Oct–23 Nov
ⓘ 26
💶 €43–€56

MÉOLANS REVEL

MAISON D'HÔTES DES MÉANS
La Fresquière, 04340 Méolans Revel
Tel 04 92 81 03 91
www.chez.com/lesmeans/
Elisabeth and Frédéric Millet's guesthouse is in a 16th-century farm at an altitude of 1,080m (3,542ft). The charming interior has furniture typical of this region. Frédéric is an official mountain guide.
🔆 Closed mid-Oct to mid-May
💶 €60, including breakfast
ⓘ 4

MONETIER-LES-BAINS

AUBERGE DU CHOUCAS
Rue de la Fruitier, 05220 Monetier-les-Bains
Tel 04 92 24 42 73
www.aubergeduchoucas.com
In the heart of the Serre-Chevalier ski area, this 17th-century farmhouse offers a comfortable base for both summer and winter stays. The restaurant serves regional cuisine and the ski lifts are within walking distance.
🔆 Closed May, 3 Nov–6 Dec
💶 €118–€180, excluding breakfast (€15)
ⓘ 12

MOUSTIERS-SAINTE-MARIE

LA FERME ROSE
04360 Moustiers-Sainte-Marie
Tel 04 92 74 69 47
www.lafermerose.fr.fm/

The pink (rose) façade gave this two-star inn its name. Inside there are beamed ceilings, a tile floor and, in the restaurant, bistro furniture and some 1950s-style pieces such as a jukebox. Enjoy breakfast in the garden in summer.
🔆 Closed mid-Jan to mid-Mar, Nov–Christmas
💶 €70–€130, excluding breakfast
ⓘ 12

LA BASTIDE DE MOUSTIERS
Chemin de Quinson, 04360 Moustiers-Sainte-Marie
Tel 04 92 70 47 47
www.bastide-moustiers.com
This cottage turned four-star inn houses one of chef Alain Ducasse's restaurants

(▷ 242). The 12 bedrooms are named after local ingredients and each is decorated according to its name.
💶 €230–€295, excluding breakfast
ⓘ 12
🏊 Outdoor

STAYING

VAUCLUSE

AVIGNON

CAMPING DE BAGATELLE

Île de la Barthelasse, 84000 Avignon
Tel 04 90 86 30 39

This camping ground, with room for 238 tents or caravans (trailers), is on the Île de la Barthelasse, an island on the Rhône connected to Avignon by a bridge and surrounded by greenery. Bring your own tent or caravan. Facilities include a grocery store, bars, a restaurant and kids' playgrounds. There's also a youth hostel.

🛏 €11 for a pitch for a two-man tent; €35 for a caravan (trailer) pitch
🌳 Outdoor

SPECIAL IN AVIGNON

HÔTEL D'EUROPE

12 place Crillon, 84000 Avignon
Tel 04 90 14 76 76
www.hotel-d-europe.fr

Follow in the steps of Napoleon Bonaparte, Pablo Picasso and Salvador Dalí, who stayed at the Marquis of Graveson's former house, built in 1580 and turned into a hotel in 1799. The luxury furnishings include antiques, candelabra, paintings and Persian carpets. The suites have a terrace with wonderful views over Avignon. There's a restaurant and parking.

🛏 €125–€398, excluding breakfast (€23)
🛏 44 rooms, 3 suites
🔲

BOLLÈNE

LE CHÂTEAU DE ROCHER

42 avenue Emile-Lachaux, 84500 Bollène
Tel 04 90 40 09 09
www.lechateaudurocher.com

This three-star hotel is in a 19th-century manor, built for the Comte de Rocher. It lies in a 4ha (10-acre) park inhabited by ostriches and peacocks. The rooms are comfortable and there is a gourmet restaurant as well as enclosed parking.

🛏 €45–€66, excluding breakfast
🛏 19

CABRIÈRES-D'AVIGNON

LA BASTIDE DE VOULONNE

D148, 84220 Cabrières-d'Avignon
Tel 04 90 76 77 55
www.bastide-voulonne.com

Behind the ochre façade and blue shutters of this 18th-century former farmhouse is a tastefully decorated interior, where wrought iron, wood and shades of terracotta dominate. Most of the rooms have king-size beds; there is a garden and an impressive bread oven in the dining room.

🔘 Closed mid–Nov to mid–Dec; reservations essential in Jan and Feb
🛏 €122–€145, excluding breakfast
🛏 7
🌳 Outdoor

GORDES

BASTIDE DES CINQ LYS

Les Beaumettes, 84220 Gordes
Tel 04 90 72 38 38
www.bastide-des-5-lys.fr

This 16th-century four-star manor stands at the end of an avenue planted with cypress trees and pink oleanders. The soft tones and subtle lighting in the bedrooms exude tranquillity. All the rooms have an attractive feature such as a four-poster bed, a terrace or even a private garden. There is also a restaurant, tennis court and golf course. Every Saturday in July and August there's a piano bar by the pool.

🛏 €154–€261
🛏 18
🌳 Outdoor

LES BORIES

Route de l'Abbaye de Sénanque, 84220 Gordes
Tel 04 90 72 00 51
www.hotelprestige-provence.com

This four-star hotel is named after the drystone buildings once used by local shepherds. The dining room is actually in a former *borie*. The bedrooms have large bay windows that open onto private terraces and have wonderful views. The hotel has its own spa, including a sauna and Turkish baths.

🛏 €160–€325, excluding breakfast (€29)
🔲 🌳 Indoor and outdoor 🔲

DOMAINE DE LA FONTAINE

Route de Murs, 84220 Gordes
Tel 04 90 72 01 36
www.lagacholle.com

This three-star hotel is in a Provençal cottage, decorated inside with wood, terracotta and wrought iron in a simple yet contemporary style. All bedrooms have a king-size bed, and some a terrace

where breakfast can be served. There are wonderful views. The restaurant serves fine regional cuisine.

🔘 Closed during Jan and/or Feb
🛏 €75–€125, excluding breakfast
🛏 11
🌳 Outdoor

LAGNES

LE MAS DES GRÈS

Route d'Apt, 84800 Lagnes
Tel 04 90 20 32 85
www.masdesgres.com
You'll be welcomed like a family friend at this restored country house. The tastefully decorated bedrooms are simple but comfortable. Breakfast and dinner are served outside, in the shade of a 200-year-old plane tree. The parking area is fully enclosed.
🅒 Closed mid-Nov to mid-Mar
🅥 €85–€190, excluding breakfast
🅘 14
🅐 Outdoor

ORANGE

HOTEL ARÈNE

Place de Langes, 84100 Orange
Tel 04 90 11 40 40
www.avignon-et-provence.com/hotel-arene
In a tree-lined square in the historic heart of Orange, the Arène offers good-value quiet rooms with a safe, air-conditioning and mini-bar and a private garage (a separate fee is charged for parking). The small breakfast room serves regional specials and there is a separate restaurant on site.
🅒 Closed 6 Nov–1 Dec
🅥 €67–€92, excluding breakfast (€8)
🅘 30
🅒

PERNES-LES-FONTAINES

MAS LA BONOTY

Chemin de la Bonoty, 84210
Pernes-les-Fontaines
Tel 04 90 61 61 09
www.bonoty.com

This 17th-century farm has been beautifully restored with tiled floors and regional furniture in the bedrooms and exposed brick walls in the living room. The surrounding park has been landscaped with lavender, olive trees and fruit trees. Fine regional cuisine is on the restaurant menu and your dinner and breakfast can be served by the swimming pool, weather permitting.
🅒 Closed Nov, Jan
🅥 €69–€85, including breakfast
🅘 8
🅐 Outdoor

LE PONTET-AVIGNON

AUBERGE DE CASSAGNE

450 allée de Cassagne, 84130
Le Pontet-Avignon
Tel 04 90 31 04 18
www.hotelprestige-provence.com
Lush gardens surround this four-star hotel, in a building dating from 1850. The elegant interior features terracotta, walnut furniture and Provençal fabrics. Some of the bedrooms have four-poster beds. The facilities on offer are those of a luxury modern hotel: internet access, satellite TV, Jacuzzi, gym, sauna and secure parking, plus a tennis court, table tennis and a pool in the garden. Golf is available nearby. Gastronomic cuisine is on offer at the restaurant.
🅒 Closed in Jan
🅥 €150–€360, excluding breakfast
🅘 30 rooms, 5 apartments
🅒 🅐 Outdoor 🆅

SAULT

HOSTELLERIE DU VAL DE SAULT

Route de St-Trinit, 84390 Sault
Tel 04 90 64 01 41
www.valdesault.com
Among pine trees and facing Mont Ventoux, this quiet three-star hotel has wonderful views. The rustic building has wooden floors and beamed ceilings. Bedrooms are simple yet the artful use of fabrics is warming. All have a private terrace. High-quality regional cuisine is served in the adjoining restaurant.
🅒 Closed Nov–end Mar
🅥 €150, excluding breakfast
🅘 11
🆅 🅐 Outdoor

VACQUEYRAS

DOMAINE DE LA PONCHE

84190 Vacqueyras
Tel 04 90 65 85 21
www.hotel-laponche.com
This 17th-century cottage is in a park dotted with cypress and olive trees. Beamed ceilings and a tiled floor set the tone of the interior. Each spacious, comfortable bedroom has a personalized detail, such as a canopy bed or a fireplace. The hotel's restaurant serves excellent regional cuisine.
🅒 Closed in Jan
🅥 €105–€200, including breakfast
🅘 6
🅐 Outdoor

VAISON-LA-ROMAINE

HOSTELLERIE LE BEFFROI

Rue de l'Evêché, Cité Médiévale, 84110
Vaison-la-Romaine
Tel 04 90 36 04 71
www.le-beffroi.com
Housed in a 16th-century mansion and an adjoining building that dates from the 17th century, this three-star hotel certainly doesn't lack character. There are beamed ceilings, tiled floors and fine furniture. You'll have panoramic views of the medieval town of Vaison-la-Romaine from some of the

bedrooms, and from the terraced garden, where breakfast is served in good weather. Facilities include a restaurant and a garage, plus satellite TV and minibar in the bedrooms.
🅥 €85–€130, excluding breakfast
🅘 22
🅐 Outdoor

HOTEL CHAINS

Name of Hotel Chain	Description	Website	Telephone
Best Western	The world's largest hotel consortium has 20 hotels in Provence.	www.bestwestern.com	0800 393 130 (UK) 800/780-7234 (US) 0800 904 490 (France)
Campanile	This chain of hotels with restaurants has nearly 50 establishments in Provence.	www.campanile.fr	0825 003 003 (France)
Châteaux & Hotels de France	An affiliation of luxury hotels and chateaux	www.chateaux-hotels.com	0820 354 725 (France)
Comfort Inn	This hotel chain claims 'luxury on a budget'.	www.comfortinn.com	0800 444 444 (UK) 877/424-6423 (US) 0800 912 424 (France)
Formule 1	Inexpensive out-of-town hotels, which have fixed-price rooms with up to 3 beds.	www.hotelformule1.com	0892 685 685 (France)
Golden Tulip	This Netherlands-based hotel group has a Golden Tulip (four-star) hotel in Monaco.	www.goldentulip.com	08705 300 200 (UK) 800/448-8355 (US)
Hilton	Quality worldwide chain with a hotel in Cannes.	www.hilton.com	08705 909 090 (UK) 800/HILTONS (US) 0800 907 546 (France)
Ibis	Hotels in this budget chain usually have a restaurant, bar and 24-hour reception.	www.ibishotel.com	0870 609 0963 (UK) 0892 686 686 (France)
Intercontinental/ Holiday Inn	The Intercontinental group includes a range of hotels from luxury Intercontinental through to Holiday Inn and Holiday Inn Express.	www.holiday-inn.com www.intercontinental.com	0800 405 060 (UK) 800/465-4329 (US) 0800 905 999 (France)
Kyriad	Comfortable, reasonably priced hotels.	www.kyriad.com	0825 003 003 (France)
Marriott	There is a Marriott hotel in Monaco.	www.marriott.com	0800 221 222 (UK) 888/236-2427 (US) 0800 908 333 (France)
Mercure	Choose from 3 grades—simple, enhanced comfort and refined.	www.mercure.com	0870 609 0965 (UK) 800/MERCURE (US) 0825 883 333 (France)
Novotel	Comfortable hotels, usually with good-sized bedrooms.	www.novotel.com	0870 609 0961 (UK) 800/NOVOTEL (US) 0825 884 444 (France)
Première Classe	Practical good-value hotels, which have rooms with up to 3 beds.	www.envergure.fr	0892 688 123 (France)
Radisson	There is a Radisson hotel in Nice.	www.radisson.com	0800 374 411 (UK) 888/201-1718 (US) 0800 916 060 (France)
Relais du Silence	This is an affiliation of peaceful, characterful hotels with good food.	www.silencehotel.com	01 44 49 90 00 (France)
Relais & Châteaux	A chain of smart hotels and chateaux.	www.relaischateaux.fr	01 42 99 80 80 (France)
Sofitel	Comfortable hotels with restaurants.	www.sofitel.com	0870 609 0964 (UK) 800/221-4542 (US) 0825 885 555 (France)

STAYING

Planning

BEFORE YOU GO

CLIMATE
● Long hot summers are the signature of Provence but winters can be bitter, especially in the mountains. Winds also play an important role: The strongest is the *mistral*, blowing south down the Rhône valley.
● There are sheltered microclimates, such as the coastal corniches near the Italian border.
● Mountain melt-water in spring and heavy rains in autumn mean there is a risk of flash floods, especially in the Rhône valley.

Enjoying the summer sun on a beach at St-Tropez

WHEN TO GO
● **Spring:** The days get longer and warmer and everything seems to be in bloom, including the flower fields that provide the raw materials for the perfume industry of Grasse. It is warm enough to take your lunchtime drinks on the terrace in April.
● **Summer:** Temperatures can rise to the mid 30s°C (93°F). School holidays in late July and August see families heading south from northern France, so make reservations for all types of accommodation. Roads are busy, particularly on the coast. Fire risk

in the forest is at its peak and some areas may be off-limits. On the plus side, all the facilities, from water sports to campsites, are open and festivals are in full swing. To escape the heat, head to the Alpes-de Haute-Provence.
● **Autumn:** High season ends when the children go back to school and Paris opens up again at the end of August. The heat tempers in September and early October but it is still warm. You can get a seat at the most popular restaurants and prices for hotel rooms drop a little. From mid-September, water sports stop and some artisans take a few weeks off, but it is *vendange* (picking time) in the vineyards.
Winter: Cool weather sets in during November, with snow arriving on high ground in early December (although the area around Nice rarely suffers snow). Inland, many restaurants and hotels close until spring and some coastal resorts empty. To avoid the dreaded *mistral*, which blows down the Rhône valley, head farther east to the Côte d'Azur.

TIMES ZONES

CITY	TIME DIFFERENCE	TIME AT 12 NOON IN FRANCE
Amsterdam	0	12 noon
Berlin	0	12 noon
Brussels	0	12 noon
Chicago	-7	5am
Dublin	-1	11am
Johannesburg	+1*	1pm
London	-1	11am
Madrid	0	12 noon
Montréal	-6	6am
New York	-6	6am
Perth, Australia	+7*	7pm
Rome	0	12 noon
San Francisco	-9	3am
Sydney	+9*	9pm
Tokyo	+8*	8pm

Clocks in France go forward one hour on the last Sunday in March, until the last Sunday in October.
* One hour less during French Summer Time.

WEATHER STATIONS

● Avignon 56m 184ft

Marseille 35m 115ft

Nice 10m 33ft

AVIGNON
TEMPERATURE
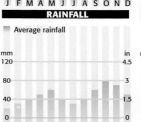
■ Average temperature per day per night

°C 30 20 10 0 — °F 86 68 50 32
J F M A M J J A S O N D

RAINFALL
■ Average rainfall

mm 120 80 40 0 — in 4.5 3 1.5 0
J F M A M J J A S O N D

MARSEILLE
TEMPERATURE
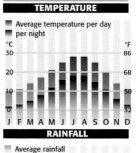
■ Average temperature per day per night

°C 30 20 10 0 — °F 86 68 50 32
J F M A M J J A S O N D

RAINFALL
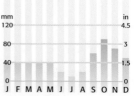
■ Average rainfall

mm 120 80 40 0 — in 4.5 3 1.5 0
J F M A M J J A S O N D

NICE
TEMPERATURE
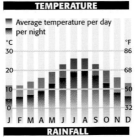
■ Average temperature per day per night

°C 30 20 10 0 — °F 86 68 50 32
J F M A M J J A S O N D

RAINFALL
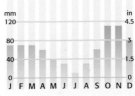
■ Average rainfall

mm 120 80 40 0 — in 4.5 3 1.5 0
J F M A M J J A S O N D

PLANNING

FRENCH EMBASSIES AND CONSULATES ABROAD		
COUNTRY	**ADDRESS**	**WEBSITE**
Australia	31 Market Street, St. Martin Tower, Level 26, Sydney, NSW 2000 tel 02 92 61 57 79	www.consulfrance-sydney.org
Canada	1 place Ville Marie, Bureau 2601, Montréal, Quebec, H3B 4S3 tel 514 878-4385	www.consulfrance-montreal.org
Ireland	36 Ailesbury Road, Ballsbridge, Dublin 4 tel 01 260 1666	www.ambafrance.ie
New Zealand	34–42 Manners Street, Wellington, 12th floor, PO Box 11-343 tel 644 384 25 55	www.ambafrance-nz.org
UK	21 Cromwell Road, London, SW7 2EN, tel 020 7073 1200	www.frenchembassy.org.uk
US (Los Angeles)	10990 Wilshire Boulevard, Suite 300, Los Angeles, CA 90024 tel 310/235 3200	www.consulfrance-losangeles.org
US (New York)	934 Fifth Avenue, New York, NY 10021 tel 212/606 3600	www.consulfrance-newyork.org

WHAT TO TAKE

● The key things to remember are passports, tickets, travel and health insurance documents, money, credit cards and any medication you'll need. If you plan to drive, take your driver's licence and, if using your own car, the vehicle registration and insurance certificates (▷ 42).

● If you go skiing, and in the sunnier months, you'll need sunscreen and sunglasses.

● You may like to take slightly more formal clothes for going out in the evening. Remember that when visiting churches you'll need to wear suitably modest attire.

● A small backpack or shoulder bag is useful for sightseeing. Bear in mind that these are attractive to pickpockets, so keep your money tucked away and an eye on your bag when you're in restaurants and other crowded places, especially in cities.

● Take the addresses and phone numbers of emergency contacts, including the numbers to call if your credit cards are stolen. Make photocopies of your passport, insurance documents and tickets, in case of loss. Keep a separate note of your credit card numbers in case you need to report a theft to the police.

● Visitors from the UK and US will need adaptors for electrical equipment (▷ 262).

● There is a language guide on pages 274–278 of this book, but if you wish to communicate in French you may find a separate phrase book helpful.

● A first-aid kit is a useful precaution.

● If you wear glasses, take a spare pair and your prescription.

● Bookstores in the cities sell English-language books, and newsstands sell English-language papers, but it is less expensive to bring your own reading material.

● Don't forget your camera! Film is widely available, but it is easier to take at least one roll with you.

PASSPORTS AND VISAS

● Entry requirements differ depending on your nationality and are also subject to change. Always check prior to a visit and follow news events that may affect your situation.

● UK, US and Canadian visitors need a passport, but not a visa, for stays of up to three months. You should have at least six months' validity remaining on your passport.

● For more information about visa and passport requirements, look up the French tourist office website (www.franceguide.com) or the French Embassy website (www.frenchembassy.org.uk or www.consulfrance-newyork.org).

● Take a photocopy of the relevant pages of your passport to carry around with you, so you can leave your actual passport in your hotel safe.

LONGER STAYS

● UK citizens who want to stay longer than three months may need to apply for a Carte de Séjour from the Préfecture de Police. US and Canadian visitors need a Carte de Séjour and a visa. For information call the Immigration Department of the French Consulate.

TRAVEL INSURANCE

● Make sure you have full health and travel insurance.

● EU nationals receive reduced-cost health treatment with the relevant documentation (form E111 or the EHIC for British visitors), but health and travel insurance is still advisable. For other visitors, full health insurance is a must.

● Check that your insurer has a 24-hour helpline.

CUSTOMS

From another EU country

Below are the guidelines for the quantity of goods you can bring to France from another EU country, for personal use:

- **800 cigarettes**
- **400 cigarillos**
- **200 cigars**
- **1 kg of smoking tobacco**

- **110 litres of beer**
- **10 litres of spirits**
- **90 litres of wine (of which only 60 litres can be sparkling wine)**
- **20 litres of fortified wine (such as port or sherry)**

From a country outside the EU

You are entitled to the allowances shown below only if you travel with the goods and do not plan to sell them.

- **200 cigarettes or**
  100 cigarillos or
  50 cigars or
  250g of tobacco

- **60cc/ml of perfume**

- **250cc/ml of eau de toilette**

- **2 litres of still table wine**
- **1 litre of spirits or strong liqueurs over 22% volume; or 2 litres of fortified wine, sparkling wine or other liqueurs**

- **Up to €175 of all other goods**

PLANNING

PRACTICALITIES

CAR RENTAL
- ▷ 47 for details of car rental companies.
- ▷ 42–47 for information on driving in France.

CHILDREN
- The French *autoroute* system has service stations at intervals of approximately 40km (25 miles), which sell food and have recreation areas. At intervals of about 10km (6 miles), there are *aires*, rest stops with toilets and recreation areas but no food or fuel, good for restless children to run around.
- Most restaurants welcome children, although not many have high chairs, and children's menus are not common outside family-friendly resorts, so it's probably best to aim for family-style bistros where facilities are better and staff are more helpful.
- If you need special facilities in your hotel, such as a cot, or a child seat in your rented car, reserve them in advance.
- For baby-changing facilities while out and about, try the rest rooms in department stores and the larger museums.
- Supermarkets and pharmacies sell nappies (diapers) and baby food, although they are often closed on Sunday so make sure you stock up.
- Entrance to museums is often free to young children.
- Don't underestimate the power of the Provençal sun. Make sure children wear a hat and sunscreen. Carry clothing to cover shoulders, arms and legs.

ELECTRICITY
- Voltage in France is 220 volts. Sockets take plugs with two round pins. UK electrical equipment will need an adaptor plug, which you can buy at airport terminals. American appliances using 110–120 volts will need an adaptor and a transformer. Equipment that is dual voltage should need only an adaptor.

LAUNDRY
- There are two options if you need a laundry service—a *laverie automatique* (laundrette) and a *pressing/nettoyage à sec* (dry-cleaners). Dry-cleaners are easier to find, but are more expensive. Some have an economy service, but this is not recommended for your best silk jacket.

LOCAL WAYS
- Greetings are often quite formal in France. Offer to shake hands when you are introduced to someone, and use *vous* rather than *tu*. It is polite to use *Monsieur, Madame or Mademoiselle* when speaking to people you don't know. For very young women and teenage girls use *Mademoiselle*; otherwise use *Madame*.
- The continental kiss is a

Café culture is part of French life

CONVERSION CHART		
FROM	**TO**	**MULTIPLY BY**
Inches	Centimetres	2.54
Centimetres	Inches	0.3937
Feet	Metres	0.3048
Metres	Feet	3.2810
Yards	Metres	0.9144
Metres	Yards	1.0940
Miles	Kilometres	1.6090
Kilometres	Miles	0.6214
Acres	Hectares	0.4047
Hectares	Acres	2.4710
Gallons	Litres	4.5460
Litres	Gallons	0.2200
Ounces	Grams	28.35
Grams	Ounces	0.0353
Pounds	Grams	453.6
Grams	Pounds	0.0022
Pounds	Kilograms	0.4536
Kilograms	Pounds	2.205
Tons	Tonnes	1.0160
Tonnes	Tons	0.9842

CLOTHING SIZES
Clothing sizes in France are in metric. Use the chart below to convert the size you use at home.

UK	Metric	US	
36	46	36	SUITS
38	48	38	
40	50	40	
42	52	42	
44	54	44	
46	56	46	
48	58	48	
7	41	8	SHOES
7.5	42	8.5	
8.5	43	9.5	
9.5	44	10.5	
10.5	45	11.5	
11	46	12	
14.5	37	14.5	SHIRTS
15	38	15	
15.5	39/40	15.5	
16	41	16	
16.5	42	16.5	
17	43	17	
8	36	6	DRESSES
10	38	8	
12	40	10	
14	42	12	
16	44	14	
18	46	16	
20	46	18	
4.5	37.5	6	SHOES
5	38	6.5	
5.5	38.5	7	
6	39	7.5	
6.5	40	8	
7	41	8.5	

PLANNING

common form of greeting between friends, and the number of times friends kiss each other on the cheek varies from region to region.
● Address waiters and waitresses as *Monsieur, Madame* or *Mademoiselle* when you are trying to attract their attention. Never use *garçon*.
● Communicating in French is always the best option, even if you can manage only *bonjour, s'il vous plaît* and *merci*. The French are protective of their language and your efforts to speak it will be appreciated. If your knowledge of French is limited, ask the fail-safe *Parlez-vous anglais?* and hope the answer is *oui*.
● Remember that it is traditional to say hello as you enter a shop, bar or café, particularly in small towns and villages, and that you are greeting your fellow customers as well as the proprietor. For a mixed audience, a *bonjour Messieurs Dames* is the appropriate phrase. When it is your turn to be served, greet the server with *Bonjour Madame* or *Bonjour Monsieur;* then don't forget to say *merci* and *au revoir* or *bonne-journée* as you leave.
● The hill villages of Provence still carry on the tradition of the siesta between lunchtime and 3pm.

MEASUREMENTS
● France uses the metric system. Road distances are measured in kilometres, fuel is sold by the litre and food is weighed in grams and kilograms.

PLACES OF WORSHIP
● Some of the most magnificent buildings in Provence are the great cathedrals found in the major cities and the tiny parish churches in towns and villages. They have become so popular as visitor attractions that it's easy to forget that they are still active places of worship. As such, it's important to respect these churches and the people who worship in them by dressing appropriately. Men should wear long trousers rather than shorts and should avoid sleeveless shirts. Women should keep their knees and shoulders covered and men should remove hats on entering the building.
● Take photos only if it is permitted and don't forget to turn off your mobile phone.

● Every town and village in France has its Roman Catholic church, usually at the physical heart of the community as well as the spiritual heart.
● There are Anglican churches around Nice and Monte-Carlo.
● Avignon, Carpentras, Cavaillon, Nice and Marseille are among the places with synagogues.
● There are mosques along the coast and in larger cities, including Marseille.

Dress appropriately when visiting churches

SMOKING AREAS
● Smoking is banned in public places such as cinemas, buses and Métro stations.
● By law, restaurants and cafés should provide a non-smoking section, although in reality it can be difficult to find a dining room, bar or café that is smoke-free.
● Some taxis display a no-smoking sign.

TICKETS
● Tourist information offices in French cities often sell a pass that gives entry to the main sights at a reduced rate. It's worth investing in one of these if you plan on spending a few days in one city.
● The French Riviera Museum Pass entitles you to entry to 65 of the region's museums and attractions. The cards are valid for 1 day, 3 consecutive days or 7 days within a 15 day period, so you can spread your sightseeing. Buy them from the tourist offices at Nice or Cannes, or from participating museums.
● For information on bus and rail tickets ▷ 39–41, 48–50.
● Students with an International Student Identity Card (ISIC) and seniors get reduced-price entry at some museums.

● For information on show and concert tickets ▷ 172.

TOILETS
● France's modern unisex public toilets are a vast improvement on previous facilities. Coin-operated and self-cleaning, you can find them in most large cities.
● In smaller towns and villages, free public toilets can normally be found by the market square or near tourist offices, although cleanliness varies.
● The two most reliable options are to take advantage of facilities in museums or other visitor attractions (almost always well maintained) or in restaurants and cafés, though you should be a customer to use the facilities, so be sure to buy a drink.
● Ask for *les toilettes*.

VISITORS WITH DISABILITIES
● France has made great headway in recent years in providing access and facilities for visitors with disabilities. All new buildings must take the needs of people with special requirements into account, and, where possible, existing buildings such as town halls, airports and train stations must be adapted with ramps and automatic doors.
● However, some tourist offices, museums and restaurants that are in historic, protected buildings are still not fully accessible. A telephone call before going to a restaurant is a good idea to arrange for an easily accessible table.
● The Association des Paralysés de France (*17 boulevard Auguste Blanqui, 75013, Paris; 01 40 78 69 00; www.apf.asso.fr*) provides information on wheelchair access. For other organizations that give advice to people with disabilities ▷ 52.

Facilities for those with disabilities are improving

MONEY MATTERS

THE EURO
● France is one of 12 European countries that have adopted the euro as their official currency. Euro notes and coins were introduced in January 2002, replacing the former currency, the French franc.

BEFORE YOU GO
● It is advisable to use a combination of cash, traveller's cheques and credit cards rather than relying on only one means of payment during your trip.
● Check with your credit or debit card company that your card can be used to withdraw cash from Automatic Teller Machines (ATMs) in France. It is also worth checking what fee will be charged for this and what number you should call if your card is stolen.

TRAVELLER'S CHEQUES
● Traveller's cheques are a safer way of bringing in money as you can claim a refund if they are stolen—but be aware that commissions can be high when you cash them.

ATMS
● ATMs are common in France, often with on-screen instructions in a choice of languages. Among the cards accepted are Visa, MasterCard and Diners Club. You'll need a four-digit PIN number.
● Your card issuer may charge you for withdrawing cash.

BANKS
● Hours vary, but usual opening hours are Monday to Friday 8.30 or 9–12 and 2–5, although banks in cities may not close for lunch.
● In smaller towns and villages banks often close on Mondays but open on Saturday mornings instead.
● Banks close at noon on the day before a national holiday, as well as on the holiday itself. Only banks with *change* signs change traveller's cheques or foreign currency and you'll need your passport to do this.

BUREAUX DE CHANGE
● Bureaux de Change have longer opening hours than banks, but the exchange rates may not be so good. You'll find them in all the major cities across Provence.
● Avoid changing large amounts of traveller's cheques at hotels, as the rates may not be competitive.

Look for the 'change' sign if you want to exchange money

BANKNOTES AND COINS

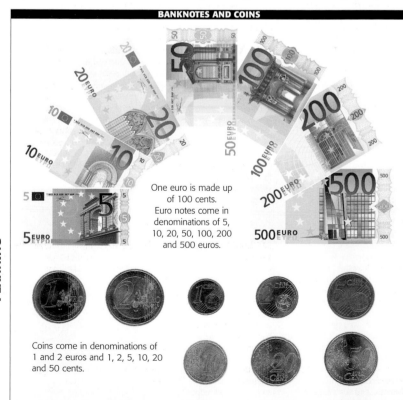

One euro is made up of 100 cents. Euro notes come in denominations of 5, 10, 20, 50, 100, 200 and 500 euros.

Coins come in denominations of 1 and 2 euros and 1, 2, 5, 10, 20 and 50 cents.

PLANNING

Most ATMs have instructions in a choice of languages

TIPPING GUIDE

Restaurants (service included)	Change *
Hotels (service included)	Change *
Cafés (service included)	Change *
Taxis	10 per cent
Tour guides	€1–€1.50
Porters	€1
Hairdressers	€1
Cloakroom attendants	30c
Toilets	Change

* Or more if you are impressed with
the level of service

CONCESSIONS

● If you are a student or teacher, apply to the International Student Travel Confederation (*www.isic.org*) in your own country for an International Student Identity Card (ISIC). This entitles you to various discounts during your visit.

● Seniors often get reduced rate tickets on public transportation and on admission to museums and sights by showing a valid identity card or passport.

● Younger children often have free entry to sights.

CREDIT CARDS

● Most restaurants, shops and hotels accept credit cards, although some have a minimum spending limit.

POST OFFICES

● Most post offices have ATMs.
● Cards accepted are listed on each ATM, and instructions are available in English.
● Money can be wired, through Western Union, via most post offices.
● International Money Orders can be sent from all post offices (a charge is applied).
● Most post offices offer exchange services in the

following currencies: American, Australian and Canadian dollars, the yen, British pound sterling, Swiss francs and Swedish, Danish and Norwegian kroners.

TAXES

● Non-EU residents can claim a sales-tax refund (*détaxe*) of 12 per cent on certain purchases, although you must have spent more than €175 in one shop, at one time.

● Ask the store for the relevant forms, which the store should complete and stamp. Give these forms to customs when you leave the country, along with the receipts, and they will be stamped. Send the forms back to the shop and they will either refund your credit card account or send you a cheque.

● Remember that you may have to show the goods to Customs when you leave France, so keep them within easy reach.

● Exempt products include food and drink, medicine, tobacco, unset gems, works of art and antiques.

● The company Global Refund offers a reimbursement service (*01 41 61 51 51; www.globalrefund.com*).

WIRING MONEY

● In an emergency, you can have money wired to you from your home country, but this can be expensive (as agents charge a fee for the service) and time-consuming.

● You can send and receive money via agents such as Western Union (*www.westernunion.com*) and Travelex (*www.travelex.fr*).

● Money can be wired from bank to bank, which takes up to two working days, or through Travelex and Western Union, which is normally faster.

TIPS

● Try to avoid using higher denomination notes when paying taxi drivers and when buying low-cost items in smaller shops.
● Never carry money or credit cards in back pockets, or other places that are easy targets for thieves.
● Keep your spare money and traveller's cheques in your hotel safe (*coffre-fort*) until you need them.
● Check the exchange rates for traveller's cheques and cash offered in post offices as well as in banks, as banks do not always offer the best rate.
● In France, Mastercard is sometimes known as Eurocard and Visa is known as Carte Bleue.
● Some smaller hotels and inns don't accept credit cards, so find out before you check in.

PRICES OF EVERYDAY ITEMS

Takeout sandwich		€2.20–€3.20
Bottle of mineral water	(from a shop, 0.5 litres)	€0.20–€0.40
Cup of coffee	(from a café, espresso)	€1–€1.85
	(*Crème*, larger cup with milk)	€1.85–€2.25
Beer	(*Un demi*, half a litre)	€1.85–€2.60
Glass of house wine		€1.85–€2.15
French national newspaper		€1–€1.20
International newspaper		€1.50–€2.30
Litre of petrol	(98 unleaded)	€1.13
	(diesel)	€0.81
Camera film	(36 pictures)	€7–€8
20 cigarettes	(on average)	€3.50

PLANNING

HEALTH

BEFORE YOU GO

● EU citizens receive reduced-cost healthcare in France (but not Monaco) with the relevant documentation. For UK citizens, this is the E111 form, which must be stamped by the post office before you travel. (This is due to be replaced by the EHIC in 2006.) Bring a photocopy with you as well as the original, as this will be kept by the hospital or doctor. Full health insurance is still strongly advised. For all other countries full insurance is a must.

● Make sure you are up to date with anti-tetanus boosters. Bring any medication you need with you and pack a first aid kit. In summer, bring sunscreen.

IF YOU NEED TREATMENT

● The French national health system is complex. Any salaried French citizen who receives treatment by a doctor or public hospital can be reimbursed by up to 70 per cent. The same is true if you are an EU citizen and have a valid E111 form or EHIC.

● If you are relying only on the E111/EHIC, rather than travel insurance, make sure the doctor you see is part of the French national health service (a *conventionné*), rather than the private system, otherwise you may face extra charges. In any case, you will have to pay up front for the consultation and treatment. To reclaim part of these costs, send the *feuille de soins* (a statement from the doctor) and your E111 to the Caisse Primaire d'Assurance-Maladie (state health insurance office) before you leave the country. Call 0820 904 175 to find the nearest office. You should also attach labels of any medicine you have to buy.

● If you have to stay overnight in a public hospital, you will have to pay 25 per cent of the treatment costs, as well as a daily charge

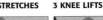
● Visitors to France from as far as the US, Australia or New Zealand may be concerned about the effect of long-haul flights on their health. The most widely publicized concern is Deep Vein Thrombosis, or DVT. Misleadingly called 'economy class syndrome', DVT is the forming of a blood clot in the body's deep veins, particularly in the legs. The clot can move around the bloodstream and could be fatal.

● Those most at risk include the elderly, pregnant women, those using the contraceptive pill, smokers and the overweight. If you are at increased risk of DVT see your doctor before departing. Flying increases the likelihood of DVT because passengers are often seated in a cramped position for long periods of time and may become dehydrated.

To minimize risk:

Drink water (not alcohol)
Don't stay immobile for hours at a time
Stretch and exercise your legs periodically
Do wear elastic flight socks, which support veins and reduce the chances of a clot forming

EXERCISES

1 ANKLE ROTATIONS   **2 CALF STRETCHES**   **3 KNEE LIFTS**

Lift feet off the floor. Draw a circle with the toes, moving one foot clockwise and the other counterclockwise

Start with heel on the floor and point foot upward as high as you can. Then lift heels high, keeping balls of feet on the floor

Lift leg with knee bent while contracting your thigh muscle. Then straighten leg, pressing foot flat to the floor

Other health hazards for flyers are airborne diseases and bugs spread by the plane's air-conditioning system. These are largely unavoidable but if you have a serious medical condition seek advice from a doctor before flying.

(*forfait journalier*). These are not refundable. It is far better to have full health insurance than to rely solely on the E111 form.

● Citizens of non-EU countries must have full health insurance.

● If you are hospitalized and have insurance, ask to see

PUBLIC HOSPITALS		
NAME	**ADDRESS**	**TELEPHONE**
Hôpital Les Broussailles	13 avenue Broussailles, 06400 Cannes	Tel 04 93 69 70 00
Hôpital St-Roch	5 rue Pierre Dévoluy, 06006 Nice	Tel 04 92 03 33 33
Centre Hospitalier du Pays d'Aix	Avenue Tamaris, 13100 Aix-en-Provence	Tel 04 42 33 50 00
Hôpital de la Timone	264 rue St Pierre, 13005 Marseille	Tel 04 91 38 60 00
Hôpital Général Joseph Imbert	Quartier Haute de Fourchon, 13200 Arles	Tel 04 90 49 29 22
Centre Hospitalier Général	305 rue Raoul Follereau, 84000 Avignon	Tel 04 32 75 33 33

OPTICIANS	
It's always a good idea to pack a spare pair of glasses or contact lenses and your prescription, in case you lose or break your main pair.	
NAME	**WEBSITE**
Opticiens Krys	www.krys.com
Lissac Opticien	www.lissac.com
Alain Afflelou	www.alainafflelou.com
Optical Center	www.optical-center.com
Optic 2000	www.optic2000.fr

the *assistante sociale* to arrange reimbursement of the costs through your insurers.

● In an emergency, dial 15 for the *Service d'Aide Médicale d'Urgence* (SAMU) unit (ambulance). They work closely with hospital emergency units and are accompanied by trained medical personnel.

● If you are able to get yourself to a hospital, make sure it has an emergency department (*urgences*).

FINDING A DOCTOR
● You can find a doctor (*médecin*) by asking at your hotel, a pharmacy or the town hall. Appointments are usually made in advance, but few doctors will refuse to see an emergency case.

● Emergency house calls (24-hours) can be arranged in the Marseille area by calling SOS Médecins (tel 04 91 52 91 52). Otherwise call 15 for emergencies or SOS Help (tel 01 46 21 46 46) for practical help in English.

FINDING A HOSPITAL
● Hospitals are listed in the phone book under *hôpitaux* and round-the-clock emergency services are called *urgences*.

● Private hospitals are a lot more expensive than public ones and treatment is not necessarily better. If you choose a private

hospital, check that you are covered for the costs before receiving treatment.

DENTAL TREATMENT
● EU citizens can receive reduced-cost emergency dental treatment with form E111, although insurance is still advised. The procedure for reclaiming money is the same as for general medical treatment.

● Other visitors should check their insurance covers dental treatment.

PHARMACIES
● A pharmacy (*pharmacie*) will have an illuminated green cross outside. Most are open Mon–Sat 9–7 or 8, but they usually post on the door details of another pharmacy that is open later (called the *pharmacie de garde*).

● Pharmacists are highly qualified and provide first aid, as well as supplying medication (some drugs are by prescription, or *ordonnance,* only). But they cannot dispense prescriptions written by doctors outside the French health system, so bring sufficient supplies of any prescribed drugs you need.

● Pharmacists also sell a range of health-related items, although it is less expensive to go to the supermarket for items such as soap, toothbrushes and razors.

● Some commonly used medicines sold in supermarkets

at home (such as aspirins and cold remedies) can only be bought in pharmacies in France.

TAP WATER
● Tap water is safe to drink and restaurants will often bring a carafe of water to the table, although most French people opt for bottled water.

● In public places look for the sign *eau potable* (drinking water). Don't drink from anything marked *eau non potable*.

LOCAL HAZARDS
● The sun can be strong so pack a high-factor sun block. You may also like to take insect repellent, although the insect bites you get in France are more likely to be irritating than dangerous.

● If you are planning on any high-altitude walks, take plenty of water, warm clothing and check weather reports before you go.

● Recent hot dry summers have led to forest fires in some areas. The nearest tourist office should be able to tell you whether the area you intend to visit is at risk. At times of high risk some roads and trails may be closed.

● Don't pick and eat wild mushrooms as some varieties are poisonous.

ALTERNATIVE MEDICINE
● Alternative medicine, such as homeopathy, is available from most pharmacies.

● Alternative treatment is on the increase, although chiropractic and reflexology are not widespread. Useful websites include www.chiropratique.org (the Association Française de Chiropratique), www.aea-org.com (Association Europe Acupuncture) and www.naturosante.com (a site about alternative medical treatments).

USEFUL NUMBERS
Emergency medical aid/ambulance
15
General emergencies
112
Police
17
Fire (Pompiers)
18
SOS Help (English crisis information hotline. Daily 3pm–11pm)
01 46 21 46 46

Pharmacies have an illuminated green cross outside

FINDING HELP

Most visits to Provence are trouble-free, but make sure you have adequate insurance to cover any health emergencies, thefts or legal costs that may arise. If you do become a victim of crime, it is most likely to be at the hands of a pickpocket, so keep your money and mobile phone safely tucked away. Petty crime is high in Provence compared with most of the rest of France, especially in the resorts.

PERSONAL SECURITY

● Make a note of your traveller's cheque numbers and keep it separate from the cheques themselves, as you will need it to make a claim in case of loss.

● Don't keep wallets, purses or mobile phones in the back pockets of trousers, or anywhere else that is easily accessible to thieves. Money belts and bags worn around the waist are targets, as thieves know you are likely to have valuables in them. Keep an eye on your bags in restaurants and bars and on trains. Carry shoulder bags across your chest to foil thieves on scooters who grab bags as they pass by.

● Thieves and pickpockets are especially fond of crowded trains, airports, rail stations, markets and beaches. Beware if someone bumps into you—it may be a ploy to distract you while someone else snatches your money.

● If you are the victim of theft, you must report it at the local police station (*commissariat*) if you want to make a claim on your insurance. Keep the statement the police give you. Contact your credit card company as soon as possible to cancel any stolen cards.

● Keep valuable items in your hotel safe (*coffre-fort*).

● Theft of cars and theft from cars are significant problems in some parts of Provence. When you park your car, don't leave anything of value inside. It's even risky to leave anything in view that could attract the attention of a thief. Carry your belongings with you or leave them in your hotel.

LOSS OF PASSPORT

● Always keep a separate record of your passport number and a photocopy of the page that carries your details, in case of loss or theft. You can also scan the relevant pages of your passport and then e-mail them to yourself at a secure e-mail account that you can access anywhere.

● If you do lose your passport or it is stolen, report it to the police and then contact your nearest embassy or consulate.

POLICE

● There are various types of police officer in France. The two main forces are the *Police Nationale,* who are under the control of the local mayor, and the *Gendarmerie Nationale,* who you often see at airports.

● You are likely to encounter the armed CRS riot police only at a demonstration.

● The police have wide powers of stop and search. It is wise to carry a photocopy of your passport in case a police officer requests your ID.

FIRE

● The French fire department deals with a number of emergencies in addition to fires. These range from stranded cats to road accidents and gas leaks. They are trained to give first aid.

HEALTH EMERGENCIES
▷ 266–267.

MAIN POLICE STATIONS IN PROVENCE		
PLACE	**ADDRESS**	**TELEPHONE**
Marseille	171 avenue Toulon, 13010	Tel 04 91 32 35 00
Nice	1 avenue Maréchal Foch, 06000	Tel 04 92 17 22 22
Arles	1 boulevard des Lices, 13200	Tel 04 90 18 45 00
Avignon	Boulevard St-Roch, 84000	Tel 04 90 16 81 00
Cannes	1 avenue de Grasse, 06400	Tel 04 93 06 22 22
St-Tropez	Rue François Sibilli, 83990	Tel 04 94 56 60 30
Aix-en-Provence	28 avenue Henri Malacrida, 13100	Tel 04 42 26 31 96
Nîmes	16 avenue Feuchères, 30000	Tel 04 66 28 33 00
Toulon	1 avenue Commissaire Morandin, 83100	Tel 04 98 03 53 00

CONSULATES IN PROVENCE		
COUNTRY	**ADDRESS**	**WEBSITE**
Canada	Rue Lamartine, 06000 Nice; tel 04 93 92 93 22 1 avenue Henry Dunnant, Monaco; tel 377 97 70 62 42	www.amb-canada.fr
Germany	La Minotaure, 34 avenue Henry Matisse, 06200 Nice; tel 04 93 83 55 25 338 avenue du Prado, Marseille; tel 04 91 16 75 20	www.amb-allemagne.fr
Ireland	152 boulevard J. F. Kennedy, 06610 Cap d'Antibes; tel 04 93 61 50 63	
Italy	Boulevard Gambetta, 06000 Nice; tel 04 92 14 40 90	www.amb-italie.fr
Spain	20 boulevard des Moulins, Monaco; tel 377 93 30 24 98	www.amb-espagne.fr
UK	24 avenue du Prado, Marseille; tel 04 91 15 72 10 26 avenue Notre-Dame, 06000 Nice; tel 04 93 62 13 56	www.amb-grandebretagne.fr
US	7 avenue Gustave V, 06000 Nice; tel 04 93 88 89 55 Boulevard Paul Peytral, 13006 Marseille; tel 04 91 54 92 00	www.amb-usa-fr

PLANNING

COMMUNICATION

TELEPHONING

French numbers Numbers have 10 digits. France is divided into five regional zones, indicated by the first two digits of the phone number. You must dial these two digits even if you are calling from within the zone. Numbers in Provence begin with 04. Monaco numbers have the prefix 377.

International Calls To call France

GUIDE PRICES		
TYPE OF CALL	**INITIAL CHARGE**	**EACH FURTHER MINUTE**
Local, peak	€0.091 (1 min)	€0.033
Local, off-peak	€0.091 (1 min)	€0.018
National, peak	€0.112 (39 sec)	€0.091
National, off-peak	€0.112 (39 sec)	€0.061
Calling the UK, off-peak	€0.11 (15 sec)	€0.12
Calling the US, off-peak	€0.11 (27 sec)	€0.15

COUNTRY CODES FROM FRANCE	
Australia	00 61
Belgium	00 32
Canada	00 1
Germany	00 49
Ireland	00 353
Italy	00 39
Monaco	00 377
Netherlands	00 31
New Zealand	00 64
Spain	00 34
Sweden	00 16
UK	00 44
US	00 1

from the UK dial 00 33, then drop the first zero from the 10-digit number. To call the UK from France, dial 00 44, then drop the first zero from the area code. To call France from the US, dial 011 33, then drop the first zero from the number. To call the US from France, dial 00 1, followed by the number.

Call charges For calls within France, peak period is from 8am to 7pm, Monday to Friday. You'll save money if you call outside this time. Numbers beginning with 08 have special rates. 0800 or 0805 numbers are free. 0810 and 0811 numbers are local rate. Other 08 numbers cost more than national calls—sometimes considerably more. The prefixes 0893, 0898 and 0899 are

particularly expensive.

Directory For national directory assistance dial 12; for international assistance, dial 3212.

PAYPHONES

- Most public payphones in France use a phone card (*télécarte*) rather than coins. Buy these at post offices, *tabacs*, newsstands and France Telecom shops. They come in units of 50 or 120. Some phones accept credit cards, although this may make the calls more expensive. You do not need to pay to call the emergency services.
- The phone gives instructions in various languages—press the flag button to select your choice. If the phone has a blue bell sign, you can receive incoming calls.
- Public phones in cafés and restaurants use cards or coins or need to be switched on by staff and you pay after the call. They tend to be more expensive than public payphones. Check the rates for hotel phones, as they can be much higher than from a public payphone.

MOBILE PHONES

- Before you leave, contact your Customer Service department to find out if you have restrictions on making calls from France.
- Make sure the numbers pre-programmed in your phone book are in the international format.
- Check the call charges, which can rise dramatically when you use your phone abroad.
- Mobile phone numbers in France begin with 06.

SENDING A LETTER

- You can buy stamps (*timbres*) for a letter (*lettre*) or a postcard (*carte postale*) at post offices and *tabacs*. Write *par avion* (by air) on the envelope or postcard if sending overseas.
- If you want registered mail, ask at the post office for the letter to be sent *recommandé*. For a

parcel (*colis*), choose *prioritaire* (priority) or the less expensive but slower *économique*.

- Mailboxes are yellow and often have two sections, one for local addresses and one for further afield (*autres destinations*).

POST OFFICES

- Post offices (*bureaux de poste*) are well signposted. The postal service is known as La Poste.
- Opening hours are generally Monday to Friday 8–5 or 6, Saturday 8–12. Some branches close for lunch and some stay open longer. Queues are worst at lunchtime and late afternoon.
- Facilities usually include phone booths, photocopiers, fax (*télécopieur*) and, sometimes, internet access. Poste Restante services are available for a fee.

POSTAGE RATES FOR LETTERS	
Within France	€0.50
To Western Europe	€0.50
To Eastern Europe	€0.75
To America	€0.90
To Africa	€0.75
To Asia	€0.90
To Australia	€0.90

INTERNET ACCESS

- You'll find internet cafés in the major towns. Some hotels and libraries have internet terminals, as do many post offices.

LAPTOPS

- Most hotels of two stars and above provide modem access. Telephone charges will apply. Remember that you may need a modem plug adaptor.

OPENING TIMES

● Banks open Monday to Friday 9–12, 2–5, but this can vary. They close at 12 on the day before a national holiday, as well as on the holiday itself.

● Shops tend to close on Sundays, even chain stores. Family-owned shops may close also on Mondays, but are often open on Sunday until 12.30 or 1. Smaller shops often close 12–2. Bakers (*boulangeries*) open on Sunday mornings and supermarkets and hypermarkets are open Monday to Saturday and have long business hours, opening at about 9am and staying open until 9 or 10pm. Some also remain closed on Monday mornings. Shops in rural areas often close from 12–3.

● Museums are generally closed on Mondays if they are municipal museums, or Tuesdays if they are national museums. Most close at lunchtime (12–2), except in August. Entrance to some museums is free on the first Sunday of the month, although

this can lead to crowds. If you plan to travel a long distance to see a particular museum, call in advance as opening hours can be idiosyncratic (some museums open on public holidays and some do not, and the renovation craze has not helped).

● Post offices open Monday to Friday 8–5 or 6 on weekdays and 8–12 on Saturday. Small branches may close for lunch.

● Pharmacies are generally open Monday to Saturday 9–7.

They all display a list of local pharmacies that open later and on a Sunday.

● Restaurants usually serve lunch 12–2 or 2.30 and dinner 7.30–10 or 11. Restaurants away from resorts and major towns close earlier, often at around 9.30, and may close on Sunday evenings and one other day, often Monday. Brasseries tend to serve food all day. Some restaurants on the coast close from November to Easter.

Nice's Musée d'Art Moderne (below) and one of its exhibits

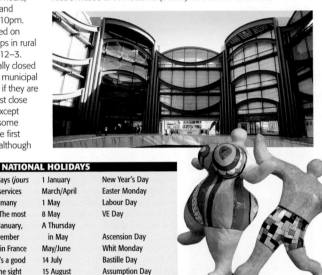

NATIONAL HOLIDAYS

France has 11 national holidays (*jours fériés*), when train and bus services are reduced and banks and many museums and shops close. The most steadfastly respected are 1 January, 1 May, 1 November, 11 November and 25 December. If you're in France during a national holiday, it's a good idea to call ahead to see if the sight you want to visit is open.

1 January	New Year's Day
March/April	Easter Monday
1 May	Labour Day
8 May	VE Day
A Thursday in May	Ascension Day
May/June	Whit Monday
14 July	Bastille Day
15 August	Assumption Day
1 November	All Saints' Day
11 November	Remembrance Day
25 December	Christmas Day

TOURIST OFFICES

FRENCH TOURIST OFFICES

Australia
Level 20, 25 Bligh Street, Sydney, NSW 2000
Tel 02 9231 5244; email: info.au@franceguide.com

Canada
1981 avenue McGill College, Suite 490, Montréal, H3A 2W9
Tel 514 876 9881;
email: mfrance@attcanada.net

Germany
Westendstrasse 47, 60325, Frankfurt;
Tel 0190 57 00 25 (€0.62 per min);
email: info.de@franceguide.com

Ireland
30 Merrion Street Upper, Dublin
Tel 15 60 235 235;
email: info.ie@franceguide.com

Italy
Via Larga 7, 20122, Milan
Tel 166 116 216 (€1.31 per min + IVA);
email: info.it@franceguide.com

Spain
Plaza de España 18, Torre de Madrid 8a
Pl. Of. 5, 28008, Madrid
Tel 906 34 36 38 (€0.35 per min);
email: es@franceguide.com

UK
178 Piccadilly, London, W1V 0AL
Tel 09068 244123 (60p per min);
email: info.uk@franceguide.com

US (New York)
444 Madison Avenue, 16th floor,
New York, NY 10022
Tel 212/838–7800;
email: info@francetourism.com

US (Los Angeles)
9454 Wilshire Boulevard, Suite 715,
90212, Beverly Hills, California
Tel 310/271–6665;
email: info@francetourism.com

PLANNING

USEFUL WEBSITES

www.aeroport.fr
Information on all of France's airports. (French)

www.angloinfo.com
A forum for English life on the Cote d'Azur, with English services and chatrooms.

www.crt-paca.fr
The website of the regional tourist organization for the French Riviera. You can order a range of brochures here or link to other sites.

www.fodors.com
A comprehensive travel-planning site that lets you research prices, reserve air tickets and put questions to fellow visitors. (English)

www.franceguide.com
Practical advice from the French Tourist Office on everything from arriving in France to buying a property. The site also has features on holidays and attractions. (French, English, German, Spanish, Italian, Dutch, Portuguese)

www.francetourism.com
The US website of the French Government Tourist Office. (English)

www.guideriviera.com
The tourist office website for the region has information on a range of attractions.

www.lemonde.fr
Catch up on current events on the site of *Le Monde* newspaper. (French)

www.meteo.fr/meteonet
Weather forecasts for France. (French, English and Spanish)

www.monum.fr
Information on France's most historic monuments. (French and English)

www.pagesjaunes.fr
France's telephone directory, online. (French and English)

www.provencebeyond.com
This website has information about Provence beyond the French Riviera.

www.provenceweb.fr
Packed with information, including links to online shopping for Provençal goods.

www.radio-france.fr
News, music and sport. (French)

www.skifrance.fr
Search for a resort, find out the latest snow conditions and see the slopes in real time via webcam. (English and French)

The internet can help you with anything from finding out about historic monuments, such as the Pont du Gard (below, left), to buying Provençal produce (right)

www.theAA.com
The AA website contains a route planner, helpful if you are driving in France. You can also order maps of the country. (English)

www.tourist-office.org
Details of every tourist office in France. (French)

Other websites are listed alongside the relevant sights and towns in The Sights section, and in the On the Move section.

KEY SIGHTS QUICK WEBSITE FINDER

Sight/Town	Website	Page
Aigues-Mortes	www.ot-aiguesmortes.fr	56
Aix-en-Provence	www.aixenprovencetourism.com	58–61
Antibes	www.antibes-juanlespins.com	102–104
Arles	www.tourisme.ville-arles.fr	62–65
Avignon	www.ot-avignon.fr	150–153
Les Baux-de-Provence	www.lesbauxdeprovence.com	66–67
Camargue	www.reserve-camargue.org	68–69
Cannes	www.cannes.com	107–108
Hyères	www.ot-hyeres.fr	94–95
Marseille	www.marseille-tourisme.com	72–78
Monaco	www.visitmonaco.com	129–136
Nice	www.nicetourism.com	117–121
Nîmes	www.ot-nimes.fr	80–82
Orange	www.provence-orange.com	160–161
Parc National du Mercantour	www.parc-mercantour.com	122–123
St-Rémy-de-Provence	www.saintremy-de-provence.com	84–86
St-Tropez	www.saint-tropez.st	98–99
Vaison-la-Romaine	www.vaison-la-romaine.com	166–168

MEDIA, BOOKS AND FILMS

TELEVISION

• France has five non-cable television stations: the nationally owned and operated channels 2 and 3, the privately owned 1 and 6, and the Franco-German ARTE (channel 5). Almost all the shows are in French. There are commercials on all these channels except ARTE.

• **TF1** has news, recent American and French films, soaps and shows.

• **France 2** has news, recent French and foreign films, soaps, shows and documentaries.

• **France 3,** a regional and national channel, has regional and national news, regional shows, documentaries, mostly French films and, once a week, a film in its original language.

• **ARTE** is a Franco-German channel with shows in French and German. International films are shown in their original language and there are also cultural documentaries.

• **M6** shows a lot of pop music videos, low-budget films and past American sitcoms and soaps. There are also some interesting documentaries.

• Digital television has now taken off in France. More than 100 channels are available either through satellite or cable.

• If the TV listings mention *VO* (*version originale*), the show or film will be in the language in which it was made, with French subtitles (Channel 3 usually screens a good film in *VO* every Sunday at around midnight).

• Note that French television channels do not always keep exactly to schedule.

• Most hotels have at least a basic cable service, which is likely to include BBC World and CNN. Cable channels now offer multilingual versions of some shows. Ask at your hotel how to use this option as the mechanics vary. The commercial-free ARTE usually offers a choice between French and German for its cultural shows.

RADIO

• French radio stations are available mainly on FM wave lengths, with a few international stations on Long Wave. Stations (with their Marseille frequencies) include:

• **Chérie FM:** 100.1 FM; French mainstream pop, news, reports.

• **France Infos:** 105.3 FM; news bulletins every 15 minutes.

• **France Musique:** 94.7 FM; classical and jazz music, concerts, operas, news.

• **NRJ:** 106.4 FM; French and International pop, techno, rap, R'n'B.

• **Radio Classique:** 100.9 FM; classical music.

• **Skyrock:** 90 FM; rap, hip-hop, R'n'B.

• **BBC Radio 4** 198 kHz MW; news, current affairs, drama.

• **BBC Five Live** 909 kHz MW; news and sport.

• **BBC World Service** morning and early afternoon 15485 kHz LW, evening 6195kHz and night 198kHz.

• **Riviera Radio** is an English-speaking station operating from Monaco. Frequencies are 106.5 FM in the Alpes-Maritimes and 106.3 FM in Monaco.

NEWSPAPERS

• In resorts and the major cities, you can buy the main British dailies, usually a day old, at a premium.

• *The Economist, USA Today* and *The Wall Street Journal* can be found at newsstands in cities, along with *The European,* which presents a pan-European perspective in English, and the *International Herald Tribune,* which reports international news from a US standpoint.

• You may be disappointed to find an international edition of your preferred paper rather than the one you would get at home.

• Local press plays an important part in the political sphere in France and there are several influential local newspapers

CABLE TV	
BBC Prime	With a mix of BBC shows, old and new
Canal+	Shows recent films (some in their original language)
MTV	Contemporary music channel
MCM	The French version of MTV
Eurosport or Infosport	For major sporting events
Planète	Nature and science documentaries
RAI Uno	Italian
TVE 1	Spanish
Euronews	A European all-news channel
LCI	All news in French
Canal Jimmy	Screens some British and American shows like *Friends* and *NYPD Blue* in English or multilingual versions
Paris Première	A cultural channel with some films in English
Canal J	With children's shows until 8pm
Téva	A women's channel that runs some English-language shows such as *Sex in the City*

NEWSPAPERS
French daily newspapers have clear political leanings.
Le Monde
This stately paper, left-of-centre, refuses to run photos and uses illustrations.
Libération
This lively youth-focused paper is more clearly leftist.
L'Humanité
Left wing.
Le Figaro
Mainstream conservative daily.
Le Parisien
This tabloid paper is written at a level of French that makes it fairly easy for non-native readers to understand.
Journal du Dimanche
Sunday newspaper.

PLANNING

published in Provence. City newspapers *La Marseillaise* and *Nice-Matin* are widely read beyond urban boundaries and reflect a southern perspective on national matters. *Département*-wide *Vaucluse* and *Var-Matin* include coverage of local issues, as does the cross-region *La Provence*.

● Local papers will normally have listings for the coming few days with movie, concert and exhibition information and contact details. Magazines with events listings include *Hello Nice* (in English) and *Proximité* (in French and English), both published monthly and available at tourist offices, and Avignon-based *Le Rendezvous*, produced monthly in English. You can pick up free listings magazines at tourist offices, music stores or cafés.

● Weekly news magazines include *Le Nouvel Observateur*, *Le Point* and *L'Express*.

● For women's fashions, options include *Elle*, *Vogue* or *Marie Claire*.

● When you want celebrity gossip and lots of pictures, buy *Paris Match*, *Voici* or *Gala*.

FILMS

● Watching a French film is a good way to get the feel of the place before you visit.

● For a classic, try *Les Enfants du Paradis* (1945) directed by Marcel Carné. For *nouvelle vague* (new wave) cinema often filmed with a hand-held camera—try *Jules et Jim* (1962) directed by François Truffaut and starring Jeanne Moreau, or *À Bout de Souffle* (1959), directed by Jean-Luc Godard. The surreal *Belle de Jour* (1967), starring Cathérine Deneuve, caused a scandal at the time due to its erotic subject matter. The 1987 weepie *Au Revoir les Enfants* tells the story of a Jewish boy in occupied France in World War II.

● No reference to French movies would be complete without mentioning Gérard Départdieu, the actor who conquered France and then Hollywood. His best known works include *Cyrano de Bergerac* (1990) and *Jean de Florette* (1986). The sequel to this, *Manon des Sources* (1986), stars Emmanuelle Béart, one of France's leading actresses.

● Jean-Pierre Jeunet's *Délicatessen* (1991) turns the

controversial subject of cannibalism into a black comedy.

● For a French feel with a Hollywood budget, watch a film directed by Luc Besson, such as *The Fifth Element* (1997) or *Léon* (1994), known for the understated performance of Jean Reno.

● Cannes hosts Europe's most prestigious film festival in May. It attracts top international actors, directors and producers, as well as hundreds of starlets and self-promoting wannabes whose antics contribute much to the atmosphere of the festival. Millions of euros of business is conducted during the 12 days of the festival. For more details, look up www.festival-cannes.fr.

● Studios de la Victoirine made Nice a player in the French and international cinema scene from 1920 until the 1960s.

● Watch out for some great Riviera mountain scenery in *Herbie Goes to Monte-Carlo* (1977), when the famed 'Love Bug' cruises the boulevards and races along the country lanes.

● *And God Created Woman* (1956) by Roger Vadim launched Brigitte Bardot onto the world stage and kick-started the

enduring reputation of St-Tropez.

● *To Catch a Thief* (1955) brought the pride of Hollywood to the Côte d'Azur in the form of Grace Kelly, Cary Grant and director Alfred Hitchcock. The film offers some great views of Monaco and the Riviera.

● Some scenes of the British film *Love Actually* (2003) were set in Provence.

BOOKS

● For those who prefer to find their atmosphere on the page, there is no shortage of choices.

● Books about Provence written from a foreigner's perspective have dominated the best-seller list over the last couple of decades. Peter Mayle's *A Year in Provence* (1989), charting the author's first months living in the area, kick-started the process, followed by the sequel, *Toujours Provence* (1991). English actress Carol Drinkwater recounts her Provençal experiences in *The Olive Farm* (2001) and *The Olive Season* (2003).

● While not autobiographical, *Voices in the Garden* (1981), by Dirk Bogarde, is set around Grasse, the British actor's French home. The story of emotional entanglement was brought to British and French television screens in 1991.

● Classic literature set in Provence includes some fine 20th-century works. Ernest Hemingway wrote much of *The Garden of Eden* (unfinished when he died and published in 1986) during a sojourn here. F. Scott Fitzgerald captures the essence of expat life on the Riviera in *Tender is the Night* (1934), which was partly inspired by his own life and social circle.

● The modern French classic *Bonjour Tristesse* (1954), a story of the flowering of a young Frenchwoman, by Françoise Sagan, is set on the Esterel Coast.

WORDS AND PHRASES

Even if you're far from fluent, it is always a good idea to try to speak a few words of French while in France. The words and phrases on the following pages should help you with the basics, from ordering a meal to dealing with emergencies.

CONVERSATION

I don't speak French.
Je ne parle pas français.

Do you speak English?
Parlez-vous anglais?

I don't understand.
Je ne comprends pas.

Please repeat that.
Pouvez-vous répéter?

Please speak more slowly.
Pouvez-vous parler plus lentement?

My name is…
Je m'appelle…

Hello, pleased to meet you.
Bonjour, enchanté(e).

I'm on holiday.
Je suis en vacances.

I live in …
J'habite à …

Good morning.
Bonjour.

Good evening.
Bonsoir.

Goodnight.
Bonne nuit.

Goodbye.
Au revoir.

See you later.
A plus tard.

May I/Can I?
Est-ce que je peux?

How are you?
Comment allez-vous?

I'm sorry.
Je suis désolé(e).

Excuse me.
Excusez-moi.

NUMBERS

1 un	6 six	11 onze	16 seize	21 vingt et un	70 soixante-dix
2 deux	7 sept	12 douze	17 dix-sept	30 trente	80 quatre-vingts
3 trois	8 huit	13 treize	18 dix-huit	40 quarante	90 quatre-vingt-dix
4 quatre	9 neuf	14 quatorze	19 dix-neuf	50 cinquante	100 cent
5 cinq	10 dix	15 quinze	20 vingt	60 soixante	1000 mille

SHOPPING

Could you help me, please?
(Est-ce que) vous pouvez m'aider, s'il vous plaît?

How much is this?
C'est combien?

I'm looking for …
Je cherche …

When does the shop open/close?
A quelle heure ouvre/ferme le magasin?

I'm just looking, thank you.
Je regarde, merci.

Do you accept credit cards?
(Est-ce que) vous acceptez les cartes de crédit?

This is the right size.
C'est la bonne taille.

Do you have anything less expensive/smaller/larger?
(Est-ce que) vous avez quelque chose de moins cher/plus petit/plus grand?

I'll take this.
Je prends ça.

Do you have a bag for this?
(Est-ce que) je peux avoir un sac, s'il vous plaît?

I'd like ….grams.
Je voudrais …grammes.

I'd like a kilo of …
Je voudrais un kilo de …

What does this contain?
Quels sont les ingrédients?

I'd like … slices of that.
J'en voudrais … tranches.

Bakery
Boulangerie

Bookshop
Librairie

Chemist
Pharmacie

Market
Marché

Sale
Soldes

Monday **lundi**	January **janvier**	August **août**	spring **printemps**	morning **matin**	day **le jour**
Tuesday **mardi**	February **février**	September **septembre**	summer **été**	afternoon **après-midi**	month **le mois**
Wednesday **mercredi**	March **mars**	October **octobre**	autumn **automne**	evening **soir**	year **l'année**
Thursday **jeudi**	April **avril**	November **novembre**	winter **hiver**	night **nuit**	
Friday **vendredi**	May **mai**	December **décembre**	holiday **vacances**	today **aujourd'hui**	
Saturday **samedi**	June **juin**		Easter **Pâques**	yesterday **hier**	
Sunday **dimanche**	July **juillet**		Christmas **Noël**	tomorrow **demain**	

HOTELS

Do you have a room?
(Est-ce que) vous avez une chambre?

I have a reservation for ... nights.
J'ai réservé pour ... nuits.

How much each night?
C'est combien par nuit?

Double room.
Une chambre pour deux personnes/double.

Twin room.
Une chambre à deux lits/ avec lits jumeaux.

Single room.
Une chambre à un lit/pour une personne.

With bath/shower/lavatory.
Avec salle de bain/ douche/WC.

Is there a lift in the hotel?
(Est-ce qu')il y a un ascenseur à l'hôtel?

Is the room air-conditioned?
(Est-ce que) la chambre est climatisée?

Is breakfast/lunch/dinner included in the cost?
(Est-ce que) le petit déjeuner/le déjeuner/le dîner est compris dans le prix?

Is room service available?
Il y a le service en chambre?

When do you serve breakfast?
À quelle heure servez-vous le petit déjeuner?

May I have breakfast in my room?
(Est-ce que) je peux prendre le petit déjeuner dans ma chambre?

Do you serve evening meals?
(Est-ce que) vous servez le repas du soir/le dîner?

The room is too hot/cold.
Il fait trop chaud/froid dans la chambre.

Will you look after my luggage until I leave?
Pouvez-vous garder mes bagages jusqu'à mon départ?

Is there parking?
(Est-ce qu') il y a un parking?

Do you have babysitters?
(Est-ce que) vous avez un service de babysitting?

Could I have another room?
(Est-ce que) je pourrais avoir une autre chambre?

Can I pay my bill?
(Est-ce que) je peux régler ma note, s'il vous plaît?

May I see the room?
(Est-ce que) je peux voir la chambre?

Swimming pool.
Piscine.

Sea view.
Vue sur la mer.

USEFUL WORDS

Yes **Oui**	There **Là-bas**	Who **Qui**	How **Comment**	Open **Ouvert**	Please **S'il vous plaît**
No **Non**	Here **Ici**	When **Quand**	Later **Plus tard**	Closed **Fermé**	Thank you **Merci**
	Where **Où**	Why **Pourquoi**	Now **Maintenant**		

PLANNING

WORDS AND PHRASES 275

Where is the information desk?
Où est le bureau des renseignements?

Where is the timetable?
Où sont les horaires?

Does this train/bus go to…?
Ce train/bus va à…?

Do you have a Métro/bus map?
Avez-vous un plan du Métro/des lignes de bus?

Train/bus/Métro station
La gare SNCF/routière/ la station de Métro.

Where can I buy a ticket?
Où est-ce que je peux acheter un billet/ticket?

Where can I reserve a seat?
Où est-ce que je peux réserver une place?

Please can I have a single/ return ticket to…?
Je voudrais un aller simple/ un aller-retour pour…, s'il vous plaît.

Is this seat free?
(Est-ce que) cette place est libre?

Do I need to get off here?
(Est-ce qu') il faut que je descende ici?

Where can I find a taxi?
Où est-ce que je peux trouver un taxi?

How much is the journey?
Combien coûte le trajet?

I'd like to rent a car.
Je voudrais louer une voiture.

No parking
Interdiction de stationner

I'm lost.
Je me suis perdu(e).

Is this the way to…?
C'est bien par ici pour aller à…?

Go straight on.
Allez tout droit.

Turn left/right
Tournez à gauche/à droite.

Cross over.
Traversez.

Traffic lights.
Les feux.

Intersection.
Carrefour.

Corner.
Coin.

Is there a bank/currency exchange office nearby?
(Est-ce qu') il y a une banque/un bureau de change près d'ici?

Can I cash this here?
(Est-ce que) je peux encaisser ça ici?

I'd like to change sterling/ dollars into euros.
Je voudrais changer des livres sterling/dollars en euros.

Can I use my credit card to withdraw cash?
(Est-ce que) je peux utiliser ma carte de crédit pour retirer de l'argent?

What is the exchange rate today?
Quel est le taux de change aujourd'hui?

brown	blue
marron/brun	**bleu(e)**
black	green
noir(e)	**vert(e)**
red	yellow
rouge	**jaune**

Where is the nearest post office/mail box?
Où se trouve la poste/la boîte aux lettres la plus proche?

How much is the postage to…?
A combien faut-il affranchir pour …?

I'd like to send this by air mail/ registered mail.
Je voudrais envoyer ceci par avion/en recommandé.

Can you direct me to a public phone?
Pouvez-vous m'indiquer la cabine téléphonique la plus proche?

What is the number for directory enquiries?
Quel est le numéro pour les renseignements?

Where can I find a telephone directory?
Où est-ce que je peux trouver un annuaire?

Where can I buy a phone card?
Où est-ce que je peux acheter une télécarte?

Please put me through to…
Pouvez-vous me passer …, s'il vous plaît?

Can I dial direct to …?
Est-ce que je peux appeler directement en …?

Do I need to dial 0 first?
Est-ce qu'il faut composer le zéro (d'abord)?

What is the charge per minute?
Quel est le tarif à la minute?

Have there been any calls for me?
Est-ce que j'ai eu des appels téléphoniques?

Hello, this is …
Allô, c'est … (à l'appareil).

Who is speaking please …?
Qui est à l'appareil, s'il vous plaît?

I would like to speak to …
Je voudrais parler à …

PLANNING

I'd like to reserve a table for ... people at ...
Je voudrais réserver une table pour ... personnes à ...heures, s'il vous plaît.

A table for ..., please.
Une table pour ..., s'il vous plaît.

Could we sit there?
(Est-ce que) nous pouvons nous asseoir ici?

Is this table taken?
(Est-ce que) cette table est libre?

Are there tables outside?
(Est-ce qu') il y a des tables dehors/à la terrasse?

Could we see the menu/wine list?
(Est-ce que) nous pouvons voir le menu/la carte des vins, s'il vous plaît?

Do you have nappy-changing facilities?
(Est-ce qu') il y a une pièce pour changer les bébés?

Where are the toilets?
Où sont les toilettes?

We'd like something to drink.
Nous voudrions quelque chose à boire.

Could I have bottled still/sparkling water?
(Est-ce que) je peux avoir une bouteille d'eau minérale/gazeuse, s'il vous plaît?

Is there a dish of the day?
(Est-ce qu') il y a un plat du jour?

I can't eat wheat/sugar/salt/pork/beef/dairy.
Je ne peux pas manger de blé/sucre/sel/porc/bœuf/produits laitiers.

What do you recommend?
Qu'est-ce que vous nous conseillez?

I am a vegetarian.
Je suis végétarien(ne).

I'd like...
Je voudrais ...

How much is this dish?
Combien coûte ce plat?

Is service included?
(Est-ce que) le service est compris?

Can I have the bill, please?
(Est-ce que) je peux avoir l'addition, s'il vous plaît?

The bill is not right.
Il y a une erreur sur l'addition.

The food was excellent.
Le repas était excellente.

Breakfast
Petit déjeuner

Lunch
Déjeuner

Dinner
Dîner

Coffee
Café

Tea
Thé

Orange juice
Jus d'orange

Apple juice
Jus de pomme

Milk
Lait

Beer
Bière

Red wine
Vin rouge

White wine
Vin blanc

Bread roll
Petit pain

Bread
Pain

Sugar
Sucre

Wine list
Carte/liste des vins

Main course
Le plat principal

Dessert
Dessert

Salt/pepper
Sel/poivre

Cheese
Fromage

Knife/fork/spoon
Couteau/Fourchette/Cuillère

Soups
Soupes/potages

Chicken soup
Soupe au poulet

Vegetable soup
Soupe de légumes

Lentil soup
Soupe aux lentilles

Mushroom soup
Soupe aux champignons

Sandwiches
Sandwichs

Ham sandwich
Sandwich au jambon

Dish of the day
Plat du jour

Fish dishes
Les poissons

Prawns
Crevettes roses/bouquet

Oysters
Huîtres

Salmon
Saumon

Haddock
Églefin

Squid
Calmar

Meat dishes
Viandes

Roast chicken
Poulet rôti

Casserole
Plat en cocotte

Roast lamb
Gigot

Potatoes
Pommes de terre

Green beans
Haricots verts

Peas
Petits pois

Carrots
Carottes

Spinach
Épinards

Onions
Oignons

Tomatoes
Tomates

Fruit
Les fruits

Apples
Pommes

Strawberries
Fraises

Peaches
Pêches

Pears
Poires

Pastry
Pâtisserie

Chocolate cake
Gâteau au chocolat

Cream
Crème

Ice cream
Glace

PLANNING

Where is the tourist information office, please?
Où se trouve l'office du tourisme, s'il vous plaît?

Do you have a city map?
Avez-vous un plan de la ville?

Where is the museum?
Où est le musée?

Can you give me some information about…?
Pouvez-vous me donner des renseignements sur …?

What are the main places of interest here?
Quels sont les principaux sites touristiques ici?

Please could you point them out on the map?
Pouvez-vous me les indiquer sur la carte, s'il vous plaît?

What sights/hotels/restaurants can you recommend?
Quels sites/hôtels/restaurants nous recommandez-vous?

We are staying here for a day.
Nous sommes ici pour une journée.

I am interested in…
Je suis intéressé(e) par…

Does the guide speak English?
Est-ce qu'il y a un guide qui parle anglais?

Do you have any suggested walks?
Avez-vous des suggestions de promenades?

Are there guided tours?
Est-ce qu'il y a des visites guidées?

Are there organised excursions?
Est-ce qu'il y a des excursions organisées?

Can we make reservations here?
Est-ce que nous pouvons réserver ici?

What time does it open/close?
Ça ouvre/ferme à quelle heure?

What is the admission price?
Quel est le prix d'entrée?

Is there a discount for senior citizens/students?
Est-ce qu'il y a des réductions pour les personnes âgées/ les étudiants?

Do you have a brochure in English?
Avez-vous un dépliant en anglais?

What's on at the cinema?
Qu'est-ce qu'il y a au cinéma?

Where can I find a good nightclub?
Où est-ce que je peux trouver une bonne boîte de nuit?

Do you have a schedule for the theatre/opera?
Est-ce que vous avez un programme de théâtre/ d'opéra?

Should we dress smartly?
Est-ce qu'il faut mettre une tenue de soirée?

What time does the show start?
A quelle heure commence le spectacle?

How do I reserve a seat?
Comment fait-on pour réserver une place?

Could you reserve tickets for me?
Pouvez-vous me réserver des billets?

I don't feel well.
Je ne me sens pas bien.

Could you call a doctor?
(Est-ce que) vous pouvez appeler un médecin/un docteur, s'il vous plaît?

Is there a doctor/pharmacist on duty?
(Est-ce qu') il y a un médecin/docteur/une pharmacie de garde?

I feel sick.
J'ai envie de vomir.

I need to see a doctor/dentist.
Il faut que je voie un médecin/docteur/ dentiste.

Please direct me to the hospital.
(Est-ce que) vous pouvez m'indiquer le chemin pour aller à l'hôpital, s'il vous plaît?

I have a headache.
J'ai mal à la tête.

I've been stung by a wasp/bee/jellyfish.
J'ai été piqué(e) par une guêpe/abeille/méduse.

I have a heart condition.
J'ai un problème cardiaque.

I am diabetic.
Je suivre diabétique.

I'm asthmatic.
Je suis asmathique.

I'm on a special diet.
Je suis un régime spécial.

I am on medication.
Je prends des médicaments.

I have left my medicine at home.
J'ai laissé mes médicaments chez moi.

I need to make an emergency appointment.
Je dois prendre rendez-vous d'urgence.

I have bad toothache.
J'ai mal aux dents.

I don't want an injection.
Je ne veux pas de piqûre.

Help!
Au secours!

I have lost my passport/ wallet/purse/handbag.
J'ai perdu mon passeport/ portefeuille/porte-monnaie/sac à main.

I have had an accident.
J'ai eu un accident.

My car has been stolen.
On m'a volé ma voiture.

I have been robbed.
J'ai été volé(e).

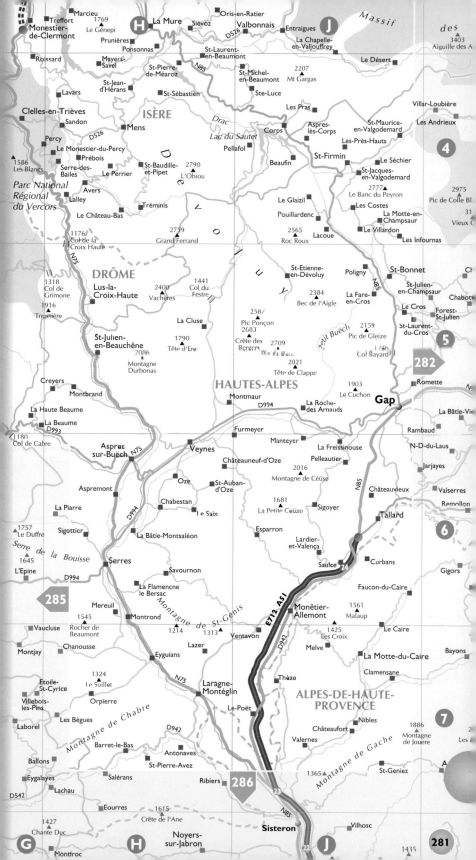

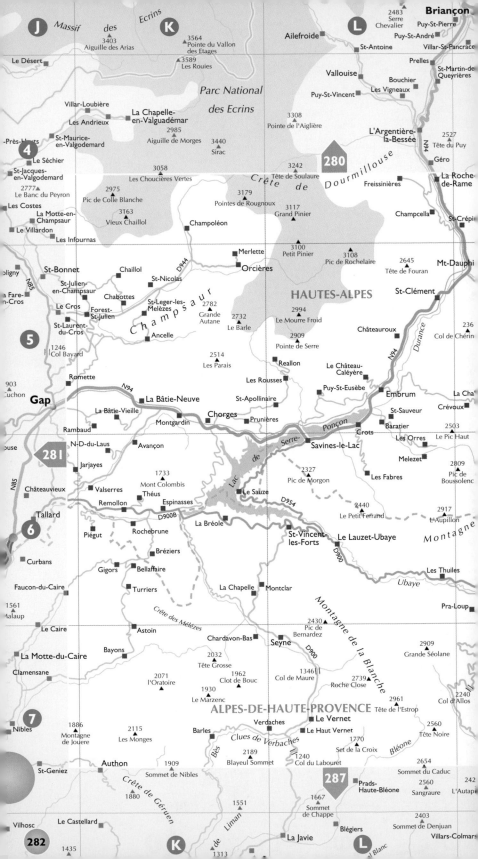

▲ 2634
Le Chenaillet

■ Cervières

3302
Bric Froid ▲

3286
Pic du
Grand Glaiza

3038
Grand Queyron ■

3325
Grand Pic
de Rochebrune ■

3083
Pic de Pic
Rochebrune ■

3216
Bric Bouchet ▲

2361
Col d'Izoard

■ La Chalp

■ Arvieux

Abriès ■

Aiguilles ■

Ristolas ■

L'Echalp ■

2912
Pic du Béal ▲
Traversier

Château-Queyras ■

2897
Pic du Fond
de Peinin ▲

2735 ▲
Monte Frioland

Q   u   e   y   r   a   s

Molines-en-
Queyras ■

Pierre-
Grosse ■

Fontgillarde ■

D947

D902

2454
Prachaval ▲

■ Montbardon

St-Véran ■

3211
Le Pain de Sucre ▲

3841 ▲
M Viso

Parc Régional
du Queyras

2846
Pointe de Rasis ▲

3176
Tête des Toillies ▲

3015 ▲
Cima delle Lobbie

■ Guillestre

soul

3035
Pointe de Saume ▲

3233
Péouvou ▲

3340
Bric de Rubren ▲

Ubaye

Vars ■

■ Ste-Marie

3387
Pic de la
Font Lauche ▲

2727
Pic de
abrières ▲

D902

3171
Dents de Maniglia ▲

2111
Col de Vars

■ Grande
Serenne

3411
Aiguille de
Chambeyron ▲

3071 ▲
Rocca la
Marchisa

I

St-Paul ■

3193
Roche Blanche ▲

2988
Grand
Parpaillon ▲

P a r p a i l l o n

■ Tournoux

St-Ours ■

Larche ■

3104 ▲
Tête de Moïse

2831 ▲
Rocca la Meja

3048
Grand Bérard ▲

■ La Condamine-
Châtelard

3032
Tête de Siguret ▲

1991
Col de Larche

■ Jausiers

2885
Tête de Fer ▲

-Pons

Faucon
D900 ●

Barcelonnette

M o n t a g n e   d e   l' A l p e

S e r r e   B o u r d o u x

2820 ▲

2955
Tête de l'Enchastraye ▲

SS21

Le Sauze ■

Super-Sauze ■

2678
Col de
Restefond

2727
Cime de Voga

2685
Le Chapeau
de Gendarme ▲

2802
Cime de la Bonette ▲

2942 ▲
Mont Vallonnet

■ Le Villard-d'Abas

839
Grand
heval
Bois ▲

Parc
National
du Mercantour

St-Dalmas-
le-Selvage ■

3031 ▲
Mont Ténibre

3051
Mont Pelat ▲

2327
Col de la Cayolle

2563 ▲
Mont Aunos

St-Etienne-
de-Tinée ■

D2205

2661 ▲
Tête de l'Autaret

Allos ●

2916
Pointe Côte
de l'Ane ▲

Auron ■

D908

2818
Cime de Pal ▲

2474 ▲
Les Donnes

Isola ■

Isola 2000

■ Clignon

▲ Entraunes

2468
Cime de l'Aspre

2673 ▲

M o n t a g n e   d e   l' A l p

ALPES-MARITIMES

2711 ▲
Mont St-Sauveur

Colmars

2817 ▲
Mont Mounier

St-Martin-
d'Entraunes ■

2434

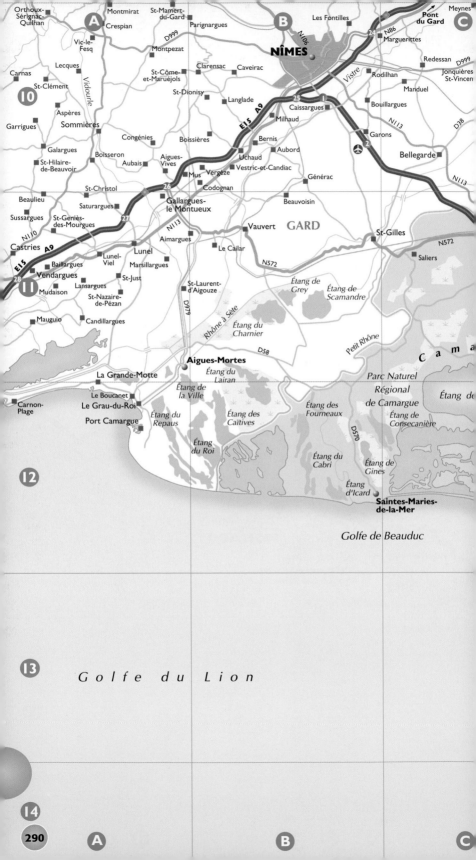

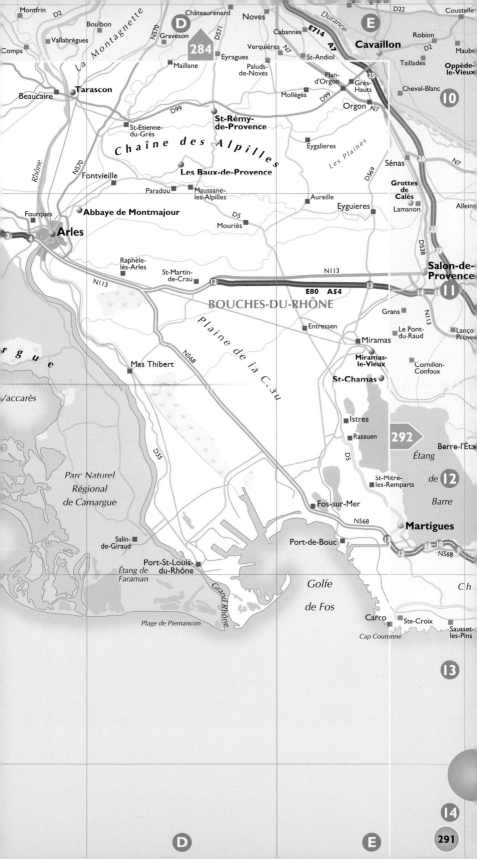

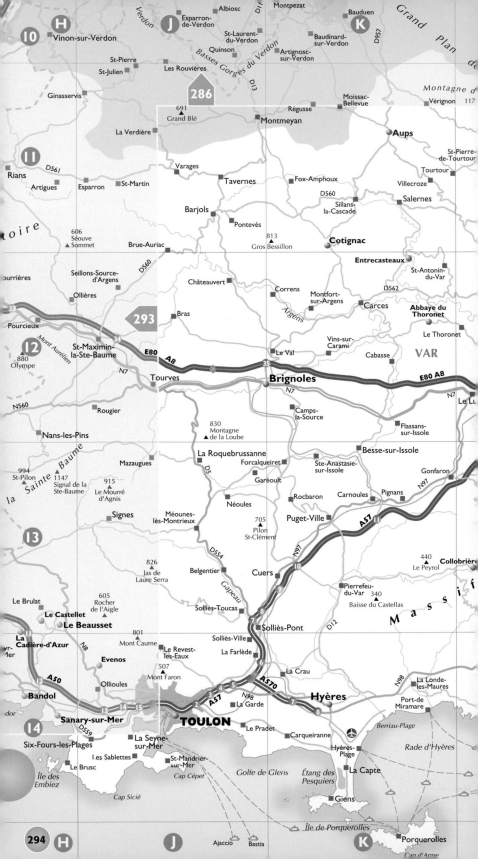

Pierre-Grosse 283 N4
Pierrelatte 284 D7
Pierrelongue 285 F7
Pierrerue 286 H9
Pierrevert 286 H10
Pignans 294 K13
Plan-d'Aups 293 H13
Plan-de-Cuques 292 G13
Plan-de-la-Tour 295 M13
Plan-d'Orgon 291 E10
Plascassier 288 N11
Le-Poët 281 J7
Le Poët-Laval 284 E6
Poligny 281 J5
Ponsonnas 281 H3
Pontamafrey 280 K1
Le Pont-du-Raud 292 E11
Pontevès 294 J11
Pont-Royal 292 F10
Pont-St-Esprit 284 C7
Porquerolles 294 K15
Port Camargue 290 A12
Port-Cros 295 L15
Port-de Miramare 294 K14
Port-de-Bouc 291 E12
Port-Grimaud 295 M13
Port-St-Louis-du-Rhône
 291 D12
Pouillardenc 281 J4
Pourcieux 293 H12
Pourrières 293 H12
Pouzilhac 284 C9
Le Pradet 294 J14
Prads-Haute-Bléone 287 L7
Pra-Loup 282 M6
Les Pras 281 J4
Prébois 281 H4
Prelles 280 L4
Le Premier-Villard 280 K1
Les Prés 285 G6
Les-Près-Hauts 281 J4
Propiac 285 F7
Prunières 281 H3
Prunières 282 K5
Puget 292 F10
Puget-sur-Argens 295 M12
Puget-Théniers 288 N9
Puget-Ville 294 K13
Puimichel 286 J9
Pujaut 284 D9
Puygiron 284 D6
Puyloubier 293 H12
Puyméras 284 E7
Puyricard 292 G11
Puy-St-André 280 L3
Puy-St-Eusèbe 282 L5
Puy-St-Pierre 280 M3
Puy-St-Vincent 280 L4
Puyvert 292 F10

Q
Quinson 286 J10

R
Ramatuelle 295 M13
Rambaud 282 K5
Raphèle-lès-Arles 291 D11
Rassuen 291 E12
Rasteau 284 E7

Le Rayol-Candel 295 L14
Reallon 282 L5
Réauville 284 D6
Rebouillon 295 L11
Redessan 290 C10
Régusse 287 K11
Reilhanette 285 G8
Reillanne 286 H9
Remollon 282 K6
Rémuzat 285 F6
Revest-des Brousses 286 H9
Revest-du-Bion 285 G8
Le Revest-les-Eaux 294 J14
Rians 293 H11
Ribiers 286 H7
Richerenches 284 D7
Riez 286 K10
Rigaud 288 N9
Rimplas 288 P8
Risoul 283 M5
Ristolas 283 N4
Roaix 284 E7
La Robine 287 K8
Robion 284 E10
Rocbaron 294 K13
Rochebrune 282 K6
La Roche-de-Rame 282 L4
La Roche-des Arnauds
 281 J5
Rochefort-du-Gard 284 D9
Rochegude 284 D7
Roche-St-Secret-Béconne
 284 E6
La Roche-sur-la-Buis 285 F7
La Rochette-du-Buis 285 G7
Rodilhan 290 B10
Rognac 292 F12
Rognes 292 F11
Rognonas 284 D9
Roissard 281 G4
Romette 282 J5
La Roque-Alric 284 E8
Roquebillière 289 Q8
Roquebillière-Vieux 289 Q8
Roquebrune 289 Q10
La Roquebrussanne 294 J13
La Roque d'Anthéron 292 F10
La Roque-Esclapon 287 M10
Roquefort-la-Bédoule
 293 G13
Roquefort-les-Pins 288 P10
Roquemaure 284 D9
Roquesteron 288 N9
Roquevaire 293 H13
Rosans 285 G6
Le Rosier 280 M3
Rottier 285 G6
Rouainette 287 M9
Roubion 288 P8
Rougier 293 J12
Rougon 287 L10
Roumoules 286 K10
Roure 288 P8
Roussas 284 D6
Les Rousses 282 L5
Rousset 293 H12
Roussillon 285 F9
Les Rouvières 286 J10

Le Rove 292 F13
Rustrel 285 G9

S
Sablet 284 E8
Les Sablettes 294 J14
Saignon 285 G10
St-Alban-des-Villards 280 K1
St-Alexandre 284 C7
St-Andiol 284 E10
St-André 280 L1
St-André-de-Rosans 285 G7
St-André-les-Alpes 287 L9
St-Antoine 280 L3
St-Antoine 289 P10
St-Antonin 288 N9
St-Antonin-du-Var 294 K12
St-Apollinaire 282 L5
St-Auban 288 M9
St-Auban-d'Oze 281 H6
St-Auban-sur-l'Ouvèze
 285 G7
St-Avre 280 K1
St-Aygulf 295 M12
St-Baudille-et-Pipet 281 H4
St-Blaise 289 P10
St-Bonnet 281 J5
St-Cannat 292 F11
St-Cézaire-sur-Siagne
 288 N11
St-Chaffrey 280 L3
St-Chamas 291 E11
St-Christol 285 G9
St-Christol 290 A11
St-Clément 282 L5
St-Clément 290 A10
St-Côme-et-Maruéjols
 290 A10
St-Crépin 282 M4
St-Cyr-sur-Mer 293 H14
St-Dalmas 289 P8
St-Dalmas-le-Selvage
 283 N7
St-Didier 284 E9
St-Dionisy 290 B10
St-Dizier-en-Diois 285 G6
Ste-Agnès 289 Q10
Ste-Anastasie-sur-Issole
 294 K13
Ste-Anne 288 P8
Ste-Cécile-les-Vignes 284 D7
Ste-Croix à-Lauze 285 G9
Ste-Croix 292 E13
Ste-Croix-de-Verdon
 287 K10
Ste-Euphémie-sur-Ouvèze
 285 F7
Ste-Jalle 285 F7
Ste-Luce 281 J4
Ste-Marie 283 M5
Ste-Marie 285 G6
Ste-Maxime 295 M13
Saintes-Maries-de-la-Mer
 290 B12
St-Estève-Janson 292 G11
St-Etienne-de-Cuines
 280 K1
St-Etienne-des-Sorts 284 D8
St-Etienne-de-Tinée 283 N7

St-Etienne-du-Grès 291 D10
St-Etienne-en-Dévoluy
 281 J5
St-Étienne-les-Orgues
 286 H8
Ste-Tulle 286 H10
St-Firmin 281 J4
St-Genies-de-Comolas
 284 D8
St-Geniès-des-Mourgues
 290 A11
St-Geniez 281 J7
St-Gilles 290 B11
St-Hilaire-de-Beauvoir
 290 A10
St-Jacques-en-
 Valgodemard 281 J4
St-Jean 285 G9
St-Jean-Cap-Ferrat 289 Q10
St-Jean-de Maurienne
 280 K1
St-Jean-d'Hérans 281 H4
St-Jean-la-Rivière 289 Q9
St-Jeannet 286 K9
St-Jeannet 288 P10
St-Julien 293 J11
St-Julien-d'Asse 286 K9
St-Julien-du-Verdon 287 L9
St-Julien-en-Beauchêne
 281 H5
St-Julien-en-Champsaur
 282 K5
St-Jurs 287 K9
St-Just 290 A11
St-Laurent-d'Aigouze
 290 A11
St-Laurent-des-Arbres
 284 D9
St-Laurent du-Cros 282 J5
St-Laurent-du-Var 289 P10
St-Laurent-du-Verdon
 286 J10
St-Laurent-en-Beaumont
 281 H4
St-Léger-du-Ventoux 285 F8
St-Leger-les-Mélèzes 282 K5
St-Lions 287 L9
St-Maime 286 H9
St-Mamert-du-Gard
 290 A10
St-Mandrier-sur-Mer
 294 J14
St-Marcel-d'Ardèche 284 C7
St-Martin 293 J11
St-Martin-de-Brômes
 286 J10
St-Martin-de-Castillon
 285 G10
St-Martin-de-Crau 291 D11
St-Martinde-la-Brasque
 293 G10
St-Martin-de-la-Porte
 280 L1
St-Martin-d'Entraunes
 288 M8
St-Martin-de-Queyrières
 280 L4
St-Martin-du-Var 289 P10
St-Martin-Vésubie 289 P8

INDEX 303

ACKNOWLEDGMENTS

Abbreviations for the picture credits are as follows:
AA = AA World Travel Library, **t** (top), **b** (bottom), **c** (centre), **l** (left), **r** (right), **bg** (background)

UNDERSTANDING PROVENCE AND THE CÔTE D'AZUR

4l AA/C Sawyer, **4c** AA/C Sawyer, **4r** AA/C Sawyer, **5l** AA/T Oliver, **5c** AA/C Sawyer, **5r** AA/C Sawyer, **5b** AA/D Ireland, **7tl** AA/T Souter, **7tlc** AA/C Sawyer, **7cl** AA/T Harris, **7btl** AA/R Strange, **7btc** AA/C Sawyer, **7bl** AA/B Smith, **7br** AA/D Ireland, **8cl** AA/A Baker, **8bl** AA/R Strange, **8tr** AA/A Baker, **8tcr** AA/C Sawyer, **8crt** AA/C Sawyer, **8btr** AA/A Baker, **8bcr** AA/C Sawyer, **8br** AA/C Sawyer, **8b** AA/C Sawyer.

LIVING PROVENCE AND THE CÔTE D'AZUR

9 AA/C Sawyer, **10/11bg** AA/C Sawyer, **10tr** AA/C Sawyer, **10tl** AA/C Sawyer, **10cl** AA/C Sawyer, **10ctr** AA/C Sawyer, **10cr** AA/C Sawyer, **11l** AA/C Sawyer, **11tl** AA/C Sawyer, **11tc** AA/C Sawyer, **11tr** AA/C Sawyer, **11cl** AA/C Sawyer, **11cr** AA, **11c** AA/T Harris, **12/3bg** AA/J Wyand, **12tl** AA/C Sawyer, **12tr** AA/C Sawyer, **12cl** AA/R Strange, **12b** Rex Features Ltd, **13tl** Rex Features Ltd, **13tc** AA/C Sawyer, **13tr** AA/C Sawyer, **13cl** Rex Features Ltd, **13c** AA/R Strange, **13tcr** AA/C Sawyer, **13cr** AA/M Chaplow, **13b** AA/C Sawyer, **14/5bg** AA/C Sawyer, **14tl** AA/C Sawyer, **14tcl** AA/C Sawyer, **14cl** AA/C Sawyer, **14tc** AA/C Sawyer, **14tr** AA/C Sawyer, **14r** AA/C Sawyer, **14c** AA/C Sawyer, **15tl** AA/A Baker, **15tc** AA/C Sawyer, **15tr** AA/C Sawyer, **15cl** Photodisc, **15c** AA/A Baker, **15cr** AA/C Sawyer, **15bl** AA/C Sawyer, **15br** AA/C Sawyer, **16/7bg** AA/A Baker, **16tl** AA/C Sawyer, **16tr** AA/C Sawyer, **16cl** AA/C Sawyer, **16c** AA/C Sawyer, **16cr** AA/C Sawyer, **17tl** AA/C Sawyer, **17tc** AA/C Sawyer, **17tr** AA/C Sawyer, **17cl** AA/E Meacher, **17c** AA/C Sawyer, **17cr** AA/R Strange, **17b** AA/C Sawyer, **18/9bg** Monaco Government Tourist Office, **18tl** AA/C Sawyer, **18tr** AA/C Sawyer, **18cl** AA/C Sawyer, **18c** Getty Images, **18b** AA/C Sawyer, **19tl** AA/C Sawyer, **19tr** AA/C Sawyer, **19cl** AA/C Sawyer, **19cr** AA/C Sawyer, **19c** Photodisc, **19b** AA/C Sawyer, **20bg** AA/C Sawyer, **20tl** AA/C Sawyer, **20tc** AA/C Sawyer, **20tr** AA/C Sawyer, **20cl** Digital Vision, **20c** AA/A Baker, **20cr** Hi-Hotel.

THE STORY OF PROVENCE AND THE CÔTE D'AZUR

21 AA, **22/3bg** AA/R Strange, **22bl** AA/R Strange, **22cr** AA/R Strange, **22/3b** AA/R Strange, **23cl** AA, **23c** AA/R Moore, **23cr** AA/R Rainford, **23bc** AA/B Smith, **23br** AA/A Baker, **23b** AA, **24/5bg** Mary Evans Picture Library, **24l** Yann Arthus-Bertrand/Corbis, **24cr** AA, **24br** AA/C Sawyer, **24/5** Mary Evans Picture Library, **25cl** A Troubadour playing lute, from the early 13th century chantefable 'Aucassin et Nicolette', 15th century, Private Collection/Bridgeman Art Library/Archives Charmet, **25c** AA/R Strange, **25cr** AA, **25br** AA/R Strange, **26/7bg** AA/A Baker, **26bl** Mary Evans Picture Library, **26cr** AA/R Strange, **26br** AA/A Baker, **27cl** Mary Evans Picture Library, **27c** AA, **27bl** AA/A Baker, **27cr** AA/R Strange, **27br** AA/A Baker, **28/9bg** AA/T Souter, **28cl** Art Archive, **28cr** AA, **28bl** Fonlupt Gilles/Corbis Sygma, **28br** AA/A Baker, **29c** Costume designed to protect doctors from the plague, 1720, by French School (18th century), Bibliotheque Nationale, Paris, France/Bridgeman Art Library/Archives Charmet, **29cl** AA/R Strange, **29bl** Bettman/Corbis, **29cr** Song sheet for the Marseillaise, mid 19th century (coloured engraving, detail), by French School, Private Collection/Bridgeman Art Library/Archives Charmet, **29br** Christie's Images/Corbis, **30/1bg** AA/A Baker, **30bl** 'Winter in Nice', poster advertising P.L.M. trains, by Hugo d'Alesi (1849-1906), Bibliotheque-Musée Forney, Paris, France/Bridgeman Art Library/Archives Charmet, **30c** AA, **30cr** AA, **30br** AA, **31cl** AA/R Strange, **30c** AA/A Baker, **30cr** Hulton Archives/Getty Images, **30bl** AA/R Strange, **30br** AA/A Baker, **32/3bg** AA/R Moore, **32bl** AA/C Sawyer, **32bc** AA, **32/3b** Rex Features Ltd, **33tcl** Rex

Features Ltd, **33c** Mary Evans Picture Library, **33cr** Getty Images, **33cl** AA/R Strange, **33b** AA/R Moore, **33br** Rex Features Ltd, **34bg** Musée de Préhistoire des Gorges du Verdon, **34cl** AA/C Sawyer, **34bl** AA/W Voysey, **34cr** Musée de Préhistoire des Gorges du Verdon, **34br** AA/C Sawyer, **34bc** AA/C Sawyer.

ON THE MOVE

35 AA/C Sawyer, **36/7** Digital Vision, **37** AA/A Baker, **38t** Digital Vision, **38c** Alamy, **39t** AA/W Voysey, **39c** AA/N Setchfield, **40/1t** AA/W Voysey, **42/3** AA/R Strange, **42c** AA/N Setchfield, **44/5** AA/R Strange, **44c** AA/R Strange, **45tl** AA/K Glendenning, **45tc** AA/J Wyand, **45tr** AA/A Baker, **45cl** AA/R Strange, **45c** AA/N Setchfield, **45cr** AA/R Moore, **45bl** AA/C Sawyer, **45bc** AA/K Glendenning, **45br** AA/A Baker, **46/7** AA/R Strange, **46c** AA/C Sawyer, **46b** Eurolines, **47** AA/P Kenward, **48** AA/M Jourdan, **49t** AA/C Sawyer, **49c** AA/B Smith, **49b** AA/R Strange, **50/1** AA/R Strange, **50** AA/N Setchfield, **52t** AA/N Setchfield, **52c** AA/C Sawyer.

THE SIGHTS

53 AA/B Smith, **54/5** AA/C Sawyer, **55l** AA/C Sawyer, **55r** AA/A Baker, **56t** AA/R Strange, **56cl** AA/C Sawyer, **56c** AA/C Sawyer, **56cr** AA/C Sawyer, **57** AA/C Sawyer, **57b** AA/C Sawyer, **58t** AA/R Strange, **58cl** AA/R Strange, **58c** AA/C Sawyer, **58cr** AA/C Sawyer, **58/9** AA/C Sawyer, **59** AA/C Sawyer, **60** AA/C Sawyer, **60/1** AA/C Sawyer, **61c** AA/C Sawyer, **61r** AA/R Strange, **61b** AA/C Sawyer, **62** AA/R Strange, **63t** AA/C Sawyer, **62/3** AA/C Sawyer, **63c** AA/C Sawyer, **63cr** AA/C Sawyer, **63b** AA/A Baker, **64** AA/C Sawyer, **65tr** AA/C Sawyer, **65cr** AA/R Strange, **65br** *The Asylum Garden at Arles*, 1889, by Vincent van Gogh, Oskar Reinhart Collection, Winterthur, Switzerland/Bridgeman Art Library, **66t** AA/A Baker, **66cl** AA/R Strange, **66c** AA/R Strange, **66cr** AA/C Sawyer, **66b** AA/R Strange, **67** AA/C Sawyer, **68/9** AA/C Sawyer, **68c** AA/R Strange, **68b** AA/C Sawyer, **69b** AA/R Strange, **70l** AA/A Baker, **70r** AA/C Sawyer, **70b** AA/C Sawyer, **71l** AA/C Sawyer, **71c** AA/C Sawyer, **71r** AA/R Strange, **72t** AA/C Sawyer, **72cl** AA/A Baker, **72c** AA/C Sawyer, **72cr** AA/C Sawyer, **73** AA/A Baker, **74** AA/C Sawyer, **74/5** AA/C Sawyer, **75l** AA/C Sawyer, **75c** AA/C Sawyer, **75r** AA/C Sawyer, **79l** AA/A Baker, **79r** AA/C Sawyer, **79b** Corbis/ Franz-Marc Frei, **80t** AA/C Sawyer, **80cl** AA/A Baker, **80c** AA/R Strange, **80/1** AA/C Sawyer, **81** AA/C Sawyer, **82** AA/A Baker, **83t** AA/C Sawyer, **83r** AA/C Sawyer, **84t** AA/A Baker, **84cl** AA/C Sawyer, **84c** AA/C Sawyer, **84cr** AA/B Smith, **85t** AA/C Sawyer, **85b** AA/C Sawyer, **86** Corbis/Chris Heller, **87t** AA/R Strange, **87b** AA/R Strange, **89t** Corbis/R Vanni, **89r** AA/A Baker, **90l** AA/A Baker, **90c** AA/R Strange, **90r** AA/B Smith, **91l** AA/C Sawyer, **91r** AA/A Baker, **92l** AA/A Baker, **92r** AA/R Strange, **92b** AA/R Strange, **93t** AA/C Sawyer, **93r** AA/C Sawyer, **94t** AA/A Baker, **94cl** AA/A Baker, **94cr** Alamy, **95tr** AA/A Baker, **95br** Alamy, **96l** AA/A Baker, **96r** AA/A Baker, **96b** AA/R Strange, **97t** AA/C Sawyer, **97cr** AA/C Sawyer, **97br** AA/C Sawyer, **98t** AA/C Sawyer, **98cl** AA/C Sawyer, **98c** AA/C Sawyer, **98cr** AA/C Sawyer, **99r** AA/C Sawyer, **99b** AA/C Sawyer, **100t** AA/A Baker, **100b** AA/A Baker, **102t** AA/C Sawyer, **102cl** AA/C Sawyer, **102c** AA/C Sawyer, **102cr** AA/C Sawyer, **102b** AA/C Sawyer, **103** AA/C Sawyer, **104l** AA/C Sawyer, **104b** *Joy of Life*, or *Antipolis*, 1946, (oil on canvas) by Pablo Picasso, Musee Picasso, Antibes, France, Bridgeman Art Library (©Succession Picasso/DACS 2004), **105l** AA/R Moore, **105r** AA/R Moore, **106** AA/C Sawyer, **107t** AA/A Baker, **107cl** AA/C Sawyer, **107c** AA/C Sawyer, **107cr** AA/C Sawyer, **108bl** AA/R Strange, **108br** AA/C Sawyer, **109l** AA/C Sawyer, **109r** AA/C Sawyer,

110l AA/A Baker, 110r AA/C Sawyer, 111l AA/C Sawyer,
111r AA/C Sawyer, 111b AA/C Sawyer, 112t AA/C Sawyer, 112l
AA/C Sawyer, 113l Photodisc, 113c AA/A Baker, 113r AA/T
Oliver, 114t Photodisc, 114c AA/C Sawyer, 115t Office du
Tourism de Menton, 115b AA/C Sawyer, 116 AA/C Sawyer,
117t AA/C Sawyer, 117cl AA/C Sawyer, 117c AA/C Sawyer,
117cr AA/C Sawyer, 118l AA/C Sawyer, 118c AA/C Sawyer,
118r AA/C Sawyer, 118b AA/C Sawyer, 119 AA/C Sawyer,
120t AA/C Sawyer, 120l AA/C Sawyer, 120b AA/C Sawyer,
121cl AA/C Sawyer, 121c AA/C Sawyer, 121cr AA/C Sawyer,
121b AA/C Sawyer, 122t AA/P Baker, 122cl AA/C Sawyer,
122c AA/C Sawyer, 122cr AA/C Sawyer, 123t AA/C Sawyer,
123b AA/C Sawyer, 124l AA/A Baker, 124r AA/C Sawyer,
125l AA/C Sawyer, 125c AA/R Moore, 125r AA/B Smith,
125b AA/A Baker, 126l AA/C Sawyer, 126r AA/C Sawyer,
127t AA/C Sawyer, 127r Culture Espaces, 128t AA/R Strange,
128cl AA/R Moore, 128bl AA/R Strange, 128br AA/R Strange,
132t AA/R Strange, 132cl AA/R Strange, 132c Monaco
Government Tourist Office, 132/3 AA/A Baker, 133t AA/A Baker,
133b AA/R Strange, 134 AA/C Sawyer, 135cl AA/C Sawyer,
135c AA/C Sawyer, 135cr AA/C Sawyer, 135t AA/R Strange,
135b AA/C Sawyer, 136l AA/C Sawyer, 136b AA/C Sawyer,
138l AA/R Moore, 138r AA/C Sawyer, 139l AA/R Moore,
139r AA/R Strange, 140t AA/C Sawyer, 140cl AA/C Sawyer,
140b AA/C Sawyer, 141t AA/R Strange, 141cr AA/A Baker,
142t AA/C Sawyer, 142b AA/C Sawyer, 143t AA/C Sawyer,
143b AA/C Sawyer, 144l AA/R Strange, 144r AA/R Moore, 145t
AA/A Baker, 145r AA/B Smith, 146t AA/A Baker, 146b AA/C
Sawyer, 148t Alamy, 148l AA/A Baker, 149l AA/C Sawyer, 149r
AA/A Baker, 150t AA/C Sawyer, 150cl AA/C Sawyer, 150c AA/C
Sawyer, 150cr AA/C Sawyer, 150b AA/C Sawyer, 151t AA/A
Baker, 151b AA/R Strange, 152 AA/C Sawyer, 153t AA/C Sawyer,
153c AA/C Sawyer, 154l AA/A Baker, 154r AA/R Strange, 155l
AA/A Baker, 155r AA/C Sawyer, 156l AA/R Strange, 156r AA/C
Sawyer, 157t AA/C Sawyer, 157r AA/C Sawyer, 157b AA/C
Sawyer, 158l AA/C Sawyer, 158c AA/C Sawyer, 158r AA/A
Baker, 159t AA/C Sawyer, 159r AA/R Strange, 160t AA/C
Sawyer, 160cl AA/C Sawyer, 160c AA/C Sawyer, 160cr AA/C
Sawyer, 161t AA/C Sawyer, 161b AA/C Sawyer, 162t AA/C
Sawyer, 162l AA/C Sawyer, 163t AA/A Baker, 163r AA/C Sawyer,
164l AA/A Baker, 164r AA/A Baker, 165l AA/R Strange, 165r
AA/R Strange, 166 AA/A Baker, 167t AA/R Strange, 167cl AA/C
Sawyer, 167c AA/C Sawyer, 167cr AA/A Baker, 168cl AA/C
Sawyer, 168cr AA/C Sawyer, 168bl AA/ABaker.

WHAT TO DO

169 AA/C Sawyer, 170/1 AA/C Sawyer, 172t Monaco
Government Tourist Office, 172cl Monaco Government Tourist
Office, 172cr Elliott et Reboul, 173t AA/J Wyand, 173cl Brand X
Pics, 173cr AA/C Sawyer, 174/5 AA/C Sawyer, 174cl AA/C
Sawyer, 174cr AA/C Sawyer, 175cl AA/C Sawyer, 175cr AA/C
Sawyer, 176t AA/C Sawyer, 176cl AA/C Sawyer, 176cr AA/C
Sawyer, 176b Image 100, 177 Monaco Government Tourist
Office, 178/9 AA/C Sawyer, 178 AA/C Sawyer, 179 AA/S
McBride, 180/1 AA/C Sawyer, 180 AA/C Sawyer, 181 AA/C
Sawyer, 182/3 AA/C Sawyer, 182 AA/C Sawyer, 183 Digital
Vision, 184/5 AA/C Sawyer, 184 AA/C Sawyer, 185 E Carecchio,
186/7 AA/A Baker, 186 AA/R Strange, 187 Photodisc, 188t AA/A
Baker, 188c AA/C Sawyer, 189t AA/C Sawyer, 189c AA/A Baker,
190/1 AA/C Sawyer, 190 AA/C Sawyer, 191 AA/C Sawyer,
192/3 AA/C Sawyer, 192 AA/C Sawyer, 193 AA/C Sawyer,
194/5 AA/C Sawyer, 194 Corbis, 195 Office du Tourisme de
Menton, 196/7 AA/C Sawyer, 196 AA/C Sawyer, 197 Monaco
Government Tourist Office, 198/9 Photodisc, 198 AA/A Baker,
199 AA/A Baker, 200t Photodisc, 200c AA/B Smith, 201t AA/C
Sawyer, 201c AA/A Baker, 202/3 AA/C Sawyer, 202 AA/C
Sawyer, 203 AA/C Sawyer, 204t AA/C Sawyer, 204c AA/C
Sawyer, 204cr AA/C Sawyer.

OUT AND ABOUT

205 AA/C Sawyer, 206 AA/R Strange, 207 AA/C Sawyer,
209tl AA/C Sawyer, 209tr AA/C Sawyer, 209b AA/C Sawyer,
210c AA/C Sawyer, 210b AA/C Sawyer, 211tl AA/C Sawyer,
211tr AA/C Sawyer, 211b AA/R Strange, 212c AA/C Sawyer,
212b AA/C Sawyer, 213t AA/C Sawyer, 213tr AA/C Sawyer,
213cl Photodisc, 213b AA/C Sawyer, 214 AA/C Sawyer,
215tl AA/C Sawyer, 215ct AA/C Sawyer, 215c AA/C Sawyer,
215cb AA/C Sawyer, 215b AA/C Sawyer, 216 AA/C Sawyer,
217t AA/C Sawyer, 217cl AA/C Sawyer, 217cr AA/R Moore,
217b AA/C Sawyer, 218 AA/R Moore, 219c AA/C Sawyer,
219cr AA/C Sawyer, 220bl AA/R Strange, 220bc AA/C Sawyer,
221 AA/C Sawyer, 222 AA/C Sawyer, 223t AA/C Sawyer,
223cl AA/C Sawyer, 223cr B Rieger, 223b D Halford, 224 AA/A
Baker, 225t AA/C Sawyer, 225c AA/C Sawyer, 225bl AA/C
Sawyer, 225br AA/C Sawyer, 226 AA/R Strange, 227t AA/C
Sawyer, 227c AA/C Sawyer, 227cl AA/A Baker, 227cr AA/C
Sawyer, 227b AA/C Sawyer, 228 AA/C Sawyer, 229tl AA/C
Sawyer, 229tr AA/R Strange, 229b AA/R Strange, 230tl AA/C
Sawyer, 230tcl AA/C Sawyer, 230tcr AA/C Sawyer,
230tr AA/C Sawyer.

EATING AND STAYING

231 AA/B Rieger, 232l AA/A Baker, 232c AA/P Kenward,
232r AA/M Short, 233l AA/C Sawyer, 233c AA/A Baker,
233r AA/C Sawyer, 234l AA/C Sawyer, 234r AA/C Sawyer,
235t AA/C Sawyer, 235c AA/C Sawyer, 235b AA/C Sawyer,
236tl AA/C Sawyer, 236tr AA/C Sawyer, 236c AA/C Sawyer,
236b AA/C Sawyer, 238cl AA/C Sawyer, 238c AA/C Sawyer,
238cr AA/C Sawyer, 238b AA/C Sawyer, 239 AA/C Sawyer,
240 AA/C Sawyer, 241tr AA/C Sawyer, 241br AA/C Sawyer,
242r AA/C Sawyer, 242b AA/C Sawyer, 243l AA/C Sawyer,
243t AA/C Sawyer, 243b AA/C Sawyer, 243r AA/C Sawyer,
244tl AA/C Sawyer, 244bl AA/C Sawyer, 245cl AA/C Sawyer,
245c AA/C Sawyer, 246l AA/R Moore, 246c AA/C Sawyer,
246r AA/N Setchfield, 246/7 AA/C Sawyer, 247c AA/R Strange,
248bl AA/C Sawyer, 248cl AA/C Sawyer, 248bc AA/C Sawyer,
248c AA/C Sawyer, 248br AA/C Sawyer, 249bl AA/C Sawyer,
249tl AA/C Sawyer, 249c AA/C Sawyer, 249tr AA/C Sawyer,
249br AA/C Sawyer, 250bl AA/C Sawyer, 250bc AA/C Sawyer,
250tl AA/C Sawyer, 250tc AA/C Sawyer, 251c AA/C Sawyer,
251br AA/C Sawyer, 252tl AA/C Sawyer, 252tr AA/C Sawyer,
252tc AA/C Sawyer, 252bc AA/C Sawyer, 252br AA/C Sawyer,
253tl AA/C Sawyer, 253tr AA/C Sawyer, 253bl AA/C Sawyer,
253bc AA/C Sawyer, 254t AA/C Sawyer, 254cr AA/C Sawyer,
254bl AA/C Sawyer, 254c AA/C Sawyer, 255l AA/C Sawyer,
255tr AA/C Sawyer, 255br AA/C Sawyer, 256tr AA/C Sawyer,
256l AA/C Sawyer, 256br AA/C Sawyer, 257bl AA/C Sawyer,
257br AA/C Sawyer.

PLANNING

259 AA/C Sawyer, 260 AA/R Strange, 262 AA/C Sawyer,
263c AA/C Sawyer, 263b AA/C Sawyer, 264 AA/R Strange,
265 AA/C Sawyer, 267 AA/C Sawyer, 268 AA/M Jourdan,
269t AA/C Sawyer, 269b AA/C Sawyer, 270t AA/C Sawyer,
270br AA/C Sawyer, 271t AA/C Sawyer, 271c AA/R Strange,
271b AA/A Baker, 272 AA/C Sawyer, 273t AA/C Sawyer,
273b AA/M Jourdan.

Project editor
Kathryn Glendenning

AA Travel Guides design team
David Austin, Glyn Barlow, Kate Harling, Bob Johnson,
Nick Otway, Carole Philp, Keith Russell

Additional design work
Katherine Mead, Jo Tapper

Picture research
Carol Walker

Internal repro work
Susan Crowhurst, Ian Little, Michael Moody

Production
Lyn Kirby, Helen Sweeney

Mapping
Maps produced by the Cartography Department of AA Publishing

Main contributors
Lindsay Bennett, Colin Follett, David Halford, Nick Hanna, Josephine Perry,
Laurence Phillips, Andrew Sanger, The Content Works

Published by AA Publishing, a trading name of Automobile Association Developments Limited,
whose registered office is Southwood East, Apollo Rise, Farnborough, Hampshire, GU14 0JW.
Registered number 1878835.

A CIP catalogue record for this book is available from the British Library.

ISBN-10: 0-7495-4514-3
ISBN-13: 978-0-7495-4514-7

Key Guide is a registered trademark in Australia and is used under license.
Binding style with plastic section dividers by permission of AA Publishing.

Colour separation by Keenes, Andover, UK
Printed and bound by Leo, China

Find out more about AA Publishing and the wide range of travel publications and services the AA
provides by visiting our website at www.theAA.com/bookshop

A01612
Maps in this title produced from:
mapping © Mairs Geographischer Verlag / Falk Verlag, D-73751 Ostfildern, Germany
and with reference to mapping © GEOnext - ISTITUTO GEOGRAFICO DE AGOSTINI, Novara

Relief map images supplied by Mountain High Maps® Copyright © 1993 Digital Wisdom, Inc
Weather chart statistics supplied by Weatherbase © Copyright 2004 Canty and Associates, LLC
Communicarta assistance with distance/time charts gratefully acknowledged

We believe the contents of this book are correct at the time of printing.
However, some details, particularly prices, opening times and telephone numbers, do change.
We do not accept responsibility for any consequences arising from the use of this book.
This does not affect your statutory rights. We would be grateful if readers would advise us of
any inaccuracies they may encounter, or any suggestions they might like to make to improve
the book. There is a form provided at the back of the book for this purpose, or you can
email us at Keyguides@theaa.com

COVER PICTURE CREDITS
Front Cover and Spine: AA/C Sawyer Back Cover, top to bottom: AA/C Sawyer; AA/C Sawyer; AA/P Kenward;
AA/C Sawyer

Dear Key Guide Reader

●

Thank you for buying this Key Guide. Your comments and opinions are very important to us, so please help us to improve our travel guides by taking a few minutes to complete this questionnaire.

You do not need a stamp (unless posted outside the UK). If you do not want to cut this page from your guide, then photocopy it or write your answers on a plain sheet of paper.

Send to: Key Guide Editor, AA World Travel Guides
FREEPOST SCE 4598, Basingstoke RG21 4GY

Find out more about AA Publishing and the wide range of travel publications the AA provides by visiting our website at
www.theAA.com/bookshop

ABOUT THIS GUIDE

Which Key Guide did you buy? _____

Where did you buy it?_____

When? _ _ month/ _ _ year

Why did you choose this AA Key Guide?
❏ Price ❏ AA Publication
❏ Used this series before; title _____
❏ Cover ❏ Other (please state) _____

Please let us know how helpful the following features of the guide were to you by circling the appropriate category: very helpful (**VH**), helpful (**H**) or little help (**LH**)

Size	**VH**	**H**	**LH**
Layout	**VH**	**H**	**LH**
Photos	**VH**	**H**	**LH**
Excursions	**VH**	**H**	**LH**
Entertainment	**VH**	**H**	**LH**
Hotels	**VH**	**H**	**LH**
Maps	**VH**	**H**	**LH**
Practical info	**VH**	**H**	**LH**
Restaurants	**VH**	**H**	**LH**
Shopping	**VH**	**H**	**LH**
Walks	**VH**	**H**	**LH**
Sights	**VH**	**H**	**LH**
Transport info	**VH**	**H**	**LH**

What was your favourite sight, attraction or feature listed in the guide?

Page _____ Please give your reason _____

_____

Which features in the guide could be changed or improved? Or are there any other comments you would like to make?

_____

_____

ABOUT YOU

Name (*Mr/Mrs/Ms*) _____

Address_____

_____

Postcode _____ Daytime tel nos _____
Please *only* give us your mobile phone number if you wish to hear from
us about other products and services from the AA and partners by text or mms.

Which age group are you in?
Under 25 ❑   25–34 ❑   35–44 ❑   45–54 ❑   55+ ❑

How many trips do you make a year?
Less than 1 ❑   1 ❑   2 ❑   3 or more ❑

ABOUT YOUR TRIP

Are you an AA member?   Yes ❑ No ❑

When did you book?   _ _ month/_ _ year

When did you travel?   _ _ month/_ _ year

Reason for your trip?   Business ❑ Leisure ❑

How many nights did you stay?_____

How did you travel?   Individual ❑ Couple ❑ Family ❑ Group ❑

Did you buy any other travel guides for your trip?_____

If yes, which ones? _____

_____

Thank you for taking the time to complete this questionnaire. Please send it to us as
soon as possible, and remember, you do not need a stamp (*unless posted outside
the UK*).

Titles in the Key Guide series:
Australia, Barcelona, Britain, Canada, Florence and Tuscany, France, Germany, Ireland, Italy,
London, Mallorca, New York, Paris, Portugal, Provence and the Côte d'Azur, Rome, Scotland, Spain.

Published in October 2005:
Costa Rica, Mexico, New Zealand, South Africa, Vietnam.
